HISTORY AND BEYOND

This classic omnibus edition of four significant works by a leading South Asian historian highlights and discusses seemingly discrete and different aspects of early Indian history, but which are in fact interconnected.

In *Interpreting Early India*, the focus is historiography, and the discussion in this book moves beyond history to provide a glimpse of explorations of new historical territories relating to early India. Time, it is argued in *Time as a Metaphor of History*, is an essential component of a historical perspective, and in India both linear and cyclic time were known. The third work in the volume, *Cultural Transactions*, suggests alternative ways of assessing early Indian tradition. Using more recent concepts of culture and tradition, it distances itself from the static notion of fixed traditions and exclusive high cultures. Finally, *From Lineage to State* discusses the history of north India from about 1000 to 400 BC. Moving away from conventional treatments of this period, it attempts to locate the processes of state formation and social configuration.

This omnibus edition is not only a necessary read for all students and scholars of early India in particular, and Indian history in general, but also a veritable collector's item.

Romila Thapar has taught early Indian history at the Delhi University, and the Jawaharlal Nehru University. She is currently Emeritus Professor of History at Jawaharlal Nehru University. She has written several books, including *Asoka and the Decline of the Mauryas*, *History of India* and more recently, *Early India*, and collections of her papers are included in *Ancient Indian Social History: Some Interpretations* and in *Cultural Pasts*.

ROMILA THAPAR

history and beyond

- Interpreting Early India
- Time as a Metaphor of History
- Cultural Transaction and Early India
- From Lineage to State

OXFORD
UNIVERSITY PRESS

OXFORD
UNIVERSITY PRESS

Oxford University Press is a department of the University of Oxford. It furthers the University's objective of excellence in research, scholarship, and education by publishing worldwide. Oxford is a registered trademark of Oxford University Press in the UK and in certain other countries

Published in India by
Oxford University Press
YMCA Library Building, 1 Jai Singh Road, New Delhi 110001, India

First Edition published in 2000
Second impression 2001
Oxford India Paperbacks 2004
Fourteenth impression 2015

ISBN-13: 978-0-19-566832-2
ISBN-10: 0-19-566832-4

Printed and bound in India at Repro India Ltd., Mumbai

Interpreting Early India

INTERPRETING EARLY INDIA

Contents

The essays included here were originally published in:

1 K.S. Krishnaswamy *et al.* (eds.), *Society and Change*. Essays in Honour of Sachin Chaudhuri. Oxford University Press, Bombay, 1977. pp. 1–19.

2. *Sociological Theories: race and colonialism*, UNESCO, Paris, 1980. pp. 93–116.

3. *Modern Asian Studies*, 1989, 23, 2, pp. 209–231.

4. *Journal of the Asiatic Society of Bombay*, 1977–78 (new series), 52–53, pp. 365–284.

5. *Proceedings of the Indian History Congress*, Forty-fourth session Burdwan University 1983, Delhi 1984. pp. 3–22.

6. S. Bhattacharya and R. Thapar, (eds.), *Situating Indian History*, Delhi 1986.

Preface

The essays in this collection were, with two exceptions, delivered originally as lectures and later marginally changed for publication. 'Ideology and the Interpretation of Early Indian History', was given at Cornell in 1974; 'Imagined Religious Communities?', was the Kingsley Martin Memorial Lecture at Cambridge in 1988; 'The Contribution of D.D. Kosambi to Indology', was delivered at the Asiatic Society in Bombay in 1980; and 'Early India: an Overview', was the Presidential Address to the Indian History Congress held at Burdwan in 1983.

All these papers, as well as those on Durkheim and Weber, and on the *Itihasa-purana* tradition, are concerned with the historiography and interpretation of facets of early Indian history and society. There is an overlap of themes in some of them and this is almost inevitable in isolated lectures. But this overlap has been retained as it serves to emphasize particular generalizations. The detailed treatment and the juxtaposing of the themes to the analyses of the authors under discussion, do make the treatment somewhat varied. The increasing interest in the historiography of the early period is an indicator of the awareness of the role of ideology in historical interpretation.

ROMILA THAPAR

Abbreviations

ABORI	Annals of the Bhandarkar Oriental Research Institute
CII	Corpus Inscriptionum Indicarum
JAOS	Journal of the American Orientalist Society
JBBRAS	Journal of the Bombay Branch of the Royal Asiatic Society
PAIOC	Proceedings of the All India Orientalists Conference

Ideology and the Interpretation of Early Indian History

It is some times said that the interpretation of the ancient periods of history has little historiographical interest, since they refer to times too distant for an ideological concern to have much meaning for contemporary society, and that the sparseness of the evidence does not provide much margin for ideological debate. This view would not however be valid for the interpretation of early Indian history, where both the colonial experience and nationalism of recent centuries influenced the study, particularly of the early period of history.

In Europe, post-Renaissance interests, which initiated the extensive study of the ancient world, brought to this study the ideological concerns of their own times.[1] These concerns are also reflected in the historiography of India,[2] if not of Asia. The interpretation of Indian history from the eighteenth century onwards relates closely to the world view of European, and particularly British historians, who provided the initial historiographical base.

[1] A. Momigliano discusses some of these in his *Studies in Historiography* (New York, 1966).

[2] C.H. Philips, ed., *Historians of India, Pakistan and Ceylon* (London, 1961), pp. 92–3; Thapar, 'Interpretations of ancient Indian history,' *History and Theory*, 1968, 7(3), pp. 318–35. For a comparative study, see D.G.E. Hall, ed., *Historians of South-East Asia* (London, 1961); Soedjatmoko, ed., *An Introduction to Indonesian Historiography* (Ithaca NY, 1965).

The resulting theories frequently reflected, whether consciously or not, the political and ideological interests of Europe—the history of India becoming one of the means of propagating those interests. Traditional Indian historical writing with its emphasis on historical biographies and chronicles was largely ignored. European writing on Indian history was an attempt to create a fresh historical tradition. The historiographical pattern of the Indian past, which took shape during the colonial period in the eighteenth and nineteenth centuries, was probably similar to the patterns which emerged in the histories of other colonial societies.

Investigation into the Indian past began with the work of the Orientalists or Indologists—mainly European scholars who had made India, and particularly Indian languages, their area of study. The majority of the Indologists, and certainly the great names among them such as Jones, Colebrooke and Wilson, were employed by the East India Company in various administrative capacities. Trained as many of them were in the Classical tradition of Europe, they were also familiar with the recent interest in philology and used the opportunity to acquire an expertise in a new area. As administrators they required a specialized knowledge of traditional Indian law, politics, society and religion, which inevitably led them to the literature in Sanskrit and Persian. Thus, scholarly and administrative interests coalesced.

The nineteenth century saw the development of not only these studies in India, but also the introduction of courses in oriental languages at various European universities and elsewhere.[3] The term Indologist now came to include those who had a purely academic interest in India and who were intellectually curious about India and the Indian past. The study of Sanskrit language and literature not only gave shape to the discipline of comparative philology, but also became the source material for the reconstruction of ancient Indian society. Vedic Sanskrit, the language of the Vedic

[3] J.F. Staal, ed., *A Reader on the Sanskrit Grammarians* (Cambridge, Mass., 1972).

literature in particular, was used extensively in the reconstruction of both Indian and Indo-European society, since the linguistic connection between the two had been established. It was now possible for scholars of Sanskrit to attempt wide-ranging interpretations of what was believed to be the beginnings of Indian history, with little or no personal experience of the Indian reality. One of the most influential of such scholars in his time was Max Müller, whose full and appreciative descriptions of contemporary Indian village communities would hardly have led one to suspect that he had never visited India. Inevitably those who were sympathetic to Indian culture tended to romanticize the ancient Indian past. These interpretations carried the imagery and the preconceptions not only of the sources, but also of those interpreting them.

By far the most influential theory to emerge from Indological studies in the nineteenth century was the Theory of Aryan Race. The word *ārya* which occurs in both the Iranian Avestan and Vedic Sanskrit texts, was given a racial connotation, as referring to the race of the Aryans. They were described as physically different from the indigenous population and their cultural distinctiveness was apparent from the fact that they spoke an Indo-European language. It was held that large numbers of Aryans, described as a branch of the Indo-European race and language group, invaded northern India in the second millennium BC, conquered the indigenous peoples and established the Vedic Aryan culture which became the foundation of Indian culture.

The identification of language and race was seen to be a fallacy even during the lifetime of Müller.[4] Although in his later writings he clarified his views on this identification, it was by then too late, and the idea had taken root. It is curious that Aryan should have

[4] J. Leopold, 'British applications of the Aryan theory of race to India, 1850–70,' *The English Historical Review*, 1974, 89(352), pp. 578–603. For various interpretations of the term *ārya*, see H.W. Bailey, 'Iranian Arya and Daha,' *Transactions of the Philological Society* (London, 1959), pp. 71–91; P. Thieme, *Der Fremdling in Rigveda*, 1938. Who has argued that the term refers to 'foreigner/stranger'.

been interpreted in racial terms since in the texts it refers merely to an honoured person of high status and in the Vedic context, this would be one who spoke Sanskrit and observed caste regulations and rituals. The racial connotation may have been due to the counter-posting of *ārya* with *dāsa*, in the *Ṛg Veda*, and it was argued that the *dāsa* is described as physically dissimilar to the *ārya*.[5] This was interpreted as representing two racial types with the *āryas* evolving later into the three upper castes and the *dāsa* remaining the lowest, included in the *śūdra* caste; the racial identity of each being preserved by forbidding inter-marriage between the castes. The pre-eminence of the *ārya* was explained as due to the successful conquest of the *āryas* over the *dāsas*. The term *varṇa*, etymologically associated with colour and occurring as a technical term referring to the caste organization of society, was used as yet another argument to support the Aryan theory of race. It was believed to provide a 'scientific' explanation for caste, namely, that the four main castes represented major racial groups, whose racial identity was preserved by forbidding inter-marriage and making birth the sole criterion for caste status. The latter half of the nineteenth century in Europe was concerned with the discussion on race in the theories of Gobineau and the growing interest in social evolution. Some of the Indologists were by no means unfamiliar with this debate.[6] The distinction between Aryan and non-Aryan, and the polarity of Aryan and Dravidian suggested by them for the Indian scene, echoes to a degree which can hardly be regarded as coincidental, the Aryan-non-Aryan distinction and the Aryan-Semitic dichotomy based on language and race, in the European context. The suggested social bifurcation is also remarkably similar; the upper castes were the Aryans and the lower castes were the non-Aryans.

The belief in the Indo-European origins of both European and Indian societies intensified the interest in Vedic sources,

[5] *Ṛg Veda* I. 130.8; 1.101.1; 10.65.11.

[6] L. Poliakov, *The Aryan Myth* (New York, 1974).

since these were seen as the earliest survivals of a common past. The village community of Vedic society was looked upon as the rediscovery of the roots of ancient European society. It was described as an idyllic community of gentle and passive people given to meditation and other-worldly thoughts, with an absence of aggression and competition.[7] Possibly some of these scholars, well disposed towards India, were seeking an escape into a utopia distant in time and place, perhaps fleeing from the bewildering changes overtaking them in their own times. Others were defending Indian society from its critics. Eventually the theory of Aryan race gave way to what has come to be called the Aryan Problem, namely, the historical role of the Indo-Aryan speaking people and their identification in early Indian sources.

But the early nineteenth century saw a new direction in the attitude of the administrator-scholars of the East India Company towards Indian history. Some, although they did not romanticize the ancient Indian past were nevertheless sympathetic in their interpretations. Others, in increasing number, became critical of what they called the values of ancient Indian society. This was in part due to the mounting problems of governing a vast colony, with an unfamiliar, if not alien culture. The nature of the relationship between Britain and India was also undergoing change, for trading stations were being substituted by colonial markets. The major intellectual influence, however, was that of English Utilitarian philosophy. James Mill, its first ideologue in the context of Indian history, completed his lengthy *History of British India* in the early decades of the nineteenth century. Mill's *History* claimed to be a critical investigation of the traditional institutions of India. These, by the standards of nineteenth century Utilitarianism, were found to be static, retrogressive and conducive to economic backwardness. He recommended a radical alteration of Indian society, to be achieved by imposing the correct legal and administrative system in India. Both the analysis and the solution suggested by

[7] M. Müller, *India, What Can it Teach Us?* (London, 1883), p. 101ff.

Mill suited the aims and needs of imperial requirements. His *History*, therefore, became a textbook on India at the Haileybury College, where the British officers of the Indian Civil Service were trained.

Further intellectual support for this view of the pre-modern history of India was found in writings of the more eminent philosophers of history of the time. Hegel, for example, remarked on the absence of dialectical change in Indian history, and consequently dismissed Indian civilization as being static, despotic in its orientation, and outside the mainstream of relevant world history.[8]

Central to this view of the pre-modern history of India, and implicit in Mill's *History*, was the theory of Oriental Despotism.[9] The genesis of this theory probably goes back to the Greco-Persian antagonism, with references in Greek writing to the despotic government of the Persians. To this was added the vision of the luxuries of the oriental courts, a vision built partly on the luxury trade with the east from early times, and partly on the fantasy world of oriental courts as described in the accounts of visitors to these regions, such as those of Ktesias at the Persian court and Megasthenes at the Mauryan court in India. The Crusades and the ensuing literature on the Turks of doubtless strengthened the fanciful notion of the all-powerful, despotic, oriental potentate. When interest in the notion was revived in the eighteenth century as an explanation for continuing empires in Asia, the focus was shifted from the doings of the despot to the nature of the despotic state. Given the concerns of eighteenth century France and England, the central question was seen as that of private property in land, and the state ownership of land.[10] Once again, the accounts of ambassadors and

[8] F. Hegel, *Lectures on the Philosophy of History* (London, 1974).

[9] R. Koebner, 'Despot and despotism: Vicissitudes of a political term,' *Journal of the Warburg and Courtauld Institutes*, 1951, 14, pp. 275–80; F. Venturini, 'Oriental despotism,' *Journal of the History of Ideas*, 1963, 24, pp. 133–42.

[10] D. Thorner, 'Marx on India and the Asiatic mode of production,' *Contributions to Indian Sociology*, 1966, 9, p. 33ff.

visitors to Mughal India such as Roe and Bernier were quoted, and they maintained that there was an absence of the right to private property in land.[11] Some, such as Montesquieu, accepted the theory of oriental despotism; others, such as Voltaire, doubted the correctness of its assumptions. By the mid-nineteenth century it had such currency in Britain that again the standard text on the traditional economy of India used at Haileybury College was that of Richard Jones, who endorsed the theory. Inevitably, the major historians of the late nineteenth century in India, who also happened to be the administrators, assumed the correctness of the theory as a precondition to their understanding of the Indian past. Even Marx, despite his concern for dialectical movement, was not averse to the idea with its emphasis on a static society and an absence of change, and worked the theory into his model for Asian society—that of the Asiatic Mode of Production.[12]

The absence of private property in land was central to this model of social and economic structure. The structure was seen in the form of a pyramid, with the king at the apex, and self-sufficient, isolated village communities at the base. The surplus was collected from the cultivators by the bureaucracy, and the process of redistribution led to its being appropriated, substantially, by the king and the court—hence the fabulous wealth of oriental courts. Control over the peasant communities was maintained by the state monopoly of the irrigation system—or the hydraulic machinery, as a more recent author has called it[13]—the control over which was crucial in arid lands dependent on artificial irrigation. The subservience of the peasant communities was ensured not only by extracting the maximum surplus from them, but also by investing the king with absolute powers and divinity. The isolation of social

[11] F. Bernier, *Voyages de F. Bernier . . .* (Amsterdam), 1699. T. Roe, *The Embassy of Sir Thomas Roe to India, 1615–1619* (London, 1926).

[12] R.A.L.H. Gunawardana, 'The analysis of pre-colonial social formations in Asia in the writings of Karl Marx,' *The Indian Historical Review*, 1976, 4.

[13] K. Wittfogel, *Oriental Despotism* (New Haven,1957).

groups was made more complete by the absence of urban centres and effective networks of trade.

The idealization of the village community from one group of scholars was now juxtaposed with the starkness of those supporting the other interpretation. This historical kaleidoscope was readjusted when a third perspective was introduced at the start of the twentieth century. The authors of this were Indian historians, using the current methodology but motivated ideologically by the national movement for independence; scholars who have been referred to in recent writings as the nationalist historians.[14] Of the two major theories, the theory of Aryan race had their approval, whereas that of Oriental Despotism was opposed for obvious reasons. The former was believed to be based on the most up-to-date philogical evidence. Its supposed 'scientific' explanation for caste was gratifying, in view of the general condemnation of caste society from the stalwarts of egalitarianism. *Homo hierarchicus*, if one may borrow the phrase, stood exonerated. The depiction of Aryan society in glowing terms was soothing to the sensitivities of Indian scholarship. There was also an appeal to some middle-class Indians that the coming of the English represented 'a reunion of parted cousins, the descendants of two different families of the ancient Aryan race'.[15]

Nationalist historical writing took up the theme, among other things, of the importance of religion to Indian society. The bipolarity of the spiritual content of Indian culture and the materialist basis of western culture was seen as an essential and inherent difference. This was in part a reaction to the earlier view, that religion was such a central factor in traditional Indian society that it obstructed progress—the latter being defined as social and economic change. This view had been eagerly taken up both by

[14] Such as for example, K.P. Jayaswal, *Hindu Polity* (Calcutta, 1924); R.K. Mookerji, *Harsha* (London, 1926); H.C. Raichaudhury, *The Political History of Ancient India* (Calcutta, 1923), among others.

[15] *Keshab Chunder Sen's Lectures in India* (Calcutta, 1923), p. 323.

Christian missionaries anxious to proselytize among the more enterprising Indian social groups, as well as by those who were looking for a single factor which would explain the backwardness of India as a colonial society.[16]

The nationalist historians concerned themselves with those ideas which were necessary to nationalist polemics. They questioned individual items of historical interpretation, rather than examining the validity of a theory as a total pattern of interpretation. Nor did they attempt to replace the existing theories by new ones, fundamentally different from what had gone before. In a sense, nationalist ideology delimited the nature of their questions. However, in spite of these weaknesses, the impact of the nationalist school was both considerable and necessary. The role of ideology in historical interpretation was recognized with the high-lighting of the ideological content of earlier interpretations. Above all, it prepared the way for questioning the accepted theories.

This has been of necessity an over-simplified sketch of the main ideological trends in modern interpretations of early Indian history. I would now like to consider at greater length the two main theories to which I have referred. In selecting the Aryan problem and Oriental Despotism for further analysis, in the light of new evidence and methods of enquiry, my purpose is not merely to indicate the inapplicability of the theories, but also to suggest the nature of possible generalizations which arise in the re-examination of accepted theories.

The questioning of the Aryan theory is based on the work in recent years from three different disciplines, archaeology, linguistics and social anthropology. The discovery and excavation of the cities of the Indus civilization has pushed back the beginnings of Indian history to the third millennium BC, and the Indus civiliza-

[16] M. Weber, *The Religion of India*, 1958. Glencoe, is the culmination of a range of such views over the nineteenth century. For a discussion of the Christian missionary position, A. Embree, *Charles Grant and the Evangelicals* (London, 1962).

tion has replaced the Vedic Aryan culture as foundational to Indian history. The cities of the Indus pre-date the Vedic culture by at least at millennium, since the decline of the cities dates to the early second millennium and the diffusion of Sanskrit as a part of the Vedic culture is believed to have begun at the end of the same millennium.[17] The Indus cities epitomize a copper-bronze-age urban civilization, based on commerce both within the north-western area of the sub-continent as well as West Asia. The earliest of the Vedic texts, th *Ṛg Veda*, reflects a pastoral, cattle-keeping people unfamiliar with urban life. If the Aryans had conquered north-western India and destroyed the cities, some archaeological evidence of the conquest should have been forthcoming. In only one part of one of the cities is there evidence of what might be interpreted as the aftermath of conquest and even this has been seriously doubted.[18] The decline of the Indus cities is generally attributed to extensive ecological changes. The repeated flooding of the Indus, the rise of the water-table and salination of the land under cultivation, the change in the course of the Sarasvatī river with a consequent encroaching of the desert and major sea-level changes affecting the ports along the west coast, seem more convincing explanations for the decline of the cities.[19] Palaeo-botanical analyses are suggesting a change in climatic conditions from humid to dry.[20] Unlike conquest, ecological change was more

[17] R. and B. Allchin, *The Birth of Indian Civilisation* (Harmondsworth, 1955); R.E.M. Wheeler, *The Indus Civilisation* (Cambridge, 1968).

[18] G.F. Dales, 'New investigations at Mohenjo-daro,' *Archeology*, 1965, 18(2), p. 18.

[19] H.T. Lambrick, 'The Indus flood-plain and the Indus Civilisation,' *Geographical Journal*, 1967, 133(4), pp. 483–95; R.L. Raikes, 'The end of the ancient cities of the Indus,' *American Anthropologist*, 1964, 66(2), pp. 284–99; 'Kalibangan:Death from natural causes,' *Antiquity*, 1965, 39(155), pp. 196–203; 'The Mohenjo-daro floods,' *Antiquity*, 1965; A.V.N. Sarma, 'Decline of Harappan cultures: A relook,' in *K.A.N. Sastri Felicitation Volume* (Madras, 1971).

[20] G. Singh, 'The Indus Valley culture (seen in the context of post-glacial climate and ecological studies in North-West India),' *Archeology and Physical*

gradual and as the cities declined there were migrations out of the cities as well as small groups of squatters moving in from the neighbouring areas. Recent evidence from excavations in western India and the Indo-Gangetic divide is pointing toward some continuity from the Indus civilization into later cultures.[21] There is little doubt now that certain facets of the Indus civilization survived into the second and first millennium cultures, in spite of the decline of the cities. The earlier hiatus between the Indus civilization and the Vedic culture is no longer acceptable, and the Indus civilization has now to be seen as the bedrock of early Indian culture.

Recent linguistic analyses of Vedic Sanskrit have confirmed the presence of non-Aryan elements, especially Proto-Dravidian, both in vocabulary and phonetics.[22] Consequently it has been suggested that Proto-Dravidian could have been the earlier language of northern India, perhaps the language of the Indus civilization, although this awaits the decipherment of the Indus script, and that Vedic Sanskrit as the language of a particular social group, slowly spread across the northern half of the sub-continent, with a possible period of bilingualism, in which Vedic Sanskrit was modified by the indigenous language.[23] It is significant that some of the Proto-Dravidian loan words in Vedic Sanskrit refer to agricultural processes. We know from archaeological evidence that plough agriculture was practised by the Indus settlements[24] and from the *Ṛg Vedic* hymns it is apparent that pas-

Anthropology in Oceania, 1971, 6(2), pp. 177–89.

[21] As for example, in the co-existence of the Black-and Red Ware culture with the late Harappan in western India and that of the Ochre Colour Pottery culture and Painted Grey Ware in the Indo-Gangetic divide and the Gaṅgā-Yamunā Doāb.

[22] A.L. Basham, *The Wonder That Was India* (London, 1954), p. 387; T. Burrow, *The Sanskrit Language* (London, 1965), p. 373ff; M.B. Emeneau, *Collected papers* (Annamalainagar, 1967), pp. 148, 155.

[23] M.B. Emeneau, *Collected papers* (Annamalainagar, 1967).

[24] B.B. Lal, 'Perhaps the earliest ploughed field so far excavated anywhere

toralism and not agriculture was the more prestigious profession among the early Aryan speakers.

Anthropological studies of Indian society have encouraged a reappraisal of the social history of early periods. The insistence on the precise meaning of words relating to social categories in the sources has been all to the good. The valid distinction between *varṇa* as caste in the sense of ritual status, and *jāti* as caste in the sense of actual status is again a help to the social historian. The most useful contribution, however, has been in the study of the formation of castes, which has made it apparent that caste society does not require the pre-condition of different racial entities, nor the conquest of one by the other. It does require the existence of hereditary groups determining marriage relations, which groups are arranged in a hierarchical order and perform services for one another. The hierarchy is dependent on occupation, on certain beliefs of purity and pollution, and on continued settlement in a particular geographical location. The formation of a new caste has therefore to be seen in terms of the historical change in a particular region. Thus, a tribe incorporated into peasant society could be converted into a caste.[25] Occupational groups often acquired a caste identity through the corporate entity of the guild or through hereditary office in administration.[26] Religious sects, frequently protesting against the caste hierarchy, often ended up as castes themselves. Possibilities of social mobility and variations in status were linked to the historical context of time and place. Social attitudes were often set; nevertheless, the opportunities for social change were exploited, and the historian can no longer dismiss the social dimension by merely referring to the unchanging rigidity of

---

in the world,' *Puratattva*, 1970–71, 4, p. 1ff.

[25] N.K. Bose, 'The Hindu method of tribal absorption,' in *Cultural Anthropology and Other Essays* (Calcutta, 1953); D. Mandelbaum, *Society in India* (Berkeley, 1970).

[26] R.S. Sharma, *Changes in Early Medieval India* (New Delhi, 1969) (Devraj Chanana Memorial Lecture.)

caste society. In this context the theory of Sanskritization has been a breakthrough in the study of social history.[27]

The combination of new evidence and fresh perspectives from all these sources raises a host of new questions with reference to the Vedic period. Evidently it was not a purely Indo-Aryan assertion over Indian culture and has to be seen as an amalgam of the Indo-Aryan and the existing culture, which in turn requires a clearer definition of each. Since the spread of Sanskrit, certainly in the Ganges valley if not in the north-west as well, appears to have occurred through a process of diffusion and less through conquest, the motivation for the diffusion would have to be sought. One of the possibilities suggested is that it coincided with the arrival of a new technology at the start of the first millennium BC. This is apparent in the use of iron in preference to copper and the introduction of the horse and the spoked wheel, both new to India.[28] The ambiguity of the word *ayas*, copper or iron in Sanskrit, creates some difficulties in an immediate acceptance of this idea. Vedic Sanskrit is closely connected with priestly groups and the belief in ritual may have accelerated the diffusion, particularly as it seems that Vedic ritual was closely associated with knowledge of the solar calendar providing, among other things, a more effective control over agricultural processes. The diffusion of a language does not require the physical presence of large numbers of native speakers. It can often be done more effectively by influential groups in the population adapting the new language and using the traditional networks of communication. The spread of Sanskrit might be more meaningfully seen as marking a point of social change, apart from merely a change of language.

The notion of historical change, other than changing dynasties, was curiously unacceptable to nineteenth century thinking on the Indian past. The unchanging nature of society is central to the

[27] M.N. Srinivas, *Religion and Society among the Coorgs of South India* (Oxford, 1952).

[28] R. Thapar, 'The study of society in ancient India,' in *Ancient Indian Social History: Some Interpretations* (New Delhi, 1978), pp. 211–39.

theory of Oriental Despotism. The span of Indian history was seen as one long stretch of empire with an occasional change of dynasty. Yet in fact, empires were of short duration and very infrequent. There was only one empire in the early period, the Mauryan empire, lasting from the end of the fourth to the early second century BC, which would even approximately qualify as an imperial system. It was not until the historical writing of the twentieth century that some concession was made to change, and imperial golden ages were interspersed with the dark ages of smaller kingdoms.[29]

In re-examining Oriental Despotism it is not new evidence which provides an alternative analysis, but the more careful questioning of existing sources. It is surprising that references to private property in land should have been overlooked. The socio-legal texts, the *dharmaśāstras* and the early text on political economy, the *Arthaśāstra*, list and discuss the laws and regulations for the sale, bequest and inheritance of land and other forms of property.[30] More precise information comes from the many inscriptions of the period after AD 500, on stone and on copper-plates, recording the grant of land by either the king or some wealthy individual to a religious beneficiary, or alternatively, by the king to a secular official in lieu of services rendered to the king.[31] These inscriptions were deciphered in the nineteenth century, but read primarily for the data which they contained on chronology and dynasties. In the last few decades, however, they have become the basic source material for the study of the agrarian structure of the first millennium AD.[32] Since these were the legal charters relating to the grants, the transfer of the land is recorded in detail. In areas where the land granted was already under cultivation, the person from whom the land was acquired and the

[29] V. Smith, *The Oxford History of India* (Oxford, 1919).

[30] P.V. Kane, *History of Dharmaśāstra* (Poona, 1942), Vol.3.

[31] e.g. B. Morrison, *Political Centres and Culture Regions in Early Bengal* (Tucson, 1970).

[32] R.S. Sharma, *Indian Feudalism* (Calcutta, 1965).

person to whom the property was transferred are mentioned, together with the location of land, the authority of the officials under whom the transfer was completed and the consent of the village within whose jurisdiction the land lay.

Not only do these inscriptions provide evidence of the categories of ownership of land, but where they refer to waste land it is possible to indicate the gradual extension of the agrarian economy into new areas. This information is of some consequence, not merely to economic history, but also to those concerned with the history of religion; for the extension of the agrarian economy was generally accompanied either by Buddhist missions or by nucleii of *brāhmaṇa* settlements, through which Sanskritic culture was introduced into the new areas and the local culture of these areas was assimilated into the Sanskritic tradition.[33] The interplay of these two levels of belief systems was a necessary process in the delineation of Indian culture. The stress so far has been on the high culture of the Sanskritic tradition which is inadequate for understanding the historical role of cultural forms.

Many of these records provide information on the rise of families of relatively obscure origin to high social status, usually through the channels of land ownership and administrative office.[34] Those who became powerful had genealogies fabricated for themselves, bestowing on the family *kṣatriya* status and, if required, links with royal lineages as well. Such periods of historical change demanded new professions, which professions finally evolved into castes. For example, administrative complexities relating to grants of land on a large scale needed professional scribes. Not surprisingly the pre-eminent caste of scribes, the *kāyastha*, are first referred to in the sources of this period.

The importance given to a centralized bureaucracy in the

[33] This is clearly reflected in the origin myths of ruling families for instance, even in areas as seemingly remote as Chota Nagpur. The origin myth of the Nāgabansis is clearly derived from Purānic sources but also incorporates local mythology.

[34] As for example, the Maitrakas of Vallabhi, during the fifth and sixth centuries AD.

model was perhaps a reflection, among other things, of the nineteenth century faith in the administrator as the pivot of the imperial system. For the bureaucratic system of early India was rarely centralized, except in the infrequent periods of empire. Recruitment was impersonal, and most levels of administration were filled by local people. And it was at the more localized levels that the effective centres of power were located. In periods of empire, the surplus did find its way into the hands of the royal court. But during the many centuries of small kingdoms, the income from revenue was distributed among a large number of elite groups, which in part explains the regional variations and distribution in art styles, where the patron was not a distant emperor but the local king. This tendency towards political decentralization was accentuated from the post-Gupta period *c.* AD 600 when grants of revenue and later grants of land became the mechanism of remuneration.

Bureaucratic control over the economy, such as it was, derived from control over revenue collection. The hydraulic machinery played only a marginal role. Large-scale, state-controlled irrigation was rare. In the main, irrigation aids consisted of wells and tanks, built and maintained either by wealthy land-owners or through the co-operative effort of the village. The more relevant question is not that of the state ownership of the hydraulic machinery, but the variation in irrigation technology and the degree to which irrigation facilities gave an individual or an institution a political edge over others.

The other mechanism of control according to the theory was a belief in the divinity of kingship, which gave the king a religious and psychological authority additional to the political. The attribution of this quality of divinity to kingship was probably the result of earlier studies on kingship and divinity in the ancient Near East. The interrelation between divinity and political authority was never absolute in ancient India. Divinity was easily bestowed, not only on kings, but on a variety of objects, both animate and inanimate. Far from emphasizing divinity, the kings of the Mauryan empire were patrons of the heterodox sects, which denied the existence of any god and ignored the notion of divinity. Divinity was appealed to initially in the rise of monarchy as a political form, in the first millennium BC.[35] But, the maximum references to kings as either incarnations or descendants of the gods coincide with the period of the rise of obscure families to kingship and the fabricated genealogies, suggesting that the appeal to divinity was a form of social validation and its significance was largely that of a metaphor. A particularly subtle aspect of the Indian notion of authority which has not so far received adequate attention has been the interaction of political authority with what may be called the moral authority of the renouncer. Time and again, the renouncer has returned to society and whilst still not fully participating in it, has played a significant role outside the realms of conventional political authority. Whereas political authority (*rājadharma*) derives in part from the power of coercion (*daṇḍa*) and religious authority from ritual and formulae (*yajña, pūjā* and *mantra*), the derivation of the authority of the renouncer is difficult to ascertain, combining as it does elements of the psychological, the social, the moral and the magical.

One of the more striking refutations of an aspect of Oriental Despotism has been that involving the absence of urban centres. The evidence for an early continuous urban economy has been pinpointed by archaeological excavation. This, combined with literary sources, suggests significant variations in the nature of urbanization. That the literary sources were not fully utilized was largely because the details of urban society occur first in the Pāli Buddhist texts, and these were not given the attention which they deserved by those using Sanskrit sources. The cities of the Indus civilization were smaller concentrations of population as compared to those of the second urbanization, linked with iron technology and which evolved in the Ganges valley in the first millennium BC. This had as its economic base trade within the

[35] J. Spellman, *Political Theory of Ancient India* (Oxford, 1964).

sub-continent. The widespread use of coins and other adjuncts to extensive trading relationships, such as letters of credit and promissory notes, not only extended the geographical reach of trade but considerably increased the volume of trade. Steps towards the growth of exchange are apparent in the Buddhist literature relating to the cities of the Ganges valley; but this is less evident in the growth of the cities of maritime south India at the end of the first millennium, where archaeology has corroborated the literary references to a lucrative trade with the Roman empire.

At another level attempts have been made to correlate certain religious movements to the needs of urban groups. The work on the rise and spread of Buddhism and Jainism in relation to the mercantile community has inspired a wider debate on aspects of the *bhakti* movements as being in part the religion of urban groups with elements of dissident thought or, for that matter, the investigation of the Hindu temple as an economic entrepreneur.[36] The outcome of such studies is likely to lead to a rather radical revision of Max Weber's thesis on the social and economic role of religion in India.

In suggesting that these two theories—the Aryan theory and Oriental Despotism—emanating from ideologies pertinent to nineteenth century Europe, are now no longer tenable, it may appear as if I am tilting at windmills. Yet, it is surprising how deeply rooted these theories are, both in India and elsewhere, and how frequently they are revived for reasons of academic study as well as in political polemics. The theory of Aryan race has not only served cultural nationalism in India but continues to serve Hindu revivalism and, inversely, anti-brahmin movements. At the academic level, the insistence on ascribing Indo-European roots to all aspects of Vedic culture has acted as a restraint on the analysis of mythology, religion and cultural symbols from the historical point of view. The intellectual history of a period as rich as that of the

[36] B. Stein, 'Social mobility and medieval South Indian Hindu sects,' *Comparative Studies in Society and History*, 1968, suppl. 3, pp. 78–94.

Upaniṣads and early Buddhism, approximately the mid-first millennium BC, has been hemmed in by the constraints of seeing it in terms of an internal movement among dissident Aryans, rather than from the more meaningful perspective of a period of seminal change. The perennial search for 'the Aryans' continues apace, with archaeologists still attempting to identify a variety of archaeological cultures as Aryan.[37]

Oriental Despotism was revived a few decades ago in Wittfogel's assessment of bureaucratic systems and in association with an oblique critique of the Soviet system. The reincarnation of the theory as the Asiatic Mode of Production has had, I believe, an even fuller transfusion in recent Soviet assessments of the Chinese past, as it has from time to time at the academic level in more general economic analyses of historical change in Asia.

That the interpretation of ancient Indian History was subject to the polemics of political ideology was inevitable. Colonial situations tend to play on the political content of historical interpretation. The sanctity of ancient culture as seen through a nationalist vision made it sensitive to historical analysis. This is not to deny, however, that over the last two centuries, at the level of the discovery of evidence, the scholarship has been both meticulous and extensive. Earlier theories of interpretation have not been replaced as there is now a concern with the need for clearer definitions of historical concepts based on a larger body of precise evidence. This is most apparent in the current debate on the periodization of Indian history. Nevertheless, for a while there was a disinclination to move away from the subject of polemics.

Symbolic of this disinclination was the consistent overlooking of one significant aspect of historical interest: the traditional Indian understanding of its own past. It has long been maintained that the Indians were an a-historical people, since there was no recognizable historical writing from the Indian tradition similar to

[37] e.g. B.B. Lal, 'Excavations at Hastinapura . . . ,' *Ancient India*, 1954–1955, 10 and 11, pp. 5–51.

that from Greece and China. This was in part because the Indian historical tradition — the *iṭihāsa-purāṇa*, as it is called — was in a form not easily recognizable to those familiar with Greek historical writing. Another reason may have been the inability of modern scholars to perceive and concede the awareness of change, so necessary to a sense of history, in the *iṭihāsa-purāṇa*, and this precluded them from seeing the historical basis of the tradition.

The early Indian historical tradition which is now receiving the attention of historians and is being analysed in terms of its ideological content does reflect a distinct image of the past, and its concerns are different from those of modern interpretations of the past.[38] For instance, the unit of history is not the empire but the *janapada*, the territory settled by a tribe, which later evolves into a state, generally a kingdom. References are made to emperors as universal rulers, the *samrāṭ* and the *cakravartin*, but these are at the abstract level. Reality revolves around the kings of smaller kingdoms. The genealogical sections of the tradition explain the settlements of tribes, and with the emergence of states, the association of dynasties.[39] But the past was not recorded as a succession of political events, for the legitimation of political authority was more important and it was to this that the historical tradition gave precedence. The records of these early genealogies were used from the first millennium AD onwards for legitimizing new dynasties who were given links with the ancient royal lineages. Recent work in social history has shown that political power was a relatively open area in early Indian society and the social antecedents of the founders of dynasties were rarely questioned, as long as they complied with the procedures necessary for legitimizing political authority.

[38] Publications on this tradition are F.E. Pargiter, *The Ancient Indian Historical Tradition* (London, 1922); V.S. Pathak, *Ancient Historians of India* (London, 1966); and A.K. Warder, *An Introduction to Indian Historiography* (Bombay, 1972).

[39] R. Thapar, 'Genealogy as a source of social history,' *op.cit.*, 1976, pp. 326–60.

In the Buddhist tradition the unit of history was the Sangha or Buddhist Church and monastic chronicles formed the core of the tradition. These were not merely the history of the Elders of the Saṅgha, for the monastery as an important socio-religious institution played an active political role and its relationship with political authority is apparent from these chronicles.[40]

Cyclic time and the change implicit in the movement of the cycle was the cosmological reflection of the consciousness of change. Even more interesting is the evolution in the form and style of the historical tradition itself, in the latter part of the first millennium AD, when the record includes details of events relating to political authority—in short, the kind of literature which is easily recognizable as historical writing, consisting of biographies of rulers and statesmen and chronicles of dynasties.[41] This new development in the tradition coincides with actual historical change, characterized by small kingdoms generally conforming to the geographically nuclear regions. These were based on a decentralized administration and economic structure, with an extension of patronage to local cultures and the emergence of the devotional religion — the *bhakti* movement—which, through its appeal to a large cross-section of social groups and its use of the regional language, strengthened the regional focus.

Yet the link with the mainstream of the tradition was not broken. Into the early history of the region or the dynasty is woven, quite deliberately, the mythology and lineages of the earlier tradition. The network of Sanskritic culture at least at the upper levels of society was a more real bond between people and places than the mere inclusion of these within the confines of an empire.

The perspective of the ancient Indian historical tradition when seen in juxtaposition with the more recent analyses of early Indian history, apart from its inherent intellectual interest, can suggest

[40] L.S. Perera, 'The Pāli chronicle of Ceylon,' in Philips, ed., *op. cit.*, 1961, p. 29ff.

[41] Such as Bānabhaṭṭa's *Harṣacarita*, Bilhana's *Vikramānkadevacarita*, Kalhana's *Rājataraṅginī* and various *vaṁśāvalis*.

the ideological concerns of the pre-colonial period. These might provide to the historian of early India a clearer vision of the priorities of the Indian past than have been provided by the polemics of more recent times.

*Durkheim and Weber on Theories of Society and Race Relating to Pre-colonial India**

This paper is concerned with the ideas of Durkheim and Weber in relation to pre-colonial India. An attempt is made to examine the colonial comprehension of India, and its influence on these two sociologists—a comprehension which included both early and contemporary India. Such a projection from one historical period onto another was, in many ways, a characteristic of eighteenth and nineteenth century European studies of India. Whatever seemed alien to the European perspective of contemporary India was often visualized as a survival from earlier times and the presumed continuity was imbued with historical authenticity. More frequently the social institutions from the past were believed to persist virtually unchanged into the present and made it legitimate for those studying contemporary Indian society to concern themselves with the texts of earlier periods. Such chronological glissandos were played by both evolutionists and functionalists.

As far as India was concerned, the focus of study was on caste which was seen as the distinctive feature of Indian civilization. This in turn required analyses of Indian religion and the racial

* I am grateful to my colleague Dr Satish Sabarwal for his helpful criticism of an earlier draft of this paper.

composition of the Indian people, since religion and race were seen as essentials of caste. Both Durkheim and Weber tended to concentrate on the former as the more important factor, but this did not preclude a discussion on the latter.

Unlike Weber, Durkheim has written little directly on India. The impact of his thinking is more apparent in the works of his disciples—the sociologists Marcel Mauss, Henri Hubert and Célestin Bouglé—and to some extent on a number of Indologists such as G. Held, G. Dumézil and P. Masson-Oursel. Nevertheless, Durkheim occasionally used the existing studies on Indian civilization to highlight some of his generalizations. The most often quoted example of this is his argument that religion cannot be defined as a belief in gods since Theravada Buddhism, widely accepted as a religion, did not postulate a belief in gods. Durkheim's concern with the origins of moral and social systems and the dichotomy of the sacred and the profane would have lent itself admirably to an analysis of the interrelations between caste and religion in India, but this clearly was a region with which he felt himself to be unacquainted.[1]

Marcel Mauss and Henri Hubert published a pioneering study on the ritual of sacrifice, *Sacrifice : its nature and function*, in which the Vedic literature with its wealth of detail on the central ritual of Vedic life, the *yajña* (sacrificial ritual) provided the authors with what was until then comparatively new data among sociologists. Earlier studies had centred on Tylor's evidence as discussed in *Primitive Culture* and that of Robertson-Smith's work in *The religion of the Semites*. These studies were based in part on observation (not always of a very systematic kind) with descriptions which were patchy and not nearly as meticulous in detail as were the Vedic texts. Above all, the Vedic texts were sacrificial manuals *per se*. Frazer's attempt to universalize the theories on sacrifice had complicated the process of analytical investigation. Hubert and Mauss

[1] E. Durkheim, 'De la definition des phenomenes religieux', *L' année Sociologique*, II (Paris, 1899), pp. 1–28.

were attempting to apply Durkheim's theories to a new area of evidence, a procedure which was to be repeated in some of the essays in the collections published as, *Mélanges d'histoire des religions*, and more specifically by Mauss in *Essai sur de Don*. Subsequently Masson-Oursel in his chapters in the collection entitled *Ancient India and Indian Civilisation* has tried to separate the magical elements from the rational in the structure of early Hinduism and has posed the problem of the expectation of worldly success in the performance of religious rituals. These ideas have been further developed by Heesterman in a study on the ancient Indian sacrificial ritual, *The Ancient Indian Royal Consecration*. Held has used the Durkheimian method more directly in an analysis of the *Mahābhārata* basing himself on a statement from Marcel Mauss, 'Le Māhabhārata est l'histoire d'un gigantesque potlatch'.[2] In *The Mahābhārata: an ethnological study*, Held argues that the Kauravas and the Pāṇḍavas were two phratries and that dicing and war were both part of the symbol of potlatch competitions; that the mythology of the epic revolves around notions of early classifications, such as the constant use of the number five and the cyclic concept of cosmic movement; and that the text distinguishes between the sacred act (*karma*) and sacred knowledge (*jñāna*) particularly in its didactic sections. More recently Dumézil has acknowledged the influence of Durkheim in his studies of Indo-European society and mythology. He argues that all Indo-European societies reflect a three-fold social division (the priest, the warrior and the commoner, what he calls the tripartite function) in the arrangement of their mythologies relating to the deities they worshipped. This in a sense overarches the religious and racial perspective.

Among the nineteenth and early twentieth century analyses of caste in India, Bouglé's work, deriving as it did from Durkheim's ideas of community, religion and stratification, introduced a new dimension and shifted the focus from race and

[2] M. Mauss, *Essai sur le Don* (Paris 1925), p. 143. (trans. *The Gift*, New York 1967).

occupation to new categories of stratification. It is unfortunate that his book *Essays on the Caste System* remained untranslated from the French for half a century; certainly its impact on studies on caste would have had a greater significance. Both Mauss and Bouglé were interested in the Indian data largely because it provided new source material on a society which had not been extensively investigated by sociologists. They were interested in the difference *per se* between Indian society and those with which they were already familiar. Caste society was for Bouglé a contrastive study in a wider area of sociological concern—the study of egalitarianism [3]: a trend which has continued until recent times as is demonstrated by Louis Dumont's *Homo Hierarchicus*.

Weber had a more clearly defined purpose in using the Indian material. He was setting up a model of Indian society in order to prove a series of theses regarding modern European society. The non-European tradition was essential to his analysis not only as a contrastive study but more specifically in order to explain the absence of the emergence of capitalism in areas other than western Europe. His study of Asian religions (India and China) focused on the intermeshing of religion and economic life. Weber was among those who subscribed to the critique of Marx by pointing to what he thought were the inadequacies of Marxist explanation. Capitalism, therefore, was not the result of an historical evolution but a unique development which had its roots in seventeenth-century western Europe. In order to demonstrate his analysis, he had to use contrastive models from traditions other than the European. A precondition to his analysis was the assumption that there were factors in the European situation which made it significantly different from all others and by implication substantially more effective in terms of world history. Weber's interest in the non-European past was not therefore in the essential difference with the European, but in testing and proving a hypothesis concerning the European past.

[3] C. Bouglé, *Essays on the Caste System* (Cambridge, 1971), p. vii. (Originally published 1908 in French).

The choice and comprehension of the Indian material was to some extent conditioned by the use which these sociologists wished to make of it. The reliability and the range of the source material which was available to them by the end of the nineteenth and early twentieth centuries when they were writing is another question which has to be considered. By this time the Indian pre-colonial past had been interpreted by a large number of sophisticated ideologues who, under the guise of the newly-found objectivity of the nineteenth century, were supporting a variety of preconceptions or what they believed were definitive models. In most cases the interpretations were highly coloured by the intellectual preconceptions current in Europe at the time.

The problem of source material operated at two levels. One was that those who were not professional Indologists had to use the sources in translation. This was crucial to the question of interpretation. Terms relating particularly to social organization could only be translated and interpreted in the light of current research. Those for example who were reliable scholars of Sanskrit were not necessarily acquainted with the nuances of social forms and stratification. Consequently, the translation of concepts could result in misunderstandings. For example, the notion of race was embedded in the European intellectual consciousness in the nineteenth century. The universality of the concept was sought to be proved by translating various words as 'race' from the literatures of non-European societies even where the concept of race did not exist. Thus Monier-Williams, an undoubtedly outstanding Sanskritist and the compiler of the standard Sanskrit dictionary, refers to race as lineage and proceeds to translate a series of terms essentially connected with descent groups and kinship relations as 'race'—*vamśa, kula, jāti, gotra, jana, varṇa.*[4] None of these words could today be translated as race. Similarly, the frequently used term, *ñāti*, in the Pāli texts, now often translated as phratry or as

[4] M. Monier-Williams, *A Sanskrit-English Dictionary* (New York, 1976), p. 652.

extended kin-group, was also earlier translated as race. The understanding of caste as described in the *Dharmaśāstra* of Manu would naturally take on a strange coloration if references to *varṇa* and *jāti* were translated as race. This particular example is interlinked with the fact that most nineteenth century theories explaining the origin of caste saw it primarily as a system of demarcating the identities of various racial groups and maintaining separation.

At the other level, the sources of India available to those who were not professional Indologists were generally limited. The primary data on caste was taken from the Census Reports and the Imperial Gazetteers for the contemporary period and from the translations of the *Dharmaśāstra*s, the socio-legal texts, for earlier times. The former category was compiled by officials of the Government of India and naturally reflected the conceptual biases then current on the pre-colonial Indian past among British administrators who were also, in the main, the scholars in the field. For the religions of India there were again the translations of the texts and the works of Indologists such as Zimmer, Oldenberg, Fick, Hopkins or historians such as Vincent Smith and Grant Duff.

The investigation of Indian society by European scholars had begun in a systematic way in the late eighteenth century. A major strand in the early interpretations was what became well known in the nineteenth century as the Aryan Theory. It derived academic sanction from the work of comparative philologists such as Max Müller, Auguste Pictet and Christian Lassen, ideological sanction from the essays of the Comte de Gobineau and political sanction by the end of the nineteenth century from the competing imperialism of the West European nations. The basis of the theory was the equation of language with race. In Europe the major dichotomy was seen as between Aryan and Semitic and in India it became Aryan and Dravidian, with the upper castes viewed as the descendants of the Aryans. The association of the theory with India had its genesis in the philological relationships noticed between Sanskrit and Greek, Latin and other European languages.

The Aryans it was argued were implicitly superior to the non-Aryans as they were the initial conquerors who had founded civilizations in Europe and Asia. In India, the arrival of the Aryans was associated with the compilation of the *Ṛg Veda* and this was believed to be the bed-rock of Indian civilization, the excavation of the Indus cities not as yet having taken place. By the late nineteenth century, the fallacy of equating language with race had been clearly demonstrated. Nevertheless, the theory remained established in European thought with reference to India. It also became acceptable to the new middle-class élite in India as it could call itself Aryan, differentiate itself from the lower castes believed to be non-Aryan and even seek a connection with the British rulers who represented European aryandom.[5]

Caste society was explained as being based on racial segregation with the Aryans forming the higher castes. The system was defended as a scientific division of society based on racial grouping, where the identity was preserved by rigid laws of marriage. The linking of caste society with racial segregation grew, in part, out of a linguistic misapprehension. The two most frequently used Sanskrit words referring to caste are *varṇa* and *jāti*. The latter quite clearly refers to descent and derives from the root **ja*—to be born. *Varṇa* on the other hand, which is used to categorize the four groups (*brāhmaṇa, kṣatriya, vaiśya* and *śūdra*), has been derived from a root meaning colour. This was immediately interpreted as a reference to human pigmentation and colour in the racial sense by the early translators of the texts. That the racial connotation is the suggestion of the translators is clear from the entry under *varṇa* in the Monier-Williams dictionary.[6] From the texts it would seem that the connotation of colour is symbolic since the four colours associated with the groups are white, red, yellow and black.[7] Social differentiation symbolized in

[5] *Keshab Chunder Sen's Lectures in India*, p. 323.

[6] M. Monier-Williams, *A Sanskrit-English Dictionary* (New York, 1976), p. 924 qv. *varṇa.*

[7] *Mahābhārata* 12.181.5ff. refers to the four *varṇas* as symbolized by the

colours is not unusual in the traditions of many early societies. Additional support for the racial basis of caste was sought from the references in the *Ṛg Veda* to the initial division of society into the *ārya-varṇa* and the *dāsa-varṇa* wherein the latter is described as being constituted of short-statured and dark-complexioned people, [8] but the description of the former is vague.

Apart from the rather simplistic racial dichotomy, other aspects were introduced gradually as caste came to be seen as the foundation of Indian social structure. Earlier, Max Müller in *Chips from a German Workshop* had argued that the racial factor was not a sufficient explanation for the evolution of caste and had added two more: conquest and political formation and professional or occupational groups. To these, Alfred Lyall had added a fourth, the religious sectarian factor, arguing that religious sectarian movements could also evolve into castes and this evolution was the reflection of the divisive tendencies inherent in Indian society.[9] Ibbetson took the argument further and suggested that three factors were important: the creation of guilds founded on hereditary occupation, the exaltation of the sacerdotal function and the importance attributed to heredity. Caste was consolidated by a series of laws regulating marriage alliances, the purity of food and

---

colours white, red, yellow and black, the differentiaion of which comes about after a preliminary period when all *varṇa*s were identical. The same sequence of colours is used in connection with the four epochs (*yugas*) 3.148.5–37.

[8] *Ṛg Veda* 1.130.8.; 5.29.10.; 9.41.1.

[9] A. Lyall, *Asiatic Studies* (London, 1889); D.C.J. Ibbetson, *Report on the Census of the Punjab taken on 17th February 1881* (Calcutta, 1883); J.C. Nesfield, *Brief View of the Caste System of the North-western Provinces and Oudh, together with an Examination of Names and Figures shown in the Census Report*, 1882. (Allahabad, 1885); H.H. Risley, *The People of India* (London, 1908). These were all officials involved in the administration of India and contributed to the collection of census data and studies of castes and tribes in British India during the late nineteenth and early twentieth centuries. In contrast to the British writing on this subject which came mainly from administrators, French studies on society and religion in India came from professional scholars of Sanskrit and from sociologists.

intercaste relations. The consolidation was largely within the framework of *brāhmaṇa* authority and power. Nesfield argued that occupation was the dominant causative factor. He favoured an evolutionary pattern from tribe to caste where marriage rules and behaviour taboos reflect tribal forms in caste and the occupation taken up by the tribe on the decline of the tribal form identified its caste status. Status was largely determined by whether the occupation was of a pre-metal working society and therefore low or of a post-metal working society and therefore high. The *brāhmana,* however, remained always the highest caste.

Risley revived the race theory in his *The People of India* (1908). He argued that there was a tribal genesis to caste, a memory of which is retained in the exogamous groups such as the *gotras*. But this soon gave way to primarily ethnological distinctions, the germ of which lies in the enemity of the white and black races as expressed in the *ārya-varṇa* and the *dāsa-varṇa* of the *Ṛg Veda*. The segregation was maintained by carefully worked out endogamous laws. He took very literally the Brahmanical idea that all low status castes are necessarily the product of interbreeding. The hierarchy of caste was based on an ethnological distinction between the Aryans retaining their purity as the highest castes and the aboriginal inhabitants of India being clustered at the lower end. Risley maintained that race was the generating principle and he used ethnographic measurement, particularly the nasal index in an attempt to prove his theory.

A rather different point of view was put forward by Senart in his *Les Castes dans l'Inde* (1896). He was dissatisfied with the racial theory. He felt that the emphasis on occupation as the crucial variable was exaggerated since caste distinctions were known even among people in the same profession. Senart sought the answer to the origins of caste in the constitution of the family. Caste has the same rights over individuals as do early families in other ancient societies such as the Greeks and the Romans. Endogamous laws were also fundamental to these societies (e.g. the *jus connubii* of Rome). Laws of commensality in caste were intended to exclude the aliens from sacrifices and religious feasts since a meal signifies sharing and equality. Even the fear of impurity and defilement has analogies from Greco-Roman parallels. The origin of caste requires a multi-causal explanation. He accepted that there was initially a conflict between the Aryans and the dark-skinned race of inferior civilization which resulted in a strengthening of the exclusiveness of the Aryans. Gradually however there was an admixture of races and apart from the extensive family groups which developed into castes, function-based groups of a mixed origin also developed into castes. The sacerdotal power strengthened itself and worked out the ideal caste system—the *varṇa* system. Notions of purity made the exclusion more rigid and prevented absorption into the indigenous population. As in the case of the Greeks, it also preserved the higher castes from performing manual labour. The unending justification of social distinctions was endorsed by the concept of metempsychosis. The continuity of caste was largely due to the absence of a political authority to cut across these divisions and unify them.

The theory of the absence of political authority derived in part from the current notion that the Indian village community contributed to the consolidation of caste since it subsumed common territory, kin and jurisdiction. It was an organic and integral unit which managed to maintain its autonomy from the political superstructure. Max Müller had described it in glowing terms as an idyllic community[10] and it became one of the tenets of nineteenth-century colonial sociology. The village community was also seen as the root of Indo-European life and it was thought that in the Indian village community Europe had rediscovered its origins. Less romantically, Marx argued that the Indian village community was one of the causes of the stagnation of Indian society.[11] Henry Maine saw it as a point along the linear form of the social growth of society from a kin-organized system to a commercial-industrial

[10] M. Müller, *India, What Can It Teach Us?* (London, 1883), pp. 15, 101.
[11] K. Marx and F. Engels, *On Colonialism* (Moscow, 1968), p. 41.

society.[12] Lyall took the argument of an absence of political authority still further and argued that India was at 'an arrested stage of development'. According to him, the evolutionary stage of the tribe was still prevalent (as in parts of Rajasthan) which was a survival from an earlier social form. The absence of political stability was due to an absence of the political institutions required to counterbalance monarchical power.

The notion of Indian society reflecting an early, if not a primitive, stage in social evolution or demonstrating a form of arrested growth was also implicit in another widely-accepted theory which pertained more closely to the nature of political and economic forms in Asia—the theory of Oriental Despotism. Its main postulates were, the existence of isolated, self-sufficient village communities, superimposed upon which was the despotic ruler and his court who creamed the surplus off the peasantry through a very efficient bureaucratic machinery. The latter was not only the mechanism for revenue collection but also ran the State-controlled irrigation system upon which all cultivation was dependent. The divine origin of the king also helped to create the appropriate distance. Since it was believed that there was no private property in land, it was argued that there were no intermediary groups between king and peasant nor, therefore, any political institutions to counterbalance the monarchy. The economic autarchy of the village community allowed it a political autonomy except for the mechanism of revenue collection which impinged on the autonomy. There was also an absence of urban centres specializing in the production of commodities for a market which, had they existed, might have been the basis for a political check on despotism and might have encouraged economic change.

The theory, partially subscribed to by historians such as James Mill in the early nineteenth century, gained ground in England over the decades and by the middle of the century was axiomatic to the understanding of Indian society and politics. Inevitably, it

[12] H.S. Maine, *Village Communities in the East and West* (New York, 1974), (reprint), p. 22ff.

was reflected to a greater or lesser degree in the reports compiled by British administrators working in the districts. Others too were not left untouched. Marx in his discussion on colonialism in India used this theory to explain what he regarded as the political stagnation and economic backwardness of India which facilitated the British conquest. The Indian village community was for Marx a survival from the past and, consequently, an anachronism which had to be done away with if the condition of arrested growth were to cease.

The assumption in these theories was that there is a contrastive difference between the Indian and the European experience. This difference can be explained by locating its causes. The methodological approach was to assume that the Indian experience had failed since Indian society had not evolved to a capitalist form and it was important to try and discover why it had failed. Basic to this assumption was the notion that Indian society reflected a stepping off, as it were, from the escalator of social evolution. This in brief was the intellectual background to the views current in Europe on Indian society. Even where these views were questioned or discarded, the rejection has to be seen in terms of the prevalent ideas. The inability of certain societies to evolve into a capitalist form became a major characteristic in differentiating various societies. This distinction also lay at the centre of sociological thought for many decades and was expressed in a variety of supposed oppositions—*gesellschaft*: *gemeinschaft*, folk: urban, status: contract and, ultimately, tradition: modernity.

Marx had earlier brought to a head the question of the primacy of ideas or social facts. The question arose repeatedly in later writing not only as part of the critique of Marxism but as a controversial issue in itself. Durkheim moved gradually from a position of regarding ideas and beliefs as a derivative of a subsect of social facts towards suggesting that symbolic thought is a condition of and explains society.[13] Durkheim's ideas on the sociology

[13] S. Lukes, *Emile Durkheim: His Life and Work* (London, 1973), p. 235ff

of religion were important in the analysis of Indian society since religion was often regarded as the crucial variable which gave a particular direction to Indian society, a point of view more fully elaborated by Weber. That the essential elements of religious thought are to be found in seminal form in primitive religion or at any rate, 'it is easier to see the forms at an early stage', is suggestive of an element of evolutionism in Durkheim's argument. There was a tendency to classify religio-social phenomena into two categories: one pertaining to pre-literate societies and the other to literate societies. The Durkheimian interest was essentially in the former with its emphasis on totemism, magic, matrilineal society, the overarching deity and pre-logical thinking, which makes this imperative as a starting point. Religion was pre-eminently a social phenomenon. Although the factual correctness of his use of interrelationships between totem and clan and his reliance on dubious ethnography have been criticized[14] nevertheless his views on religion have been used to correlate religious forms and social realities in Indian society, which have further strengthened the hypothesis of the particular role of religion in Indian society. Since Durkheim's views were largely limited to the religion of primitive societies, their application to Indian data was mainly in the form of recognizing primitive survivals in religious rites and beliefs of the early historical period. Few attempts have been made to apply them to the religious systems of 'tribal India' current even today. The application of his views to more advanced forms of religion in India were limited owing partially to his own initial hesitations in extending his ideas to more complex religious forms.

Durkheim's own analysis did not pertain centrally to Indian religion and even where he uses the absence of deity in Buddhism to point up his definition of religion he is not concerned with any detailed understanding of Buddhism. He argues that the turning in of man upon himself in the process of meditation allows the absence of a deity, a point made by earlier Indologists such as

[14] *Ibid.*, p. 477ff.

Oldenberg and Barth.[15] Nevertheless, Buddhism is a religion since it admits of the existence of sacred things. Buddhism, Jainism and Hinduism enter the discussion again when Durkheim argues that altruistic suicide is a form of sacrifice arising out of a sense of duty and not unrelated to pantheistic beliefs. Durkheim's division of religious phenomena into beliefs and rites reappeared in later studies of the Vedic sacrifice.

Hubert and Mauss analysed the ritual of sacrifice in some detail with frequent reference to the texts on the early Vedic sacrifices. They asserted that the ritual implied the consecration of a common object to a religious plane and that it symbolized the separation of the sacred and the profane. This separation is inherent all the time but can only be actualized through the mediation of religious agents. The separation is apparent at many levels: the area where the sacrifice takes place is demarcated as sacred, the priest communicating with the god is sacred in the sacrificial context as also is the sacrifiant and the mundane animal now consecrated as the sacrificial victim. Outside of a sacred place immolation is murder. As the texts put it, he who performs the sacrifice, 'passes from the world of men into the world of gods'.[16] The preparation for consecration is as elaborate as that of desacralisation. The sacrificer purifies himself by being in a condition of sanctity and redeems himself by substituting the victim in his place. Sacrifice therefore also becomes a procedure of communication between the sacred and the profane worlds. Mauss elsewhere develops the argument with reference to *dāna* (gift giving) which is generally treated as a purely religious action, but he views it as a form of gift-exchange. Using the lengthy discussion on the ritual of *dāna* as stated in the Anuśāsanparvan of the *Mahābhārata* as his data, Mauss argues that a routine action of making a gift can

[15] H. Oldenburg, *The Buddha* (London, 1922), p. 214ff; M. Weber, *The Religion of India* (Glencoe, 1958), p. 146; Quoted in W.S.F. Pickering, *Durkheim on Religion* (Boston, 1975), p. 80ff.

[16] *Śatapatha Brāhmaṇa*, 1.1.1.1ff.

become a sacred rite depending on the donor, the recipient, the place and the intention with which the gift is made, all of which are listed in the text as important factors in the process of *dāna*. Alternatively, the same ritual can be seen as establishing the secular relationships implicit in a gift-exchange.

The bipolarity of the sacred and the profane in the Vedic sacrificial ritual can be seen as embodying social representations in as much as it can be argued that this was also germinal to the idea of purity and pollution with reference to caste groups. The purity of the *brāhmaṇa* was partly derived from his condition of sanctity at the time of the *yajña*, and the exclusion of the other castes may have been measured in terms of their social distance from the sacrificial enclosure. Thus, the *kṣatriya* was frequently the *yajamāna*, he who has the sacrifice performed, and could therefore be admitted as a participant. The other castes were at best observers from a distance.

Clearly, this was but one aspect of caste differentiation and for Bouglé it was by no means the central. Closer to his interest was Durkheim's distinction between mechanical solidarity and organic solidarity underlying which was the notion of pre-industrial and industrial society. The morphological structure of the first which Durkheim characterized as the segmental type—a clan-based society moving to territorial identity—was to be a repeated feature in the discussion on caste. Such societies according to Durkheim, were not based on a division of labour and lacked a fusion of markets and the growth of cities both of which were noticeable in organic solidarity. Other characteristics of the first category were the relatively weak interdependence between the segments, rules with repressive sanctions and the prevalence of penal law and absolute collective authority with little room for individual initiative. Such a society also placed a premium on values relating to society as a whole in its ethical forms, manifested a highly religious conscience and emphasized the transcendental. The transformation from mechanical solidarity to organic solidarity was for Durkheim the central focus of social change with its attendant social integration.[17]

Bouglé examined caste in the light of the definition of mechanical solidarity. He began by investigating whether caste was indigenous to Hindu society alone or was common to all societies at some stage. He includes among the characteristics of caste the following four: hereditary specialization; hierarchy and the inequality of rights; a clear opposition between elementary groups which isolate themselves through a series of taboos relating to food, contact, clothing etc., and which resist unification; and the incidence of mobility being collective rather than individual. When considering the roots of the system, Bouglé disagrees with the explanation that the *brāhmaṇas* were the originators of caste using it to divide and control society which he felt laid too great an emphasis on religion. The theories of some Indologists who saw caste evolving out of industrial guilds and therefore gave prominence to hereditary specialization were also unacceptable to Bouglé, for this would require an equation of caste with economic function and occupation, and such an equation is thwarted by a series of overlapping relations in caste. Senart had listed three groups among the *ārya*s: the sacerdotal who had appropriated the sacrificial ritual, the aristocracy founding itself on heredity, and the common people. These three divisions provided the impetus for further divisions and the separation of the Arya from the non-Arya. Senart was looking at the origins of caste with reference to *varṇa*. For Bouglé the protypes of caste were not the *varṇa*s but the *jāti*s which were lineage descendants and indicated the dominance of ancient familial exclusivism. Such exclusivism was not specifically Aryan; tribal societies are known to have had rigid rules of exogamy and commensality and fraternity taboos are also to be found among the Semites.

The pre-eminent status of the *brāhmaṇa* was not secured from

[17] It has been suggested that Durkheim understated the degree of interdependence and reciprocity in mechanical solidarity and overstated the role of repressive law. Lukes, *op.cit*, p. 159ff.

the start, but was gradually usurped by the *brāhmaṇa* after an initial competition for status between the *brāhmaṇa* and the *kṣatriya*. Bouglé argued that since the *brāhmaṇa* caste could not accumulate riches its essential strength lay in religious power which it exploited and in this was encouraged by an absence of political organization. The prestige of the *brāhmaṇa* arose out of many factors. The racial superiority of the Aryans who conquered the Dravidians was partly responsible since the *brāhmaṇa*s salvaged what they could of their Aryan inheritance by careful marriage regulations. However, he qualified this by stating that it could not be based on physical types but on the perception of differences among ethnic groups. In addition, the *brāhmaṇa*s had become the guardians of the sacrifice and as such were in a perpetually consecrated condition (a view rather similar to Hubert and Mauss) which was reiterated by an emphasis on avoiding pollution through food and touch, all of which strengthened the exclusivity of the *brāhmaṇa*.

Caste therefore resulted from a concurrence of spontaneous and collective tendencies subject for the most part to the influence of ancient religious practices. The closed cult of the first familial groups prevented castes from mingling and the respect for the mysterious effects of sacrifice finally subordinated them to the castes of priests. The ideas which generated the caste system argued Bouglé, are not peculiar to the Hindus or to the Aryans, but were the common patrimony of primitive peoples. They survived in India because they managed to resist the influence of any unifying forces cutting across the exclusive groups. Thus, Hindu civilization is characterized by an arrested social development. Indian society has moved in an inverse direction and has continued to divide, specialize and hierarchize whereas other societies have unified, mobilized and levelled. Thus, caste society had the same roots and origins as egalitarian societies, but unlike the latter, which underwent changes in the egalitarian direction, caste society deliberately remained inegalitarian.

The lack of social and historical change is specifically noted by Bouglé who uses this as a partial explanation as to why there are neither historians nor historical records in pre-colonial India. He maintains that superficially political forms have changed and there have been administrative monarchies and feudal politics, but beneath this the caste structure has preserved a constant form. Even religion does not succeed in destroying caste since religious sects take on the characteristic identities of castes. The only exception to this was Buddhism and significantly Buddhism did not survive in India. Its disappearance wa not due to Hindu intolerance, since intolerance requires political dogmatism which was lacking in India. Rather it was the abstracting of the Buddhist community from social life which prevented it from denting the caste system and furthermore the monastery was closed to those in opposition to authority. Philosophies of detachment and inaction are not conducive to change and the theory of transmigration encourages neither reform nor revolt nor change.

On the question of race Bouglé did not totally discard racial identities in caste although he was unsympathetic to the theories of Risley and anthropometry arguing that castes are not pure races and are racially mixed. To correlate caste and race in accordance with Brahmanical theory (of course assuming that this *was* in fact Brahmanical theory) is to superimpose the theory on observed data. Further, hereditary specialization has not deposited essentially different properties in different castes, as was occasionally suggested by other commentators on Indian society. Bouglé was of the view that the philosophy of race remains unproven, although castes as strictly enclosed groups may have preserved primitive repulsions of a racial nature.

In his discussion on law and caste Bouglé appears to have relied heavily on Durkheim's description of mechanical solidarity. Bouglé maintains that rules relating to behaviour are governed by notions of purity and are therefore largely ritual prescriptions. Unlike western law which is restitutive, the *dharmaśāstras* of India in which the laws are coded, are repressive. The legal system did not seek to cut across caste distinctions and instead supported the hierarchy of castes and the stress on inequality by assuming an ascending scale of punishment. Hindu law was able to preserve its religious colouring because no political power arose to counterbalance the power of the priestly caste nor did economic life change caste. Caste did not obstruct economic production—if anything it assisted in perfecting the dexterity of the craftsman based on hereditary specialization and the intensive practice of skills. But caste did obstruct economic change in that it retained the primitive clan character of society and mechanical solidarity could not give way to organic solidarity. In the terminology of Henry Maine, status repels contract. Since caste is essentially divisive and separatist, economic groups could not arise which would cut across caste boundaries and the organization of authority left little place for the institutions of liberty. There was never a body of towns large enough and numerous enough for the production and circulation of wealth and at the same time the production and circulation of ideas acting as the necessary centres of co-ordination. Centres of production were associated with political capitals and were therefore transitory. Commerce was never predominant in law, action and style. The city requires a unity among citizens to safeguard its independence, but this was inimical to caste. Guilds were rooted in caste since they could not adopt new members or associate socially among themselves. Thus, there was an arrested development of economic formations, a generalization on which Weber was to expand.

Some of Bouglé's views on India are shared by Weber. His focus was not on caste however but on the absence of the emergence of capitalism. European capitalism was seen as the watershed or the divide separating pre-capitalist from capitalist societies and the dichotomy was emphasized by many theorists at the time such as Tönnies, Simmel and Maine.[18] Marx saw it as a stage in historical development, but Weber saw it as a totality, as a 'civilization'. Central to this totality was the role of rationality in western capitalism which made it a unique experience in world

[18] S. Hughes, *Consciousness and Society* (New York, 1961).

history.[19] This was not to deny the rationality of other civilizations but to point to the generally more static role of rationality in these as compared to its dominant role in western capitalism. Weber tended to pose rationality and irrationality as bipolarities which are present in every situation. Rationality permeated the whole of capitalist culture. It dominated science, law (a written constitution regulating political activity), music, architecture and above all economics, where it is evident not only in the more obvious technological basis of industrialization, but also in the separation of industrial from household economics and the precise analysis of cost and profit which lies at the core of capitalist enterprise. All these in turn tend to impersonalize relationships and conduct (and perhaps even dehumanize certain segments of society). In addition to rationality, there was also the historical factor of the simultaneous emergence of free labour without any land and the industrialist who had accumulated capital through the mercantile activities of the pre-capitalist world.[20] This was a major element in the rise of capitalism which Weber conceded to the Marxist model. The third factor which Weber stressed was the Protestant religion which he felt embodied the spirit of capitalism. Weber's emphasis was on the role of Protestantism in developing capitalism rather than on Protestantism reflecting the rise of capitalism.[21] Weber did not accept the possibility of establishing laws of social development and thereby predicting social change as had been proposed explicitly by Marx and suggested implicitly by Durkheim. He rejected evolutionary theories and maintained that the best analysis was based on categories and 'ideal-types'. The social scientist was also not in a position to make a representation of reality. Methodology was merely a means of understanding—hence the exaggeration implicit in his 'ideal type' was deliberate in order to highlight differences and clarify the model.

[19] J. Freund, *The Sociology of Max Weber* (London, 1968), p. 5ff.

[20] J. Lewis, *Max Weber and Value-Free Sociology* (London, 1975), p. 67.

[21] R.H. Tawney, *Religion and the Rise of Capitalism* (Harmondsworth, 1961), pp. 89–142.

Weber's explanation for the absence of capitalism in India required a detailed examination of religion in India, the two being intertwined. But, apart from examining the religions of Asia, he also argued for certain historical situations in Europe having provided some base for the growth of capitalism. His attempt to locate the latter was by discussing the absence of capitalism in antiquity. It was from this perspective that he viewed the historical development of the pre-capitalist world, both the agrarian structures of ancient civilizations and the rise of the medieval city.

Weber's discussion on the absence of capitalism in antiquity appears to be somewhat anachronistic and arises no doubt from his refusal to make concessions to alternate forms of historical evolution. Yet at the same time he does speak of stages in the social organization of agricultural societies. These he describes as the walled settlements of household and village, the fortress, the aristocratic city-state, the authoritarian liturgical state, the hoplite polis and the democratic citizen polis.[22] The initial stage was characterized by a distinction between free members and slaves and the emergence from among the former of princely clans, their justification being based on division of spoils, voluntary gifts and special allotments of land enhanced by divine legitimacy. The second stage sees the emergence of the king and greater dependence on rent from land. The aristocratic city-state emphasized the status of those who owned land and debt slaves (often peasants who could not pay rents). The feudal nobility of the fortress stage became the urban community, although Weber does not explain the emergence of either. The fifth stage refers to the power of the state and its imposition of duties on the subject. The hoplite polis, a derivative of the aristocratic polis, was subject to the domination of the clan and was characterized by a self-equipped citizen army dependent on ownership of land. This, in turn, gave way to the final stage of the democratic citizen polis where land ownership

[22] M. Weber, *The Agrarian Sociology of Ancient Civilisations* (London, 1976), p. 69ff.

was closely regulated but at the same time separated from military service. Communal forms of land ownership were abolished and rent alone remained. This led to the rise of capitalism since slaves were not debt slaves but purchased. Sharecroppers and slave agriculture gave way to yeomanry and mercenary armies replaced the hoplites. Ultimately city-states declined and were replaced by monarchical state systems with their major structural unit in the manor, channelling land relations, taxes and military recruitment. Weber saw the large empires of Asia such as the Assyrian and the Persian as conglomerates of urban and manorial areas. Yet at the same time he accepted the theory of the absence of private ownership of land in Asian civilization. He argues that, whereas in Europe the pattern of settlement moved from cattle breeding to agriculture and private ownership of land emerged on the basis of communal grazing grounds, in Asia it changed from nomadism to horticulture and the notion of private ownership was thus by-passed.[23]

Weber argues against the possibility of a capitalist economy emerging in the ancient past because the cities were centres of consumption rather than production. The urban economy of cities was limited since they were dependent on grain imports, their export articles were based on high labour inputs which required the purchase of slaves and their policies were solely determined by commercial interests. The development of capitalism was not based on rent from land but on commodity production. Slave agriculture could be regarded as capitalist although here Weber would be subjected to the same criticism as that made of Rostovtzeff's views on capitalist agriculture in Greco-Roman antiquity.[24]

[23] *Ibid.*, p. 37ff. Horticulture implies a mixture of food-gathering and primitive food production requiring neither technological innovations nor substantial changes in demographic structure and land-rights as were necessary in the transition from cattle breeding to agriculture.

[24] M. Reinhold, 'Historian of the classic world: a critique of Rostovtzeff,' *Science and Society*, 1946, 10, pp. 361–91.

In his study *The City*, with particular emphasis on the medieval city, Weber moves away from earlier theorists who had emphasized religion, legal structure replacing kinship, contract replacing status and economic institutions providing the theoretical basis of the city. Weber argues that it is the evolution of the urban community as an institution which characterizes the basis of the city. Above all that the urban community is typical of Occidental society and is virtually absent in the Orient (except in the ancient Near East). It is based on the dominance of trade-commercial relations and characterized by the presence of fortifications, a market, a court reflecting partially autonomous law, association of city members with partial autonomy and administration by authorities in whose election the burghers participate. With reference to India, Weber argued that only guilds and castes developed courts and special legal structures but even here trial by law and courts were absent. Autonomous administration was virtually unknown. The Indian urban dweller remained a member of the caste, guild or city-ward, but not a citizen of the city. There was no joint association representing the city and this was prevented by the segregating necessities of the system. Endogamous castes with their exclusive taboos were an obstacle to the fusion of the city dwellers into a status group enjoying social and legal equality and the ban on commensality among castes prevented the display of solidarity and fraternity of those sharing a common table. The only exceptions to this were that in periods of salvation religions, guilds could sometimes cut across town loyalties if they subscribed to the religion; and in the periods prior to the rise of bureaucratic kingdoms there were autonomous cities governed by clan elders. Indian cities were essentially royal centres or political capitals with market places and fortifications.

Medieval Occidental cities (and especially those north of the Alps) were strikingly different from Asian cities. They grew as a result of immigration so that local ties were eroded and the city became an administrative district within which all inhabitants irrespective of differences shared the same administration. Taboo barriers of totem, caste and clan were absent. On the contrary, the *conjuratio*, the oath-bound fraternity of burghers, broke through some of the earlier tendencies towards separation. Weber's rather glowing account of the medieval Occidental city tends to blur the distinctions within the citizens where both fraternity and autonomy tended to belong to limited groups. For Weber, the most important aspect of the city, namely civic development, emerged neither in the Asian city nor in the medieval European city. It emerged later in the West European city. He gives among possible reasons for its absence the lack of city fraternization which encourages the growth of the urban community. Clans and castes were mutually exclusive. There were no urban military interests and the burgher was not a military man. The guilds in the cities of India and China could bring pressure on royal power, but could not oppose it in a military manner. In the later European cities the guilds could not only combine and assert civic power, but the *conjurationes* could take up arms independently of the king. It was this ability to unite as citizens, demonstrate independence and defy royal power which made the difference. The legalization of privileges encouraged political autonomy. In Weberian terms traditional domination gradually gave way to legal domination. The occurrence of a charismatic figure was not precluded, but the potential for a reciprocal relationship so necessary to the theory of domination would be reduced in a society built on legal domination and the bureaucracy.

Charismatic leadership was more apparent in the role of the prophet in early societies.[25] Here Weber differentiates between the exemplary and the ethical prophet. The Buddha typifies the first where there is no divine mission, the prophet merely showing his followers the path to salvation. Moses as an ethical prophet highlights the claim to communion with God and demands obedience as an ethical duty. The exemplary prophet is common in India and

[25] *The Sociology of Religion* (London, 1965), p. 46ff.

China because of the absence of a personal transcendental and ethical god and also because the rationally regulated world had its point of origin in the ceremonial order of sacrifice. The difference between Asia and Europe is spotlighted by another fundamental notion, that of predestination. In Europe predestination strengthened the idea of vocation and gave the Christian a justification for his activity as being ordained. Success was a sign of God's blessing. Whereas in Asia it provided a negative impulse where salvation lay not in vocation but in escape from the sufferings of the terrestrial world. Similarly, there were basic differences in the nature of asceticism. Christianity culminated in asceticism of the inner-worldly category not the contemplative withdrawal of the world-rejecting type in Asia. Man had to ethically justify himself before the Christian God and not submerge himself. Christian monasteries placed a premium on labour and work rather than on meditation and the bureaucracy of the Christian church required an involvement in life. Some of these contrasts filled out the dichotomy which Weber was posing between Europe and Asia, a dichotomy which he analysed at greater length in his detailed studies of religion in China and India.

It is evident from looking at the sources which Weber consulted in writing *The Religion of India* that he was influenced by the current theories of nineteenth century Indologists and historians, relying as he had to on secondary works.[26] Weber's analysis of the social structure of India was a background to his understanding of both the orthodox doctrines of Hinduism and the heterodox doctrines of Buddhism together with the influence of popular religion on these. Caste and religious beliefs were therefore linked and, ultimately, he was concerned with the impact of religious beliefs on the secular ethic of Indian society. Weber sees caste as a status group with rigid rules of intermarriage and social intercourse and with pollution acting as a discriminatory factor between castes.

[26] *Ibid.*, p. 344ff.

According to Weber, the spread of caste society was brought about by three agencies: conquest, the conversion of tribes into castes, and the sub-division of castes. As a result of conquest racial differences led to segregation and prevented intermarriages, although Weber did not believe that racial differences were inherited. Whereas for Weber race was not the basis of caste as Risley had argued, the juxtaposition of racial differences were significant for the development of caste in India. The conquerors claimed rights in land and the conquered became subservient and lost their rights. Weber makes much of the difference between what he calls 'guest' and 'pariah' people without realizing than many 'guest' peoples were not given the lowest status in caste as he assumes. The conversion of tribes into castes was a commonly held theory among the ethnographers of the time. Tribes and castes had a totally opposite structure and the gradual conversion began with the assimilation of ruling groups among tribal societies into Hindu society generally by their being given *kṣatriya* status.[27] It was also said that food-gathering tribes who had lost their land as a result of the expansion of the agrarian economy were sometimes assimilated *en masse* as a single caste, usually that of peasants. The sub-division of castes meant that a new caste could branch off from an existing one by migration, a change in ritual duties, entry into a new religious sect, inequality of property possession where the better-off would imitate high caste social norms or a change of occupation arising out of economic or technological change. A difference of caste was established with the denial of connubium and commensalism by the original caste and the renunciation of ritual duties by the new caste.

Weber argued that the formation of castes was fundamental to the Indian social order which is based on clan charisma. Even feudal state formation did not rest on land grants but derived from

[27] E.W. Hopkins, 'The social and military position of the ruling caste in ancient India as represented in the Sanskrit epics,' *Journal of the American Oriental Society*, 1899, 13, p. 57ff.

sib, clan, phratry and tribe. The historical evidence however indicates that it was the making of land grants from the first millennium AD that broke the clan charisma. This evidence was available to Weber in the translations of epigraphical data but he, like the historians of the time evidently overlooked this. In the absence of genuine feudalization he argued that there was a prebendalization of the patrimonial state.

The *śūdras* as craftsmen he described as helots of single villages receiving a fixed wage or artisans in self-governing villages selling their products directly or through traders, or artisans settled by the kings, the temple, the landlord and, whether bondsmen or free, subject to servitude, or, finally, independent artisans settled in well-defined parts of the city and working as wage earners. For the *vaiśya*s the caste of traders and merchants, Weber drew his information from the description given by Baden-Powell, and maintained that they could not struggle against the patrimonial prince because of the caste system as well as the pacifism preached by the salvation religions. The stress on pacifism degraded the status of the peasant and inhibited the traders from creating an urban militia. Caste had a negative effect on the economy since it was anti-rational and traditionalistic. Ritual laws stood in the way of economic and technical revolutions. The trader remained a merchant incapable of using a new form of labour power and of diverting his wealth into capitalist forms. Neither was there any chance of cross-caste associations leading to the autonomy of the city nor was there any fraternization of castes as in European guilds followed by the seizing of political power. Caste emphasized distance rather than association. Cities were fortresses rather than urban centres with a weak market nucleus.

Enveloping the social totality was the theory of *samsāra* and *karma* (transmigration and rebirth) which developed into a system for the first time in Buddhist thought. Although Buddhism denied the existence of the soul and merely postulated the continuity of consciousness through a cycle of rebirths, it nevertheless related the ethics of rebirth to caste and this became axiomatic to both

Hindu and Buddhist social philosophy. *Karma* transformed the world into a strictly rational, ethically determined cosmos representing the most consistent theodicy ever produced in history. But it also required the strict fulfilment of caste obligation. Ethnic and economic factors were no doubt significant to caste structure, but *karma* reinforced it at the ethical level. There was no universally valid ethic but a compartmentalization of private and social ethic with each caste having its own ethic and, therefore, men were forever unequal. The absence of ethical universalism led to striving for individual salvation based on attempts to escape the wheel of rebirth. Even asceticism was a striving for personal, holy status where gnosis and ecstasy were sublimated to personal salvation as also were the natural sciences. Rational methods of asceticism were directed towards irrational goals. Yogic and ascetic techniques had two purposes: they had to accommodate the holy through the emptying of consciousness and they sought gnostic knowledge through meditation and techniques conducive to meditation. The salvation doctrines within which Weber included Buddhism, Jainism and the Bhāgavat-*bhakti* aspects of Hinduism, showed scant interest in the ethic for life on a temporal plane. For them reality consisted of the eternal order of the universe and the rebirth of souls.

Weber described Buddhism as the polar opposite of Islam and Confucianism: it was an unpolitical and anti-political status religion of wandering and intellectually schooled mendicants. It was a salvation religion—an ethical movement without cult or deity and centred on the personal salvation of the single individual. Above all, it advocated that the will to life has to be destroyed in order to achieve *nirvāṇa*. Although Buddhism did have a levelling, democratic character, it nevertheless did not attempt any rational method in life-conduct. Weber explains the schisms in Buddhism from the fourth century BC onwards as being due to a lack of strong roots in society, its marginal demands on the laity and its essentially monastic and itinerant way of life. When the monks became materialist minded and accepted gifts and proselytized, the religion declined. This decline was helped by the antagonism of secular rulers to Buddhist monasteries and the rising power of the town guilds. The Brahmanical restoration as Weber saw it continued to emphasize irrational ends. Ritualistic activities were strengthened because the *brāhmaṇas* wished to protect their fees and prebends. Instead of a drive towards the rational accumulation of capital, Hinduism created irrational accumulation chances for magicians, mystagogues and the ritually oriented strata. Brahmanism was supported by rent from land and fees for religious services which were inheritable and given in perpetuity. This encouraged a bifurcation of religious and secular authority and led to the weakening of the latter. In addition, local autonomy was strengthened as against a centralized system. The absence of a secular ethic was particularly apparent from an equal absence of the characteristics of European Protestantism. There was no devotion to a calling in Calvinistic terms with its attendant economic success nor could a rational transformation of the world be postulated as an act of Divine Will. The other-worldliness of Indian religion did not diminish an interest in this world, but the aim of this interest was different. Therefore, even if people were materialistic by nature, they were influenced by non-materialistic ideology into channelling their materialism to ineffective ends.

Perhaps the most frequently used word in Weber's analysis of the religion of India is 'absence'—reflecting a sharp distinction in his mind between the characteristic features of the Occidental civilization and their absence in the Asiatic/Oriental. To this extent he was echoing a common belief among nineteenth-century European thinkers for whom the dichotomy between Occidental and Oriental was very real. This was enhanced by the supposed duality between materialist and spiritualist civilizations, a duality which was to play an even more dominant role in the ideology of Asian nationalism in the twentieth century. The stress laid by Weber on the rationality of developments in Europe came under attack and such analyses were seen as part of a larger racial framework in which ideologues other than Weber attached value judgements of *a priori* superiority to the rationality. This was of course quite apart from the question of whether rationality was the prime motive in the development of European capitalism, a question which has been legitimately raised by some of those examining the place of Weber's thought within the European ideological tradition.[28]

Weber's understanding of capitalism has its own limitations. He fails to distinguish between the two major phases of capitalism—merchant capitalism and industrial capitalism. Thus, the characteristics of the first tend to get extended into the second. Hence the stress on the Protestant ethic, which undoubtedly was significant in the crystallization of the first phase but of only marginal significance to the second phase. What was central to the second phase was colonialism; both in its early form resulting from the colonization of Latin America and industrialization in the second phase dependent on the colonization of Asia and Africa. The ploughing in of the profits of colonialism into the development of European capitalism made a qualitative difference to the nature of capitalism. This not only accelerated industrialization but provided to capitalism precisely the kind of momentum which made it of consequence to world history and more than just a localized European phenomenon. Had the latter been the case, sociological theory in nineteenth-century Europe would not have regarded capitalism as the great divide in the classification of societies. Up to a point this reflects the inadequacies of the understanding of the process of industrialization and capitalism current in Europe at the time. Weber's ideal-type draws on the second phase, but he seeks to explain it by reference to the characteristics of the first phase. The uniqueness of western capitalism became apparent to him when the consequences of the second phase were being felt in Europe. The advance of Europe against the arrested growth of Asia was an established postulate in European thought in the nineteenth century. It was the nature of colonialism which

[28] S. Hughes, *op. cit.*, p. 330ff.

was seen as the historical manifestation of the advance. The initial inadequacy of Weber's theory is the absence of any reference to the role of colonies in the development of capitalism. Even if seen as a unique civilization, Weber's analysis of capitalism was restricted to its nascent phase and to that extent it was incomplete. His dismal prognostications for the future as envisaged in bureaucratic systems, tended to jump from the nascent to the mature without adequately examining the intervening phases.

It is doubtless Weber's refusal to concede historical evolution which led him to inquire into the possibility of capitalist forms in antiquity, both European and Asian. His historical probings would have been more apposite had he analysed non-European history during periods immediately prior to the rise of capitalism in Europe. This he was probably prevented from doing as he did not visualize historical change in Asian societies. Weber was clearly influenced by the concept of Oriental Despotism and, although he does not elaborate on this point, he saw Indian society basically as a static society. Whereas he does see at least three faces to the form of Modern Europe in Judaism, Greco-Roman antiquity and medieval Europe, in the case of India and China, he views them almost as faceless monoliths. This leads to his underplaying even though aware of it, the change within religious movements or social groups as, for example, his repeated references to Buddhist monks as itinerant mendicants even for periods when some were well-settled property owners. This weakness also relates to the discrepancy in the source material which he consulted for Europe and India. In the former case his generalizations are based on data recorded by the actual groups under discussion but in the Indian case he uses the media of Brahmanical texts for virtually all his major generalizations.

Weber accepts the primacy of religion above all other facets in Indian society. This is perhaps what prevented him from examining the more clearly-defined economic aspects at the root of capitalism in his study of Indian society. Whereas the availability of free labour and the existence of accumulated capital is a prior requisite for the emergence of capitalism, he nowhere attempts to assess the availability of these in India. To this extent Weber subscribed to the current lack of interest in the economic institutions of Indian society. Indian civilization was defined as Hindu and Buddhist with a sprinkling of Jainism. Yet it was precisely in the period of what has recently been called incipient capitalism in India, i.e. the seventeenth and eighteenth centuries, that the Islamic ethic, both religious and political was an important factor. A study of merchant capitalism in India would have involved the need to look at Islam in India, particularly at communities such as the Bohras and Khojas of Guajarat and the west coast, of for that matter even non-Islamic communities such as the Parsis. The exclusion of Islam stemmed from the nineteenth-century tendency to identify religions with their areas of origin and therefore Islam was limited to West Asia. To search for the roots of capitalism in the religious ethic of India during the first millennium BC and the first millennium AD is, to say the least, an anachronistic exercise.

Weber's study of India was a by-product of his main thesis and it would be unfair to be too critical of his theories, particularly as he was relying on secondary material for data. It is strange, though, that he should not at any point have questioned the contextual bias of his sources. One can only assume that his faith in the rationality of contemporary scholarship was as axiomatic to him as his faith in the rationality of capitalism. One cannot criticize him for the limitations of his source material but only for accepting unquestioningly the current interpretations and for not applying his own methodology to these sources—an accusation which can equally well be levelled at Marx in his writings on Asia.

In their analyses of caste both Bouglé and Weber were basing themselves on the existing theories without questioning too closely the premises of these. That the argument was often circular did not seem to matter too much, as for instance, in the Census Reports where the model of caste often related to the Brahmanical *Dharmaśāstras*. It has however to be remembered that they were writing over half a century ago with no access to the more recent insights into the social and economic history of India. Early models without the advantage of detailed research tended to result in over-simplification. Thus, in spite of arguing quite correctly that caste formation often took the form of the conversion of a tribe into a caste, there was all the same an acceptance in Weber's writing of the racially distinct character of upper and lower castes.

Caste is seen as divisive and separatist, but it can be maintained that at another level it is associative and this is expressed for example in the uniformity of certain cultural patterns over extensive geographical areas. This aspect is not analysed. The horizontal perspective played a significant role in the spread of 'Hindu civilization' at the élite levels, and was crucial to the extension of caste society. It was again the associative character of caste which was fundamental to major social and economic changes from the late first millennium AD onwards, particularly in periods of state formation. It could be argued that the nature of caste underwent a fundamental historical change during this period—a change which has not been fully recognized by historians and sociologists.[29] So strong was the preconception of the unchanging character of Indian society that generalizations based on the sources of the Vedic period (1000 BC) were considered adequate for the pre-colonial period up to the eighteenth century AD. For example, the status of the *brāhmaṇa* is rightly linked with his control over the sacrificial ritual in the Vedic period. However, with the extensive granting of property to the *brāhmaṇa* in livestock, in gold and ultimately in land there was a qualitative change in the status of the *brāhmaṇa* by the end of the first millennium AD as also in the sacrificial ritual. Far from abstracting a community from social life, the monasteries (the Buddhist *vihāra*s and the Hindu *maṭhas*) were also to take on the role of social institutions with substantial political and economic functions. These institutions became parallel seats of power. Alienation from society would have been one reason for joining the monastery but ac-

[29] Romila Thapar, *The Past and Prejudice* (New Delhi, 1975).

celerated social and political mobility could as well have been another. The renouncer rapidly acquired both social status and charisma and frequently built on it a worldly ambition. The 'this-worldly' role of the renouncer seems to have been missed by these sociologists.

From the monastic centres, both Hindu and Buddhist in their time and later even Islamic, there arose the foci of sectarian and political orthodoxy as well as heterodoxy and opposition which led them into varying relationships vis-à-vis political authority. Such religious centres often doubled for networks of trade and were therefore in close contact with merchants and guilds. The nature of the relationship between guilds and political authority was earlier believed to be one of subservience from the former towards the latter, but this view requires re-examination with the availability of more specific and local source material relating to the seventeenth and eighteenth centuries. The jockeying for power between political authority and merchant interests in India during this period suggests a more complex relationship than had been supposed earlier. The crucial question may remain the same as the one posed by Weber, namely, the inability (real or seeming) of the merchants to make an open bid for political power. The answers to such questions lie perhaps less with caste as the crucial variable and more with the role of the European trading companies in Asia. It is curious that Weber did not examine the sources for this period in detail. Had he done so his analysis may have been sharper. But perhaps this would have required of Weber too great an emphasis on historical perception.

From the perspective of the limitation of source materials perhaps the greatest injustice is done to the analysis of Buddhism. Theravada Buddhist sources composed in Pāli were generally regarded by Indologists as somehow not as reliable as Brahmanical, Sanskrit sources. The former were assumed to be *parti pris* but strangely enough not the latter. Since Buddhism had died out in India, Buddhist texts were not given the same importance even though at the time of their composition or soon after, Buddhism was as important, if not more so, as Brahmanism. Had Weber looked more fully at Buddhist sources he would have seen a different epistomology with an emphasis on the universal ethic within which the caste structure was adjusted (and not just the absence of the former and an insistence only on the caste ethic), a movement in time from a pristine utopia to a well-defined future, a strong sense of sectarian historiography impinging on political history of a more secular nature and a monastic life deeply embedded in a society of lay-followers. The three major characteristics as defined by Weber seem doubtful since Buddhism was often closely associated with political authority, at the level of popular support it assimilated local cults and far from advocating a destruction of the will to life it endorsed a programme for the householder and lay-followers which precluded monasticism. Many of the sectarian splits within Buddhism arose because of its having to adjust to changing social mores as it spread across India and Asia. The decline of Buddhism in India had more to do with the changing role of the monastery as an institution, together with competition from other religious sects and a decline in patronage with the decrease of trade in the middle of the first millennium AD.

Weber makes a distinction between early Buddhism, a religion of salvation-striving monks and the later phase with the emergence of what he calls monastic landlordism. The salvation-striving monks were from the start part of a monastic order and the monasteries were segments of what might be called parallel societies. The development of monastic landlordism is seen by Weber essentially in terms of change within the Buddhist structure and to a lesser degree as the interplay between Buddhist institutions and the other institutions of society. Monastic landlordism tends to take on a static form which does not conform to the historical evidence; nor is the emergence of monastic landlordism merely the result of extensive support from the laity since the nature of the institution was such that it made demands both on political authority and the economy. When, even the forest-dwelling monks, theoretically seeking isolation were willing to accept royal patronage and become the nuclei of political centres, the role of such monasteries takes on various political dimensions.

It is not the intention of this paper to attempt to refute the interpretations of Bouglé (as linked to Durkheim) and Weber. Both studies have been seminal to much that is new and meaningful in the sociology and social history of India. A more serious concern with the validity of these interpretations would undoubtedly result in still newer areas of research and analysis. Its intent was to suggest that both Bouglé and Weber in their studies on India were influenced by the prevailing preconceptions about India, which preconceptions they surprisingly tended to accept without too much questioning. One wishes that Weber had applied some of his more innovative categories of thought to the pre-colonial Indian past as he did to the European past.

ADDITIONAL BIBLIOGRAPHY

Baden-Powell, B.H., *The Indian Village Community*, New Haven, 1957 (originally published in 1896)

Bendix, R., *Max Weber, An Intellectual Portrait*, London, 1960.

Dumezil, G., *Mythe et Epopée*, I and II, Paris, 1968, 1971.

Dumont, L., *Homo Hierarchicus: The Caste System and Its Implications*, New York, 1972.

Durkheim, E., *The Division of Labour in Society*, New York, 1964 (reprint and trans).

——, *Primitive Classification*, Chicago, 1963 (reprint and trans).

——, *The Elementary Forms of Religious Life : A Study in Religious Sociology*, London, 1915 (reprint and trans).

Heesterman, J.C., *The Ancient Indian Royal Consecration*, The Hague, 1957.

Held, G.J., *The Mahabharata : An Ethnological Study*, London, 1935.

Hubert H., and M. Mauss, *Sacrifice : Its Nature and Function*, London, 1964 (reprint and trans).

——, *Melanges d'histoire des Religions*, Paris, 1909.

Mill, J., *History of British India*, London, 1818–1823.

M. Müller, *Chips from a German Workshop,* I and II, London 1867–75.

D. Kantowsky has edited of papers entitled, *Recent Research on Max Weber's studies of Hinduism,* London 1986, in which he argues that many scholars working on Weber's theories on India have misunderstood Weber because the translation of his study on the religion of India has misrepresented the original German text. This may well be. One expects therefore a more correct translation to be made available. A recent study which touches on many aspects of this essay is T. Trantmann's *Aryans and British India* which demonstrates the "twinning" as he Calls it of Sanskrit studies and ethnology in the nineteenth century understanding of early India.

*Imagined Religious Communities? Ancient History and the Modern Search for a Hindu Identity**

My choice of subject for this lecture arose from what I think might have been a matter of some interest to Kingsley Martin; as also from my own concern that the interplay between the past and contemporary times requires a continuing dialogue between historians working on these periods. Such a dialogue is perhaps more pertinent to post-colonial societies where the colonial experience changed the framework of the comprehension of the past from what had existed earlier: a disjuncture which is of more than mere historiographical interest. And where political ideologies appropriate this comprehension and seek justification from the pre-colonial past, there, the historian's comment on this process is called for.

Among the more visible strands in the political ideology of contemporary India is the growth and acceptance of what are called communal ideologies. 'Communal', as many in this audience are aware, in the Indian context has a specific meaning and primarily perceives Indian society as constituted of a number of

* I would like to thank K.N. Panikkar, Neeladri Bhattacharya and B.K. Matilal for their helpful criticism of an earlier draft of this lecture.

religious communities. Communalism in the Indian sense therefore is a consciousness which draws on a supposed religious identity and uses this as the basis for a political and social ideology. It then demands political allegiance to a religious community and supports a programme of political action designed to further the interests of that religious community. Such an ideology is of recent origin but uses history to justify the notion that the community (as defined in recent history) and therefore the communal identity, have existed since the early past. Because the identity is linked to religion, it can lead to the redefinition of the particular religion, more so in the case of one as amorphous as Hinduism.

Such identity tends to iron out diversity and insists on conformity, for it is only through a uniform acceptance of the religion that it can best be used for political ends. The attempt is always to draw in as many people as possible since numbers enhance the power of the communal group and are crucial in a mechanical view of democracy. This political effort requires a domination over other groups and where the numbers are substantially larger, there is a deliberate emphasis both on superiority and the notion of majority, a notion which presupposes the existence of various 'minority communities'. In the construction of what have been called 'imagined communities',[1] in this case identified by religion, there is an implied rejection of the applicability of other types of divisions in society, such as status or class.

In the multiplicity of communalisms prevalent in India today, the major one obviously is Hindu communalism since it involves the largest numbers and asserts itself as the dominant group. I shall therefore discuss only the notion of the Hindu community and not those of other religions. Nevertheless my comments on communal ideology and its use of history would apply to other groups claiming a similar ideology. I would like to look at those constituents of Hindu communal ideology which claim legitimacy from the past, namely, that there has always been a well-defined

[1] B. Anderson, *Imagined Communities* (Vaso, 1983).

and historically evolved religion which we now call Hinduism and an equally clearly defined Hindu community. Implicit in this are the historical implications of Hindu communalism and I shall argue that it is in part a modern search for an imagined Hindu identity from the past, a search which has drawn on the historiography of the last two centuries. The historical justification is far from being the sole reason for the growth of communalism, but recourse to this justification fosters the communal ideology.

The modern description of Hinduism has been largely that of a *brāhmaṇa*-dominated religion which gathered to itself in a somewhat paternalistic pattern a variety of sects drawing on a range of Buddhists, Jainas, Vaiṣṇavas, Śaivas and Śāktas. The texts and the tradition were viewed as inspirational, initially orally preserved, with multiple manifestations of deities, priests but no church, a plurality of doctrines with a seeming absence of controversies and all this somehow integrated into a single religious fabric. Differences with the Semitic religions were recognized and were seen as the absence of a prophet, of a revealed book regarded as sacred, of a monotheistic God, of ecclesiastical organization, of theological debates on orthodoxy and heresy and, even more important, the absence of conversion. But somehow the logic of these differences was not built into the construction of the history of the religion. Hinduism was projected largely in terms of its philosophical ideas, iconology and rituals. It is ironic in some ways that these multiple religious sects were seldom viewed in their social and historical context even though this was crucial to their understanding. Histories of the 'Hindu' religion have been largely limited to placing texts and ideas in a chronological perspective with few attempts at relating these to the social history of the time. Scholarship also tended to ignore the significance of the popular manifestation of religion in contrast to the textual, a neglect which was remedied by some anthropological research, although frequently the textual imprint is more visible even in such studies.

The picture which emerges of the indigenous view of religion from historical sources of the early period is rather different. The prevalent religious groups referred to are two, Brahmanism and Śramanism with a clear distinction between them. They are organizationally separate, had different sets of beliefs and rituals and often disagreed on social norms. That this distinction was recognized is evident from the edicts of the Mauryan king Aśoka[2] as well as by those who visited India and left accounts of what they had observed, as, for example, Megasthenes;[3] the Chinese Buddhist pilgrims Fa Hsien and Hsüan Tsang;[4] and Alberuni.[5] The Buddhist visitors write mainly of matters pertaining to Buddhism and refer to the *brāhmaṇas* as heretics. Patañjali the grammarian refers to the hostility between Brahmanism and Sramanism as innate as is that between the snake and the mongoose.[6] Sometimes the *brāhmaṇas* and the *śramaṇas* are addressed jointly as in Buddhist texts and the Aśokan edicts. Here they are being projected as a category distinct from the common people. Such a bunching together relates to a similarity of concerns suggestive of a common framework of discourse but does not detract from the fundamental differences between the two systems. It might in fact be a worthwhile exercise to reconstruct Brahmanism from the references to it in Sramanic and other non-Brahmanical sources.

A historical view of early Indian religion would endorse this dichotomy and its continuity even in changed forms. Early Brahmanism demarcates the twice-born upper castes from the rest. The twice-born has to observe the precepts of *śruti*—the *Vedas* and of *smṛti*—the auxiliary texts to the *Vedas* and particularly the *Dharmaśāstras*. *Dharma* lay in conforming to the separate social observances and ritual functions of each caste. The actual nature

[2] J. Bloch, *Les Inscriptions d'Asoka* (Paris, 1950), pp. 97, 99, 112.

[3] J.W. McCrindle, *Ancient India as Described by Megasthenes and Arrian* (London, 1877); Arrian, *Indica*, XI.I to XII.9; Strabo XV 1.39–41, 46–9.

[4] J. Legge, *Fa-hien's Record of Buddhistic Kingdoms* (Oxford, 1886); S. Beal, *Si-yu-ki:Buddhist Records of the Western World* (London, 1884).

[5] E.C. Sachau (trans. and ed.), *Alberuni's India* (Delhi, 1964 reprint), p. 21.

[6] S.D. Joshi, ed., *Patañjali Vyākaraṇa Mahābhāsya* (Poona, 1968), II. 4.9; I. 476.

of belief in deity was left ambiguous and theism was not a requirement. The focus of worship was the sacrificial ritual. Brahmanism came closest to having a subcontinental identity largely through its ritual functions and the use of a common language, Sanskrit, even though it was prevalent among only a smaller section of people.

Śramanism, a term covering a variety of Buddhist, Jaina, Ājīvika and other sects, denied the fundamentals of Brahmanism such as Vedic *śruti* and *smṛti*. It was also opposed to the sacrificial ritual both on account of the beliefs incorporated in the ritual as well the violence involved in the killing of animals. It was characterized by a doctrine open to all castes and although social hierarchy was accepted it did not emphasize separate social observances but, rather, cut across caste. The idea of conversion was therefore notionally present. The attitude to social hierarchy in most Śramanic sects was not one of radical opposition. In Buddhism, for example, recruitment to the *saṅgha* and support from lay followers was initially in large numbers from the upper castes and the appeal was frequently also made to such groups.[7] Nevertheless there were no restrictions on a lower caste recruitment and in later periods support from such groups was substantial. The founders of the Śramanic sects were not incarnations of deity. Buddhism and Jainism had an ecclesiastical organization, the *saṅgha*, and in most cases there was an overall concern with historicity.

In terms of numbers there appears to have developed even greater support for the Śākta sects which were in many ways antithetical to early Brahmanism. The essentials of Śāktism are sometimes traced back to Harappan times and some of these elements probably went into the making of popular religion from the earliest historical period. Recognized sects gradually crystalized from the first millennium AD when they come to be referred to in the literature of the period. The centrality of worshipping the goddess was initially new to upper caste religion. Some of these

[7] N. Wagle, *Society at the Time of the Buddha* (Bombay, 1966), p. 74.

sects deliberately broke the essential taboos of Brahmanism relating to separate caste functions, commensality, rules of food and drink and sexual taboos.[8] That some of the beliefs of the Śākta sects were later accepted by some *brāhmaṇa* sects is an indication of a break with Vedic religion by these *brāhmaṇa* sects although the legitimacy of the Vedic religion was sometimes sought to be bestowed on the new sects by them. Such religious compromises were not unconnected with the brahmanical need to retain social ascendency. However, some brahmanical sects remained orthodox.

As legitimizers of political authority, the *brāhmaṇas* in the first millennium AD were given grants of land which enabled them to become major landowners. The institutions which emerged out of these grants such as the *agrahāras* became centres of control over rural resources as well as of Brahmanical learning and practice. It was probably this high social and economic status of the *brāhmaṇa* castes which encouraged the modern idea that Brahmanism and Hinduism were synonymous. But that Brahmanism had also to compromise with local cults is evident from the religious articulation of text and temple and from the frequency with which attempts were introduced into Brahmanism to purify the religion in terms of going back to *śruti* and *smṛti*. In the process of acculturation between brahmanic 'high culture' and the 'low culture' of local cults, the perspective is generally limited to that of the Sanskritization of the latter. It might be historically more accurate on occasion to view it as the reverse, as, for example, in the cult of Viṭhṭhala at Pandharpur or that of Jagannātha at Puri.[9]

[8] Curiously, the eating of meat and the drinking of intoxicants was part of the rejection of Brahmanism for these were now abhorent to Brahmanism, a rather different situation from that described in the Vedic texts where *brāhmaṇas* consumed beef and took *soma*.

[9] G.D. Sontheimer, 'Some Memorial Monuments of Western India,' in *German Scholars in India*, II (New Delhi, 1976); S.G. Tulpule, 'The Origin of Viththala: A new Interpretation,' *ABORI*, 1977–78, vols. 58–59, pp. 1009–15; A. Dandekar, 'Pastoralism and the Cult of Viṭhṭhala,' M. Phil. Dissertation,

In such cases the deities of tribals and low caste groups become, for reasons other than the purely religious, centrally significant and Brahmanism has to adapt itself to the concept of such deities. The domain of such deities evolves out of a span spreading horizontally, moving from a village to its networks of exchange and finally encompassing a region. The focal centre of such a cult takes on a political dimension as well in the nature of the control which it exercises, quite apart from ritual and belief. Pilgrimage then becomes a link across various circumferences.

The increasing success of Brahmanism by the end of the first millennium AD resulted in the gradual displacement of Śramanism—but not entirely. Local cults associated with new social groups led to the emergence of the more popular Puranic religion. Vedic deities were subordinated or ousted. Viṣṇu and Śiva came to be worshipped as the pre-eminent deities. The thrust of Puranic religion was in its assimilative and accommodating processes. A multitude of new cults, sects and castes were worked into the social and religious hierarchy. Religious observance often coincided with caste identities.

By the early second millennium AD a variety of devotional cults—referred to by the generic label *bhakti*—had come to form a major new religious expression. They drew on the Puranic tradition of Śaivism and Vaiṣṇnavism but were also in varying degrees the inheritors of the Śramanic religions. Their emphasis on complete loyalty to the deity has been seen as a parallel to feudal loyalties. But what was more significant was that *bhakti* cults and the sects which grew around them sought to underline dependence on and release from rebirth through the deity. To this extent they indicate a departure from earlier indigenous religion. These cults were god-centred rather than man-centred. The ritual of sacrifice had been substituted by the worship of an icon. Some sects accepted, up to a point, brahmanical *śruti* and *smṛti* whereas others

JNU; H. Kulke, *Jagannātha kult und Gajapati-Königtum* (Wiesbaden, 1979), p. 227; H. Kulke and D. Rothermund, *A History of India* (London, 1986), p. 145ff.

vehemently denied it, a debate which continues to this day. Those sects in opposition to Brahmanism which sought to transcend caste and differentiated social observances, insisting that every worshipper was equal in the eyes of the deity, often ended up as castes, thus once again coinciding sect with caste. With the arrival of Islam in India some drew from the ideas of Islam. Most of these sects were geographically limited and bound by the barriers of language. Possibly the beginnings of larger religious communities within what is now called the Hindu tradition, date to the middle of the second millennium, such as perhaps some Vaiṣṇava sects, where, for example, the worship of Kṛṣṇa at Mathura drew audiences from a larger geographical region than before. This also heralds a change in the nature of Puranic religion, for Mathura attracts Vaiṣṇavas from eastern and southern India and becomes like Ayodhya (for the worship of Rāma[10]) the focus of a search for sacred topography. It might perhaps be seen as an attempt to go beyond local caste and sect and build a broader community. The historical reasons for its happening at this juncture need to be explored.

Initial opposition from those of high caste status also encouraged *bhakti* sects to inculcate a sense of community within themselves, particularly if they were economically successful, such as the Vīraśaivas. Even when such religious sects attempted to constitute a larger community, the limitations of location, caste and language, acted as a deterrent to a single, homogeneous Hindu community. In the continuing processes of either appropriation or rejection of belief and practice, the kaleidoscopic change in the constitution of religious sects was one which precluded the emergence of a uniform, monolithic religion.

The multiplicity of cults and sects also reflects a multiplicity of beliefs. Even in Brahmanism we are told that if two *śruti* traditions are in conflict then both are to be held as law.[11] This is a

[10] A. Bakker, *Ayodhya* (Groningen, 1984).

[11] Manu II. 14–15.

fundamentally different approach from that of religions which would like to insist on a single interpretation arising out of a given theological framework. This flexibility together with the emphasis on social observance rather than theology allowed of a greater privatization of religion than was possible in most other religions. Renunciatory tendencies were common, were respected and often gave sanction to private forms of worship. The renouncer opted out of society, yet was highly respected.[12] The private domain of belief was always a permissible area of early Indian religion: a religion which is perhaps better seen as primarily the religious belief of social segments, sometimes having to agglomerate and sometimes remaining sharply differentiated. The coexistence of religious sects should not be mistaken for the absorption of all sects into an ultimately unified entity. But the demarcation was often more significant since it related both to differences in religious belief and practice as well as social status and political needs. The status of a sect could change as it was hinged to that of its patrons. Political legitimation through the use of religious groups was recognized, but the appeal was to a particular sect or cult or a range of these and not to a monolithic religion. Royal patronage within the same ruling family, extended to a multiplicity of sects, was probably conditioned as much by the exigencies of political and social requirements as by a religious catholicity. This social dimension as well as the degree to which a religious sect had its identity in caste or alternatively was inclusive of caste, has been largely ignored in the modern interpretation of early Hinduism. With the erosion of social observances and caste identity, there is now a search for a new identity and here the creation of a new Hinduism becomes relevant.

The evolution of Hinduism is not a linear progression from a founder through an organizational system, with sects branching off. It is rather the mosaic of distinct cults, deities, sects and ideas

[12] Romila Thapar, 'Renunciation: The making of a Counter-Culture?,' in *Ancient Indian Social History: Some Interpretations* (Delhi, 1978), pp. 63–104.

and the adjusting, juxtaposing or distancing of these to existing ones, the placement drawing not only on belief and ideas but also on the socio-economic reality. New deities could be created linked genealogically to the established ones, as in the recent case of Santoshi Ma, new rituals worked out and the new sect could become the legitimizer of a new caste. Religious practice and belief are often self-sufficient within the boundaries of a caste and are frequently determined by the needs of a caste. The worship of icons was unthought of in the Vedic religion, but the idol becomes a significant feature of Puranic religion and therefore also in the eyes of contemporary Muslim observers. The consciousness of a similarity in ritual and belief in different geographical regions was not always evident. Thus *bhakti* cults were confined to particular regions and were frequently unaware of their precursors or contemporaries elsewhere. Recourse to historicity of founder and practice was confined within the sect and was not required of a conglomeration of sects which later came to be called Hinduism. This is in part reflected in the use of the term *sampradāya* for a sect where the emphasis is on transmission of traditional belief and usage through a line of teachers. The insistence on proving the historicity of human incarnations of deity, such as Rāma and Kṛṣṇa, is a more recent phenomenon and it may be suggested that there is a subconscious parallel with the prophet and the messiah. The identification of the *janma-bhūmis*, the location of the exact place where Kṛṣṇa and Rāma were born, becomes important only by the mid-second millennium AD.

Religions such as Buddhism, Jainism, Islam and Christianity, see themselves as part of the historical process of the unfolding and interpreting of the single religion and sects are based on variant interpretations of the original teaching. They build their strength on a structure of ecclesiastical organization. In contrast to this, Hindu sects often had a distinct and independent origin. Assimilation was possible and was sometimes expressed in the appropriation of existing civilizational symbols. What needs to be investigated is the degree to which such civilizational symbols were originally religious in connotation.

Civilizational symbols are manifested in many ways: from the symbol of the *svāstika* to the symbol of the renouncer as the noblest and most respected expression of human aspirations. The history of the *svāstika* goes back to the fourth millennium BC where it occurs on seals and impressions from northwest India and Central Asia. In the Indian subcontinent it is not a specifically Hindu symbol for it is used by a variety of religious groups in various ways, but in every case it embodies the auspicious. The Bon-po of the Himalayan borderlands reverse the symbol to distance themselves from the Buddhists. The two epics, the *Mahābhārata* and the *Rāmāyaṇa*, frequently treated as primarily the religious literature of the Vaiṣṇavas, are in origin as epics, civilizational symbols. They were, at one level, the carriers of ethical traditions and were used again by a variety of religious sects to propagate their own particular ethic, a situation which is evident from the diverse treatment of the theme of the *Rāmāyaṇa* in Vālmīki, in the Buddhist *Vessantara* and *Dasaratha Jātakas* and in the Jaina version—the *Paumacaryam* of Vimalasūri.[13] The epic versions were also used for purposes of political legitimation. The primarily Vaiṣṇava religious function of the epics develops gradually and comes to fruition in the second millennium AD with clearly defined sects worshipping Rāma or Kṛṣṇa coinciding with the development of what has been called the Puranic religion. Subsequent to this were various tribal adaptations of the *Rāmāyaṇa*, and these were less concerned with the Vaiṣṇava message and more with articulating their own social fears and aspirations.

Even on the question of beliefs about the after-life, although the concept of *karma* and rebirth was commonly referred to, there were distinct and important groups who believed in a different concept. The life after death of the hero in the heaven of Indra or

[13] Romila Thapar, 'The Rāmāyaṇa: Theme and Variations,' in S.N. Mukherjee, ed., *India: History and Thought* (Calcutta, 1982), pp. 221–53.

Śiva, waited upon by *apsaras*, goes back to the Vedic belief in the *pitṛloka* or House of the Fathers. This belief is a major motivation in the widespread hero cults from the mid-first millennium AD onwards.[14] Here even the concept of after-life was conditioned by social birth and function. A different idea influences the way in which the ritual of *satī* changes its meaning over time. Initially a ritual which ensured that the faithful wife accompanied her hero-husband to heaven, and therefore associated largely with *kṣatriya* castes and those dying heroic deaths, its practice by other castes in the second millennium AD involved a change in eschatology. Ultimately the *satī* was defied, which meant that she neither went to heaven nor was subjected to the rules of *karma*.[15]

It has been suggested that there was a structural similarity in various rituals practised by people in different regions and therefore shared myths and shared ritual patterns can account for some unity in the varieties of the religious beliefs that we find in India over a long time.[16] This is certainly true. But nevertheless it is different from a shared creed, catechism, theology and ecclesiastical organization.

The definition of Hinduism as it has emerged in recent times appears not to have emphasized the variant premises of Indian religion and therefore the difference in essence from the model of Semitic religions. This definition was the result of various factors: of Christian missionaries who saw this as the lacunae of religions in India and which they regarded as primitive; of some Orientalist scholarship anxious to fit the 'Hindu' process into a comprehensible whole based on a known model; the efforts also of Indian reform movements attempting to cleanse Indian religion of what they regarded as negative encrustations and trying to find parallels with the Semitic model. Even in the translation of texts from

[14] Romila Thapar, 'Death and the Hero,' in S.C. Humphreys and H. King, *Mortality and Immortality: The Anthropology and Archaeology of Death* (London, 1981), pp. 293–316.

[15] Romila Thapar, 'Sati in History,' *Seminar*, no. 342 (February 1988).

[16] Personal Communication, B.K. Matilal.

Sanskrit into English, where religious concepts were frequently used the translation often reflected a Christian undertone. The selection of texts to be studied had its own purpose. The East India Company's interest in locating and codifying Hindu law gave a legal form to what was essentially social observance and customary law. The concept of law required that it be defined as a cohesive ideological code. The Manu *Dharmaśāstra*, for example, which was basically part of Brahmanical *smṛti* was taken as the laws of the Hindus and presumed to apply universally. In the process of upward social mobility during the late eighteenth and early nineteenth centuries, traders and artisanal groups emerged as patrons of temple building activities and the trend to conform to the brahmanical model was reinforced by this comprehension of Hinduism.[17] The growth of the political concepts of majority and minority communities further galvanized the process.

The degree to which castes and sects functioned independently even in situations which would elsewhere have been regarded as fundamentally of theological importance, can perhaps be seen in attitudes to religious persecution and the manifestations of intolerance. Among the normative values which were highlighted in the discussion of Hinduism in recent times, has been the concept of *ahimsā* or non-violence. It has been argued that nonviolence and tolerance were special features of Hinduism which particularly demarcated its ethics from those of Islam and to a lesser extent Christianity. Yet *ahimsā* as an absolute value is characteristic of certain Śramanic sects and less so of Brahmanism. The notion appears in the *Upaniṣads*, but it was the Buddhists and the Jainas who first made it foundational to their teaching, and their message was very different from that of the *Bhagavad-Gītā* on this matter. That Brahmanism and Śramanism were recognized as distinct after the period of the *Upaniṣads* further underlines the significance of *ahimsā* to Śramanic thinking. This is also borne out by the evidence of religious persecution.

[17] H. Sanyal, *Social Mobility in Bengal* (Calcutta, 1981).

In spite of what historians, ancient and modern, have written, there is a persistent, popular belief that the 'Hindus' never indulged in religious persecution. However, the Śaivite persecution of Śramanic sects is attested to and on occasion, retaliation by the latter. Hsüan Tsang writing in the seventh century refers to this when he describes his visit to Kashmir.[18] That this was not the prejudiced view of the Buddhist pilgrim is made clear by the historian Kalhaṇa in the *Rājataraṅginī,* who even in the twelfth century refers to the earlier destruction of Buddhist monasteries and the killing of Buddhist monks by the Hūna king Mihīrakula and other ardent Śaivites.[19] That Mihīrakula was a Hūna is used by modern historians to excuse these actions, but it should be remembered that he gave large grants of land, *agrahāras*, to the *brāhmaṇas* of Gandhāra, which Kalhaṇa in disgust informs us they gratefully received. Clearly there was competition for royal patronage and the Śaiva *brāhmaṇas* triumphed over the Buddhists. The Buddhist association with the commerce between India and Central Asia was one of the reasons for the material prosperity of the Buddhist *saṅgha.*[20] The Hūna disruption of the Indian trade with Central Asia may well have resulted in an antagonism between the northern Buddhists and the Hūnas.

Elsewhere there is a variation on this story. In Tamil Nadu, for example, from the seventh century onwards, Śaiva sects attacked Jaina establishments and eventually succeeded in driving out the *śramaṇas*.[21] In neighbouring Karnataka, at a somewhat later date, the Vīraśaivas or Lingāyatas acquiring wealth and status in commerce, persecuted Jaina monks and destroyed Jaina images.[22] In

[18] S. Beal, *Si-yu-ki*, I. xcix.

[19] I. 307.

[20] Xinru Liu, *Ancient India and Ancient China* (Delhi, 1988).

[21] Romila Thapar, *Cultural Transaction and Early India* (Delhi, 1987), p. 17ff.

[22] P.B. Desai, *Jainism in South India* (Sholapur, 1957), pp. 23, 63, 82–3, 124, 397–402; *Epigraphia Indica* V, p. 142ff, 255; *Ep. Ind.* XXIX, pp. 139–44; *Annual Report of South Indian Epigraphy*, 1923, p. 4ff.

some inscriptions the Vīraśaivas claim that the Jainas began the trouble. In this case the hostility can be traced not to competition for royal patronage but rather to control of the commercial economy over which the Jainas had a substantial hold. A further reason may also have been linked to the fact that the Jainas, maintaining high standards of literacy, may have been seen by the Vīraśaivas as rivals in the role of advisers and administrators at the royal court.

What is significant about this persecution is that it involved not all the Śaivas but particular segments of sects among them. The persecution was not a *jehād* or a holy war or a crusade in which all Hindu sects saw it as their duty to support the attack or to wage war against the Buddhists or the Jainas. Nor was there room for an inquisition in the Indian situation, for there dissidents could found a new sect and take on a splinter caste status. The notion of heresy evolved gradually. The term *pasamda* in the Aśokan edicts refers merely to any religious sect or philosophical school. By the time of the Puranic literature, *pāṣaṇḍa* quite clearly referred to sects in opposition to Brahmanism and carried with it the clear connotation of contempt.[23] Untouchability was also a form of religious persecution, for this exclusion was common to Brahmanism as well as to some Śramanic sects, the *caṇḍāla* being a category apart. Vaiṣṇavism, although it had its episodes of enemity with Śaivism and others, seems to have been less prone to persecuting competitors. Instead it resorted to assimilating other cults and used the notion of the *avatāra* or incarnation of Viṣṇu to great effect in doing so. But even Vaiṣṇavism was less given to assimilating the Śramanic sects, preferring to absorb tribal and folk cults and epic heroes. Thus in spite of the reference to Buddha as among the ten incarnations, this, interestingly, does not become the focus of a large body of myths or Puranic texts as do the other incarnations. If acts of intolerance and violence against other religious sects reflecting the consciousness of belonging to a religious community

[23] Romila Thapar, 'Renunciation'.

did not form part of a Hindu stand against such sects, then it also raises the question of how viable is the notion of a Hindu community for this early period.

The notion of a Hindu community does not have as long an ancestry as is often presumed. Even in the normative texts of Brahmanism, the *Dharmaśāstras*, it is conceded that there were a variety of communities, determined by location, occupation and caste, none of which were necessarily bound together by a common religious identity. The term for village, *grāma*, referred to the collective inhabitants of a place and included cultivators and craftsmen. The control of this community lay in the hands of the *grāma-saṅgha*[24] and the *mahājana* and, in some cases, the *pañcakula*. Customary law of the village is referred to as *grāma-dharma*.[25] The sense of the village as the community was further impressed by the grants of land to *brāhmaṇas* and officers in the late first millennium AD when they began to be given administrative and judicial rights over the villages granted to them. Community therefore had one of its roots in location and the law of the *janapada* / territory is listed among those which a king should observe.

In urban centres, craftsmen of the same profession or of related professions formed organizations and guilds, such as the *pūga*, *goṣṭhi* and *śrenī*. They were responsible for production and sale and gradually took on a community character. Thus donations were made at Buddhist *stūpas*, as the one at Sanchi, by *goṣṭhis* and *śrenīs* which identified themselves as such.[26] These communities were part of the larger Buddhist community and the same *stūpa*

[24] Manu VIII. 41.

[25] *Aśvalāyana Gṛhasūtra* I.7.I.; *Aśvalāyana Śrauta-sūtra* XII.8; Pāṇini 6.2.62; *Amarakośa* 2.3.19; Buddhist texts speak more specifically of village boundaries (*Vinaya Piṭaka* I. 109. 10; III. 46.200). This was necessary in a system where the limits of areas for collecting alms had to be defined for each monastery.

[26] See inscriptions from Sanchi as given in J. Marshall and A. Foucher, *Monuments of Sanchi* (Calcutta, 1940); also H. Lüders, *Ep. Ind.* X. nos. 162–907; See also the Bhattiprolu inscription, Luders no. 1332.

was embellished from donations by a number of other such communities and by individuals. One can therefore speak of a Buddhist community which cuts across the boundaries of caste and locality. In contrast is the silk-weavers guild at Mandasor which built a temple to Sūrya, the Sun-god, and rennovated it in the late fifth century AD.[27] Even though the members of this guild had taken to a variety of alternative professions they retained their identity as a guild for the purpose of building a temple. This religious edifice was built through the effort of a single group, identified as a guild and worshipping Sūrya, for no other Sun-worshippers were involved nor any other religious group which today would be called Hindu. It is unlikely that such a group saw itself as part of a larger Hindu community as its identity seems to have been deliberately limited. The Hūnas established themselves in the region soon after and were known to be Sun-worshippers. A temple to the Sun was built at Gwalior in the early sixth century AD by a high-ranking individual.[28] Curiously there is neither contribution from nor reference to other Sun-worshipping communities in the area in the later inscription, barring the reference to the Hūna kings.

In urban life the guild was a commanding institution acting as the nucleus of the urban community. The coins and seals of such guilds point to economic power and social status.[29] The *Nārada-smṛti* clearly states that a guild could frame its own laws and these laws related both to administration and social usage.[30] The customary law of the guild, the *śrenī-dharma*, is particularly mentioned in the *Dharmaśāstras* and to which kings are required to conform. The importance of the guild also lies in the fact that some evolved into *jāti*s or castes, becoming units of endogamous mar-

[27] J.F. Fleet, ed., *Inscriptions of the Early Gupta Kings and their Successors*, Corpus Inscriptionum Indicarum, III (Varanasi, 1970 reprint), p. 79ff.

[28] *Ibid.*, p. 162ff.

[29] *Bṛhaspati* I. 28–30; *Kātyayaṇa* 2.82; 17.18; I. 126; Archaeological Survey of India, Annual Report, 1903–04; 1911–12.

[30] *Nārada-smṛti*, X. 1–2; *Ep. Ind.* XXX, p. 169.

riage uniting kinship and profession. Those not following a Śramanic religion maintained their own separate religious identity. We are also told that the king must respect *jāti-dharma*. The emphasis on the *dharma* of the *janapada* (locality or territory) *śreṇī* (guild) and *jāti* (caste) and the absence of reference to the *dharma* of various religious sects or of a conglomeration of religious sects are a pointer perhaps to what actually constituted the sense of community in the early past.

Identities were, in contrast to the modern nation state, segmented identities. The notion of community was not absent but there were multiple communities identified by locality, languages, caste, occupation and sect. What appears to have been absent was the notion of a uniform, religious community readily identified as Hindu. The first occurrence of the term 'Hindu' is as a geographical nomenclature and this has its own significance. This is not a quibble since it involves the question of the historical concept of 'Hindu'. Inscriptions of the Achaemenid empire refer to the frontier region of the Indus or Sindhu as Hi(n)dush.[31] Its more common occurrence many centuries later is in Arabic texts where the term is initially used neither for a religion nor for a culture. It refers to the inhabitants of the Indian subcontinet, the land across the Sindhu or Indus river. Al-Hind was therefore a geographical identity and the Hindus were all the people who lived on this land. Hindu thus essentially came to mean 'the other' in the eyes of the new arrivals. It was only gradually and over time that it was used not only for those who were inhabitants of India but also for those who professed a religion other than Islam or Christianity. In this sense Hindu included both the *brāhmaṇa*s and the lower castes, an inclusion which was contrary to the precepts of Brahmanism. This all-inclusive term was doubtless a new and bewildering feature for the multiple sects and castes who generally saw themselves as separate entities.

The people of India curiously do not seem to have perceived

[31] The Persepolis and Naqsh-i-Rustam inscriptions of Darius, in D.C. Sircar, *Select Inscriptions*, vol. I (Calcutta, 1965), p. 7.

the new arrivals as a unified body of Muslims. The name 'Muslim' does not occur in the records of early contacts. The term used was either ethnic, Turuṣka, referring to the Turks,[32] or geographical, Yavana,[33] or cultural, *mleccha*. Yavana, a back formation from *yona* had been used since the first millennium BC for Greeks and others coming from West Asia. *Mleccha* meaning impure, goes back to the Vedic texts and referred to non-Sanskrit speaking people often outside the caste hierarchy or regarded as foreign and was extended to include low castes and tribals. Foreigners, even of high rank, were regarded as *mleccha*.[34] A late fifteenth-century inscription from Mewar refers to the Sultan of Malwa and his armies as *Śakas*, a term used many centuries before for the Scythians, and therefore reflecting a curious undertow of historical memory.[35] These varying terms, each seeped in historical meaning, do not suggest a monolithic view, but rather a diversity of perceptions which need to be enquired into more fully.

For the early Muslim migrants Indian society was also a puzzle, for it was the first where large numbers did not convert to Islam. There was, further, the unique situation that they were faced with a society which had no place for the concept of conversion, for one's birth into a caste defines one's religious identity and conversion is outside the explanation of belief.

Historians have posited two monolithic religions, Hinduism

[32] Similarly Muslim women were often referred to as *turuṣki*, as, for example, in Hemādri, *Caturvarga-cintāmaṇi*, Prāyaścitta-kāṇḍa.

[33] e.g. Chateśvara temple inscriptions, where in the thirteenth century a reference is made to a campaign against the *yavanas*. *Ep. Ind.* 1952, XXIX, pp. 121–2.

[34] Romila Thapar, 'The Image of the Barbarian in Early India,' in *Ancient Indian Social History*, pp. 152–92. A fourteenth-century inscription from Delhi refers to Shahab-ud-din, as a *mleccha*, who was the first Turuṣka to rule Dhillika/Delhi. D.R. Bhandarkar, ed., Appendix to *Epi. Ind.* XIX–XXIII, no. 683.

[35] Udaipur inscription of the time of Rajamalla in *Bhavnagar Inscriptions*, p. 117ff. And see Bhandarkar, ed., Appendix to *Ep. Ind.* XIX–XXIII, no. 862. It is ironic that it was earlier thought that these Rajput ruling families may in some cases have had their origin in the Śakas!

and Islam, coming face to face in the second millennium AD. This projection requires re-examination since it appears to be based on a somewhat simplistic reading of the court chronicles of the Sultans. These spoke of Hindus sometimes in the sense of the indigenous population, sometimes as a geographical entity and sometimes as followers of a non-Islamic religion. Such references should be read in their specific meaning and not as referring uniformly to the religion of India. Possibly the germ of the idea of a Hindu community begins when people start referring to themselves as Hindus, perhaps initially as a concession to being regarded as 'the other'. Such usage in non-Islamic sources is known from the fifteenth century. The literature of the *bhakti* sects registers a variation on this. Much that was composed in an indigenous tradition such as the *Rāmacaritamānas* of Tulsidās seems not to use the term Hindu. That which was clearly influenced by Islamic ideas such as the verses of Kabīr refers to Hindus and counterposes Hindus and Turuṣkas in a religious sense. Curiously both Tulsidās and Kabīr belonged to the Rāmanandin sect, yet expressed themselves in very different idioms.

Rānā Kumbha of Mewar ruling in the fifteenth century, on defeating the sultans of Dhilli and Gurjarātra, takes the title of *himdu suratrāna*,[36] *suratrāna*, being the Sanskrit for sultan. In the context of the inscription in which it occurs, it is less a declaration of religious identity and more a claim to being a sultan of *al-hind*, superior to the other sultans. In another inscription the sultan of Gujarat is referred to as the *gurjareśvara* and the *gurjarādhīṣvara*, but the virtually hereditary enemy, the sultan of Malwa, merely as *suratrāna*,[37] a subtle but significant distinction.

It would also be worthwhile to investigate when the term Muslim came to be used in what would now be called Hindu sources. One's suspicion is that Turuṣka and its variants and

[36] Sadadi Jaina inscription of the time of Kumbhakarṇa of Medapata in *Bhavnagar Inscriptions*, p. 114ff and D.R. Bhandarkar, *op. cit.*, no. 784; D. Sharma, *Lectures on Rajput History and Culture* (Delhi, 1970), p. 55.

[37] Kīrtistambha-praśasti, *ASIR*, XXIII, p. 111ff.

certainly *mleccha* were more commonly used as they are to this day. *Mleccha* does not have a primary religious connotation. It is a signal of social and cultural difference. Indian Muslims of course did not discontinue caste affiliations, particularly as the basis of marriage relations and often even occupations. Thus the gulf between the high caste Muslims claiming foreign descent, such as the *ashrafs*, and the rest was not altogether dissimilar to the social difference between *brāhmaṇas* and non-*brāhmaṇas*. But the rank and file were often converted from lower castes, where an entire *jāti* would convert. These Muslims retained their local language in preference to Persian, were recognized by minor differences of dress and manner and often incorporated their earlier rituals and mythology into Islamic tradition. Some of the *mangal-kābyas* in Bengali, for instance, are an example of such interlinks in the creation of what might be seen as a new mythology where Puranic deities intermingled with the personalities of the Quran.[38] This becomes even more evident in the folk literature of regions with a large Muslim population. Elsewhere in Tamil-Nadu, for instance, the guardian figures in the cult of Draupadi are Muslim.[39] This is not an anomaly if it is seen in terms of local caste relations.

This is not to suggest that the relationship was one of peaceful coexistence or total cultural integration but rather that the perception which groups subscribing to Hindu and Islamic symbols had of each other was not in terms of a monolithic religion, but more in terms of distinct and disparate castes and sects along a social continuum. Even the recognition of a religious identity does not automatically establish a religious community. Tensions, confrontations and even persecutions at the level of political authority were not necessarily repeated all the way down the social scale nor were all caste and sectarian conflicts reflected at the upper levels. Clashes which on the face of it would now be interpreted as between Hindus and Muslims, would require a deeper investiga-

[38] Ashim Roy, *The Islamic Syncretistic Tradition in Bengal* (Princeton, 1983).
[39] A. Hiltebeitel, *The Cult of Draupadi* (Chicago, 1988).

tion to ascertain how far they were clashes between specific castes and sects and to what degree did they involve support and sympathy from other castes and sects identifying with the same religion or seeking such identity.

The nineteenth-century definition of the Hindu community sought its justification in early history using Mill's periodization which assumes the existence of Hindu and Muslim communities and takes the history of the former back to the centuries BC. Its roots were provided by yet another nineteenth-century obsession, that of the theory of Aryan race.[40] It was argued that the Indo-Aryans conquered India and created the Hindu religion and civilization. In the theory of Aryan race the nineteenth-century concern with European origins was transferred to India. The theory as applied to India emphasized the arrival of a superior, conquering race of Aryans who used the mechanism of caste to segregate groups racially.[41] It underlined upper caste superiority by arguing that they were the descendants of the Aryans and it therefore became an acceptable explanation of the origin of upper castes, who could now also claim relationship to the European Aryans.[42] The lower castes were seen as the non-Aryan, indigenous people and were said to be of Dravidian and Austric origin. Aryanism was seen then to define the true and pure Hindu community. Other groups recruited into the caste structure at lower levels were regarded as polluting the pristine Hindu community.

Because of its centrality to both the notion of community and religion, the theory of Aryan race requires to be looked at critically by historians working on nineteenth-century ideas as well as historians of ancient India. The earlier evidence quoted in support of the theory as applied to India begins to fade with information

[40] Romila Thapar, 'Ideology and the Interpretation of Early Indian History,' of this volume, p. 1ff.

[41] H. Risley, *The People of India* (London, 1908).

[42] As, for example, in the writings of Keshab Chunder Sen, 'Philosophy and Madness in Religion,' in *Keshab Chunder Sen's Lectures in India* (London, 1901).

from archaeology and linguistics. The notion of an Aryan race has now been generally discarded in scholarship and what we are left with is essentially a linguistic category: the Indo-Aryan speaking people. The archaeological picture takes the foundation of Indian civilization back to proto-history and the Harappa culture. The characteristic features of the latter do not mesh with those of the Vedic texts associated with the culture of the Indo-Aryan speakers.[43] The culture depicted in the Vedic texts seems increasingly to have drawn on local practices and beliefs, some going back to the Harappa culture or earlier, others drawing perhaps from the then contemporary society in India. There is virtually no evidence of the invasion and conquest of northwestern India by a dominant culture coming from across the border. Most sites register a gradual change of archaeological cultures. Where there is evidence of destruction and burning it could as easily have been a local activity and is not indicative of a large-scale invasion. The border lands of the northwest were in communication with Iran and Central Asia even before the Harappa culture with evidence of the passage of goods and ideas across the region.[44] This situation continued into later times and if seen in this light then the intermittent arrival of groups of Indo-European speakers in the northwest, perhaps as pastoralists or farmers or itinerant traders, would pose little problem. It is equally plausible that in some cases local languages became Indo-Europeanized through contact. Such situations would require a different kind of investigation. If cultural elements from elsewhere are being assessed, then during the Harappan period excavated evidence for contact with West Asia via the Gulf was more significant than that with eastern Iran and Central Asia and this raises another set of possibilities.

[43] Romila Thapar, 'The Study of Society in India,' in *Ancient Indian Social History*, pp. 211–39; also, 'The Archaeological Background to the Agnicayana Ritual,' in F. Staal, *Agni*, vol. II (Berkeley, 1983), pp. 3–40.

[44] J. Jarrige, 'Excavations at Mehrgarh: their Significance for Understanding the Background of the Harappan Civilisation,' in G. Possehl, ed., *Harappan Civilisation* (New Delhi, 1982), p. 79ff.

The more basic question for the historian is to explain the slow and gradual spread of the Indo-Aryan language across a large part of the Indian subcontinet. Here again the evidence from linguistics provides an interesting pointer. The claim that the earliest of the Vedic texts, the *Ṛg Veda* dating back to the second millennium BC is linguistically purely Indo-Aryan is now under question for it is being argued that the text already registers the presence of non-Aryan speakers. The later Vedic texts show an even greater admixture of non-Aryan and specifically when dealing with certain areas of activity, such as agriculture.[45] The emergent picture might suggest that the speakers of Indo-Aryan may have been in a symbiotic relationship with speakers of non-Aryan languages, with a mutual adopting of not only vocabulary and linguistic structures in a bi-lingual situation but also technologies and religious practices and beliefs.[46] The exclusivity of *brāhmaṇa* ritual does not have to be explained on the basis of a racial segregation, but can be viewed as derived from the will to retain a certain kind of priestly power, which, claiming bestowal by the deities would ensure a separate and special status. Possibly the political hold of priestly power has its roots in the Harappa culture. In charting the spread of Indo-Aryan it is worth remembering that Sanskrit not only underwent change in relation to other languages with which it had to co-exist and in relation to social change but that its use was initially restricted to *brāhmaṇa* ritual and elite groups.

The focus therefore is shifting to an investigation of the many ways in which a language gains acceptability. This would involve detailed studies of the juxtaposition of new technologies particularly in relation to ecological contexts, of demography, of kinship systems and the ways in which social groups interact where stratification relates to lineage rather than to race. So deep has been the modern obsession with race that Pargiter as late as in the 1920s suggested the identification of even the traditional de-

[45] T. Burrow, *The Sanskrit Language* (London, 1965), p. 379: M.M. Deshpande and P.E. Hook, eds., *Aryan and non-Aryan in India* (Michigan, 1979).

[46] Romila Thapar, *From Lineage to State* (New Delhi, 1984), p. 21ff.

scent groups from the genealogies of the Puranic texts as Aryan, Dravidian and Austric.[47] Thus the spread of the Indo-Aryan languages and the changes they manifest are a far more complicated study than that implied in the theory of spread by conquest. There is also a need to see the evolving of early Indian society as suggested by archaeological evidence independent of the attempt to impose Aryan identities on archaeological cultures. Only then can we hope to understand the social processes which went into the creation of early Indian society. In the text the term *ārya* generally refers to status indicating one who is to be respected. Whereas the connotation of *dāsa* may be said to contain racial elements, as for example, in the emphasis on physical characteristics, such elements are not in the forefront of references to *ārya*. Thus in the Vedic texts there are *ārya*s of *dāsa* descent, the *dāsi-putrāḥ brāhmaṇas*,[48] or, politically powerful *dāsa* chiefs making gifts to the *brāhmaṇas*.[49] (It is interesting that one of the most respected lineages, that of the Pūrus is associated with sub-standard Sanskrit.[50] It is also said that Pūru was an ancient king who was an Asura Rākṣasa and was overthrown by Bharata,[51] which can hardly be said to place the Pūrus in the category of the pure Aryans! In the *Dharmaśāstras* it is the observance of the complex *varnāśrama-dharma* which defines the *ārya*. To trace the emergence of caste would also involve a study of access to resources, kinship and clan networks and notions of pollution.

Early history suggests the existence of multiple communities based on various identities. The need to create the idea of a single, Hindu community appears to have been a concern of more recent times which was sought to be justified by recourse to a particular

[47] F.E. Pargiter, *Ancient Indian Historical Tradition* (London, 1922).

[48] *Bṛhaddevatā* 4.11–15; 21–3; describes the birth of Dīrghatamas and his son Kakśivant as the son of a *dāsi*. The *Aitareya Brāhmaṇa* 2.19 and the *Kauśītaki Brāhmaṇa* 12.3 describe the Ṛg Vedic seer Kavasa Ailusa as a *dāsi-putraḥ*.

[49] Romila Thapar, *From Lineage to State*, p. 43.

[50] *Ṛg Veda*. VII. 18.13.

[51] *Śatapatha Brāhmana* VI. 8.I.14.

construction of history. The new Hinduism which is now sought to be projected as the religion of this community is in many ways a departure from the earlier religious sects. It seeks historicity for the incarnations of its deities, encourages the idea of a centrally sacred book, claims monotheism as significant to the worship of deity, acknowledges the authority of the ecclesiastical organization of certain sects as prevailing over all and has supported large-scale missionary work and conversion. These changes allow it to transcend caste identities and reach out to larger numbers. Religions indigenous to India which questioned brahmanical belief and practice such as Buddhism and Jainism have been inducted into Hinduism and their separateness is either denied or ignored. Pre-Islamic India is therefore presented as a civilization characterized by an inclusive Hinduism, whereas it would seem that the reality perhaps lay in looking at it as a cluster of distinctive sects and cults, observing common civilizational symbols but with belief and ritual ranging from atheism to animism and a variety of religious organizations identifying themselves by location, language and caste. Even the sense of religious identity seems to have related more closely to sect than to a dominant Hindu community.

The modern construction of Hinduism is often acclaimed as in the following defence of Orientalism: 'The work of integrating a vast collection of myths, beliefs, rituals and laws into a coherent religion and of shaping an amorphous heritage into a rational faith known now as "Hinduism" were endeavours initiated by Orientalists.'[52] Given that religious traditions are constantly reformulated, the particular construction of Hinduism in the last two centuries has an obvious historical causation. Deriving largely from the Orientalist construction of Hinduism, emergent national consciousness appropriated this definition of Hinduism as well as what it regarded as the heritage of Hindu culture. Hindu identity was defined by those who were part of this national consciousness

[52] D. Knopf, 'Hermeneutics versus History,' *Journal of Asian Studies*, 1980, 39.3, pp. 495–505.

and drew on their own idealized image of themselves resulting in an upper-caste, *brāhmaṇa*-dominated identity. Even the counterposing of Hindu to other religious identities as an essential fact of social and historical reality grew out of this construction. But this construction not only deviates from the history of the religious groups involved but fails to encapsulate the essential differences within what is called the Hindu tradition whose presuppositions were distinct from other religions and closely entwined with social articulation. The search for coherence and rational faith was in terms of a perspective familiar to those who came from a Christian religious tradition and hardly reflected any attempt to understand the coherence of a different, indigenous religious tradition. The shape thus given to the latter has changed what originally existed and has made it difficult to recognize the actual earlier form.

The need for postulating a Hindu community became a requirement for political mobilization in the nineteenth century when representation by religious community became a key to power and where such representation gave access to economic resources. The competition for middle class employment brought with it the argument that in all fairness the size of the community should be taken into consideration. Communal representation of the religious kind firmed up the image. Once this argument was conceded it became necessary to recruit as many people as possible into the community. Here the vagueness of what constitutes a Hindu was to the advantage of those propagating a Hindu community. It encouraged an almost new perception of the social and political uses of religion. Conversion to Hinduism was invented largely to bring in the untouchables and the tribals. The notion of purification, *śuddhi*, permitted those who had been converted to Islam and Christianity to be reintroduced to the Hindu fold. A Hindu community with a common identity would be politically powerful. Since it was easy to recognize other communities on the basis of religion, such as Muslims and Christians, an effort was made to consolidate a parallel Hindu community. This involved a change from the earlier segmented identities to one which encompassed caste and region and identified itself by religion which had to be refashioned so as to provide the ideology which would bind the group. In Gramsci's terms, the class which wishes to become hegemonic has to nationalize itself and the new 'nationalist' Hinduism comes from the middle class.

The change implicit in the various levels of what is called modernization inevitably results in the refashioning of communities. Given that the notion of expansive communities may well be imagined, nevertheless the premises on which such communities are constructed are open to analysis and where they claim an historical basis, there the historian has perforce to be involved. This involvement becomes even more necessary when the concept of communities is brought into play in assigning positions to them in history either close to or distant from what are regarded as national aspirations. Thus the majority community tends to define national aspirations. The minority communities in varying degrees are viewed as disrupting society by their refusal to conform. The projection of such communities historically is that of their always having been alien to the dominant culture and therefore refusing to assimilate with the majority.

Minority communities pick up their cue in a similar reconstruction of history seeking to project a unified community stance in all historical situations. The fear of being overwhelmed by the majority community is expressed even in opposition to the making of homogeneous civil laws. These are treated as threats to a specific culture and practice, and there is a tendency to preserve even that which is archaic in an effort to assert a separate identity.

If the history of religions in India is seen as the articulation not only of ideas and rituals but also the perceptions and motivations of social groups, the perspectives which would follow might be different from those with which we are familiar. The discourse and the play between and among religious sects of various kinds, has been a central fact of Indian religion and would reflect a more realistic portrayal of the role of religion in society. A historically analytical enquiry into the definition and role of religion and the concept of religious communities in pre-modern India could be juxtaposed with the way in which these have been perceived by interpreters of the past in the last couple of centuries. Incidentally such an assessment would be valuable not only to contemporary society in India but also to those societies which now host the vast Indian diaspora. Communal ideologies may be rooted in the homeland but also find sustenance in the diaspora.

It is possible now to look more analytically at the perspectives on early Indian society as available in the sources, keeping in mind the insights which we have, arising from research which, in a sense, is being gradually liberated from the polemics of the colonial age. Where institutions and ideologies of modern times seek legitimacy from the early past, at least there, the dialogue between historians working on these time periods becomes imperative.

The Contribution of D.D. Kosambi to Indology

It has recently been argued that a revolution in scientific knowledge comes about not through the accumulation of data alone but through a change in the paradigm.[1] When the framework of explanation or the hypothesis is altered or a new set of questions are posed only then can there be a breakthrough in scientific knowledge. This applies as much to history and the social sciences. The accumulation of data is of course a necessary first step and includes the deriving of fresh data from new sources, but an advance in knowledge is dependent on using the data to present new formulations.

Histories of the Indian sub-continent, such as were to become germane to the perception on the Indian past, have subscribed to three major changes of paradigm. The first comprehensive history was James Mill's *History of British India*[2] published in the early nineteenth century, where he set out his theory of Indian history evolving out of three civilizations, the Hindu, the Muslim and the British. The first two of these he described as backward, stagnant and ahistoric. His theory was to become axiomatic to the periodization of Indian history and is with us still, though sometimes in a disguised form. A change came about with Vincent Smith's

[1] T. Kuhn, *The Structure of Scientific Revolutions* (Chicago, 1970).
[2] J. Mill, *History of British India* (London, 1918–23).

History of India[3] published in 1919, which tried to avoid the sharpness of Mill's value judgements. Smith concentrated more on a chronological overview which was in any case less charged with colonial and anti-colonial sentiment and argued for the rise and fall of dynasties as being crucial to the study of Indian history. By the early twentieth century chronological data had accumulated to the point where such a treatment of history was possible. Where Mill's assessment was seeking to justify the British conquest of India, Smith was justifying colonial rule. The infrequency of explicitly negative value judgements on the pre-British period was largely an indication of his awareness of Indian national sentiment in the matter. Nationalist historians writing on early India reversed the value judgements but adhered to the paradigm of dynastic and chronological concerns.

Kosambi's first book, *An Introduction to the Study of Indian History*[4] published in 1956, was a major shift in the paradigm. He had little use for a chronological narrative since he argued that chronology for the early period was too obscure to be meaningful. For him history was the presentation in chronological order of successive developments in the means and relations of production.[5] Because of the absence of reliable historical records he argued that Indian history would have to use the comparative method.[6] This meant a familiarity with a wide range of historical work and his own familiarity with classical European history is evident in his writing; it also meant the use of various disciplines and interdisciplinary techniques to enable the historian to understand the pattern of social formations. His definition of the comparative method required the historian to be an inter-disciplinary creature in himself with the ability to use a large number of

[3] V. Smith, *The Oxford History of India* (Oxford, 1919).

[4] D.D. Kosambi, *An Introduction to the Study of Indian History* (Bombay, 1956). Henceforth *ISIH*.

[5] *Ibid.*, p. 1ff.

[6] *Ibid.*, p. 5ff; 'Combined Methods in Indology' *Indo-Iranian Journal*, 1963, VI, pp. 177–202.

investigative techniques. This ability he demonstrated to the full in his writings on Indology. Added to this was his conviction that the historian in India was in a particularly happy position since so much of the past survives in the present. As he puts it,' . . . the country has one tremendous advantage that was not utilised till recently by the historians: the survival within different social layers of many forms that allow the reconstruction of totally diverse earlier stages.'[7] For him this amply made up for the absence of reliable historical records.

Kosambi's acknowledged status as an Indologist was all the more remarkable, in that by profession he was a mathematician. Indology to begin with was a subsidiary interest, perhaps inherited from his father, a scholar of Pāli and Buddhism who taught at various centres in India, apart from a period at Harvard. The older Kosambi walked the countryside in an effort to relate the texts to their original milieu, an approach which was followed by his son. A quick perusal of the younger Kosambi's many publications, points to a telling trend. His earliest papers in the 1930's sare mainly on various aspects of mathematics. In the 1940's his interest in Indology become apparent in the form of occasional papers. (This was also the period when he wrote on Soviet contributions to mathematics and genetics and was enthusiastic about the Soviet attempt to build a socialist society). He was appointed to the Mathematics Chair at the T.I.F.R. in 1946. During the 1950's however and until his death in 1966, most of his publications were on Indology and early Indian history although his mathematical interests remained constant.

Given the fact that Indology is now viewed as rooted in a colonial perception of the past, and since Kosambi's writing challenged this perspective, it would be more appropriate to refer to him as a historian, the field in which his major contribution lay and where he has been strikingly influential. But he was prolific and researched into other related areas as well, hence the continuing use of the label, Indologist. His first venture into early Indian sources was a critical assessment of Bhartṛhari which can be regarded as a model

[7] D.D. Kosambi, *The Culture and Civilisation of Ancient India in Historical Outline* (london, 1965). Henceforth *CCAIHO*.

for such analysis.[8] At a later stage he edited, jointly with V.V. Gokhale, the Vidyākara *Subhāśita-ratna-koṣa* for the Harvard Oriental Series.[9] Apart from applying the norms of higher criticism to such texts he also tried to place them in historical context not merely through a chronological analysis but by referring them to the society from which they emanated. He argued that from the first millennium AD Sanskrit should be seen as a measure and expression of upper class unity when it replaced Prākrit in the royal courts and was patronized, particularly in the initial stages, by foreign rulers. This is of course evident in the change from Prākrit to Sanskrit as the language of royal inscriptions between the Mauryan and the Gupta periods. He stressed the feudal background of many Sanskrit texts which brought him into a lively controversy with one of his closest friends, the Harvard Sanskritist, Daniel Ingalls. Kosambi maintained that Sanskrit was deliberately kept restricted to a small number of people, even though the excellent early grammar of the language by Pāṇini, commented upon by Patañjali, converted it into an orderly and systematic language, open to anyone who was taught it properly. However he felt that it froze in the hands of what he called, 'a disdainful priest class',[10] and much of the real world was byepassed in the courtly literature.

The relation of text to context was examined at greater length in his papers on the *Bhagavad Gītā* where he attempted to relate ideology to society.[11] He argued that the *Gītā* in propounding the concept of

[8] 'Some Extant Versions of Bhartrhari's *Śatakas*' *JBBRAS*, 1945, XXI, pp. 17–32; *The Śatakatrayam of Bhartṛhari with the commentary of Rāmarṣi*, ed., in collaboration with Pt. K.V. Krishnamoorthi Sharma, Anandāsrama Sanskrit Series No. 127 (Poona, 1947); *The Southern Archetype of Epigrams ascribed to Bhartṛhari*, Bharatiya Vidya Series, 9 (Bombay, 1946); 'The Quality of Renunciation in Bhartṛhari's Poetry,' in *Exasperating Essays* (Poona, 1857), p. 72ff.

[9] Harvard Oriental Series No. 44 (Cambridge Mass., 1956).

[10] *ISIH*, p. 266.

[11] 'The Avatāra Syncretism and possible sources of the Bhagavad Gītā' *JBBRAS*, 1948–9, XXIV-XXV, pp. 121–34; 'Social and Economic Aspects of the Bhagavad Gītā' in *Myth and Reality* (Bombay, 1962), p. 12ff.

bhakti laid emphasis on unquestioning faith in, and personal loyalty and devotion to, a deity, and these values were in conformity with the ideology of feudalism which also required a chain of unquestioning loyalties. The text emphasized caste functions and the requirement to do one's ordained duty as a member of a particular caste which he saw as a message in support of caste society and the conservatism which such a society entails; a message propounded by the upper castes to keep the rest of society passive. He further suggests that religious sects supporting a synthesis of gods and of tolerance are expressions of a period of a social surplus, when wealth was more widely distributed; whereas the ideology of *bhakti* is more frequent in periods of crisis, but that it nevertheless acted as a means of inter-relating the scattered religious beliefs of a region. It could be argued however that the *bhakti* endorsed by the *Gītā* is not identical with that which was taught by later *bhakti* teachers. Whereas the single minded devotion to a deity is retained, the social context changes substantially and is expressed in a concern with a universal ethic which echoes that of the Buddhist and Jainas and which permits the *bhakti* movements to become powerful mobilizers of various social groups. There is an almost apparent contradiction between the emphasis on caste-duty in the *Gītā* and the universal ethic of the later *bhakti* movement.

In his handling of Buddhist texts Kosambi uses them mainly to draw out data on social and economic life and much of his discussion on early trade, for instance, is based on these sources. This was not new as such data had earlier been extracted from these sources by scholars of Buddhism such as Rhys Davids[12] and Fick.[13] Kosambi co-related this data with evidence from Sanskrit sources but above all from archaeological excavations and contemporary inscriptions and brought the Buddhist material into the wider orbit of reconstructing the history of the late first millennium BC. The fact that the Buddhist sources do at times contradict

[12] *Buddhist India* (London, 1903).

[13] *The Social Organisation in North East India in Buddha's Time* (Calcutta, 1920).

the brahmanical tradition was for him a particularly important aspect of the Pāli texts and invested them with the kind of authenticity which he found invaluable. The recognition of this feature he owed to his father's work on the Buddhist texts.[14]

His knowledge of Sanskrit led Kosambi to a series of etymological analyses which he used to great effect in reconstructing the social background, particularly of the Vedic period.[15] Thus he argued that the names of many of the established *brāhmaṇas* in Vedic literature and the Purāṇic tradition clearly pointed to their being of non-Aryan origin. Some were given the epithet, *dāsi-putraḥ* (such as Kakṣivant) or else their names suggested totems, as for instance, Ajigarta or Kaśyapa. Further, that the original seven *gotras* of the *brāhmaṇas* were of mixed Aryan and non-Aryan priests. His analysis of the *gotras* led him into a debate with John Brough.[16] From the study of the *gotras* he went on to the logical point that the language of the Vedic texts could not have been pure Aryan and must have had an admixture of non-Aryan elements reflecting the inclusion of non-Aryans as *brāhmaṇas*. This theory is now more acceptable to those who have worked on Indo-Aryan linguistics, on the basis of the linguistic analyses of the texts and language which clearly indicates non-Aryan structures and forms both in syntax and vocabulary.[17] Kosambi's own use of linguistic analyses bears the stamp of philology and he was evidently less familiar with the changes in linguistic practices of the mid-twentieth century. His etymological reconstruction of Sātakarni as Indo-Austric is an example of this where he makes no attempt to

[14] *ISIH*, p. 174, f.n.1.

[15] 'Early Brahmans and Brahmanism' *JBBRAS*, 1947, XXIII, pp. 39–46; 'On the Origin of the Brahman Gotra,' *JBBRAS*, 1950, XXVI, pp. 21–80. 'Brahman Clans,' *JAOS*, 1953, 73, pp. 202–8.

[16] J. Brough, *The Early Brahmanical System of Gotra and Pravara* (Cambridge, 1953); D.D. Kosambi, 'Brahman Clans' *JAOS*, 1953, 73, pp. 202–8.

[17] T. Burrow, *The Sanskrit Language* (London, 1965); B.M. Emeneau, *Collected Papers*, (Annamalai University, 1967); M.N. Deshpande and P. Hook, *Aryan and non-Aryan in India* (Ann Arbor, 1979).

support his argument by providing other Austric links.[18] The same problem arises with his attempt to equate the Hittite *khatti* with the Sanskrit *kṣatriya* and the Pāli *khettiyo.*[19]

An area in which he successfully utilised his mathematical knowledge was Indian numismatics and more especially in the one coinage system on which he worked in great detail, namely, the punch-marked coins which were in circulation between c. 500-100 BC. These were coins cut from a sheet of silver, each coin bearing a set of symbols but with no legend. Hence their chronology and the agency which issued them was an enigma. Kosambi wished to demonstrate the application of scientific methods for obtaining information from numismatic evidence. He worked initially on a statistical analyses from one hoard with a meticulous weighing of each coin to ascertain loss of weight by wear and tear and with a careful analysis of their fabric and alloy. By arranging the coins in accordance with their weight and their set of symbols he hoped to provide a chronological sequence of the coins and believed that this would in turn provide a clue as to the source of their issue.[20] For the method to be ultimately successful the coins to be used as control had to come from stratified excavations. These could be tested against coins from hoards provided they were free from encrustations. His analyses revealed that the average weight decreases when the symbols on the reverse increase. From this he argued that coins in constant circulation would also be the ones to be weighed and valued more frequently. He maintained that they were originally issued by traders but were ratified by the kings' valuers and marked with the kings' symbols. The next step was the identifying of particular symbols as the marks of particular kings. Whereas the statistical analyses of the coins is generally accepted, the identifications of certain symbols with royalty re-

[18] *ISIH*, pp. 229–30.

[19] *CCAIHO*, p. 77.

[20] 'Study and Methodology of Silver Punch-Marked Coins' *New Indian Antiquary*, 1941, 4, pp. 1–35 and 49–76; 'The Effect of Circulation upon Weight of Metallic Currency,' *Current Science*, 1942, XI, pp. 227–30; *ISIH*, p. 162ff.

main controversial with some numismatists still arguing that the coins may not bear any royal marks. It does seem curious that with major changes in the nature of the state and of royalty during this period, the coins, if connected with royalty, should have remained without any appreciable change in style. It seems implausible that the Mauryan kings would not have issued special coins and would have been content to merely ratify these issued by traders, for, if nothing else they would at least have imitated the Persian and Greek coins which were circulating in West Asia and with which area Indian kings and traders were in contact. It seems more likely that the coins continued to be issued and ratified by guilds as legal tender, a suggestion which has been linked to the occasional legend of *negama* (from *nigama*?) on some issues from Taxila. The evaluation of coins by the king's valuer as described in the *Artha-śāstra* would doubtless have applied to all coins irrespective of where they were issued.

Kosambi's use of archaeology was in part to reconstruct the prehistoric period where he literally walked the stretch around Pune in an effort to record the archaeological data. On the basis of his extensive fieldwork on microlithic sites and through his typology of microlithic artefacts he was able to suggest the routes which herders, pastoralists and incipient traders would have taken across the western Deccan in the pre-historic period.[21] Relating to a more developed culture, he looked for continuities of archaic artefacts and sought to explain these in their fullest function, for example, the function of the saddle-quern which he explained both with reference to those found in archaeological excavations and as well as those in current use.[22] By the term 'use' he meant not merely the technological function but also the role of the object in religious ritual. He was also among the earliest scholars to recognize the significance of the megalithic material and the

[21] 'Pilgrim's Progress: a contribution to the Prehistory of the Western Deccan' in *Myth and Reality*, p. 110ff.

[22] *ISIH*, p. 43ff.

potentialities which it held in the discussion on the origins of many institutions.

Added to the fieldwork was an intelligent understanding of geo-morphology and topography. In many cases his assessment of the historical importance of a site was based on the logic of geography. This he felt should indicate to the historian where to look for sites and the likely nature of the sites. This approach is demonstrated in what can only be called a brilliantly insightful discussion of the trade routes from the west coast upto the plateau and across the *ghats* in the western Deccan.[23] Geographical considerations were partially responsible for the location of urban centres and Buddhist monasteries in this area during the first millennium AD with a continuity of Maratha forts and British railway links in the second millennium.

It was the recognition of cultural survival which led Kosambi to weave so much material from ethnology and anthropology into his historical narrative. This is perhaps best demonstrated in the pages of his *Introduction to the Study of Indian History,* where he describes what he sees in the vicinity of his house in Pune.[24] Here we have history virtually on the door-step, what with the encampment of a nomadic group, the presence of a tribe which had once given rise to a *jāti,* and of another which became a quasi-guild. He noticed trees and sacred groves, stones marking a sacrificial ritual, caves and rock shelters which may have been occupied successively by prehistoric men, by Buddhist monks and later by practitioners of Hindu cults. Such places have a remarkable continuity as sacred centres and often provided a greater historical continuity both in object and ritual than many written texts. These for him were primary areas for archaeological and historical investigation. It is important to clarify that Kosambi was not arguing that religion played a more significant part in Indian culture than has been the case in other cultures, as has been the stand of those who maintain

[23] *Ibid.*, p. 246ff.
[24] *Ibid.*, p. 24ff.

the greater spirituality of the Indian past; but rather, Kosambi's position is that there was a greater survival of the archaic in religious ritual than in other areas of Indian life which speaks of a certain conservatism but at the same time makes it worth investigating historically. This perspective on culture is again demonstrated in the discussion on the probable Harappan religious forms and their continuity into later periods.

Kosambi had little use for physical anthropology. For him, both the measuring of nasal indexes and the theories on the racial identities of India derived therefrom, were worthless.[25] At a wider anthropological level he maintained that one of the clues to understanding the Indian past was the basic factor of the transition from tribe to caste, from small, localized groups to a generalized society.[26] This transition was largely the result of the introduction of plough agriculture in various regions which changed the system of production, broke the structure of tribes and clans and made caste the alternative form of social organization. This process he traced in part from the evolution of clan totems into clan names and then into caste names. The agency through which plough agriculture was introduced would therefore become the major factor of control in caste society. This agency he saw as the brahmanical settlements in various parts of the country. These led to an assimilation of local cults into the brahmanical tradition as is evident from the various *Purāṇas* and *Māhātmyas*. But equally important it led to the sanskritization of local folk cults with the incorporation of *brāhmaṇa* priests and rituals, the association of epic heroes and heroines, and by the inclusion of such cults in Sanskrit mythology.

The interpretation of myths is essential to any study of early cultures and Kosambi's work is peppered with such interpretations. In a detailed discussion of the story of Purūravas and Urvaśi which he traces through its many varients in the texts,[27] he dismis-

[25] *Sovetskaya Etnografia,* Ak. Nauk USSR, No. 1., 1958, pp. 39–57.
[26] *ISIH.*, p. 24ff.
[27] 'Urvaśī and Purūravas' in *Myth and Reality,* p. 42ff.

ses the simplistic nature-myth interpretation of Max Müller and his contemporaries who saw the disappearance of Urvaśi as symbolic of the vanishing dawn on the rising of the sun. Kosambi attempts a functional anthropological analysis in which he argues that it reflects the institution of sacred marriage in prehistoric societies as well as the ritual sacrifice of the hero by the mother goddess.[28] One of the frequent strands in his explanations of myths was related to his belief that societies were matriarchal in origin and many gradually changed to patriliny and that myths therefore reflect the transition from the one to the other. This view was largely derived from the writings of F. Engels[29] and what one might call the 'mother-right school of anthropology.'[30] He applied the same argument to explain the *kumbha* symbol or birth from a jar of certain *brāhmaṇa gotra*s and of the Kauravas in the *Mahābhārata* where the jar has an obvious symbolic equation with the womb. Bride-price is also for him a survival of matriliny.[31] The insistence on a transition from matriarchy to patriliny in every case is not now acceptable since many societies are known to have been patrilineal from the beginning. It is curious that the structural study of myths was known at that time but Kosambi shows little interest in it.

I have tried to indicate the various ways in which Kosambi contributed to Indological studies in his handling of the various sources and data. That his scholarship ranged over a variety of aspects was in conformity with the best Indological tradition which required a many faceted scholar who could claim familiarity with different source materials. What distinguished Kosam-

[28] 'At the Crossroads: a study of mother goddess cult sites,' *Myth and Reality*, p. 82ff.

[29] *The Origin of the Family, Private Property and the State* (London, 1946).

[30] e.g. R. Briffault, *The Mothers* (New York, 1927); O.R. Ehrenfels, *Mother Right in India* (London, 1941).

[31] *ISIH*, p. 27. In his letters to Vidal-Naquet dated 18.9.1965 and 27.9.1965 he provides further examples of this in the wealth paid by Bhīṣma for the marriage of Pāṇḍu to Mādri, the Madra princess, *Mahābhārata* I. 105.1. and also in the form of the marriage of Arjuna to Subhadrā, of the Yadu tribe.

bi from other scholars was that his ultimate concern was with an overall theoretical frame-work, into which, not only was his scattered research directed, but which he propounded as an attempt to comprehend the totality of Indian history. His first book, *An Introduction to the study of Indian History*, drew together the many themes on which he had researched in earlier years and which he had published as papers in various journals of Oriental Studies. This book was to prove his claim not merely to being a historian but to changing the paradigm for early Indian history.

For Kosambi, Marxism provided the clue to understanding the past and he identified his method unambiguously with Marxism. Kosambi would doubtless have accepted the judgement of Jean Paul Sartre that Marxism is the 'necessary' philosophy of our time, by which Sartre meant that even if Marx's particular conclusions are un-acceptable, the method of analysis which he had worked out is virtually unavoidable in the social sciences. Many among the non-Marxist and anti-Marxist historians in this country tried to dismiss the book with the predictable critique of all Marxist histories, that the author was forcing the facts to fit a preconceived theory: a critique which is applied *ad nauseam* to many versions of knowledge which are intellectually uncomfortable for those who are incapable of changing the paradigm and who are fearful of scholars attempting to do so. A few among the more intellectually gifted realized that what Kosambi was doing was not forcing the facts to fit the received Marxist pattern on Indian history, but was instead using a Marxist methodology to investigate a possible pattern and suggest a new framework; that in fact he was using the method creatively. As he himself states elsewhere, Marxism was not being "proved" or "justified", but simply being used as a tool of professional investigation. And this was also part of the reason why he was regarded with suspicion by the then Marxist political establishment in this country, the people whom he has referred to in his writings as the OM—the Official Marxists![32]

[32] In the introduction to *Exasperating Essays* (Poona, 1957), pp. 3–4 and on

Enthusiastic support came to him from intellectuals interested in Marxism and in history and from liberal intellectuals in Europe and America. It is significant that Kosambi was invited to give a series of lectures on the history of Hinduism at London University and to lecture at the Oriental Institute in Moscow in 1955, and this was before any Indian University took such a step.

I would like now to consider his approach to early Indian history with which he was centrally concerned. In the context of his general argument of the transition from tribe to caste, socio-economic formations were his primary interest. He draws his evidence on tribal forms both from literary sources as well as from the survival of such groups into recent centuries and from their interaction with peasant groups. The earliest of such transitions occurred in the Indus valley; hence Kosambi's concern with agrarian technology at that time.[33] He assumed that it was a culture without the plough, that the river bank was cultivated with a harrow and that the seasonal flood water was utilized for irrigation with dams and embankments helping in retaining this water and the river silt for a longer period. The decline of the Indus civilization is attributed to the Aryans who destroyed the agricultural system by breaking the embankments, which action he maintains, is symbolically referred to in the Ṛgvedic descriptions of Indra destroying Vṛtra, and releasing the waters. Kosambi was of the opinion that the plough was brought by the Aryans [i.e. the speakers of Indo-Aryan] who thereby changed agricultural technology. Recent evidence on the Indus civilization makes it clear that plough agriculture was practised even as early as the pre-

p. 18. He says of them, 'These form a decidedly mixed category, indescribable because of the rapidly shifting views and even more rapid political permutations and combinations. The OM included at various times several factions of the CPI, the Congress Socialists, the Royists and numerous left splinter groups . . . The OM Marxism has too often consisted of theological emphasis on the inviolable sanctity of the current party line, or irrelevant quotations from the classics.'

[33] *Ibid.*, p. 62ff.

Harappan period and that the plough was known to the non-Aryan since the more commonly used word, for the plough in Vedic literature is of non-Aryan etymology.[34] The theory of the destruction of the embankments is conjectural and may have greater application to dams built to prevent the flooding of the cities rather than for agricultural purposes. Nevertheless the question posed by Kosambi as to why the agrarian base of the Harappan culture declined and was unable to support an urban civilization in the later stages still remains a valid one and is now sought to be answered by evidence of a far reaching ecological change with which Harappan technology could not cope and which eventually resulted in the location of new urban centres in the Ganges valley.

Although he had no use for any theory of an Aryan race, Kosambi did support the idea of the Aryan speaking peoples having settled in north-western India and spreading gradually into the Ganges valley, in both cases initially as conquerors.[35] Such a theory of conquest had been questioned by those working in Indo-Aryan linguistics and it is now being proposed that conquest should be replaced by considering the possibility of migrations and technological changes being responsible for the arrival and the dominance of the Aryan speakers, the resulting long period of co-existence between them and the indigenous peoples being suggested by the evidence of bi-lingualism. Even the archaeological data which was once put forward to support the destruction of the Harappan cities by invaders is now discounted.[36] The new evidence however tends to strengthen the more important point made by Kosambi that much of the Indian tradition from the earliest Vedic texts is already an amalgam of Aryan and non-Aryan as indeed are even those of the highest caste.

Plough agriculture and iron technology when it was intro-

[34] Romila Thapar, 'The Study of Society in Ancient India' in *Ancient Indian Social History: Some Interpretations* (New Delhi, 1978) p. 211ff.

[35] *CCAIHO*, p. 41.

[36] Romila Thapar, *op. cit.*

duced into the Ganges valley led ultimately to the growth of urban centres as well as the recognizable forms of caste. Recent views would include as causal factors in this development, the role of a change in crop patterns with a dependence on rice agriculture, the diversity of irrigation systems, the use of labour in the new technologies and the range of control over these factors by different social groups. This is a fleshing out, as it were, of Kosambi's argument by extending the span of causal factors. Analyses of the structure of caste at this time in terms of the theoretical form given to the actuality, gives further rein to the question implicitly raised by Kosambi, namely, the degree to which ideology and social structure are inter-connected.

The Mauryan monarchy which controlled the Indian sub-continent was a feasible political system according to Kosambi because of the expansion of the village economy through *śūdra* agriculturalists being settled on state lands and by the deportation of prisoners-of-war who were used for the same purpose.[37] He argues against the use of slavery in production in early India and prefers the theory of *śūdra* helotage, although he does not develop this theory in detail. The decline of the Mauryan empire is attributed to an economic crisis, the details of which are debatable. His argument that the currency was debased devolves from his own chronological interpretation of the coins, which as we have seen, is not entirely acceptable, as also the argument that double cropping indicated an economic crisis, for we now know from archaeological sources that double cropping was an established practice even in earlier centuries.[38] However, that the inability of the Mauryan polity to survive must be attributed to causes which in part were certainly economic, cannot be doubted. A more plausible analysis would be to examine the nature of the Mauryan polity in terms of whether the existing man power and agricultural

[37] *ISIH*, p. 176ff.

[38] K.A. Chaudhuri, *Ancient Agriculture and Forestry in Northern India* (Bombay, 1977).

resources were conducive to such a system. Equally important is the question of whether the polity was as centralized as has been made out in historical studies.

Kosambi's treatment of the rise of the Buddhist, Jaina and other sects of that time links them to major technological changes and to urbanism. But above all he maintains that they reflect a situation of detribalization in which they attempt to reach out across castes to a wider social range through their universal ethic. He argues forcefully in support of a mercantile patronage extended to these sects which rooted them in society more firmly than did the help they received from royal patronage. The punch-marked coins are for him an indication of developed commodity production[39] which provided a high status for artisans and traders as members of urban society and their link with religions propagating a universal ethic would not be surprising. This link was demonstrated in his discussion of the post-Maurya period where he examines the role of guilds and artisans as donors to the Buddhist *saṅgha* in the light of the expansion and diffusion of trade. The emergence of occupational *jātis* in urban areas can frequently be associated with this development.

An evident departure from the orthodox Marxist pattern of historical periodization is Kosambi's refusal to apply either the Asiatic Mode of Production or the Slave Mode of Production to early Indian history without modifications of a major kind. For Karl Marx the Indian past conformed, by and large, to what he called the Asiatic Mode of Production characterized by a static society, an absence of private property in land, self-sufficient villages, a lack of a commercial economy and by a state control over the irrigation system. Although he and Engels recognized deviations from this pattern, they saw this pattern as a contrast to that prevalent in Europe and argued that historical stagnancy in India was broken by the coming of colonialism. This was not altogether acceptable to Kosambi, for whom the key to the Indian

[39] *CCAIHO*, p. 125.

past in the advance of plough agriculture over tribal society made a static history impossible. Of the notion of the self-sufficient village economy he writes, '. . . acute and brilliant as these remarks are, they remain misleading nevertheless . . .'.[40] The dependence of the village on external sources for salt and metals would automatically preclude self-sufficiency. Elsewhere he has argued for the existence of the tenant and of the landowning peasant.[41] He did however concede that from the end of the Gupta period there was a relative increase in self-sufficiency and this brought with it a static mode of production which was not the Asiatic mode for it came about during a period of feudalism.[42] He also argued that the lack of a sense of history and the power of myth further reduced individuality. A static mode of production could not have co-existed with a form of feudalism since the latter breeds its own contradictions. Perhaps if he had been questioned on this ambiguity he may have modified his position to argue that the degree of self-sufficiency increased, but not to the extent of the static mode of production becoming the dominant feature.

Elaborating his views on the Asiatic Mode of Production he wrote

> The real difficulty here (not in China) is the misleading documentation. Ancient Indian records derive from the brahman caste and those who read them pay no attention to the function of caste in ancient—(as well as modern and feudal) Indian society. Indian history is, to me, a very fine example of Marxist theory working very well in practice. Unfortunately, Marx had only the solitary report of Buchanan-Hamilton on Karnatak villages, not even the *Foral* of 1640 by the king of Portugal guaranteeing the rights of Goa village communities, which existed in a much more primitive form, and which could not be called 'hydraulic', in view of the torrential rainfall. The Goan organisation (which I have studied elsewhere, *Myth and Reality*, Chapter V) was actually the model for the Karnatak settlement, and survived almost to this day.

[40] *ISIH*, p. 244.
[41] *CCAIHO*, p. 101.
[42] *ISIH*, p. 244ff.

It follows that 'Oriental Despotism' has to be looked at from some other points of view than Wittfogel's hydraulic social aberrations. It seems to me that the two main Marxist considerations are: (1) The incidence of commodity production (per head) with the relative ease of food-gathering. This becomes vital when you consider Africa. By the way, the Pharoah's main function was not regulation of water or irrigation, but distribution of the numerous materials which had all to be imported from a long distance, including wood, metals, and so on. Henri Frankfort has a very neat answer to Toynbee, where he brings this out, in contrast to Mesopotamian development of numerous warring cities. (2) The need to use overriding force to compel the people (in an environment where food-gathering was, however irregular, always possible) to change over to food-production i.e. agriculture with the plough. In Egypt food-gathering was different except in the delta, but the cultivator had to be kept at his work. You will find that the British had to impose a poll-tax in Africa in order to get cheap labour for the mines and the white man's farms.

If you grant this, then it follows that despotism, even of the so-called oriental type, was a tool (however disgusting) used to bring a more productive form of society into existence. But during this very process, there came into being a class of state servants, state nobility or administrators—at times priests, who reduced the need for violence and helped develop the back-lands (as did my own ancestors in Goa and the Buddhist monasteries in China as well as in the Deccan). This class then used the absolute, despotic monarchy and the more or less passive substratum for its own purposes. Hence the changeless appearance of the country, seeing that the actual tools of production need not become more efficient. Under such circumstances, feudalism is a special development used to keep the rule in the hands of a ruling warrior caste-class, often conquerors. Don't be misled by the supposed Indian *kshatriya* caste, which was oftener than not a brahmanical fiction . . . .[43]

His rejection of the Slave Mode of Production as applicable to the Indian past arose from a hesitation in applying the accepted Marxist periodization of European history. Marx had suggested that primitive communism gave way to a slave mode of production predominant in Greco-Roman antiquity and this in turn gave

[43] Letter to Pierre Vidal-Nāquet dated 4.7.1964.

rise to feudalism in Europe from which evolved the capitalist mode of production. Kosambi was averse to the mechanical application of this model to India as had been done by various historians in Soviet Russia and in India, as for example, by S.A. Dange. Kosambi was caustic in his evaluation of Dange's book, *From Primitive Communism to Slavery*, which he said followed the Russian analysis and which analysis, '... saves a certain type of "left intellectual" the trouble of reading anything else or thinking for himself.'[44] Kosambi's analysis differed from any existing model. He maintains that the statement of the Greek ambassador Megasthenes (of the fourth century BC) that there was an absence of slavery in India was correct because Megasthenes makes a comparison with Sparta which suggests helots instead of slaves.[45] Kosambi states that at this period the *śūdra*s were essentially helots. He does not however discuss in greater detail the nature of *śūdra* helotage. Whereas the origin of the *śūdra* caste could perhaps be traced to a form of helotage, the classification cannot hold for the entire past. At the ideological level it would be clearly contradicted by the early *Dharmaśāstra* exposition of the *varṇa* theory where the origin of the *śūdra* is attributed to mixed caste marriages including those involving the upper castes. Such a theory even if not based on actuality would have undermined the notion of helotage. The possibility of a Slave Mode of Production in early India is problematical since it is difficult to assess the ratio of slaves to other forms of labouring men nor is there a clear distinction between slaves in domestic employ or in agricultural and craft production. Doubtless these numbers would also have varied in the *gaṇasaṅgha* chiefships where they were probably higher and in the kingdoms where with a diversity of labour, slavery for production may have been smaller. It would also be important to consider

[44] *Ibid.*, p. 6; see also, 'Marxism and Ancient Indian Culture'. *ABORI*, 1949, 29, pp. 271–77. Kosambi's views on his relations with the Communist Party of India over his review of Dange's book and his relations with Dange are described in his letters to Vidal Naquet dated 22.11.1963 and 4.12.1963.

[45] *ISIH*, p. 187.

the degree of unfreedom of the *dāsa* in relation to the *karmakāra, bhṛitaka* and *śūdra* which would involve questions of the legal status of these categories.

The Feudal Mode of Production Kosambi accepts as relevant to pre-modern Indian history, although even here he makes his own distinction between what he calls, 'feudalism from above' and 'feudalism from below', and which he regards as the peculiar features of Indian feudalism. Feudalism from above was his characterization of the changes which came about in the late first millennium AD subsequent to the Gupta period.[46] Incidentally he has little time for the Gupta period and is justifiably contemptuous of the nationalist historians who described it as the golden age of Hindu revivalism. His contempt is summed up in the sentence, 'Far from the Guptas reviving nationalism, it was nationalism that revived the Guptas.'[47] Recent research has not only tarnished some of the golden quality of this age, but has on occasion even revealed that a part of it was mere tinsel. The changes noticeable in the post-Gupta period were mainly those of an increase in the granting of land with a greater frequency of transition from tribe to caste through the introduction of plough agriculture, a decline in trade and commodity production which adversely affected the growth of urban centres, the decentralization of the army and a concentration of wealth at local courts. With this was associated the spread of *bhakti* cults whose emphasis on loyalty and devotion he saw as a characteristic feature of feudal society. In a discussion on private property in land, central to the concept of the Asiatic Mode of Production, he argues that it should be viewed in the Indian context which implies, firstly, that actual cultivators were ex-tribals who still regarded land as territory deriving from kinship rights, and secondly, the holding of a field was proof of membership of community rather than ownership of land and thirdly, that is a non-commodity producing village or one located near waste

[46] *Ibid.*, p. 275.
[47] *Ibid.*, p. 291.

land, land would have no sale value. The only conditions were the regular payment of taxes to either the grantee or the king. These arguments read more like an attempt to somehow salvage the notion of the absence of private property without a willingness to admit the pattern of the Asiatic Mode of Production as an explanatory model. Nor are these arguments wholly convincing because although in some areas the cultivators were recent converts to peasantry in others they were peasants of long standing since many of the grants of land were made in villages of well-established cultivators. The statement that land had no sale value in newly settled areas is contradicted by inscriptional evidence in some areas where, in Bengal for example, land is sold and the price is stated in districts which were regarded as being on the edge of waste land.[48] Part of the problem with his analysis of the two phases of feudalism, and this is a problem of which he is well aware, is that no generalization can cover the entire sub-continent since the changes varied from region to region.[49]

In his discussion on feudalism from below he draws his evidence mainly from Kashmir and Rajasthan and depicts a more clearly recognizable form of feudalism but with specific Indian features.[50] This phase is characterized by political decentralization accompanied by a low level of technology with production for the household and the village and not for a market, and the holding of land by lords on a service tenure who also have judicial or quasi-judicial functions in relation to the dependent population. The Indian features were the absence of demesne farming on the lord's estate by forced labour where in many cases, slaves were used instead, leading to an increase in slaves; there was also an absence of guilds and of any organized church. The backwardness of technology allowed of an easy conquest of northern India by those with a more advanced military technology. Changes in the

[48] B. Morrison, *Political Centres and Culture Regions in Early Bengal* (Tucson, 1970).

[49] *CCAIHO*, p. 177ff.

[50] *ISIH*, p. 326ff.

ruling class did not substantially affect the nature of feudalism in India and it continued until the coming of colonialism.

Kosambi's definition of feudalism would today find its critics as also would its general applicability to the sub-continent be debated. On the latter point one would have to consider whether other systems prevalent in other parts of the sub-continent would seriously subtract from the generalization.[51] The nature of control over land was different in parts of the peninsula as also was the condition of trade, where the rise of powerful guilds was characteristic of this period. The increase in the number of slaves was not such as to constitute a Slave Mode of Production and as Kosambi maintains quite correctly there was no slave economy of the Roman kind to initiate the institution of the manor. The existence of serfdom has also been suggested for many areas. Although there was no organized church nevertheless there is what Max Weber has called 'monastic landlordism' both among Buddhist and Hindu sects, which at some levels was a parallel system to that of church lands in Europe. The monastic centres of this period were opulent and powerful. Kosambi argues that religious sects frequently failed to provide the ethical and religious values by which they had once held the society, but he does not consider the monastic institution as the foci of political and economic control, a role which it often played at this time.[52]

It is curious that Kosambi takes as his model feudalism in England and shows no familiarity with the classic work on feudal society by Marc Bloch which would have been far more pertinent to his analyses. (His facility in French would have enabled him to have read Marc Bloch in the original). In a sense, this points to something of a narrowness in his wider historical reading. Although far from being an orthodox Marxist he nevertheless showed little interest in schools of analyses other than the Marxist

[51] R.S. Sharma had argued for a substantial similarity in many parts of northern India, *Indian Feudalism* (Calcutta, 1965).

[52] An example of the analysis of this role can be found in H. Kulke, *Jagannātha Kult und Gajapati Königtam* (Weisbaden, 1979).

as far as interpreting early societies was concerned. He does not for example indicate any familiarity with the works of those who were critical of Lewis Morgan and Frederick Engels inspite of using Marxist analyses as a starting point for the study of early societies, such as Karl Polyani. It is also curious that inspite of his interest in French scholarship (arising out of a concern with French colonial activities in Vietnam and North Africa) he was not introduced to the writings of French historians such as Fernand Braudel with which, one suspects, he would have found a rapport. Whereas his respect for the works of Gordon Childe and George Thomson is evident in his own studies, his acquaintance with Moses Finley's work on the Greeks came later[53] and one wonders whether he would have analysed the Indian epics in a manner similar to Finley's analysis of the Greek epics. Convinced as he was of the correctness of one methodology, Kosambi seems to have found the debate on methodology unnecessary. His utilization of Indian anthropological literature was more as a source of ethnology and a study of survivals and indigenous forms rather than as a means of examining the validity of any anthropological method. Possibly this limitation may also have been due to the tendency among Indian Marxists at that time to confine themselves to the writings of British Marxists, which can perhaps be explained as a curious reflection on the limitations of colonial scholarship where, even in radical circles the intellectual metropolis remained British with occasional forays into the writings of Soviet scholars. This is in striking contrast to more recent years in which the translations of European Marxist writing and that from other parts of the world are as widely read as the works of British Marxists.[54] A more

[53] M. Finley, *The World of Odysseus*, was first published in 1954. The fact that he was initially working in the United States would at that time have made his books less easily available in India. Kosambi refers to his study *Ancient Greeks* as being most stimulating, rather than to his more acclaimed work on the Greek epics.

[54] The easy availability of English translations has helped in this, such translations resulting mainly from the interest in Neo-Marxism on the part

mundane explanation may be the paucity of new books at that time and Kosambi was very conscious of this lack of availability of up-to-date research. In his personal correspondence with scholars in fields other than Indology he makes repeated requests to be kept informed of new studies since such information was not available in India. Where he could obtain such works he read them with great thoroughness and commented at length on them, as for example, on Maurice Godelier's views on early societies, many of which views he endorsed. That the deepest intellectual influence on Kosambi came from the writings of Frederick Engels is evident from both his books on Indian history.[55]

Such limitations, as these may be, are marginal to the serious quality of Kosambi's work, a quality which is enhanced by the intellectual honesty with which he justifies his use of Marxist methodolgy. His was a mind which by any standards would be considered outstanding. He combined in himself the best of a rigorous Indian intellectual tradition and rejected the facile revivalism and cultural chauvinism which in recent decades have emasculated Indian thinking. In changing the paradigm Kosambi presented a view of Indian history which sought answers to the fundamental questions of how and why Indian society is what it is today. He provided a new theoretical framework which was not a mechanical application of theories derived from elsewhere but was hammered out by his proficiency in handling a variety of sources and the intellectual perceptions and originality of thought

---

of American radicals and academics. It is significant that some of the most stimulating debates on precapitalist societies emanating from new Marxist writing are to be found in the issues of the last fifteen years of *Current Anthropology* and *American Anthropologist*.

[55] A view put forward in the course of a conversation by Charles Malamoud (who translated *CCAIHO* into French) and with which view I am in agreement. In a letter to Vidal-Naquet dated 4.6.1964 Kosambi writes, 'I learned from these two great men [Marx and Engels] what questions to ask and then went to fieldwork to find the answers, because the material did not exist in published books.'

which he brought to bear on his explanations. Fresh evidence may well lead to a reconsideration of the answers which he gave to these questions but his questions and his concerns still remain valid. Even in this reconsideration we are often dependent on the leads which he initially gave and which he indicated were worth pursuing. Kosambi raised the debate on early Indian history from variations in narrative to contending theoretical formulations.

Above all he was concerned with the contemporary relevance of his understanding of the past. But he insisted that the relevance was never to serve any doctrinaire purpose;[56] rather, it should stem from what he thought was the natural function of the historian. I can only conclude with what he himself quoted as the summation of the role of the historian. E.H. Carr writes: 'The function of the historian is neither to love the past nor to emancipate himself from the past, but to master and understand it as the key to the understanding of the present. Great history is written precisely when the historian's vision of the past is illuminated by insight into problems of the present . . . . The function of history is to promote a profounder understanding of both past and present through the inter-relation between them.'[57]

[56] *CCAIHO*, p. 24.
[57] *What is History?* pp. 20, 31, 62.

Early India: an Overview

The scope of ancient Indian history is undergoing some modification and the erstwhile ancient period, which stretched from Harappan times to the early second millennium AD is now being sub-divided into the ancient and the early medieval period. The nomenclature 'early medieval' does little towards either explaining itself or the subsequent medieval period: but the differentiation between pre-Gupta and post-Gupta history is a necessary and welcome change as also is the continuity between the late first millennium and the second millennium AD.

Harappan society remains enigmatic. There have been few attempts at detailed reconstruction from the archaeological evidence. This is in part because the variety of data required from studies such as palaeo-botany, ecology and hydrology remains limited for such a reconstruction and partially also because there are few archaeologists working on India willing to attempt a theoretical reconstruction in which the use of concepts from other disciplines such as anthropology, demography and statistics would be a prerequisite.[1] Such a reconstruction is especially re-

[1] An exception to this is the recent study of Harappan and West Asian trade by Shereen Ratnagar, *Encounters: The Westerly Trade of the Harappan Civilisation* (Delhi, 1981). A primary requirement relating to ecology and hydrology would be a series of studies along the lines of those Robert Mac Adams on Mesopotamia, particularly *The Heartland of Cities* (Chicago, 1981). Evidence from other disciplines can be utilized more effectively through a larger input of scientific techniques into excavation and analyses

quired with the fading of the so-called 'dark age' between the Harappa Culture and subsequent societies.[2] The question as to how far Vedic society is entirely Indo-Aryan or draws on the Harappan tradition in language, ritual and institutions becomes even more apposite than before.[3]

It is in the study of the many sub-periods within the broad boundaries of the ancient period that fundamental questions arise, providing scope for wide-ranging discussion. For a better definition of these sub-periods and in the interests of historical clarity a considerable refining of concepts and theories becomes necessary. Many of the crucial terms used in the definitions have been ap-

---

as well as data gathered from such disciplines. This may well happen in the near future now that archaeology the world over is drawing increasingly on scientific sources and less on the study of the classics. This calls for a little more theoretical daring on the part of archaeologists working on India and a concern with questions relating to the nature of Harappan society. The decipherment of the Harappa script, still a long way off, would of course be a help and would involve using the more conventional techniques of linguistics and cultural symbols. But the reconstruction of Harappan society could be met half-way by an approach which tries to intelligently reconstitute the society on the basis of material remains, environment and ecology. That the interest in ecology and environment does not have a relevance limited to archaeological data alone is clear from the recent Harris-versus-Heston debate on why the cow is sacred in India. M. Harris, 'The Cultural Ecology of India's Sacred Cattle,' *Current Anthropology*, 1966, 7, pp. 51–60; A. Heston, 'An Approach to the Sacred cow of India,' *Current Anthropology*, 1971, 12, pp. 191–209; S. Odend'hal, 'Energetics of Indian Cattle in their Environment,' *Human Ecology*, 1973, I.I. pp. 3–22.

[2] Archaeological continuities are being discovered between Harappan and post-Harappan societies as for example, in the repeated occurence of the Black-and-red Ware from Harappan to proto-historic times and more recently the overlap in the Punjab between Late Harappan and the Painted Grey Ware culture (associated by some with Vedic society) J.P. Joshi and Madhubala, 'Life During the Period of Overlap of Late Harappan and PGW Cultures,' *Journal of the Indian Society of Oriental Art*, 1977–78, NS, IX, pp. 20–9.

[3] Romila Thapar, 'The Archaeology of the Agnicayana,' in F. Staal, ed., *AGNI—The Vedic Ritual of the Fire Altar*, vol. I (Berkeley, 1982).

plied to such diverse social forms that they cease to have a specific meaning and tend to mask the diversities. This sharpening of focus becomes particularly necessary with the growing interest in social and economic history. It will also help in understanding the process of historical mutation over time. Although there is now a rich literature describing segments of the period, the explanation of change from one to the next and the linkages between these require a fuller consideration. A creatively critical discussion is called for on the terms used to translate categories mentioned in the sources since much of the interpretation depends on such discussion.

The nineteenth century was the age of the grand edifices of historical explanation and theoretical construction. While some of these edifices still stand firm, others are tottering. Even those which still stand often require repair and renovation, sometimes of a structural kind, in the light of new knowledge and fresh theories. The refining of concepts and theories therefore becomes a necessary part of the historical exercise and is particularly incumbent on those who, as conscientous historians, build their explanations on the basis of theoretical frameworks.[4] It is of this need for the refining of concepts that I would like to speak.[5]

Among the early sub-periods, Vedic society has been de-

[4] In the refining of concepts and theories the comparative method can be a useful tool. This involves an awareness of the historical analyses of other cultures and the use of specific categories of explanation which may not be directly applicable to early Indian history, but which would nevertheless generate questions and comparisons which can in turn assist in fresh analysis. It is to be deeply regretted that serious expertise on the ancient history of areas outside the Indian sub-continent is generally unavailable in Indian centres of research.

[5] I have elsewhere analysed in greater detail some of the themes which I am touching upon here. Questions relating to lineage-based societies, the sacrificial ritual and the peasant economy were considered by me in *From Lineage to State*. A summary of these ideas was contained in a paper, 'State Formation in Early India, *International Social Science Journal*, 1980, XXXII, No. 4, pp. 655–669.

scribed as tribal. The term 'tribal', which we have all used in the past, has rightly come in for some questioning.[6] In its precise meaning it refers to a community of people claiming descent from a common ancestor. In its application however, it has been used to cover a variety of social and economic forms, not to mention claims to biological and racial identities; and this tends to confuse the original meaning. Even as a convention it has lost much of its precision. The more recently preferred term, lineage, narrows the focus. Although the economic range remains, lineage does emphasize succession and descent with the implication that these are decisive in determining social status and control over economic resources. It also helps differentiate between chiefships where lineage dominates and kingship, which as a different category, evokes a larger number of impersonal sanctions. The concept of *vaṃśa* (succession) carries a meaning similar to lineage and is central to Vedic society with its emphasis on succession even as a simulated lineage. Thus *vaṃśa* is used to mean lineage or descent group among the *rājanya*s and *kṣatriya*s but is also used in the list of Upaniṣadic teachers where succession does not appear to be by birth but by the passing on of a tradition of knowledge.[7] Lineage also becomes important in the structure of each *varṇa*, defined by permitted rules of marriage and kinship and by ranking in an order of status, the control over resources being implicit. In this sense the emergence of the four *varṇas* is closely allied to the notions of a lineage-based society.[8]

In a stratified society the reinforcing of status is necessary. But where there is no recognized private property in land and no effective state such reinforcing has to be done by sanctions which often take a ritual or religious form. In the absence of taxation as a system of control in the Vedic period, sacrificial ritual functioned as the occasion for renewing the status of the *yajamāna*, initially a

[6] M.H. Fried, *The Notion of Tribe* (Menlo Park, 1975).
[7] *Bṛhadāranyaka Upaniṣad*, II. 6. 1ff; IV. 6. 1ff; VI. 5. 1ff.
[8] Romila Thapar, *From Lineage to State*, pp. 37–69.

rājanya or a *kṣatriya*. Apart from its religious and social role sacrificial ritual also had an economic function. It was the occasion when wealth which had been channelled to the *yajamāna* was distributed by him in the form of gifts to the *brāhmaṇa* priests which strengthened their social rank and ensured them wealth. The ritual served to restrict the distribution of wealth to the *brāhmaṇa*s and the *kṣatriya*s but at the same time prevented a substantial accumulation of wealth by either, for whatever came in the form of gifts and prestations from the lesser clans, the *viś*, to the ruling clans, the *kṣatrīya*s, was largely consumed in the ritual and the remainder gifted to the *brāhmaṇa*s. Generosity being important to the office of the chief, wealth was not hoarded. The display, consumption and distribution of wealth at the major rituals such as the *rājasūya* and the *aśvamedha*, was in turn a stimulus to production, for the ritual was also seen as a communication with and sanction from the supernatural. Embedded in the sacrificial ritual therefore were important facets of the economy. This may be a partial explanation of why a major change to the state system and a peasant economy occurred initially in the mid-first millennium BC not in the western Ganga valley but in the adjoining area of the middle Ganga valley. This change was occasioned not only by an increase in economic production and a greater social disparity but also by the fact that the prestation economy associated with the lineage-based society became more and more marginal in the latter region and in some areas was altogether absent.

The term 'peasant economy' is frowned upon by some scholars as an imprecise concept.[9] However it is of some use as a measurement of change. The label of 'peasant' has been applied to a variety of categories some of which are dissimilar. The use of a

[9] J. Ennew *et al.*, 'Peasantry as an Economic Category,' *Journal of Peasant Studies*, 1977, IV, 4, pp. 295–322; M. Harrison, 'The Peasant Mode of Production in the work of A. V. Chayanov,' *Journal of Peasant Studies*, 1977, IV, 4, pp. 323–36; Utsa Patnaik, 'Neo-Populism and Marxism: The Chayanovian View of the Agrarian Question and its Fundamental Fallacy,' *Journal of Peasant Studies*, 1979, VI, 4, pp. 375–420.

single word as a portmanteau description confuses the categories and therefore a differentiation is necessary. Eric Wolf at one point defines peasants as:

> . . . rural cultivators whose surpluses are transferred to a dominant group of rulers that uses the surpluses both to underwrite its own standard of living and to distribute the remainder to groups in society that do not farm but must be fed for their specific goods and services in turn.[10]

This definition seems to me inadequate even in terms of Wolf's study of peasants, for the important point is not merely the existence of a surplus but the mechanism by which it is transferred and it is to this that I would relate the emergence of a peasant economy. That the recognition of an incipient peasant economy in various parts of India is significant to the study of social history hardly needs stressing, since, concomitant with this is also the establishing of particular kinds of state systems, varient forms of *jātis* and new religious and cultural idioms in the area.

For the early period of Indian history the term peasant has been used to translate both the Ṛgvedic *viś*[11] as well as the *gahapati* of Pāli sources. But some distinction is called for. The Vedic *viś* was primarily a member of a clan although this did not preclude him from being a cultivator as well. The transferring of surpluses, in this case the voluntary prestations of the *viś* to the *kṣatriya*, points to a stratified rather than an egalitarian society and the simile of the *kṣatriya* eating the *viś* like the deer eating the grain[12] would indicate greater pressures for larger prestations. But the transfer was not through an enforced system of taxation. In the absence of private ownership of land, the relationship of the *viś* to the *kṣatriya* would have been less contrapuntal with little need of an

[10] E. Wolf, *Peasants* (New Jersey, 1966), pp. 3–4.

[11] This was popularized through A.A. Macdonell and A.B. Keith's *Vedic Index of Names and Subjects*, 1912. The technical term for the cultivator was *kīnāśa* and the root *kṛṣ* is used more frequently in association with cultivation.

[12] *Śatapatha Brāhmaṇa*, VIII. 7.1.2; VIII. 7.2.2; IX. 4,3,5.

enforced collection of the surplus. The context of Vedic references to *bali*, *bhāga* and *śulka* (the terms used in later periods for taxes) suggest that they were voluntary and random although the randomness gradually changed to required prestations, particularly at sacrificial rituals. However the three major prerequisites governing a system of taxation—a contracted amount, collected at stipulated periods by persons designated as tax collectors—are absent in the Vedic texts. The recognition of these prerequisites in the post-Vedic period and the collection of taxes from the cultivators by the state would seem decisive in registering the change from cultivators to peasants in which the existence of an economy based on peasant agriculture becomes clear.

The introduction of taxation presupposes the impersonal authority of the state and some degree of alienation of the cultivator from the authority to whom the surplus is given, unlike the lineage-based society where prestations are more personalized. Taxation reduced the quantity of prestations and became the more substantial part of what was taken from the peasant, but prestations were not terminated. The sanction of the religious ritual becomes more marginal and that of the state more central, the change occurring gradually over time. The formation of the state is therefore tied into this change. For the cultivator land becomes property or a legal entity and the pressures on cultivation have to do not only with subsistance but also with a provision for ensuring a surplus. This highlights the difference between appropriation in the earlier system and exploitation in the latter.

The Vedic *viś* was more a generalized term in which herding, cultivation and minimal crafts adequate to a household were included. Such groups were germane to the later peasant household. In effect, because the relationship with the dominant *kṣatriya* was based on gifts and prestations rather than on taxes, these cultivators would seem part of a lineage society in which their subservience to a dominant group arises more out of the exigencies of kinship or the ordering of clans than out of exploited labour, although the latter can be seen to increase in time.

The gradual mutation which took place becomes evident from the frequent references in the Pāli sources to the *gahapati*. The existence of the *gahapati* focuses more sharply on the presence of what might be called a peasant economy. But to translate *gahapati* as peasant is to provide a mere slice of its total meaning. Derived from *gṛhapati*, the head of the household, the term *gahapati* includes a range of meanings such as, the wealthy *mahāśālā-brāhamaṇas* addressed as *gahapatis* by the Buddha,[13] who had received as donations extensive, tax-free, arable land as well as those who paid taxes—the wealthy land-owners who cultivated their large farms with the help of slaves and hired labourers (*dāsa-bhṛtaka*).[14] Those at the lower end of the scale who either owned small plots of land or were professional ploughmen are more often referred to as the *kassakas*.[15] An intermediate group is also implied in one of the *Dharmaśūtras*.[16] The *Arthaśāstra* mentions tenants as *upavāsa* and also refers to another category, the *śūdra* cultivators settled by the state on cultivable or waste land on a different system of tenure from the above; as also the range of cultivators employed on the state farms supervised by the overseers of agriculture, the *sītā-dhyakṣa*.[17]

Gahapati with reference to agrarian society, therefore, is perhaps better translated as the landowner of some substance who would generally pay taxes to the state except when the land which he owned was a religious benefice. Private land ownership and

[13] e.g. *Majjhima Nikāya*, I. 401.

[14] As for example the *gahapati* Meṇḍaka, *Mahāvagga*, VI. 34.

[15] *Dīgha Nikāya*, I. 61; *Saṁyukta Nikāya*, I.172; III. 155; IV. 314; *Aṅguttara Nikāya*, I. 241; 229; 239.

[16] The *Baudhāyana Dharmasūtra* III. 2. 1–4 refers to householders of the upper *varṇas* who can in some cases be tenants and who cultivate six *nivartanas* (*bīghās*) of land. These were not poor peasants for they are also described as *śālina*, living in well-to-do homes, and would probably constitute an intermediary category between the *gahapati* and the *kassaka*. That this was a recognized category seems evident from their mode of subsistance being described as *ṣannivartana* (six *nivartanas*).

[17] III. 10.8; II. 1.1.

the payment of taxes demarcates this period as one in which a peasant-based economy is evident. Traces of the lineage based society continued in the marking of status by *varṇa* and the performance, although by now of marginal economic significance, of the sacrificial rituals.

That the *gahapati* was not even just a landowner but more a man of means is supported by the fact that it was from the ranks of the *gahapatis* that there emerged the *seṭṭhis* or financiers.[18] The two terms are often associated in the literature and this is further attested in the votive inscriptions recording donations to the *sangha* in central India and the western and eastern Deccan from the late first millennium BC.[19] *Gahapati* fathers have *seṭṭhi* sons as well as the other way round. It would seem that *gahapati* status was acquired through the practice of any respectable profession which provided a decent income, although the most frequent references are to land-ownership and commerce.

This is not to suggest that trade originated with the land-owning groups but rather that the large-scale commercialiaztion of exchange was tied to the emergence of the *gahapati*. In examining the origins of trade it is necessary to define more clearly the nature of the exchange involved. Broadly, there are some recognizable forms of exchange which can either develop into commercialized exchange or supplement it. There is evidence of luxury goods exchanged by ruling groups as a part of gift-exchange. Marriage alliances between *kṣatriya* families involved an exchange of gifts. Thus when Bharata visits his maternal kinsmen, he returns with gifts.[20] This is not an exchange based on need but is a channel

[18] *Aṅguttara Nikāya* IV. 282; VIII. 1.16.

[19] *Epigraphia Indica*, X. 1909–10. Lüders List Nos: 1056, 1062, 1073, 1075, 1121, 1127, 1209, 1281, etc. The inscriptions are later than the Pāli texts and may indicate the repetition of a process which had occurred earlier in the Gaṅgā valley.

[20] *Rāmāyaṇa* VII. 90. 1–5. Among the gifts were horses, probably imported from Gandhāra which was close enough to the Kekeya territory. The trade in horses from the north-west would doubtless have been accelerated by

through which status and kinship is confirmed. It may in addition lead to other forms of exchange. The major royal sacrifices required tributes and gifts and the *rājasūya* of Yudhiṣṭhira provides an interesting inventory of valued items.[21] The more ordinary sacrificial rituals involved the giving of gifts such as cattle, horses, gold, *dāsis* and chariots by the *yajamāna* to the priests.[22] These gifts became part of a distribution and exchange of wealth which in the lineage based societies formed the salient part of the wealth of those who ruled, whereas in the change to an economy based on peasant agriculture, they were merely a part of the wealth accumulated by the ruling families and the more wealthy *gahapatis.*

Less spectacular but more essential was another form of exchange, that of raw materials and commodities brought by itinerant groups such as smiths and pastoralists. It has been argued that the itinerant metal smiths formed a network of connections between villages.[23] Metal, particularly iron, was also a major item of regular trade. The role of pastoralists in trading circuits is now coming in for considerable attention particularly with reference to those groups which had a regular pattern of transhumance.[24] Exchange through sources of itinerant professionals was probably

---

forms of exchange. Romila Thapar, 'The *Rāmāyaṇa*: theme and variation,' in S.N. Mukherjee, ed., *India History and Thought* (Calcutta, 1982), pp. 221–53.

[21] *Mahābhārata,* Sabhā Parvan, 47.5; Romila Thapar, 'Some Aspects of the Economic Data in the Mahābhārata, *ABORI* (Poona, 1977–78), LIX, pp. 993–1007; 'The Historian and the Epic,' *ABORI*, 1979, LX, pp. 199–213.

[22] Romila Thapar, '*Dāna* and *dakṣinā* as forms of exchange,' *Ancient Indian Social History : Some Interpretations*, p. 105ff.

[23] D.D. Kosambi, *Introduction to the Study of Indian History*, Bombay, 1956. pp. 11, 91.

[24] Apart from the question of whether or not the Ṛgvedic Aryan speakers introduced iron technology to northern India, it would be worth examining whether as pastoralists there were patterns of movement which permitted them to maintain a symbiotic relationship with pre-existing agricultural communities. This would perhaps explain the factor of bi-lingualism in Vedic Sanskrit.

the starting point of the beat of pedlars which is a continuing feature of one level of exchange in India.

Yet another category is what might be called exchange between one settlement and the next. This is a useful basis for plotting the gradual diffusion of an item, as for example, the better quality varieties of pottery from excavations. Such an exchange provides evidence not only on local trade but also on the geographical reach of intra-regional contacts. Some of these settlements may then have come to play the role of local markets, the equivalent perhaps of what the Pāli texts refer to as *nigama*. These in turn are likely to have been the nuclei of urban growth as in the case of Rājagṛha and Śrāvastī.[25]

Distinct from all these is the familiar picture of trade which dominates the scene in the post-Mauryan period. This is the commercial exchange between two or more centres processing and producing commodities specifically destined for trade. The organization of this more complex form involved a hierarchy of producers and traders some of whom were sedentary while others were carriers of the items traded but of a different order from pedlars and pastoralists. The picture of commercialized exchange emerges from Buddhist texts and by the time of the *Arthaśāstra*, it is regarded as a legitimate source of revenue for the state. The question then arose of the degree of state interference and control which would be conducive to increasing the finances of the state.[26] The major artefact in this trade (other than the commodities) is coined metallic money, providing evidence of the degree of complexity and the extent of such trade and trading circuits. These early coins in some instances were issued by the *nigama* and in other cases may have been issued by local authorities or possibly by ruling families. In the post-Mauryan period dynastic issues gain currency, a clear pointer to the importance of commercialized exchange. However even in this period local issues remain in circulation suggesting multiple levels of exchange.

[25] N. Wagle, *Society at the Time of the Buddha* (Bombay, 1966), p. 22.
[26] *Arthaśāstra* IV. 2.

With such commercialized exchange the control of trade routes becomes a significant factor in political policy and military annexations. A recent analysis of the Silk Trade, involving a variety of levels of exchange from gift-exchange to sophisticated emporia, in the context of political relations between tribal groups and established centres of political power, suggests ways in which the complicated question of trade, often treated as a uniform monolith by historians of ancient India, may be investigated.[27] The trade of the Roman empire with India, as is clear from both commodities and the function of money, also spans a similar range. Diverse forms of exchange suggest the coexistence of various economic levels within larger trading systems and sharpen the social contours of the groups involved.

The analysis of trade also requires locating those involved in these exchanges in the social hierarchy of the time. In the production of goods for exchange, artisans, whether individuals or in guilds, relate to merchants and financiers in forms as diverse as the various categories of cultivators to land-owners. The role of the *śilpin* (artisan) and the *śreṇī* (guild) is quite distinct from the *seṭṭhi*. Their presence registers a change in the nature of the trade as also does the differentiation between categories of professionals such as the *vānija*, the *seṭṭhi* and the *sārthavāha*. Clearly there is a sea change when commercialized exchange becomes active. The investment required for an elaborate trade can only be provided

[27] M.C. Raschke, 'New Studies in Roman Commerce with the East,' in H. Temporim and W. Haase, eds., *Aufsteig und Niedergang der Romischen Welt* (Berlin, 1978). The Silk Trade spanning Central Asia, northern India and the eastern Mediterranean drew on a variety of exchange systems and Raschke's discussion on the role of silk as part of the exchange of gifts in Central Asia provides a new perspective on that section of the trade. An almost graphic representation of the varieties of exchange comes from the recent discoveries of rock engravings and inscriptions, the latter from the Kuṣāna period onwards along the Karakorum Highway in Gilgit. K. Jettmar, *Rock Carvings and Inscriptions in the Northern areas of Pakistan* (Islamabad, 1982); A.H. Dani, *Chilas* (Islamabad, 1983).

by a well-endowed social group which can invest its surplus in risk-taking ventures. The obvious category was the *gahapati* who could fall back on land if the venture failed. That it turned out to be highly successful is clear from the fact that not only did the *seṭṭhis* emerge from the ranks of the *gahapatis*, but, by the post-Mauryan period, had an independent identity as financiers and gradually superceded the *gahapatis*.[28] The wealth of the *seṭṭhis* became in turn an avenue to power, for some of them were known to be the financiers of kings and obtained in return rights to collect revenue, perhaps the proto-type of what was later to become the regular form of emoluments to administrative officers.[29] On the manifestations of trade, Buddhist and Jaina sources together with epigraphic and archaeological evidence provide a useful counterpoint to the *Dharmaśāstra* literature.

The link between agriculture and commerce is important for understanding the changes in the subsequent period. The opulence of those involved in commerce was poured into the adornment of religious monuments, monasteries and images and in the conspicuous consumption which is associated with the wealthier towndwellers of these times. This tends to obscure the agrarian scene where one notices less of *mahāśālā* landowners and large estates and more of those with small holdings. Small plots of land could be purchased and donated to religious beneficiaries and it seems unlikely, as has been argued, that such sales were restricted to religious donations.[30] Smallholdings together with the alienation of land could point to some degree of impoverishment among peasants. The inclusion of debt bondage (*āhitaka* and *ātmavikreta*), as a regular if not frequent category of slavery,[31] as well as the increasing references to *viṣṭi* (forced labour or a labour tax), sug-

[28] I. Fiser, 'The Problem of the Seṭṭhi in Buddhist Jātakas,' *Archiv Orientali* (Prague, 1954), XXII, pp. 238–66.

[29] *Ibid.*, p. 261.

[30] The *Arthaśāstra* refers clearly to the sale of land. II. 1.7; III. 9.3, 15–17; III. 10.9.

[31] *Arthaśāstra* III. 2.; Nārada I. 128; V. 29; Manu XI. 59.

gest a different rural scene from that of the preceding period. That oppressive taxation had become a recognized evil is explicitly mentioned in various texts.[32]

This mutation was endemic to the evident change in the post-Gupta period. Where trade flourished there the resources of the urban centres and the trade routes bouyed up the system; but this period points to a declining trade in many areas.[33] Internal commercialized trade requires the ballast of agrarian settlements and where lineage based societies could be converted into peasant economies there the agrarian support to trade would be strengthened. Earlier networks of exchange had permitted an easier co-existence with lineage based societies. Their resources, generally raw materials such as timber and gem-stones could, as items of exchange, be easily tapped by traders through barter and direct exchange without disturbing the social structure to any appreciable degree. On the other hand because of the requirement of land and labour, state systems more heavily dependent on a peasant economy had to absorb these societies and convert them into peasant economies in order to extract the benefits. Where trade declined or where new states were established the need to develop the agrarian economy became urgent. The granting of land appears to have been the mechanism adopted for changing the agrarian situation. The reasons for this change in the post-Gupta period need more detailed investigation particularly at a regional level.[34] In the very useful work done so far substantial

[32] *Viṣṇu Purāṇa* IV. 24; *Mahāsupina Jātaka* No. 77; *Mahābhārata* Aranyaka Parvan 188.18ff; Śānti Parvan 254. 39ff.

[33] That the external trade—the Silk Trade and the Roman trade—played a significant role in northern India is also clear from the negative evidence. Areas where trade declined as in the Gaṅgā valley shows a decline in the urban economy which has been pointed out by R.S. Sharma. Areas on the northern borders of the sub-continent, arterial to the Central Asian trade flourished in the post-Gupta period.

[34] A comparative regional analysis has become necessary with the recognition not only of regional environmental differences but also variations in the processes of change and the nature of change, particularly the fact that

data has surfaced. What is now required is a sifting and classifying of the data to provide more precise answers and to evoke fresh questions.[35]

---

not all changes coincide chronologically and completely in form. This makes the study of regional history significant not only in terms of regional variations but also as a prerequisite to broader generalizations about the history of the sub-continent.

[35] This work ties in with the debate on feudalism in India, and studies of this period such as those of D.D. Kosambi, R.S. Sharma, B.N.S. Yadava, B.D. Chattopadhyaya, D.N. Jha and H. Mukhia, in addition to many detailed regional studies of the post-Gupta period, too numerous to list here.

Much of the argument on the debate on feudalism in India so far has been of a generalized form. Perhaps what is required at this stage is comparative regional views which could better cope with the areas of investigation which call for analysis. Initially a few selected regions could be analysed in depth for both the urban and the agrarian aspects of the economy, but a start could be made with the agrarian. A tabulation of the data might sharpen the focus. Grants in a region could be classified in accordance with the type of grantee and the nature of the grant. Categories could be defined such as grants of waste land or cultivated land, grants converting lineage-based societies into peasant economies where the grant would be made to the lineage chief, or grants of state-owned lands already cultivated where cultivators were transferred along with the land, and other such categories where data is available. The chronological order and quantum of each would be useful information. Proprietory rights could also be part of this tabulation. At another level the analyses of the titles of grantees and changes therein might provide clues. The question of whether the peasantry was free hinges not only on the technical and legal definitions but also requires a discussion of the actual status of the peasant. Rights, obligations and dues of the grantees vis-à-vis the peasants would need to be tabulated in detail. These would provide some indications of the essentials of the prevailing system.

A worms's eye view of agriculture also needs to be investigated since some aspects of the debate involve questions relating to soil fertility and control over water resources. Some of these questions could be better handled through inter-disciplinary research if historians were to work jointly with specialists in soil analysis, and hydrology. The expertise of a wide range of agricultural scientists has entered into debates on the archaeological evidence relating to agriculture, but curiously has not been invited by agrarian historians into their domain. Now that the study of these subjects has become

It is curious that there is little resort to the policy recommended by the *Arthaśāstra* and other texts of establishing colonies of cultivators on land owned by the state so as to extend agriculture and thereby increase the revenue.[36] Was the state unable to do so because it lacked the administrative infrastructure or was it because it did not have the power to implement such a policy? Instead the state increases the grants of land to religious beneficiaries and later to administrative officers in lieu of a salary. This points to a need for an evaluation of the nature of 'early medieval' states with the possibility that their formation and structure were different from the previous ones. Was this type of state attempting to restructure the economy to an extent greater than the previous which appear to have been more concerned with revenue collecting functions, judging by the model advocated by Kauṭilya? Did the system of granting land predominate (perhaps initially) in

---

so specialized this reluctance as well as the absence of field studies is to be regretted. Considering that the data from survivals of various forms would be much richer for medieval history than for the ancient period one only hopes that a trend in this direction will develop soon. An increase in data of the technical kind can assist the quality of theoretical analysis. Questions more specific to the history of agriculture relate to investigating cultivation techniques, crop patterns, crop rotation, irrigation systems and water cesses, the percentage of arable land available in an area which would condition decisions about starting new settlements or intensifying existing agriculture, variations in the system of fallow for particular crops, the size of holdings in relation to the quality of the soil and the crops, the subsistence level of the peasant, labour input into land and crops and other similar questions. Many of these questions would involve extrapolating back from revenue records as well as considerable field work in the area under study, in order to sharpen the questions and gain insights into possibilities for an earlier period. It is not for nothing that R.H. Tawney is believed to have said that the first essential of research into agrarian history is a pair of stout boots.

[36] Some grants are given of waste land and this would be a case of extending the area under cultivation, but the revenue from this goes to the grantee and not to the state, which makes it different from the situation described in the *Arthaśāstra*. *Śūdra* cultivators are mentioned but in some cases as labourers of land-owners, e.g. Manu IV. 253.

areas where lineage based societies were prevalent so as to facilitate their conversion to a peasant economy (where lineage could also be used for economic control) and to a *varṇa* and *jāti* network? The identification with *varṇa* status would have acted as a bridge to a peasant economy and prevented a rupture with the lineage system. Elements of lineage have often continued even in some areas where peasant agriculture became the norm.

Religious benefices were on the pattern of earlier grants and were not strictly an innovation except that now grants were made increasingly to *brāhmaṇas* and ostensibly in return for legitimizing the dynasty and for acquiring religious merit.[37] These were the stated reasons for the grant but were not sufficient reasons. Grants of this nature, as has been pointed out, were a channel of acculturation. They could also be used as foci of political loyalty.

If the grants were made initially from state-owned lands they amounted to a renouncing of revenue. If the state was unable to administer the extension of agriculture, was the system of grants also introduced to encourage settlements in new areas where the grant was of waste land, or alternatively, of cultivated lands to stabilize the peasantry and induce increased production? Given the fact that slaves were not used in any major quantitative degree in agricultural production at this time, was the system of grants an attempt at converting the peasantry into a stable productive force through various mechanisms of subordination and a chain of intermediaries? Interestingly the term *gahapati*/*gṛhapati* drops out of currency for the system had changed and terms incorporating *rājā*, *sāmanta* and *bhogin* become frequent. The recipients of land grants had the right to receive a range of taxes and dues previously collected by the state and were soon given administrative powers as well. This permitted them to act as a 'back-up' administration where the grant was in settled areas and to introduce the system

[37] Legitimacy was necessary where the dynasty was of obscure origin or was described as having served the previous one e.g., F.E. Pargiter, *The Purana Texts of the Dynasties of the Kali Age*, Oxford, 1913, pp. 38, 45, 47, 55, 56.

where new settlements were being established. It may in origin have been a fiscal measure but in effect became the means of controlling the peasantry. The apparent increase in debt bondage and the fear of peasant migration would point to this being one of the functions of the large-scale grants. That the possibility of peasant migration to alleviate discontent was being slowly stifled is suggested by the fact of peasants taking to revolt as well from the early second millennium onwards.[38] A rise in brigandage may well have been a possibility for this period.[39] A qualitative change occurs when the state begins to grant villages or substantial acreages of land already under cultivation; a change which reflects both on the economy and on the nature of the state.

The need to fetter the peasantry would seem an evident departure from the earlier system and this in turn introduced a change in the relationship between the cultivator and the land now riveted in legalities and liabilities, with tax or rent no longer being the sole criterion of a peasant economy. The *karṣaka* of this period found himself in a different situation from the *kassaka* of earlier times. The term 'peasant' therefore cannot have a blanket usage or meaning since the variations within it have to be distinguished.

The secular grantees were part of a hierarchical system in which they mirrored the court at the local level. This is evident from their attempts to imitate the courtly style as depicted in the art and literature of the time. Grants of land to the *brāhmaṇas* as

[38] Instances of such revolts are mentioned in R.S. Sharma, *Indian Feudalism* (Delhi, 1980), pp. 127, 220; cf. N. Karashima, *South Indian History and Society* (New Delhi, 1984). Prior to this the more common form of protest was peasant migration which is referred to in the *Jātaka* literature and which is held out as a threat to a king who demands excessive taxes. Romila Thapar, 'Dissent and Protest in the Early Indian Tradition,' *Studies in History*, 1979, I. No. 2, p. 189ff.

[39] The increasing frequency in hero-stones commemorating a heroic act in defence of a village would point to uncertain conditions in certain areas. These tend to be in the interstices between kingdoms and between settled and forested areas. Romila Thapar, 'Death and the Hero,' in S.C. Humphreys and H. King, eds., *Mortality and Immortality* (London, 1981).

the major religious grantees rehabilitated them to a position of authority and their anguished invocation of Kalki as a millennial figure becomes less urgent.[40] A new religious ideology gained popularity focusing on the image and the temple and asserting an assimilative quality involving the cults and rituals of Purāṇic Hinduism and the genesis of the *bhakti* tradition. Ideological assimilation is called for when there is a need to knit together socially diverse groups. It is also crucial when there is an increase in the distancing between such groups as well as the power of some over others and the economic disparity between them. The significance of these new cults and sects may lie in part in the focus on loyalty to a deity which has a parallel to the loyalty of peasants and others to an overlord. But it would be worth examining the rudiments of each sect in its regional dimension, its grouping towards a *jāti* status and the use of an ostensibly cultural and religious idiom to express a new social identity. Were these also mechanisms for legitimizing territorial identities drawing on sacred geography and pilgrimage routes with the temple as the focal point?[41] The egalitarian emphases of the devotees in the eyes of the deity has rightly been viewed as the assertion of those lower down the social scale in favour of a more egalitarian society. But its significance grows when the social background to this belief is one of increasing disparity. Movements of dissent which had religious forms were often gradually accommodated and their radical content slowly diluted. The move away from community participation in a ritual to a personalized and private worship encourages the notion of individual freedom, even if it is only at the ideological level.

In the justifiable emphasis on social and economic history there has been too frequently a neglect among historians of the

[40] *Viṣṇu Purāṇa* IV. 24; *Mahābhārata*, Śānti Parvan, 254.39ff.

[41] This appears to have become important in a later period judging from the Jagannātha cult at Puri and the Viṭhobā cult at Pandarpur. H. Kulke, *Jagannātha-kult and Gajapati Königtum* (Weisbaden, 1979); G.A Deleury, *The Cult of Viṭhobā* (Poona, 1960).

analysis of ideology. To study ideology without its historical context is to practice historical hydroponics, for ideas and beliefs strike roots in the humus of historical reality. To restrict the study of a society to its narrowly social and economic forms alone is to see it in a limited two-dimensional profile. The interaction of society and ideology takes a varied pattern and to insist always on the primacy of the one over the other is to deny the richness of a full-bodied historical explanation.

Ideas are sometimes analysed as a response to social pressures and needs. This is particularly pertinent for those dealing with social history. Some of the more important literature is suffused with a theoretical representation of society even in symbolic or ideational forms. Meanings very often do not stem from just the vocabulary but require familiarity with the cultural context of the word. Examples of this would be the levels of meaning of words such as *varṇa* and *jāti* as they travel through time in texts such as the *Dharmaśāstras*. The ideological layers in the latter as codes of behaviour have to be peeled in order to obtain a better comprehension of their ordering of society.

Central to any concern with ideology in the ancient past is the critique of religious thought (as distinct from religious practice or organization). Some analyses of the *Upaniṣads* for instance, can provide an interesting example of this. One of the major strands in Upaniṣadic thought is said to be a secret doctrine known only to a few *kṣatriyas* who teach it to select, trusted *brāhmaṇas*.[42] Even the most learned among the latter, the *mahāśālā mahāśrotriya*, are described as going to the *kṣatriyas* for instruction.[43] The doctrine involves the idea of the soul, the *ātman* and its ultimate merging with the *brahman* as well as metempsychosis or the transmigration of the soul: in fact a fundamental doctrine of this age which was to have far-reaching consequences on Indian society. That it should have been secret and originally associated with the *kṣatriyas* raises

[42] S. Radhakrishnan, *The Principal Upaniṣads* (London, 1953). Introduction.

[43] *Chāndogya Upaniṣad*, V. 11.1ff.

many questions, some of which have been discussed by scholars.[44] It is true that the *brāhmaṇas* and the *kṣatriyas* were both members of the 'leisured classes' in Vedic society and could therefore indulge in idealistic philosophy and discourse on the niceties of life after death. But this is only a partial answer and much more remains to be explained. Was the ritual of sacrifice so deeply imprinted on the *brāhmaṇa* mind and so necessary to the profession at this point that it required non-*brāhmaṇas* to introduce alternatives to salvation, other than the sacrificial ritual? The adoption of meditation and theories of transmigration had the advantage of releasing the *kṣatriyas* from the pressures of a prestation economy and permitting them to accumulate wealth, power and leisure. Alternatively, was the accumulation of these already present in the fringe areas, described as the *mlecha-deśa* (impure lands) in Vedic texts, where the sacrificial rituals for various reasons had become less important? Thus Janaka of Mithilā, Aśvapati Kaikeya and Ajātaśatru of Kāśī could reflect on alternative ways to salvation. This also places a different emphasis on the function of the *kṣatriya* who had now ceased to be primarily a cattle-raiding, warrior chief.

These are not the only kinds of connections relevant to a history of the period. Upper and lower groups or even classes treated as monolithic, belie social reality. The tensions within these should also be noticed where the evidence suggests this. The competition for status between *brāhmaṇas* and *kṣatriyas* and the separation of their functions, as well as their mutual dependence, is symbolized in the sacrificial ritual which becomes a key articulation of the relationship. The new belief was the reversal of the sacrificial ritual in that it required neither priests nor deities but only self-discipline and meditation. At another level, the transmigrating of the soul through the natural elements and plants to

[44] P. Deussen, *The Philosophy of the Upanisads* (Edinburgh, 1906), p. 17ff; A.B. Keith, *Religion and Philosophy of the Vedas* (HOS, 1925), p. 495ff; D.P. Chattopadhyaya, *Indian Philosophy* (New Delhi, 1964), p. 85ff.

its ultimate rebirth, carries an echo of shamanism which may have remained popular outside priestly ritual.

There is in the new belief the first element of a shift from the clan to the individual in as much as the sacrificial ritual involves the clan but meditation and self-discipline, perhaps in opposition to the clan, involves only the individual. It symbolizes the breaking away of the individual from the clan. It also introduces an element of anomie which becomes more apparent in the later development of these beliefs by various sects. These reflections were seminal to what became a major direction in Indian thought and action, the opting out of the individual from society and where renunciation is a method of self-discovery but can also carry a message of dissent.[45] That the new ideas were attributed to the *kṣatriyas* and yet included in a brahmanical text was probably because for the *brāhmaṇas* to author a doctrine openly questioning the sacrificial ritual would, at this stage, have been an anomaly. That the doctrine stimulated philosophical discussion would in itself have required that it be recorded. But its inclusion may also partially have been motivated by the fact that when the doctrine was appropriated by heterodox teachers such as the Buddha, it could be maintained that even the roots of heterodoxy stemmed from the Vedic tradition. This was to become yet another technique by which orthodox theory in subsequent centuries sought to disguise ideas contradicting its own position. The Buddha not only democratized the doctrine[46] but also nurtured the idea of *karma* and *saṃsāra* and related it, among other things, to social inequities. But his negation of the soul (*ātman*) introduces a contradiction of the doctrine as visualized in the *Upaniṣads*. Such theoretical contradictions were current at this time.[47] The positing of a thesis and an anti-thesis becomes a characteristic feature of

[45] Romila Thapar, 'Renunciation: the making of a Counter-Culture?' *Ancient Indian Social History: Some Interpretations*, p. 63ff.

[46] S. Radhakrishnan, *op. cit.*

[47] K.N. Jayatilleke, *The Buddhist Theory of Knowledge* (London, 1963), p. 49ff.

philosophical debate and is reflected both in empirical disciplines such as grammar as well as in more abstract analysis.[48]

The relating of ideology to historical reality can result not only in new ways of examining a historical situation and be used to extend or modify the analysis from other sources but can also help in confirming the reality as derived from other sources. (It might also stir the still waters of contemporary interpretations of early Indian thought). Such a study, incorporating elements of deconstructing thought, would sharpen the awareness of concepts and theoretical frameworks. Historical explanation then becomes an enterprise in which the refinements of concepts and theories are a constant necessity, not only because of the availability of fresh evidence from new sources but also because of greater precision in our understanding of the categories which we use to analyse these sources. It is a bi-focal situation where the frame of reference provided by the analysis of ideology remains the distant view while the historian's use of a theoretical explanation of the data indicates the nearer reading.

[48] S.D. Joshi (ed.) *Patañjali's Vyākaraṇa Mahābhaṣya* (Poona, 1968), pp. i–xiv. At the more abstract level it is evident in the Brahmajālasutta in the *Dīgha Nikāya* I.1. The method of *pūrvapakṣa-uttarapakṣa-siddhānta,* although reminiscent of Hegel's dialectic should not be taken as an equivalent as it appears to have been limited to categories of logical analysis.

*Society and Historical Consciousness: The Itihāsa-purāṇa Tradition**

The expression of historical consciousness, it has often been assumed, takes the form of historical writing, clearly recognizable as a genre of literature. More frequently, however, the geological analogy of a particular vein embedded in rock seems more apposite, in that such consciousness is not always visible and has to be prised from sources which tend to conceal it. Within the vein lies information purporting to relate to events of the past, and enveloping this vein is the commentary which arises from concerns of the present. The form it takes tends to reflect the kind of society from which it emanates.

Historical consciousness, therefore, can change over time. Historians tend to view historical writing as conforming almost entirely to the format and pattern familiar from the last couple of centuries, or from models borrowed from particular societies such as ancient Greece and China. The more important but neglected aspect is the search for historical consciousness, irrespective of how immediately recognizable or evident it may be, in its literary form. This perhaps requires a distinction between what might be termed 'embedded history'—forms in which historical conscious-

*I am grateful to my colleagues Satish Saberwal and B.D. Chattopadhyaya for comments on an earlier draft of this essay.

ness has to be prised out—and its opposite, 'externalized history'—which tends to bring embedded consciousness into the open, as it were, and to be more aware of its deliberate use of the past. The need for such a deliberate use suggests a changed historical situation. This distinction can be apparent not only between societies but also within the same society as it undergoes change. The attempt in this essay is not to analyse historical consciousness in relation to society as a whole, but in relation to a more restricted view of its expression among those who successfully aspired to power. It relates therefore only to historical writing in terms of changing forms in the perception of power.

Each version of the past which has been deliberately transmitted has a significance for the present, and this accounts for its legitimacy and its continuity. The record may be one in which historical consciousness is embedded: as in myth, epic and genealogy; or alternatively it may refer to the more externalized forms: chronicles of families, institutions and regions, and biographies of persons in authority. There is no evolutionary or determined continuum from one form to the other and facets of the embedded consciousness can be seen as a part of the latter, whether introduced deliberately or subconsciously. The degree to which forms change or overlap has a bearing on dominant social formations. Similarly, major social and political changes influence the form of historical consciousness even though there is no mechanical correlation between the two.

Evident historical texts such as chronicles of families, institutions and regions often incorporate mythical beginnings which act as charters of validation. The tracing of links with established lineages through genealogical connections, and frequently with epic heroes, plays the same role of drawing upon embedded history. I shall consider some forms of embedded history, such as the prevalent myths in the *itihāsa-purāṇa* tradition, which encapsulate features of what might be seen as historical experience; the eulogies and hero-lauds which were gradually expanded into epic literature; the genealogical sections or *vaṁśānucarita* of the Puranic texts which, by implication, carry a commentary on the social status of ruling families.

In contrast to these the more externalized forms draw upon the embedded but have other primary concerns and carry a different type of historical information. Thus historical biography or the *carita* literature has as its germ the hero-laud and the epic hero. Family chronicles and *vaṃśāvalīs* assimilate myth and genealogy to other events. Chronicles of institutions and regions maintain a variant form of mythology and genealogy, and are aimed at recording the history of the institution or the area. The distinction made between the two forms is not arbitrary; I am arguing that the embedded form is closer to what have been called lineage-based societies and the externalized form to state systems incorporated in monarchies. Or, to put it in another way, the existence of the state requiring its own validation encourages the creation of an externalized historical consciousness.

In the articulation of historical consciousness in early north-Indian society the truly embedded forms are evident in the literature of the lineage-based society characterized by an absence of state formation, and the more free-standing or externalized forms emerge with the transition to state systems. The terms 'lineage society' and 'state systems', used here as a short-hand, represent not merely a change in political forms but a multiple social change. Thus the term 'state' would refer to a society registering political polarities, an increasingly vertical hierarchy of authority, social inequalities, differentiated economies and distinct ideological identities; not that these characteristics are completely absent in lineage societies, but there are endemic differences between the two. Sometimes these differences are blurred in the texts. Lineage society derives its validity from different sources of authority as compared to state systems, with which we are in any case more familiar.[1] The central role of lineage in the earlier society has

[1] I have discussed these differences as they pertain to early Indian society, specifically to Vedic and post-Vedic times prior to the rise of the Mauryan state, in *From Lineage to State* (Delhi, 1984). The term 'lineage' is used in

reference to more than just the ordering of kinship for it dominates virtually every aspect of activity.

I

The deepest layer of the embedded form is myth. Events are assumed to have happened, and time is almost proto-chronos since it involves gods and the supernatural in an active role with humans and animals. The significance of myth to the historian lies more in its being the self-image of a given culture, expressing its social assumptions. The role of myth in this context is often explanatory. Origin myths are concerned with cosmogony and the start of events such as the Flood myth.[2] The *Śatapatha Brāhmaṇa* version of the Flood myth carries obvious traces of association with the Sumerian Flood myth. Manu, when performing his morning ablutions, finds a fish in his cupped hands and rears the fish until it reaches an enormous size. The fish explains the intention of the gods to drown the earth in a deluge and, wishing to save Manu and the seven *ṛṣis* (in whom vests all knowledge) from this disaster, it orders Manu to build a boat for this purpose. This is tied to its horn and it swims through the deluge. The boat and its passengers remain safely on a mountain until the flood subsides, after which they return. By means of sacrifical rites Manu creates a series of sons for himself and one androgynous daughter, his children being the founders of the various lineages. The eldest son, Ikṣvāku, establishes the Sūryavaṁśa or Solar lineage, and the androgynous daughter, Ilā/Iḍa, establishes the Candravaṁśa or Lunar lineage.

---

preference to the more commonly employed term 'tribe', as lineage whether fictive or real is central to such societies, is more precise and points to the crux of such societies where descent and birth are in fact the major focus of social ordering.

[2] '*Śatapatha Brāhmaṇa* I.8.1.1–10; *Mahābhārata*, Sabhāparvan, 185; *Matsya Purāṇa* I.11–34; Romila Thapar, 'Puranic Lineages and Archaeological Cultures,' in *Ancient Indian Social History: Some Interpretations* (New Delhi, 1978) (hereafter referred to as *AISH*), p. 240 ff.

The *Matsya Purāṇa* version links the fish with the incarnation of Viṣṇu, thus bringing the gods more directly into the story, and at the same time using what was obviously a familiar myth to demonstrate the power of the new god, Viṣṇu. Manu, as the name suggests in its association with *mānava* (mankind), is the primeval, archetypal man who is the eponymous ancestor of all the lineages. The emphasis on origins is again stressed in the deluge, where the flood is seen as a time-marker. Floods tend to wipe away earlier conditions and society can start afresh.[3] The survival of Manu and the *ṛṣis* links the new creation with the old, in spite of the deluge washing away the old, since Manu is the seventh in a succession of pre-Flood Manus. The link is important to the genealogical records. The status of the earlier Manus is conveyed through it to the new lineages. All the eponymous ancestors of the lineages are the children of Manu.

Other myths provide social sanctions, one such being the Puruṣasūkta story in the *Ṛg Veda* describing the origin of the four castes.[4] The Puruṣasūkta hymn occurs in a late section of the *Ṛg Veda* and describes the sacrifice of the god Prajāpati, from whose body the four *varṇa*s are said to have sprung: the *brāhmaṇa*s from his mouth, the *kṣatriya*s from his arms, the *vaiśya*s from his thighs and the *śūdra*s from his feet. The symbolism of each bodily part relates to the ritual status and function of the particular *varṇa*. That the origin and hierarchy go back to a ritual occasion underlines the nature of the ranking. The evolution of *varṇa* stratification is rooted in the lineage-based society of Vedic times. In a sense the *brāhmaṇa* and the *kṣatriya varṇa*s were to evolve as distinct lineages with their separate rules of marriage and descent: exogamy in the *brāhmaṇa gotra*s and the more frequent endogamy of the *kṣatriya*s. The *śūdra varṇa* is excluded by its very origin, which is a denial of lineage since it is said more often to include groups identified by the status of the two parents.

[3] M. Eliade, *The Myth of the Eternal Return* (Princeton, 1971).
[4] *Ṛg Veda*, x. 97.

Some myths legitimize a changed social and political condition, as is apparent from the much repeated story of Pṛthu.[5] The various versions of this story begin by referring to the wickedness of Vena who had to be killed by the *ṛṣis* because of his unrighteous rule. From his left thigh they churned a successor, Niṣāda, who was inadequate and was expelled to the forest as a hunter-gatherer. From the right arm of Vena they churned another successor, the righteous *rājā* Pṛthu, who introduced cattle-keeping and agriculture and bestowed so many benefits on the earth, Pṛthvī, that she in gratitude gave him her name. Vena was wicked because he ceased to perform the sacrificial ritual and had to be killed by the *ṛṣis* (and not expelled by his subjects), who alone had the right to depose a ruler. The dark, short, ugly Niṣāda became the prototype of all forest-dwelling people. The myth sought to legitimize the expulsion of such groups when land was cleared and settled by agriculturists.

In each of such cases an attempt is made to explain social origins and assumptions which are significant to historical reconstruction. Myth was transmitted orally in its earliest phase. With the evolution of a more heterogeneous and stratified society, myths were questioned and explanations sought. Some myths were replaced with new or different versions and others added to and embellished, often to such a degree that the original myth became almost opaque. That myths in some ways mirrored society was not their sole function, but for our purposes this aspect is significant.

Myths of descent often serve to integrate diverse groups by providing common origins. Among competing groups a myth can be used for the reverse process of distinguishing one from the other. Origin myths posit beginnings authoritatively and are therefore central to embedded history. The degree to which myths reflect different social assumptions can be demonstrated by a comparison of origin myths from the *Ṛg Veda* and from Buddhist

[5] *Mahābhārata*, Śāntiparvan, 59: *Viṣṇu Purāṇa*, I.13; *Matsya Purāṇa*, x.4–10.

sources, a comparison which also demonstrates the degree to which historical consciousness is embedded in myth.[6] The origins of the Śākyas, Licchavis, Mallas and Koliyas are all described in stories which have a common format, which format suggests a tradition deviant from the brahmanical origin myths. The clans are of the Ikṣvāku lineage, are said to be of the families of *rājās* (which could mean royal descent but more likely refers to families of lineage chiefs) and are often the exiled children of such families, thus suggesting a lineage migration or fission. The new settlement is in a forest clearing with a town as its nucleus. The name of the lineage is frequently associated with an object such as the *kol* or *śaka* tree. More interestingly, the original founders have a system of sibling marriages and in each case sixteen pairs of twin children are born: it is from these that the lineage expands. Sibling incest, since it is never actually referred to as prevalent, would point to a symbolic concern with purity of lineage, a demarcation between the families of the *rājās* who owned land and the rest of the people, by the assertion of origins otherwise taboo; or perhaps an endorsement of cross-cousin marriage, which, because it was prohibited by brahmanical codes referring to northern India, may have been seen as a form of sibling incest. That the origin myth was of some consequence is evident from its inclusion in the history of every lineage and by the considerable emphasis given to it in the biographies of the Buddha. There is an absence of any reference to ritual status.

II

Apart from myth, other embedded forms are associated with various fragments of literature moving towards the emergence of the epic. The evolution is traceable via the *dāna-stuti* (eulogies on

[6] *Sutta Nipāta*, 420ff; *Sutta Nipāta Commentary*, I.352ff; *Sumaṅgalavilāsinī*, I, pp. 258–60; Romila Thapar, 'Origin Myths and the Historical Tradition,' *AISH*, p. 294ff.

gift-giving), *gāthā*, *nārāśaṁsi* (eulogies on heroes) to the *ākhyāna* and the *kathā* (cycles of stories generally involving heroes). The *dāna-stuti* hymns scattered throughout the *Ṛg Veda* are eulogies on chiefs and deities who act as would chiefs bestowing generous gifts on grateful bards and priests.[7] The prototype of the gift-giver was the god Indra. The Indra-*gāthā*s express the gratitude of the *jana* (tribe) whom he has led successfully in a cattle-raid and subsequently in distributing the wealth bestowed, much of it on the priests. The same was expected from the ideal *rājā* (chief) in a society where raids were a major access to property and where wealth was computed in heads of cattle and horse, in chariots, gold and slave girls. The *dāna-stuti*s mentioned the names of their patrons, who were doubtless actual chiefs, but, equally important, the hymns indicated the purpose of the gift and the items of wealth. They were not only eulogies of past actions but also indicators of what was expected from the chiefs.

The *ākhyāna*s, commemorating *rājā*s and heroes, were the cycles of stories recited at the time of the *yajña*s (sacrificial rituals).[8] Some heroes underwent a metamorphosis in time and came to be remembered for reasons quite different from those of the earliest stories. Thus Purūravas in the *Ṛg Veda* is a mortal who loves a celestial woman, Urvaśi; in the *Śatapatha Brāhmaṇa* he is shown as aspiring to become a celestial being himself in pursuit of his love; and finally in the *Mahābhārata* he is not only a celestial being but is among the more important ancestors of the Candravaṁśa lineage.[9] The protagonists in these stories are members of the chiefly families (*rājanya*s and *kṣatriya*s); the stories narrate their lives and activities and incidentally provide information on the lineages as

[7] *Ṛg Veda*, VI. 63; V. 27; V. 30; VI. 47; VIII. 1; VIII. 5; VIII.6.

[8] Both the terms *ākhyāna* and *kathā* have the meaning of recitation or oral narration, and the purpose of the form is clear from these words. Some of the bardic fragments in the form of stories are also to be found in the *Jātaka* literature.

[9] *Ṛg Veda*, X. 95; *Śatapatha Brāhmaṇa*, XI. 5.1.1ff; *Mahābhārata*, Ādiparvan, VII. 70–71.

well. An example of the latter is the transformation of single lineages into confederacies of tribes—the Bharatas and the Pūrus of the *Ṛg Veda* confederating with others into the Kurus of later times. The genealogies tend to be shallow and activities centre around the lineages rather than the succession of hereditary status.

A common feature of these many embedded forms is that they are linked to the ritual of sacrifice, the *yajña*. This imparts sanctity to the story and ensures it a continuity coeval with the performance of the ritual; it also imbues it with what were believed to be transcendental powers associated with the accurate and precise performance of the ritual. Even if the events were limited to the activities of the *kṣatriyas*, the audience was much wider and incorporated the entire tribe. Apart from the obvious ritual and religious function of the *yajña* its relevance also lay in its being the occasion for the redistribution of wealth, both from cattle raids and from agricultural production. Up to a point certain rituals had elements of a potlatch in which wealth was not merely redistributed but was also consumed. Both the redistribution as well as the destruction of wealth were directly concerned with claims to status.[10]. When the ritual was enlarged to include representation from other *janas*, either in the form of honoured guests or as tribute bearers, its function as a potlatch gradually gave way to its symbolizing status on a grander scale. The claims of individual lineages or their segments as descent groups could be established on such occasions, as for example the famous *rājasūya* sacrifice of Yudhiṣṭhira[11] which raises a complex set of problems concerning the status of various lineages, not least among them that of Kṛṣṇa as the chief of the Vṛṣṇis. The *yajña* therefore stated, as it were, the ranking order of the lineages. The stories which related to these lineages became social charters recording status *vis-à-vis* other lineages, or changes of status, as for example from segment to confederacy, or the migration and fissioning off of a segment from

[10] Romila Thapar, '*Dāna* and *dakṣiṇa* as forms of exchange,' in *AISH*, p. 105ff.

[11] *Mahābhārata*, Sabhāparvan, 30ff; 34ff.

a lineage, as in the case of the Cedis migrating from the western Ganga valley to central India.[12] The record of such migrations was crucial not only to territorial claims but also to genealogical links with established lineages by those newly formed. The *yajña* was a conduit of gift-exchange as well where the wealth of the lineage brought as *bali* or tribute (initially voluntary and later less so) by the *viś* (clan) to the *kṣatriya* or the *rājā*, or else the wealth captured in a raid would be ceremonially used in the ritual and what remained of it would be gifted to the *brāhmaṇas* performing the *yajña*. The exchange was at many levels. Wealth was offered to the gods in return for the success and well-being both of the *kṣatriya* and the *viś*, the well being guaranteed by the *brāhmaṇas*. Tangible wealth moved from the household of the *kṣatriya* to that of the *brāhmaṇa*. Such a limited exchange was economically non-productive in the sense that it was self-perpetuating with little chance of breaking through to new social forms. But its actual significance lay in its being an operative process in maintaining the lineage society.

III

It was doubtless these fragments of eulogies (*praśasti*s) on the heroes and the cycles of stories which led to the first gropings towards epic forms in India, referred to as the *kathā*. Both the *Mahābhārata* and the *Rāmāyaṇa* had their earlier and perhaps more truly epic versions in what have been referred to as the *Rāma-kathā* and the *Bhārata*[13] or *Jaya*. In their later forms, as we have them

[12] *Mahābhārata*, Ādiparvan, 57.

[13] V.S. Sukthankar, *On the Meaning of the Mahabharata* (Bombay, 1957); 'Epic Studies,' *ABORI*, XVIII, pp. 1–76; C. Bulke, *Rāma-kathā* (Allahabad, 1972); H. Jacobi, *The Ramayana* (trans. S.N. Ghoshal), (Baroda, 1960). It is a moot question as to how much of the original epic persists in the now heavily inflated and interpolated versions, which, despite the critical editions of both texts, still require substantial pruning to be brought anywhere near the original. The interpolations have been both of substance and form: hence the

now, each of the two epics has a distinct locale and the narrative is woven around one of the two main lineages. Thus the *Mahābhārata* focuses on the western Gaṇgā valley, referred to as *madhya-deśa* in the literature, and is concerned with the Aila lineage. The *Rāmāyaṇa* as the epic of the Ikṣvāku lineage has its nucleus in the middle Gaṇgā valley, in Kośala and Videha, and is concerned with migrations southwards into the Vindhyan region, with Dakṣina Kośala perhaps providing the clue to the area of exile.

The epic continued to be recited, initially on ritual occasions; the *Mahābhārata* is said to have been recited at the *yajña* in the Naimiśa forest and the *sarpa-yajña* of Janamejaya, the *Rāmāyaṇa* by Lava and Kuśa in the Vālmīki-*āśrama*. But it also became the stock for court poetry, the *kāvya*, in the newly emerging courts of the monarchies of the late first millennium BC, or for that matter in more elaborate literary fashions in the courts of the various kingdoms of the first millennium AD.

The epic form carries within it the germs of a more conscious and less embedded historical tradition.[14] Its historicity lies in the fact that it is a later age reflecting on an earlier one, the reflections frequently taking the form of interpolations interleaved among the

---

reference to the *Rāmāyaṇa* as a *kāvya* or literary poem and to the *Mahābhārata* as *itihāsa*, more closely approximating history, although the historical content remains internalized.

[14] This is in part reflected in the perennial search by archeologists for 'epic ages'. The financially flourishing 'Ramayana archaeology', even though without any tangible results, continues to be discussed seriously in some archaeological and historical circles, despite the near absurdity of the idea. That epic archaeology is an almost non-existent category becomes clear from a discussion of the encrustations which go into the making of an epic. E.W. Hopkins, *The Great Epic of India: Its Character and Origin* (New York, 1901); V.S. Sukthankar, *Prolegomena* to the Critical Edition of Adi Parvan (Poona, 1933); Romila Thapar, *Exile and the Kingdom: Some Thoughts on the Rāmāyaṇa* (Bangalore, 1978); 'The Historian and the Epic,' *Annals of the Bhandarkar Oriental Research Institute*, 1979, vol. LX, pp. 199–213; B.D. Chattopadhyaya, 'Indian Archaeology and the Epic Tradition,' *Puratattva*, VIII, 1975–6, pp. 67–71.

fragments of the oral, bardic tradition. When epic literature ceases to be a part of the oral tradition and is frozen into a written form, reflections begin to tail off. The pastoral-agricultural society of the world of the heroes structured around lineage gives way to the more clearly agrarian societies and to the rise of urban centres controlled by what is visibly emerging as a state system—which in the Gaṅgā valley at this time was mainly monarchical.

Many of the seeming contradictions in the stances and configurations characterizing the epics can perhaps be explained by these texts (and particularly the *Mahābhārata*), reflecting something of a transitional condition between two rather different structures, the societies of the lineage-based system and that of the monarchical state. Idealized characters are seldom the gods but rather the heroes who occupy the centre of the stage and the gods remain in the wings. Sometimes the earlier deities even come in for a drubbing.[15] The importance of the heroes is further endorsed by their being almost the terminal descendants in the major lineages of the past, a matter of some despair for their death is seen as the wrapping up and putting away of the lineage society, which, in certain areas, was being replaced by monarchies. However, some elements of the lineage society did persist and among them was the continuation of *varṇa* ranking. In many areas outside the *madhya-deśa*, lineage society continued for longer periods and the transition to monarchical states was a gradual process. Nevertheless the change to monarchy meant a substantial alteration of social configurations.

Unlike myth, epic does not attempt to explain the universe or society. It is sufficient that the problems of society are laid bare, and even solutions are not sought since the ultimate solution is the

[15] The treatment of Indra in the epics, for example, records a sea change from the Indra-*gāthās* of the *Ṛg Veda*. Indra is now subservient not only to the rising status of Viṣṇu but is unequal even to the superior power of the *ṛṣis*. Leaving aside the deliberate incarnating of Viṣṇu as the epic heroes Rāma and Kṛṣṇa, there is little doubt that they are now more central than the older gods.

dissolution of the system. Societies experiencing greater stratification require an overall authority to maintain the cohesion of lineage and strata. When such an authority comes into being and is eulogized, that eulogy becomes the dirge of a truly epic society. In laying bare the conditions in the transition from lineage society to state systems, a number of bi-polarities are reflected in the literature which give an added edge to the image of the past and the contours of the present. Thus *grāma* (settlement) is contrasted with *aranya* (forest), the kingdom with exile; the orderliness of the *grāma* is opposed to the disorder of the *aranya*; the kingly ethic arises out of governing a people and claiming land, the heroic ethic emerges from war and confrontation. The monarchical state is seen as the superior and is the successor to lineage society, irrespective of whether this is clearly spelt out—as in the conflict between the kingdom of Kośala and the *rākṣasas* in the *Rāmāyaṇa*—or whether it is left more ambiguous—as in the diverse assumptions of the narrative and didactic sections of the *Mahābhārata* where the Sabhāparvan, encapsulating the essence of a lineage society, stands in contrast to the Śāntiparvan with its rhetoric on the monarchical state. The new ethic is sustained in part by the popularizing of new sources of authority. Among them and significant to the political arena were the king, the *brāhmaṇa* and the *ṛṣi*. None of these were entirely new in that the chief, the priest and the shaman were dominant figures in lineage society. But it is the tangible authority of the king based on land as the source of revenue, or of the *brāhmaṇa* as the sole performer of and manual on rituals, and of the *ṛṣi* and *saṁnyāsi* as symbolizing an intangible moral authority almost as a counterweight to that of the first two, which gives a fresh dimension to their role and their interrelations. The changed situation is reflected in a shift in the kind of authority exercised. From a more diffused, equitable authority there is a movement towards a hierarchical, vertical authority.[16] This was

[16] Cf. W.B. Miller, 'Two Concepts of Authority,' *American Anthropologist*, April 1955, vol. 57, pp. 271–89.

mitigated somewhat by the countervailing presence of the renouncer and the charisma attached to renunciation.

The epic as the literature of one age looking back nostalgically on another can become a literature of legitimation. Interpolations are often the legitimation of the present but are attributed to the heroes of the past. The bards were perhaps providing the models of what patrons should be like. But, more important, it is the kingdoms looking back on an age of chiefships: where recently founded dynasties were seeking ancestry from the *kṣatriya* lineages through actual or, more often, imagined genealogical links; where such ancestry would also bestow social legitimacy and validate kingship. That legitimacy and validation are essential to the epic is clear from the central event of the narrative, namely the legitimacy of succession, involving elder and younger sons and the problems of disqualification.[17] Legitimacy also relates to using the past to explain the present. Perhaps the most dramatic example of this is the series of explanations in favour of accepting the strangeness of Draupadī marrying five brothers, fraternal polyandry not being a commonly practised form of marriage. Among the explanations is predictably a reference to an earlier birth of Draupadī.[18] Fortunately the doctrine of transmigration, referring to events and situations in a previous birth, makes the use of the past more plausible. The interplay of the past and the present is thus not only part of the implicit epic idiom but is made more explicit by recourse to the theory of transmigration. At another

[17] J.A.B. van Buitenan refers to the problem of the 'disqualified eldest' in his introduction to the translation of the Ādiparvan. The *Mahābhārata. The Book of the Beginning* (Chicago, 1973), p. xviii. The problem goes back to earlier antecedents. Thus the Candravaṁśa lineage starts with the replacement of Yadu, the eldest son of Yayāti, by his youngest son, Pūru. The *Mahābhārata* war, which involves virtually all the *kṣatriya* lineages and becomes the last heroic act of a lineage society, is again motivated by the problem of succession where physical ailments further complicate the question. The exile of Rāma is over the issue of succession, which, in spite of the heavier emphasis on primogeniture, is still subject to the whims and wishes of the parents.

[18] *Mahābhārata*, Ādiparvan, 189.

level the past validates the present in the long discourses on what constitutes good government or the correct functioning of the *kṣatriya* as king: perhaps best exemplified in the dying Bhīṣma delivering the lengthy *mokṣadharma* perorations, lying on his bed of arrows. Legitimacy makes the claim to historicity more feasible and the association with myth is weakened.[19]

IV

The gradual prising of historical consciousness becomes visible in the compilation of what came to be called the *itihāsa-purāṇa*.[20] The phrase remains difficult to define, veering between the perceived past and historicity. It is described as the fifth Veda but was an oral tradition for many centuries until it was compiled in the form of the *Purāṇa*s in the mid first millennium AD. The genealogical sections of the *Purāṇa*s were a reordering of the earlier material in a new format. The lesser and multiple *Purāṇa*s borrowed the format of the earlier major *Purāṇa*s, although their contents differed. The *Purāṇa* was to become a recognized literary form. To the extent that it recorded history, it was initially transitional from embedded to externalized history. It was linked to the bardic tradition, where the *sūta* and the *māgadha* are said to have been its earliest authors.[21] In the Vedic texts the *sūta* has a close relation with the *rājā* and was of high status, but by the time of the Manu *Dharmaśāstra* the *sūta* had been reduced to the level of a *sankīrṇa*-

[19] Romila Thapar, 'The *Rāmāyaṇa*: Theme and Variation,' in S.N. Mukherjee, ed., *India: History and Thought* (Calcutta, 1982), pp. 221–53.

[20] The *itihāsa-purāṇa* is referred to in the *Arthaśāstra*, 1.5. Its literal meaning is 'thus it was'—*iti-hi-asa*. The events of the past were to be so related as to link them with the goals and purposes of the tradition which was being historicised.

[21] The *sūta* and the *māgadha* are said to have arisen from the sacrifice of Pṛthu, and immediately on appearing began a *praśasti* of the *rājā*. *Atharvaveda*, V.3.5.7; *Taittirīya Brāhmaṇa*, II.4.1. In texts such as *Gautama*, IV.15; *Manu*, X.11, 26; *Nārada*, 110, the status of the *sūta* has changed. This change is made explicit in the *Mahābhārata*, Ādiparvan, 122.4ff. and 126.15ff., in which the *sūta* is inferior to the *kṣatriya*.

jāti or mixed caste. Doubtless by now the tradition had been appropriated by the literate *brāhmaṇas* who had also seen the potential value of controlling oral information on the past and recording it in a literary form relevant to emergent contemporary requirements.

There is evidence to suggest that the Purāṇic texts were translated from the oral Prākrit to the literate Sanskrit.[22] The structure of the *Purāṇas* was an attempt to provide an integrated world view of the past and present, linking events to the emergence of a deity or a sect, since each *Purāṇa* was dedicated to such a one, the *Viṣṇu Purāṇa* being regarded as the model. The historical epicentre of the *itihāsa* tradition was the *vaṁśānucarita,* which, as the name suggests, was the genealogy of all the known lineages and dynasties upto the mid-first millennium AD. It was not a parallel tradition to the earlier *kathās* and *ākhyānas* since it incorporated many of these forms of embedded history. The genealogical core pertaining to those who were believed to have held power in the past was carefully preserved after it had been worked out into a systematic pattern. This was because it not only purported to record the past but was also later to become essential to future claims to lineage status, and was therefore linked with historical writing. Evidently there was a need for a recognizable historical tradition at this time. In the transition from lineage to state, which was occurring in many parts of north India, monarchy had emerged as the viable political form.

The major dynasties recorded in the *Purāṇas* upto the mid-first millennium AD start with descendants of recognized *kṣatriya* lineages, but by the mid-first millennium BC begin to refer to families of non-*kṣatriya* origin. Some are specifically said to be *śūdras,* such as the Nandas and possibly the Mauryas. Others, judging by their names, were *brāhmaṇa,* such as the Śuṅgas and Kāṇvas. The lesser dynasties dating to the early centuries AD are stated to be *vrātya-dvija, śūdra* and *mleccha,* and this is explained as resulting from the

[22] F.E. Pargiter, *The Ancient Indian Historical Tradition* (London, 1922), p. 77ff; *Dynasties of the Kali Age* ..., 1913, reprint, (Delhi, 1975), p. 77ff.

inevitable degeneration of all norms in the Kaliyuga. Successor dynasties are frequently referred to as the *bhṛtyas* or servants of the previous ones, suggesting that the founders of dynasties may often have been administrators, high in the hierarchy of office who overthrew weak kings. This may well account for the rise of *brāhmaṇa* dynasties. The gradual increase in references to *śūdra* rulers would indicate that political power, although in theory restricted to *kṣatriyas*, was infact open to any *varṇa*. It required force and administrative control to establish a dynasty. Claims to territory were established through strength of arms. Legitimation through brahmanical ritual was evidently not required since some dynasties are described as not conforming to Vedic rites. This may well have been due to the influence of Buddhism and Jainism at this time. The Brahmanical refusal to bestow *kṣatriya* status on such families may have been in part due to their being patrons of non-brahmanical religious sects. Buddhist and Jaina literature on the other hand insists on the *kṣatriya* status of some of these dynasties. Thus the Mauryas are not only listed as *kṣatriyas* but are linked to the clan of the Buddha, the Śākyas, which would automatically have related them to the prestigious Sūryavaṁśa as well.[23] The absence of proper status in the brahmanical sources did not detract from the importance of these families. If anything it points to the relative independence of the state as a political form from the clutches of traditional validation during this period. The need for legitimation through lineage status was apparently not required at this time.

The encroachment of foreign rulers in the post-Mauryan period led to some indigenous families having to recede into the background. Claims to power and to actual status were conceded to the Indo-Greeks, Śakas, Parthians and Kuṣāṇas, but claim to *varṇa* status was denied them and they continued to be called *vrātya-kṣatriyas* (degenerate), having no indigenous land-base in the sub-continent nor being able to claim kinship links with earlier

[23] *Mahāvaṁsaṭīkā*, p. 180ff.

established lineages.[24] This was despite the fact that some among them did claim *kṣatriya* status in their own inscriptions.[25] The lack of genealogical connections was a form of exclusion, effective in a society where ritual status still drew heavily on the values of a lineage-based social organization and where genealogical links had played a crucial role.

Although dynastic status was not confined to any particular *varṇa*, those who succeeded to kingship from the mid-first millennium AD onwards often observed the formality of claiming *kṣatriya* status, or at least of participating in a common *kṣatriya* past as embodied in the *itihāsa-purāṇa* tradition. The question may well be asked as to why such a practice becomes more necessary during this period, and the answer covers a range of possibilities. The making of land grants to *brāhmaṇa*s and the consequent spread of Sanskritic culture provides an obvious reason. But it would be as well not to overlook the reality on the ground, as it were, and examine the actual process of state formation at a time when it related to secondary (if not tertiary) states, or new states emerging from association with established states. Land grants of a substantial size to non-religious grantees would have provided the base for the grantee establishing a network of political control over the area through his lineage connections.[26] The partial *brāhmaṇa* ancestry of some ruling families as given in their genealogies would suggest that even *brāhmaṇa* grantees were not averse to participating in this process. Where unoccupied land was still available and the migration of peasants feared, political control would be less effective if dependent on force and more effective if drawing its strength from legitimacy. The expression of power in the sense of controlling resources and seeking compliance through persuasion, influence and support[27] would be better achieved by

[24] *Viṣṇu Purāṇa*, IV. 21–4: *Manu*, X. 43–5.

[25] *Epigraphia Indica*, VIII, pp. 59, 86; E.J. Rapson, ed., *The Cambridge History of India*, vol. I, *Ancient India* (Cambridge, 1935), p. 577.

[26] For a later period, cf. R.G. Fox, *Kin, Clan, Raja and Rule* (Berkeley, 1971).

[27] Miller, *op cit*.

legitimacy than by force. The legitimation of lineage origins therefore became a necessity.

The granting of land, apart from its other functions, served also to incorporate areas under lineage systems into the society dominated by the state. Lineage-based agrarian activity was assimilated into the new economy and erstwhile clansmen or else their chiefs were converted into tax-paying peasants. Lineage traditions continued up to a point and could be adjusted to the *varṇa* framework, which acted as a bridge between the earlier society and its later form.

It would be worth investigating whether the process of state formation in the late first millennium AD provided a different emphasis from that of the earlier period. The overlap between lineage and state continued, but the political form was perhaps not so reliant on institutions of the state and included a more substantial dependence on lineage. Would it then be correct to argue that the post-Gupta state did not attempt to uproot the *kṣatriya*s (to use the phrase of the *Purāṇa*s) and reduce the importance of lineage societies, but rather that it attempted to encourage the emergence of a new role for lineages through which it sought to extend its control?

With the kaleidoscopic formation of states in the post-Gupta period, new ruling families relied heavily on genealogical links, fabricated genealogies providing them with claims to being *kṣatriya*s: claims which were carefully stated in the then legal charters, i.e. the inscriptions recording the grants of land by these families to *brāhmaṇa*s and other grantees. Such claims became even more crucial in a situation of competition for status by horizontal marriage alliances among the 'new' *kṣatriyas*. Matrimonial links sealed the claims to status. Thus the possible tribal Gond and Bhil associations of the Candella and Guhilot ruling families did not eventually stand in the way of their claims to *kṣatriya* status, which were backed not merely by land-ownership but also by claims to genealogical links with the Candravaṁśa and the Sūryavaṁśa: the claim being recognized with marriage into other established *kṣatriya* families.[28] The sixteenth century marriage of a Gond *rājā* into the Candella family is an interesting example of how the system worked. The acceptance by other competing families of the origin myth and of the genealogy of the family successfully installed in power was largely because political power was relatively open and individual families were concerned with succeeding to power, not with altering the framework within which status was conferred. The narrowing down of legitimation to one family meant that others could aspire to the same power in changed circumstances.

The earlier states from the Mauryan to the Kuṣāṇa tended to develop administrative structures in which local regions were left relatively untampered as long as they provided the required revenue.[29] When revenue requirements became oppressive, peasants could threaten to migrate from the state and establish new clearings in the forest and on waste land. Migration was the alternative to peasant revolt and kings are cautioned against oppressive taxes lest peasants migrate. From the Gupta period onwards there was a gradual and increasing tendency to intensify the revenue demands and tie down the peasantry.[30] The economic restructuring of the local region was regarded as part of the state's legitimate right to revenue. The ability of the peasant to migrate was hampered, and even though there is little apparent evidence of peasant

[28] J.N. Asopa, *Origin of the Rajputs* (Delhi, 1976) pp. 102ff., 208ff; J. Tod, *Annals and Antiquities of Rajasthan*, vol. I, (London, 1960), p. 173ff. Asopa argues that 'Guhila' means a forest and that it is to be located in the area between Guhila-bala and the Mahi river. See also B.D. Chattopadhyaya, 'Origin of the Rajput: The Political, Economic and Social Processes in Early Medieval Rajasthan,' *The Indian Historical Review*, July, 1976, vol. III, no. 1, pp. 59–82. Claims to *kṣatriya* status were also made by ruling families and politically powerful groups in south India. Thus the Colas claimed to be Sūryavaṁśi, the Pāṇḍyas Candravaṁśi, and the *vel* chieftains sought Yādava descent.

[29] Romila Thapar, 'The State as Empire,' in H. Claessen and P. Skalnik, *The Study of the State* (The Hague, 1981), p. 409ff.

[30] R.S. Sharma, *Indian Feudalism* (Delhi, 1980).

revolts the earlier flexible relationship between peasants and the state would have changed—with the intermediate grantees playing the difficult role of keeping the peasants tied since it was not only the revenue demands of the state but also their own revenue rights which were at stake. This points towards an urgent need on the part of grantees and landowners and clan chiefs, the potential ruling families, to not only insist on their high status but to be able to prove it whenever necessary. An emphasis on status, with the insistence on service by the lower orders inherent in the formulation of *varṇa,* became in some areas an adjunct to coercion by those who had succeeded in rising to higher levels of political power. The *itihāsa-purāṇa* tradition became one of the means of legitimizing status and the *vaṁśānucarita* sections had to be carefully preserved.

Lists of succession (*vaṁśa*)—whether of teachers as in the Vedic texts, or of Elders in the *saṅgha,* or of descent groups as in the case of the Sūryavaṁśa and the Candravaṁśa, or of dynasties—encapsulate perceptions of the past. Genealogy as a record of succession lay at the core of the epic tradition and linked epic to embedded history as well as to the *itihāsa-purāṇa* and later historical forms. Genealogy is used by new groups in the ascendant to legitimize their power and claim connections with those who were earlier in power. Links were therefore sought in the post-Gupta period by new ruling families with the Sūryavaṁśa and the Candravaṁśa. The epics embodying the stories of these lineages were thus assured continuity, quite apart from the infusion of a religious dimension through the theory of epic heroes being *avatāras* of Viṣṇu. The less obvious information from genealogical data indicates kinship patterns, marriage forms, geographical settlements and migration.[31]

The pattern or structure of a genealogy is often indicative of social integration where competing groups are shown through a

[31] Romila Thapar, 'Genealogy as a source of Social History,' *AISH,* p. 326ff.

listing of descent. Among these the successful ones claim a larger share of the genealogical structure, parallel to their claim to inheritance and power. In the Aila genealogy, for example, the Pūrus and the Yādavas claim the major part of the genealogy and the lines of Turvaśa, Anu and Druhyu peter out fairly soon. The ideological function of the genealogy is to legitimate those who have succeeded to power or to subvert the claims of those who for various reasons are unacceptable. That genealogy was of considerable consequence is indicated not only by the *Purāṇas* but also by other sources.[32]

The *vaṁśānucarita* section has three distinct constituent parts.[33] The first is the mythical section of the rule of the seven Manus, which is wiped away by the action of the Flood. This is followed by the detailed listing of the generations in each of the two major lineages. The Ikṣvāku is the senior and more cohesive. Descent is recorded only from eldest son to eldest son with a tight control over a well demarcated territory, indicative of a stronger tendency towards monarchy and primogeniture. The Aila lineage is more akin to the pattern of a segmentary system with a wide geographical distribution involving northern, western and central India. Possibly it reflects a more assimiliative system in which the segments are less the result of branching off or migrating away from the main lineage and more a record of alliances with existing clans. The spread of the Haihaya group in central India would suggest this. It might also be the result of an element of the 'tidying up' of lineages by the authors of the *Purāṇas*. Two sub-lineages

[32] Pliny in *Natural History*, VI. 21.4–5, quotes Megathenes as stating that the Indians count 154 kings upto the time of Alexander. Genealogical data is also contained in the seals and in most land-grant inscriptions from the Gupta period onwards, e.g. Sonpat Copper Seal of Harshavardhana, in J.F. Fleet, ed., *C.I.I.*, vol. III, Inscriptions of the Early Gupta Kings (Varanasi, 1970), p. 231: Ralanpur Stone Inscription of Jajalladeva I, V.V. Mirashi, ed., *C.I.I.* vol. IV, Inscriptions of the Kalacuri-Cedi Era (Ootacamund, 1955), p. 409; the Lakhamandala inscription, *Epigraphia Indica.*, I, 1892, p. 10ff.

[33] Romila Thapar, *op. cit.*

among the Candravaṁśa are given pre-eminence, those of the Purus controlling the western Ganga valley and the more diffused Yādavas migrating to western and central India. The segments are all treated as *kṣatriyas*, even though at times this status conflicts with the status assigned to some of them in other sources.[34] Thus the genealogy was a method of legitimizing all those who had held power. However, they had to have performed the brahmanical sacrificial ritual in order to be included in the *itihāsa-purāṇa*, for those who were lax in this matter were either dropped altogether, such as the Licchavis, or like the Śākyas were merely mentioned *en passant*.[35]

The *Mahābhārata* war acts as another time-marker and brings to the battlefield virtually all the lineages of the Candravaṁśa, and a few others as well, and marks the death of the lineages. That it was a terminal event is reflected in the switch to the future tense after the war, suggesting a prophetic form, and is followed by details on dynastic succession in the kingdom of Magadha, an area which emerged in fact as the most powerful kingdom of the Ganga valley. Descent lists now become king lists mentioning historically attested dynasties—Nandas, Mauryas, Śuṅgas, Kāṇvas, Āndhras, and so on, as well as the regnal years of kings. The genealogical record thus indicates a change to monarchies during this period, a change which was of considerable historical importance. Those dynasties which did not claim links with earlier descent groups such as the Indo-Greeks, Śakas, Kuṣāṇas and Kṣatrapas receive short shrift at the hands of the genealogists. The Yavanas as a

[34] Pargiter, *The Ancient Indian Historical Tradition*, p. 109ff; *Manu*, X. 8, X. 23 refers to the Āndhras and Sātvats as *śūdras*. the Āndhras are identified with the Andhaka of the Andhaka-Vṛṣṇi group and the Vṛṣṇis married the Sātvats. Pāṇini, II.2.95 and VI.2, 34, refers to the Andhaka and the Vṛṣṇis as being *kṣatriya gotras*. The events of the *Mahābhārata* suggest that the Vṛṣṇis were of a lower status, judging by the objection of some of the *kṣatriyas* present to giving Kṛṣṇa the status of the honoured guest. Sabhāparvan, pp. 33.26ff; 34.1ff.

[35] *Viṣṇu Purāṇa*, IV. 22.

generalized term are described as the descendants of the Turvaśa, who, as a segment of the Candravaṁśa, become relatively insignificant fairly early in the genealogical listing.[36] The entry of *śūdras* as kings, be they Indian or foreign, was of course seen as the inevitable consequence of social imbalances foretold for the Kaliyuga. The *vaṁśānucarita* section therefore becomes a preservation of the record of social and political relations as perceived at a crucial historical moment, and incorporates much of what was believed to be historically accurate. This is put together in a distinctive structure which not only gives form to the past but also becomes a charter of sanction for existing social institutions as well as a potential charter for future claims to legitimacy and status.

Purāṇic literature, in the sections other than the *vaṁśānucarita*, reflects facets of change which impinged upon the historical tradition. It comprises essentially assimilative texts where the Sanskritic tradition and the local tradition are sought to be intermeshed. This was inevitable in a situation where those of a Sanskritic cultural milieu received grants of land and settled in areas where the exposure to Sanskritic culture had been relatively sparse, if at all. Some degree of mutual interchange was required, even if for no other purpose than that of establishing dominance. The Purāṇic texts with their various sub-categories are facets of this development. The culture of the dominant and of the subordinate remained distinct, but proximity and some degree of absorption smoothened the edges of an otherwise angular relationship in many areas. The rhetoric of the Great Tradition and the systematizing of substratum cultures, both of which are reflected in the *Purāṇas*, made the literature acceptable to the audience and useful in mobilizing social and political action.[37]

[36] *Mahābhārata*, Ādiparvan, 80.1ff.

[37] Examples of such adjustments extend even to the literal Sanskritization of non-Sanskrit names, and to the story which relates the event, e.g. the Śailodbhava dynasty in its origin myth relates the story of how a *brāhmaṇa* was requested to create a man out of chips of rock, and thus the ancestor of the Śailodbhavas was created, the story evidently explaining the Sanskriti-

V

A more clearly recognizable historical tradition is evident in the post-Gupta period, linked in part to the historical changes of the early and mid first millennium AD. The states of this period were territorially not as large as the Mauryan and the Kuṣāṇa, for example. There was a multiplicity of state formation, particularly in areas hitherto regarded as peripheral or marginal and often characterized by a lineage society. Many of these new states emerged as a consequence of the changes in agrarian relations in the earlier established states, when the system of making grants of land became current. These changes required new processes of authority, law and revenue collection in areas which earlier were either outside the state system or on the edge of it. The change was not limited to the political arena but also introduced new forms of a wider social mobility. There was a growth of sectarian religious groups, some of which professed a doctrinal cult (*bhakti*, narrowing in on an individual's devotion to a particular deity); others which attempted to systematize more earthly cults of fertility and magic; and still others which remained loyal lay supporters of the Buddhist and Jaina *saṅgha*. It was also perhaps in part a reaction to this last group which motivated the increasing interest in an *itihāsa-purāṇa*. Both the Buddhists and the Jainas had shown a sense of centring their sects in avowedly historical events which imparted a certain historicity and added to the intellectual strength of their institutions. The historicity of the Buddha and Mahāvīra was emphasized, major events in the history of the respective *saṅghas* were linked to political events and personalities, chronology was often calculated on the basis of the date of the death of the Buddha and of Mahāvīra. This point was not missed by other groups and in the latter half of the first millennium AD when Vaiṣṇava and Śaiva sects competed for royal patronage, they not only established monastic institutions but also introduced

---

zation of a non-Sanskrit name. R.G. Basak, *History of North-Eastern India* (Calcutta, 1967), p. 211ff.

a historical dimension into the discussion on the evolution of the sect. It can be argued that Buddhist and Jaina sects arose as a part of a counter-culture and therefore as groups in dissent had a clearer sense of their historical purpose.[38] This is a partial explanation of a far more complex question: why Buddhism has a more recognizable sense of externalized history—a question which cannot be discussed in this brief essay. Be it said in passing that apart from considerations of eschatology and epistemology, all of which have their own significance, it is as well to consider also that Buddhism and Jainism were quite early on institutionally based and moved fairly soon to becoming property holders on a considerable scale. As such the records of their evolution did not merely narrate the life of the Buddha and the history of the *saṅgha* (with its various divergent sects, each claiming status and authenticity), but also described the building of monasteries, the amassing of property and the rights to controlling these—rights which became complex and competitive with the fissioning off of sects from the main stems. The sense of the historicity of the sect becomes evident even in Śaiva and Vaiṣṇava sects when they begin to locate themselves in *āśrama*s and *maṭha*s and become immensely wealthy property holders, and when intensified competition for patronage has to be supported by claims to legitimacy—which require a substantial input of historically phrased argument.

Implicit in the genealogical form is the notion of time and chronology. The arrangement of events in a chronological order is less precise for earlier times and only when sequential causation becomes important does chronological precision enter the focus of history. Genealogical generations indicate time periods, as also do regnal years. The latter move from fanciful figures to more credible ones as the dynastic lists approach historically attested time. Thus the chronology given for the Śiśunāga, Nandas, Mauryas and other dynasties is feasible. The arrangement of chronological

[38] Romila Thapar, 'Renunciation: the making of a Counter-culture?,' in *AISH*, p. 63ff.

order becomes more important as historical memory becomes less embedded. The cosmological time of the *mahāyuga* and the start of the Kaliyuga gives way to historical time.[39] The accuracy of historical time increases by the reference to dateable eras—the Kṛta (c. 58 BC), Śaka (AD 78), Gupta (AD 319–20), Cedi (c. AD 249), Harṣa (AD 606), and so on: and by the very precise dates recorded in era, regnal year, season, month, lunar fortnight and day in the inscriptions. The era, apart from commemorating an event, can also be seen as a capturing of time, symbolic of an articulation of power in a context where time is viewed as part of an eventual point of destruction. The word for time is *kāla* from the root *kal* 'to calculate', which suggests a meaning indicative of measurement.

[39] Cosmological time moves in the Mahāyuga of 4,320,000 years and the complete cycle is then divided into four *yugas*: the Kṛta of 1,728,000 years; the Tretā of 1,296,000 years, the Dvāpara of 864,000 years and the Kaliyuga of 432,000 years, the size of the *yugas* declining in arithmetical progression. The Kaliyuga is crucial and there is a regular reduction by substracting the length of the Kaliyuga from each preceding *yuga*, an orderliness which is basic to the concept. The numbers used are quasi-mathematical, a mixture of magic and astronomy. Numbers such as 3,7,12 and 72 are considered magical and constitute the fractions in the figures. Thus 432,000 = 60 × 7200, and this further introduces the sexagesimal unit of 60, frequently used in ancient West Asia as well as in south Indian astrology. The Babylonian tradition also uses 72,1,200 and 432,000 for its chronology (J. Campbell, *The Masks of the Gods*, vol. II, New York, 1959, p. 128ff.) and the *Jyotiṣa-vedāṅga* shows a familiarity with Babylonian astronomy and mathematics. (D. Pingree, 'The Mesopotamian Origin of Early Indian Mathematical Astronomy,' *Journal for the History of Astronomy*, 1973, IV, pp. 1–12.) The figure of 72 years is taken to calculate the processional lag moving over one degree and 432,000 is the basis of calculating the epicycle. Was cosmological time the earlier and more popular astronomical knowledge which was deliberately preserved in this manner, as distinct from the mathematics and the solar-based astronomy of the period reflected in the more formal writings of scientists of later times? As a contrast to these majuscule dimensions there are also the miniscule fractional parts of time listed in Jaina texts of the late first and the early second millennia AD. Interestingly, the description of the *yugas* and *kalpas* is spatial, e.g. *Saṁyutta Nikāya*, XV.1.5–8.

Perhaps because of the cyclical theory it was also associated with destruction in the sense of the end of time.

The inevitability of time is strengthened by the use of prophecies in genealogies, for time is the ultimate destroyer, *mahākāla*. Cosmological time is distinct from historical time not only by its mathematical pattern and the spatial form in its description, but also by its total orderliness, an orderliness which emphasizes its unreality. This in part might also explain the marginality of chiliastic and millenarian movements in such a pattern as compared to the Judaeo-Christian tradition in which they play a distinctive role. The coming of Viṣṇu as Kalkin arises out of an anxiety relating to the present—the wish to terminate the inequities of the Kaliyuga through Viṣṇu yet again being incarnated as a saviour figure. But such a termination is predetermined by the length of the cycle and will in any case lead to the ultimate ending of the cycle. It is more to the weakness of the eschatology that the marginality of millenarian movements can be attributed. The interplay of cosmological and historical time in the brahmanical tradition can perhaps be explained partially by the *yajña* and *varṇa* requirements which were part of the process of legitimizing families and cults. Cyclical time it has been argued, goes counter to an eschatology which would point to a historical change towards a directed goal.[40] Yet within the *mahāyuga* there is an emphasis on change. It is change rather than repetition which is inherent in the concept, and within this the explanation of change is also implicit.[41]

The notion of change is even more central to the Buddhist concept of time.[42] Because of the claim to the historicity of the Buddha there is a single, central point to which all events relate chronologically, namely the Mahāparinirvāṇa, the death of the

[40] M. Eliade, *Cosmos and History* (New York, 1959).

[41] Kalhaṇa, *Rājataraṅginī*, V. 21.

[42] A.L. Basham, *The Wonder That Was India* (London, 1964), pp. 272–3; *Dīgha Nikāya*, III, p. 75ff.

Buddha. Buddhist eschatology envisages the extinction of consciousness in *nirvāṇa*, which, although seemingly negative, is the aim of human endeavour since it is a release from rebirth. Change within cosmological time is emphasized further by the cyclic movement of time taking the form of a spiral, in that the cycle never returns to its point of origin: and a spiral if fully stretched can become a wave, if not a linear form. The rise and fall within the cycle purports constant change and even the fall carries within it the eventual upward swing of the cycle, and this is conducive to the idea of a coming millennium, an idea envisaged in the Buddha Maitreya. This in turn is paralleled by decay carrying within it the seeds of regeneration.

The precision of historical time as recorded in inscriptions probably derived from the more widespread use of the solar calendar from the first millennium AD. But it also had to do with the legitimacy of the individual in authority, for the inscription was frequently a legal charter. Not only was the authority of the king time bound in such charters, but so also was his claim to the property which he was donating in as much as later kings could revoke these grants in spite of the insistence in the inscriptions that they were given in perpetuity. An additional factor was the influence of the idea that all actions are conditioned by the auspiciousness of the moment when they are carried out, and in the case of donations and grants this would be particularly apposite.[43] The multiple use of historical time focused on the individual and gave

[43] Some of the dates for inscriptions were provided by astrologers, and these include astronomical details. However they are not always correct. D.C. Sircar, *Studies in Society and Administration of Ancient and Medieval India*, vol. I (Calcutta, 1967), pp. 171–2. It is worth noting that apart from the legal charters, another sphere of life in which time was very precisely recorded was the horoscope. As a corollary to this it is interesting that an almost exact counterpart to the careful record of time in inscriptions is to be found in discussions on the precise time for conducting a *yajña*, where the time is again indicated in terms of the year, season, month, lunar fortnight, constellation, date and time of day.

sharper definition to the individual as a figure of authority: an idea by no means unfamiliar by now in the historical consciousness of the period. A fuller exposition of this idea had come from Buddhist sources. Aśoka Maurya, as a patron of Buddhism, acquired an accretion of legends, some of which were gathered into the *Aśokāvadāna.* The attempt was to give historicity to the Buddhist *saṅgha* by linking it to a powerful political personality, a notion which was not alien to the emergence of much of the other non-Buddhist *carita* literature. The need to write the biography of the Buddha, *buddha-carita,* had been felt since the time of the early monastic movement and the first missions. It changed from being a part of the canonical texts to a separate genre of literature.[44] Gradually the idea of biography was extended to the 'hero' in a wider context. A historical background is also helpful to organized missionary activity in new areas where antecedents have to be explained; this was useful to the entry of Buddhism into Asia, as indeed it was useful to brahmanical centres in the more remote parts of the Indian subcontinent. The *carita* tradition doubtless also drew on the *praśasti*s incorporated in a number of early inscriptions, such as that of Khāravela at Hāthigumphā and Rudradāman at Junagadh; a style which became more elaborate in time as evidenced by the Udaipur *rāj-praśasti.*[45]

VI

Those in authority seek validation from the past, and this validation was the starting point of a new category of texts, the *vaṁśāvalī*s and the *caritas* of the post-Gupta period. The *vaṁśāvalī*s were the histories of the ruling families in specific geographical regions, the latter often coinciding with the new kingdoms and states in

[44] This change is reflected in the difference between the *Suttas* and the *Vinaya,* where the life of the Buddha is part of canonical scripture, and Aśvaghoṣa's *Buddhacarita,* which is a biography *per se.*

[45] D.C. Sircar, *Select Inscriptions,* second edition (Calcutta, 1965), pp. 213–19, 175–80; *Epigraphia Indica,* vol. XXIX, 1951–2, parts 1–5, pp. 1–90.

areas previously either unoccupied or settled by groups of tribes. As a genre they lay between the lineage lists of the *Purāṇas* and the historical biographies of individual rulers. The *carita* or historical biography was a complement to the *vaṁśāvalī* and focused on the king, who was seen as the centre of authority in a more radial state system. Bāṇabhaṭṭa's *Harṣacarita* led off the biographical form and was followed by a large number of others.[46] Most of the better known ones were written between the eighth and twelfth centuries AD, but as a form *carita* literature continued into later times, in each case commemorating the rise of new kings. The *carita* was unashamedly the eulogy of the patron, but the persons chosen were those who had a special status and function in the ruling family and were contributors of a more than ordinary kind, not only to their own families but also to the consolidation of kingdoms and kingship. The rhetoric of eulogy when deconstructed would doubtless reveal multiple relationships within a courtly edifice of norms and actions, and despite the ambiguity in presenting hard historical data much of the subtlety of historical nuance can be gathered from these biographies. *Carita* literature also focuses on other aspects of the individual in society. Cyclic time carries a certain inevitability but the individual can opt out of it, and on a lesser level this is demonstrated in biographies where the *karma* of the individual may play a larger role than the inevitability of the time cycle: and the individual *karma* and its historic role was central to the doctrine of Buddhism as well as the ideology of the *bhakti* tradition.

On occasion the subjects of the biographies were younger brothers who had come to rule (as for example, Harṣavardhana and Vikramāditya VI), and their legitimacy over other claimants

[46] Such as Vākapati's *Gauḍavāho* on Yaśovarman of Kannauj; Bilhaṇa's *Vikramāṅkadevacarita* on Vikramāditya VI, the Cālukya king; Sandhyākaranandin's *Rāmacarita* on Rāmapāla; Jayānaka's *Pṛthvīrājavijaya;* Nayacandra Sūri's *Hammīra-mahākāvya;* Someśvaradeva's *Kīrtikaumudi*, a biography of Vastupāla, who, although not a king, was a person of great political importance; and Hemacandra's *Kumārapālacarita*.

had to be established. The royal patron was linked with the major lineages of the *itihāsa-purāṇa* or with a new lineage which had acquired status since then, such as the Agni-kula among Rajputs or the Nāgavaṁśa among certain central Indian dynasties. The *carita* was essentially a literary form in origin and thus a far cry from the bardic fragments of epic times. The most sophisticated courtly tradition found expression in this literature and the courtly values of chivalry, heroism and loyalty were at a premium.[47] Two obvious characteristics of this form were the depiction of the king as the focus of the court and a clear awareness of a well-defined geographical area which constituted the kingdom and was identified with the dynasty. Obeisance is made to the lineage but it plays a secondary role in relation to the king who is now most clearly the figure of formal political authority in both state and society.

Political decentralization inherent in the granting of land on a large scale encouraged a competition among families aspiring to dynastic status. Dynasties survived through an assertion of power, legitimacy and recourse to marriage alliances with ambitious feudatories. Attempts to restructure the economic potential within certain areas of the state and to balance the intricate relationship between royal power, brahmanical authority and the dominant religious cults of the region become a further support to power. The emphasis on territory had again to do with the jostling of new states and with the legitimizing of the economic and administrative changes which the system of land grants introduced into the kingdoms.

The *vaṁśāvalī* was the chronicle of a dynasty, and inevitably also the chronicle of the territory controlled by the dynasty. The *vaṁśāvalī* therefore used as source material the various local *Purāṇa*s as well as the oral tradition.[48] It became the characteristic

[47] V.S. Pathak, *Ancient Historians of India* (Bombay, 1966), p. 21ff.

[48] The sources drawn upon by the authors of the *vaṁśāvalī*s included the *sthala-purāṇas, upa-purāṇas, tīrtha-purāṇas,* caste *purāṇas* and *mahātmyas,* all of

literature of the new states in various parts of the subcontinent in the early second millennium AD. This is indicative of some elements of similarity in historical change, which in turn reflects a degree of cultural uniformity. These elements do not indicate the influence of one dominant regional culture over the others, but rather the expression of a similar historical situation, which, formulated in a certain kind of literature, was common to many regions.

The structure of the *vaṁśāvalī* was almost identical in all these regions. The earliest section narrated the origin myths pertaining to the region and the dynasty. In this there was a recording of local lore as well as a borrowing from the *itihāsa-purāṇa* tradition. Attempts were made to link local history with themes from the

---

which were texts recording the past and the evolution of places, sects and deities, locations of pilgrimage, dominant castes and local history. Such texts were part of the larger Purāṇic tradition and, although conforming to the major *Purāṇas* in sprit if not in form, included a large amount of local and regional data. The oral sources consisted of bardic fragments and ballads on local heroes and events of significance, not to mention the genealogies and marriage alliances of land-owning families, for the bardic tradition was still alive, as it remains to this day. It has been argued that Kalhana's *Rājataraṅginī*, a fine example of a *vaṁśāvalī*, was a unique document in that it was the only genuine piece of historical writing from India (A.L. Basham, 'The Kashmir Chronicle,' in C.H. Philips, *Historians of India, Pakistan and Ceylon* (Oxford, 1961), p. 57ff). Yet the *vaṁśāvalī* form occurs in various parts of the country—from the neighbouring Chamba *vaṁśāvalī* (Ph. Vogel, *The Antiquities of Chamba State*, Calcutta, 1911, *A.S.I.*, vol. 36) to the most distant *Mūṣakavaṁśa* or chronicle of the Ay dynasty in Kerala. Gopinath Rao, 'Extracts from the Mūṣakavaṁśam . . . ,' *Travancore Archaeological Series*, 1916, II.1, no. 10, pp. 87–113; See also M.G.S. Narayanan, 'History from Muśakavaṁśa-kāvya of Atula,' *P.A.I.O.C.* (Jadhavpur, 1969). Curiously in both cases the founder is born in a cave (*guhā*) and is associated with a *mūṣakavaṁśa* (literally: 'mouse lineage'). A better known cave association is of course that of the Guhilots of Mewar (J. Tod, I, p. 173ff.). For further lists of *vaṁśāvalīs* see A.K. Warder, *Introduction to Indian Historiography* (Bombay, 1972), and J.P. de Souza and C.M. Kulkarni, eds., *Historiography in Indian Languages* (Delhi, 1972).

Purāṇas incorporating the myths and the genealogies of the Great Tradition with local persons and places. The *Purāṇas* were the prototypes and local personalities were the protagonists. This required the continued availability of the *Purāṇas* as sources from which the *vaṁśāvalīs* could draw. The major part of the text, however, dealt with more contemporary events, and a history of the ruling dynasty was narrated giving its genealogy and referring to important events associated with the dynasty. The veracity of this information can often be ascertained by comparing it with the evidence of inscriptions, since many of the grants of land were recorded on copper plates or on temple walls. Whereas the need for a *vaṁśāvalī* was motivated by the acquisition of power, the historically authenticated section would appear to coincide with the constitution of power, often articulated in the taking of royal titles such as *mahārājādhirāja*. Concomitant with this was the acceptance of responsibilities of power by the family. The authors of the *vaṁśāvalīs* were court poets and officials and were therefore familiar with political and administrative concerns. The *vaṁśāvalīs* would also be important to those who received grants of land in vouching for the legitimacy of the granting authority.

The *vaṁśāvalī* differs from the earlier tradition in that it legitimates a particular family and not an entire lineage, and to that extent the legitimation of lineage is indirect. The family was not seen merely as a household of agnatic and affinal kinsfolk but was the hub of power. It drew its strength both from claims to high descent as well as to property. Marriage alliances were controlled because dowry and inheritance were a part of the property structure. Such forms of the legitimation of families in power and of regions was of more immediate necessity to newly risen families in small states. The *vaṁśāvalī* therefore was by its very nature not a record of expansionist states. The major dynasties of the past, such as the Nandas and Mauryas, were not the models and only the very early lineages were considered possible sources of status. The appeal was not to the political system of the state but to sources of power which could back up the economic reality of aristocratic families with visions of dynastic ambition. It is significant that the *caritas* and the *vaṁśāvalīs* take up the narrative, as it were, from where the major *Purāṇas* leave off. The Purāṇic accounts of the ruling dynasties come to a close soon after the Guptas. The dynasties listed prior to these are mainly of the core regions of the Ganga valley and western and northern India. That the account was not continued in these *Purāṇas* was probably because there was a bigger distribution of centres of power in the post-Gupta period, and in each of such areas local *Purāṇas* and chronicles of various kinds began to be maintained. These texts often incorporate both the Purāṇic tradition and the local tradition, as is exemplified in those cases where legitimation is sought by reference to local myths of descent—as in the case of the Agni-kula Rajputs and the Nagavaṁśis of central India.

As a form the *vaṁśāvalī* was not restricted to dynastic chronicles and was adapted to the history of other institutions as well. Some of these were monastic institutions where not only was the succession of elders chronicled but also their relations with political authority. This dynastic and political information pertained either to royal patrons of the institution or recorded relations between the institution and political authority, generally in the context of the institution establishing its own legitimacy. An early expression of this relationship is evident from the Buddhist tradition where monastic chronicles were a regular part of the historical tradition.[49]

[49] The *Mahāvaṁsa*, as the chronicle of the Mahāvihāra monastery in Sri Lanka composed in the mid first millennium AD, is primarily concerned with establishing its legitimacy both as the fount of the pristine teaching of the Buddha as well as in its interaction with political authority. Thus the Theravāda sect, which was established in the Mahāvihāra monastery, is said to have originated from the schism at the Council of Pāṭaliputra, called at the initiative of Aśoka Maurya, and was established in Sri Lanka largely through the patronage of Devānampiya Tissa. Buddhist chronicles do tend to show a greater degree of historical determinism. Sri Lanka is predestined for the establishment of Buddhism. Events move towards proclaiming the

In attempting to establish the legitimacy of the dynasties or institutions whose history they are recording, chronicles stress the uniqueness of historical events relating to the origin and history of the subject of the chronicle, with indications of its growth and change. Actions are directed towards a goal, often resulting in the success of the subject. Chronicles are therefore compiled when a dynasty or institution has established itself and is recognized as powerful. The chronicle helps to establish its claims to authority over competing groups, especially those which are politically important. The borrowing from the *itihāsa-purāṇa* tradition suggests continuity and also stresses legitimacy, for the new group is seen as being related to those who were in power in the past and can also claim antiquity by maintaining these connections with earlier lineages. The chronicle is again the statement of the successful group and manages to deflect if not erase the presence of competitors. This becomes a particularly useful aspect of the chronicle in a society where not only dissent but even protest often takes the form of opting out or migration away, in preference to confrontation.[50]

If changing forms in the expression of historical consciousness symbolize historical change, and if changes in the political forms of society are reflected in the nature of historical expression, then the *itihāsa-purāṇa* tradition would point to three phases in the unfolding of early Indian history. Initially, in lineage societies, historical consciousness was embedded and recorded the perception of the ordering of lineages. With the evolution of states in northern India the second phase was inaugurated, focusing on dynastic power and the supremacy of the state as a system which in the political arena seems to have overridden caste ordering. The

primacy of the *saṅgha*. L.S. Perera, 'The Pali Chronicles of Ceylon,' in C.H. Philips. p. 29ff. This is further emphasized by the notion of causality and contract so central to Buddhist ethics, and by the historical role of the missionaries who propagate Buddhism in new areas.

[50] Romila Thapar, 'Dissent and Protest in the Early Indian Tradition,' *Studies in History*, 1979, vol. I, no. 2, pp. 177–95.

post-Gupta period saw a change in the structure of the state, accompanied by the need in many cases for the legitimation of status of ruling families.

Historical consciousness in early India took a form which grew out of embedded history. Part of the explanation for this may lie in the fact that the *varṇa* ordering of society, which never fully coincided with a clearly defined socio-economic stratification, carried a large element of the lineage-based structure and therefore also the embedded history of that structure. Where *kṣatriya* legitimation became necessary, the *itihāsa-purāṇa* tradition was strengthened with a drawing upon embedded history for origins. In such cases the past in relation to political power became a *kṣatriya* past. But at the same time it did not remain embedded. Although the origin myths of the dynasties recorded in the *vaṁśāvalī*s become something of a *mantra* or a formula, this should not hide the fact that despite the continuing idiom from the past there is a substantial historical core in the *vaṁśāvalī* which is distinguished from the embedded section, and which is therefore a break from the past and takes the form of historical consciousness expressed as externalized history.

Index

Time as a Metaphor of History

THE KRISHNA BHARADWAJ MEMORIAL LECTURE

Time as a Metaphor of History: Early India

For Kaushalya

The Heras Memorial Lectures honour the memory of the Reverend Henry Heras, S.J., who came to India from Spain in 1922 to be Professor of Indian Historical Research Institute, now renamed the Heras Institute of Indian History and Culture. He died in Bombay in 1955, after spending more than half his life digging up India's past in order to display to the world the history and culture of the land he made his own and whose citizen he became. Sponsored by the Heras Society and organized by the Heras Institute, the 1980 Heras Memorial Lectures, seventeenth in the series, were delivered by Professor Romila Thapar, a scholar of the history of ancient India.

PREFACE

This is an expanded version of the Heras Memorial Lectures on the subject of lineage and state systems in early India, delivered at St. Xavier's College, Bombay in February 1980. I am grateful to Father John Correia-Afonso and the authorities of the Heras Institute and the Heras Society for inviting me to deliver these lectures.

An attempt has been made in these lectures to define the nature of early Indian society during the mid-first millennium B.C. and relate it to the ancient Indian historical tradition in its earliest forms. I have also sought to indicate the particular character of social formations, their genesis and continuity as part of the later Indian social landscape. The data for this book was collected whilst I was on a Jawaharlal Nehru Fellowship during the years 1976 and 1977.

I would like to express my gratitude to my colleagues in the Centre for Historical Studies of the Jawaharlal Nehru University and in particular to Neeladri Bhattacharya, Bipan Chandra, B.D. Chattopadhyaya and Satish Saberwal for their helpful comments on an earlier draft. I would also like to thank Leslie Gunawardana and Sirima Kiribamune at the University of Peradeniya for discussions on the Ceylon Chronicles.

Romila Thapar

ABBREVIATIONS

AISH.	Romila Thapar, *Ancient Indian Social History : Some Interpretations*, New Delhi, 1978
Ait.	*Aitareya*
Ang.	*Anguttara*
Āpa.	*Āpastamba*
Brāh.	*Brāhmaṇa*
D.S.	*Dharma-sūtra*
D.Śā.	*Dharma-śāstra*
DED.	T. Burrow and M.B. Emeneau, *A Dravidian Etymological Dictionary*, Oxford, 1961
Dīp.	*Dīpavaṃsa*
G.S.	*Gṛhya-sūtra*
H.O.S.	Harvard Oriental Series
IHR	*Indian Historical Review*
IRRI	International Rice Research Institute, Philippines
JAOS	*Journal of the American Oriental Society*
JESHO	*Journal of the Social and Economic History of the Orient*
Maj.	*Majjhima Nikāya*
Manu	*Mānava Dharma-śāstra*
Nik.	*Nikāya*
PED	T.W. Rhys Davids and W. Stede, *Pali-English Dictionary*, P.T.S., London, 1966
PIHC	*Proceedings of the Indian History Congress*
P.T.S.	Pali Text Society
Ṛg. V.	*Ṛg Veda*
Śat.	*Śatapatha*
Sam.	*Saṁhitā*
SBE	Sacred Books of the East
Sm.	*Smṛti*
Tait.	*Taittirīya*
Up.	*Upaniṣad*
Vedic Index.	A.A. Macdonell and A.B. Keith, *Vedic Index of Names and Subjects*, Delhi, 1967 (reprint)

Contents

Time as a Metaphor of History: Early India*

*This is a much expanded version of the Krishna Bharadwaj Memorial Lecture delivered at Jawaharlal Nehru University in March 1993. I would like to express my appreciation for comments on an earlier draft by David Pingree and Neeladri Bhattacharya.

I

The Argument

James Mill, writing what has been described as the hegemonic history of India in the nineteenth century,[1] begins his discussion of what he calls Hindu civilization with the statement:

> Rude nations seem to derive a peculiar gratification from pretensions to remote antiquity. As a boastful and turgid vanity distinguishes remarkably the oriental nations, they have in most instances carried their claims extravagantly high.[2]

Mill was being critical not only of early Indian notions of time and history but also of those Indologists who were attempting a chronological reconstruction of Indian history from these concepts. Yet early Indian notions of time as described in the Manu *Dharmaśāstra*, the *Mahābhārata* and the *Purāṇas*, had attracted much attention even from earlier scholars such as Alberuni in the eleventh century. Alberuni was astute enough to observe the difference between popular views and those of astronomers and mathematicians, even though he otherwise caustically describes Indian astronomy as a mixture of pearls and dung.[3]

This difference was not observed by the early Orientalists, particularly the scholar administrators working in India and commenting on Indian notions of chronology, such as William Jones, Francis Wilford, John Bentley and Thomas Colebrooke. There were also some expectations that unravelling the

[1] R. Inden, 'Orientalist Construction of India', *Modern Asian Studies*, 1986, 20, 3, 401–6.

[2] James Mill, *The History of British India*, Vol. I, London 1858 (fifth ed.), Book II, Chapter 1, 107.

[3] E. C. Sachau, *Alberuni's India*, Delhi 1964 (rep.), I, 25.

traditional knowledge of India might lead to another renaissance, as with the earlier 'discovery' of Greek civilization.[4] Furthermore, such knowledge was also seen as an asset to colonial power in India. Their primary concern was with the texts which they perceived as central to this knowledge, the texts on social codes and on religion. Among these the Manu *Dharmaśāstra* was given priority by local pandits and it is this which they used as their exploratory text into concepts of time and history, gradually extending their interest to other writings.[5]

They searched for works easily recognizable as history backed by at least a skeletal chronology. Such an enterprise yielded little and the unity of Chronos and Clio which they ascribed to the Graeco-Roman world seemed non-existent in Indian civilization. After repeated and unsuccessful attempts at cross-referencing Biblical and Classical information with Indian texts, it was generally conceded that there was an absence of both a sense of history and of the notion of linear time.

At the turn of the eighteenth century and shortly thereafter, the theory which emerged was that the Indian sense of time was entirely cyclic, was tied into an infinity of recurring cycles, and did not therefore recognize historical change; and in the absence of a sense of history there was no differentiation between myth and history. This in part explains the statement by James Mill who endorsed this view of time in early India. Cyclic time was seen as diametrically

[4] R. Schwab, *La Renaissance Orientale*, Paris 1950.

[5] William Jones, 'The Third Discourse', *Asiatic Researches*, 1789, Vol. 1, 354 ff. F. Wilford, 'On the Chronology of the Hindus', in ibid., 345 ff. 1794, Vol. 2, 88–113; 1808, Vol. 5, 241 ff.; J. Bentley, 'Remarks on the Principal Eras and Dates of the Ancient Hindus', in ibid., 1808, Vol. 5, 315 ff.; 'On the Hindu system of Astronomy' in ibid., 1809, Vol. 8, 195 ff. S. Davis, 'On the Indian cycle of sixty years', in ibid., 1794, 3, 289 ff.; H. T. Colebrooke, 'Hindu Astronomy. Mr Colebrooke's Reply to the Attack of Mr Bentley', *Asiatic Journal*, 1826, Vol. 21, 360 ff.

opposite to linear time and linear time was associated with dialectical change. Cyclic time with immense cycles was said to be characteristic of primitive and archaic societies, a particularly galling indictment given the uncomplimentary definition of 'primitive' in those days. This view of Indian time was strengthened by the then current insistence among some Christian sects on a short chronology between the creation of the universe up to the present, many calculating it as a period of about as little as six thousand years.[6] The direction in linear time went from Adam and Eve, via the Jewish prophets to Christ and ultimately to Judgement Day, when the souls of the dead would be awarded everlasting life, either in heaven or hell. This eschatology, relating to the beginning and end of time, was not paralleled in early Indian sources. Linear time therefore came to be viewed as characteristic of the Judaeo-Christian and Islamic traditions. The secularization of linear time in Europe incorporated the notion of change in time and the belief that change was progress as defined in nineteenth-century terms. The challenge to Biblical chronology first posed by geology and biology and later by archaeology, and which was to introduce an infinitely longer time span, was yet to come.[7]

Two hundred years later the received wisdom on the subject remains largely unchanged, even if the reasons for the continuance of these views differ. In the intellectual fashion set by the historian of religion, Mircea Eliade, the fundamental assumptions about time in early India are: that there is an eternal cyclic repetition of time, so huge in concept that human activities become minuscule and insignificant in comparison. Cyclic time is continuous, without a beginning or an end. The cycle returns with unchanging regularity and in unchanging form. This amounts to a refusal of history, for no

[6] S. Toulmin and J. Goodfield, *The Discovery of Time*, Harmondsworth 1967, 92–3.

[7] Ibid., 172 ff.

event can be particular or unique and all events are liable to be repeated in the next cycle. Such a sense of time, based on what has been called an orgy of figures, can only support the philosophic notion of the world being illusory.[8] Time—*kāla*—derived from the root *kal*, to calculate, can also mean to destroy, and is seen in this second meaning as an agency of destruction, resulting in a negative eschatology.

Cyclic time in this argument pertains to the sacred because it is also mythical time, and linear time relates to the profane. The persistence in ascribing cyclic time alone to non-monotheistic religions and ignoring the evidence for other categories of time in the history of their societies was in part because the texts selected emphasized cyclic time in mythology. But the more subtle argument was that such societies live in another time, and this was a device to define the otherness of those societies.

The linear form by contrast was said to have a beginning and an end and emphasized the uniqueness of the particular which made events non-recurring. This was said to liberate history from repetition, deny the reversibility of time, and distinguish history from myth, where myth belonged to a distant time or even timelessness. Whereas change as 'progress' was linked to linear time, it is said to be absent in cyclic time. Thus a close connection was postulated between time concepts as pointers to the centrality of history in society.

This view has very recently been endorsed by some historians of religion, anthropologists and commentators on Indian culture.[9] This is evident in their discussions on perceptions of

[8] M. Eliade, 'Time and Eternity in Indian Thought,' in *Man and Time*, Bollingen Series, xxx, 3. Princeton University Press, New Jersey. *Cosmos and History: The Myth of the Eternal Return*, New York 1959.

[9] An argument derived from grammar states that in Sanskrit the verb from the root **bhu* can be translated both as 'to become' and 'to exist'. Time is conceived statically rather than dynamically. Phrases used for cause and effect read as a compound, effect-and-cause, e.g. *phalahetu*. H. Nakamura, 'Time in Indian and Japanese Thought', in J.T. Fraser (ed.), *The Voices of Time*, London 1986, 77–85.

the past in India, particularly those relating to politics and religion. The argument is often made that because there is no distinction between myth and history in early Indian thought, therefore resort to history even today is irrelevant and meaningless to the Indian mind. Since the dichotomy of cyclic and linear time, projected in the imagery of the phoenix and the ladder, has been basic to this argument, it is worth investigating the forms of time in early Indian texts.

Some attempts have been made to question what has become a stereotype on Indian views of time.[10] Diverse philosophical perceptions of time within the Indian tradition are beginning to be noticed. A study of time in various schools of philosophy points to an evident difference of views where some relate time to the reality of change, others emphasize the distinctiveness of the instant to the point of negating tense, or speak of the subjective construction of sequence, and yet others describe time as flowing like a river which never rests. Such views resemble to some degree the philosophical debates elsewhere between what have been called process philosophers who argue that there is a flow of time and man's advance through it is an important metaphysical fact, and the philosophers of the manifold for whom the flow of time is an illusion and the concept of past, present and future, unreal.

Equally crucial to the discussion is the detailed study of time in India from texts of astronomy and mathematics and what might be called the technology of time in the use of horology, calendars and dating systems. This reveals the construction of knowledge, especially in astronomy and mathematics, and their distance, in some cases, from popular beliefs and also underlines the dialogue between Indian and

[10] A. N. Balslev, *A Study of Time in Indian Philosophy*, Wiesbaden 1983. G. Cardona, 'A Path Still Taken: Some Early Indian Arguments Concerning Time', *Journal of the American Oriental Society*, 1991, 3, 3, 445–64. K. K. Mandal, *A Comparative Study of the Concepts of Time and Space in Indian Thought*, Banaras 1968. A. K. Coomaraswamy, *Time and Eternity*, Ascona 1947.

Greco-Babylonian views.[11] But notions of time are also cultural signals. The reading of these would involve the visualization of the form of time, the degree to which mythical time is distinct from historical time, the association of time with eschatologies, with utopias or with moral and social decline as reflected in golden ages or the decline of *dharma* and the simultaneous use of different time reckonings. It is on these latter aspects that I shall be speaking. They also touch on the question of whether the rhythm of social life can be seen as the basis of categories of time and whether cultures with differing conceptions of time can communicate.[12]

The link between time and history is evident if history is a narrative of human activities of the past, purported to have happened and narrated in the present. Such narrative has an underlying sense of time: it is sequential, moving from the earliest to the most recent. There is a consciousness of change with conjunctures or disjunctures underlying events. Because time is irreversible, the events of the past cannot be altered. However, the assessment of what constitutes an event and its interpretation as history as well as the altering of history through changing causal explanations, is open to discussion. Time concepts and historical change interact in as much as change can be projected as either repetitive, recurrent or periodic, pointing to a wide stretch of time concepts, ranging from what are viewed as the cyclical to the continuously progressive and directional, suggesting a linear form, with many in-between positions such as a wave or a spiral. In terms of eschatology there is an evident difference of form between cyclic and linear time. But not only does cyclic time have a genesis and a predicted termination (as does linear time), it can also encompass segments of time consisting of historical chronologies. Cyclic time does not

[11] D. Pingree, 'Astronomy and Astrology in India and Iran', *Isis*, 1963, 54, 2, 176, 229–46. *Jyotiḥśāstra* (History of Indian Literature Series), Wiesbaden 1981.

[12] J. Fabian, *Time and the Other*, New York 1983.

preclude other categories of time, some more apposite to historical chronology and taking on the functions of linear time. The sharp demarcation between cyclic and linear is made somewhat indistinct by these chronological forms which therefore introduce a range of mediatory positions. The dichotomy weakens if there is a recognition that the one does not negate the other and the two can co-exist. It is also feasible that in some cultures there are grey areas where the two may overlap, as, for example, in Purāṇic time concepts, as I hope to show. These features tended to be ignored in earlier discussions on time and history in India.

II

Time-reckoning

Both cyclic and linear time are at one level linked with ideas of cosmology — the theory of the universe as an ordered whole and of the possible laws which govern it. Cosmological time, therefore, relates to the universe, is almost infinite, ano where it is cyclic, consists in constructions of many cycles of time, setting out as it were, a calendar for the universe.

Initially those who make the calendar control the reckoning of time. Calendars are part of a larger system of time measurement and calendar-makers were proficient in astronomy. Concepts of time and the theories of astronomers sometimes run parallel, although they are not necessarily interdependent. Astronomers calculated time and conceptualized it. This took the form of extensive computations relating to planetary distances, orbits, asterisms, eclipses and such like, the accumulated knowledge of endless years of observing the night skies and daily shadow readings. These could become patterns in cosmic time. Cosmological time need not be either complete fantasy, or intuitive. It could draw on the existing notions of time current in the calculations of astronomers and mathematicians, although imagination would also be brought into play in the final construct.

Units of time are often initially natural units, such as the cycle of day and night, the cycle of the month based on phases of the moon — the synodic month and lunar fortnights — and the seasonal cycle of the year, starting generally with the spring equinox with segments named after the seasons: what are referred to in the early Indian texts as *ahorātra*, *māsa* and *pakṣa* and the *ṛtus*. The year was also divided into the northern and southern course of the sun on the basis of the solstice —*uttarāyana* and *dakṣināyana*. The lunar day or *tithi* consisted of *muhūrtas*, sometimes refined further to finer measurements as minute as the blinking of an eye.

What may be called ritual time revolved around the cycles of nature. Seasonal rituals often evolved from the routine activities of a given society over the year, e.g. the grazing circuits of herders or the sowing and harvesting periods of cultivators. Some of these were also moments for the gathering of wealth. Ritual time is broadly predictable. Ritual texts sometimes describe the year in terms of the seasons.[13] It comes to be treated as more precise when it is tied to astrology. With reckoning in *muhūrtas* for example, the notion of the auspicious moment comes into existence. Where the ritual is meticulously observed, it suspends the performers of the rituals into a threshold condition where only the parameters of their time-reckoning prevail. Cyclical theories of time arise from the observance of rhythm based on the sequences in relation to the sun and the moon or the seasons.[14] The concept of *ṛta* as a law guiding the universe to ensure regularity and predictability, also derives from the notion of rhythm.

In the early Indian literature, where the need to determine

[13] *Śatapatha Brāhmaṇa*, 6. 7. 1. 18; 13. 6. 1. 10–11; 1. 7. 2. 21; 2. 4. 2. 24; *Atharvaveda*, 6. 55. 2.

[14] *Ṛg Veda*, I. 164. 2; 10. 90. 6; 7. 88. 4; for a more poetic rendering, 10. 72.

time was also linked to the efficacy of sacrificial rituals, time is described as a five-spoked wheel, constantly revolving,[15] evoking regular spacing and cyclic movement. In a five-year cycle the solar and lunar calendars were adjusted.

The *nakṣatras* or constellations called for particular attention and this remained a significant activity in early Indian astronomy. The path of the sun and the moon were marked on the basis of a stellar frame. Initially, the five-year cycle was referred to as a *yuga* although later it was extended to a much longer period.[16] The term *yuga*, literally a yoke, is intended to suggest a binding together as an entity. Its usage connected with time refers to a period in which planetary bodies are in conjunction, both at the start and at the end. In the early period the major planets were of course the sun and the moon which had already figured in stellar astronomy. A far more extensive span of time than a five-year cycle was required with planetary movements becoming important. The *yuga* carried not only the notion of a natural cycle and was therefore benign and harmonious but the conjunction of planets carried another meaning, in that it suggested a variety of bi-polarities — good and evil, divine and human, life and death.

Time reckoning was generally based on a luni-solar calendar. The earliest sense of a calendar had to do with time-markers, both of the individual life cycle and involving the environment, which were gradually ritualized. Some had been established in accordance with the lunar calendar with easily comprehensible calculations based on the phases of the moon. The precision of the solar calendar was useful in agricultural activities and also in horoscopy and in either case it became an agency of social control. Measurements of time were required by astrology in the making of horoscopes. These were further activated by the introduction, in the early Christian era, of Hellenistic ideas derived from the obsession with horoscopy and divination among the

[15] *Ṛg Veda*, 1. 164. 13–14

[16] P.V. Kane, *History of Dharmaśāstra*, Poona 1958, Vol. 5, 1, 486.

Graeco-Romans. Predictions based on the signs of the zodiac and the seven-day week — still so prominent in our Sunday newspapers — appear to have been Hellenistic in origin. The urgency to determine time now included the need to know the proper moment for ceremonies and observances — *saṃskāras* — particularly important to the identity of upper castes — as indeed also to improve upon calendars and horoscopes.[17] This became an aspect of ritual time which soon evolved its own forms and rules.

Indian interest in astronomy is revealed in texts dating to the fifth century BC and often included in the category of *Jyotiḥśāstra.* The measurement of time was an important aspect in these studies. The basic unit was initially the five-year *yuga.* Infusions from west Asia introduced further calculations of cyclic time as developed in Greek astronomy based in turn on Babylonian ideas.[18] This interest was an indirect result of the substantial trade and contacts, both overland and maritime, between the eastern Mediterranean and Hellenistic west Asia with northern and western India. Yavanas from the former areas were the visiting traders and some seem to have settled for long periods in India, perhaps even being associated with office.[19] The mingling of Indian and Graeco-Babylonian ideas enhanced activity in astronomy and mathematics in India. This took the form of extensive calculations relating to planets, orbits, eclipses and the like. It has been argued that there was a radical change after *c.* AD 400 when the *Siddhānta-jyotiṣa* replaced the *Vedāṅga-jyotiṣa* and calculations earlier based on stellar and lunar observations now preferred to incorporate planetary motions and solar reckonings.[20]

[17] Pingree, *Jyotiḥśāstra.*

[18] Ibid.

[19] Pingree, *Isis.*

[20] Y. Krishan, 'The Astronomical Revolution in India about AD 400 and its Implications', *Vishveshvaranand Indological Journal,* 1977, 15, 2, 265–84. S.N. Sen, 'Astronomy', in D.M. Bose *et. al.* (eds.), *A Concise History of Science in India,* New Delhi 1971, 81–2.

III

Cosmological Time

In the construction of the large cycles of cosmological time the figures used both in cosmology and in astronomy came to be central. In what has been called the *yuga* astronomy of the fifth century AD Indian astronomers calculated that a *kalpa*, the longest period of time, consisted of 4320 million years. The astronomers may have borrowed the notion of a *kalpa* from Puranic sources since they required a long period of time as the basis of their calculations.[21] This raises two questions, one relating to the current theories of cosmological time and the other concerning the dialogue between the authors of a variety of texts.

Cosmological time is described in Manu's *Dharmaśāstra* and in the *Mahābhārata* and is further elaborated upon in the *Purāṇas.* Concepts of time, integrated with ideas on creation, go into the making of what might be called cosmological time. Manu quotes the *mahārṣi* Bhṛgu in describing these concepts which are linked to the notion of the *yugas* calculated in terms of humanly manageable time, as well as the larger unit of divine time associated with Brahmā.[22] It is said that there were six Manus before the present one and this provides one kind of time scale. This is followed by a detailed working out of the smaller units of time from the blinking of an eye to a human year with their equivalents in the enhanced time scale used by the *pitṛs*/ancestors and the *devas*/gods. Given the propensity to classification, different time units were associated with a hierarchy of persons in ascending orders of magnitude. A human month is a day and a night for the ancestors and a human year is the same for the gods. Manu

[21] D. Pingree, personal communication.

[22] Manu, I. 60–86.

continues with the description of the four *yugas*: the first, the Kṛta lasts for four thousand years with a preceding and subsequent twilight period of four hundred years each. The next three, the Tretā, Dvāpara and Kali, are calculated by reducing one thousand from each with a corresponding reduction of one hundred in the twilight period.

Kṛta	4000	+	400	(X 2)	=	4800
Tretā	3000	+	300	(X 2)	=	3600
Dvāpara	2000	+	200	(X 2)	=	2400
Kali	1000	+	100	(X 2)	=	1200
	10,000	+	2000		=	12000

The total of twelve thousand years constitutes an age of the gods. A thousand of these constitutes a single day of Brahmā and a night of Brahmā is of equal length. The age of Manu, *manvantara*, consists of seventy-one times the age of the gods.

A similar description of the four *yugas* occurs in the *Mahābhārata*, where, at the end of the cycle of four ages or the *mahāyuga*, the Kṛta returns.[23] The emphasis here, as in Manu, is on the change in the character of the four ages accompanied by the increasing decline of *dharma* in each, with a graphic picture of deterioration in the Kali age. At one point it is stated that the world turns upside down in the Kali age.[24] It goes on to list the *mleccha* and other kings who will rule and the list seems to echo the more detailed lists of the *Purāṇas*. Parts of the *Mahābhārata* are regarded as later additions and some of these could well be contemporary with the early *Purāṇas* or at least were borrowing from a common source of ideas, current by the second or third centuries AD.

The theory of the four ages as a conceptualization of cosmological time is more elaborate in the *Purāṇas*, which are generally dated to around the mid-first millennium AD. In the *Viṣṇu Purāṇa*, for instance, it is discussed in the sections on the creation of the world and concepts of cosmography.

[23] Vanaparvan, 186. 17 ff. Śāntiparvan, 224, 6 ff.
[24] Vanaparvan, 186. 28 ff.

The sentiment on the significance of *dharma* remains evident, although there is a greater play with numbers in these texts. The twelve thousand years are treated as divine years and conversion to human years requires multiplication by three hundred and sixty.[25] The length of the *mahāyuga* is therefore calculated as 4,320,000 human years. The *kalpa* which incorporates the *mahāyuga* is calculated as one thousand ages or fourteen *manvantaras.*[26] The *manvantara* is equal to seventy-one times the number of years in a *mahāyuga* with some to spare. This we are told is equal to 852,000 (1200 x 71) divine years or 306,720,000 (360 x 852,000) human years. It has been suggested that this is an imperfect synthesis of more than one independent doctrine and perhaps the *manvantaras* derive from a source different to that of the *mahāyugas.*[27] Kali, the smallest of the ages, extended to 432,000 years. According to one view, the number 432,000 is of Babylonian origin and appears to have been combined with Greek epicycle theory.[28] The *mahāyuga* was a category of time reminiscent of what geologists in the last century termed 'deep time' and perhaps what Fernand Braudel in our century would have recognized as 'la longue durée' — the time of long duration.

The projection of the *kalpa* as cosmological time in non-astronomical texts was almost calculated to defeat any controllable sense of time. Could the mathematical innovations of that period, namely, the concept of the zero and of decimal place value notation have encouraged this formulation of figures and numbers? The magnification to millions was almost a fantasy on ciphers. There is perhaps something ironic in time constructs such as these, playing with the concept of the zero which, as *śūnya,* could refer to emptiness or the void.

[25] *Viṣṇu Purāṇa,* 1. 3. 11 ff.

[26] *Viṣṇu Purāṇa* 3. 2.

[27] A. L. Basham, *The Wonder That was India,* London 1954, 321.

[28] Pingree, *Isis.*

In the cosmology of the *Purāṇas*, the *kalpa* is the period through which creation lasts and is calculated in figures. The dissolution at the end of the *kalpa* occurs when fire and flood engulf creation. In Buddhist, Jaina and Ājīvika texts, the *kalpa* was made unreal not just by the use of the fantasy of figures but also by a spatial description which made it virtually inconceivable. A Buddhist text describes the *kalpa* thus : if there is a mountain in the shape of a cube, measuring one *yojana*[29] and if every hundred years the mountain is brushed with a silk scarf, then the time that is taken for the mountain to be eroded by the scarf is the equivalent of a *kalpa*.[30] Alternatively, if there is a city of iron walls, measuring one cubic *yojana*, and is filled with mustard seeds, and if one seed is taken out every hundred years, the seeds would all be removed before the *kalpa* ended.[31] In Jaina texts the wheel of time, *kālacakra*, is said to consist of zillions of atoms of time, *palyopmas*, calculated to 20 x 10,000,000 (2) x 10 x 10,000,000. The measure of each atom is again described spatially: it is the number of years it would take to empty a cylinder, four miles in length and width, tightly packed with the body hair of humans, if every hundred years a single hair is taken out.[32] The Ājīvika description of a *mahākalpa* states that if there was a river 117,649 times (that is, seven to the seventh power) the size of the Ganga, and if every hundred years one grain of sand is removed from the bed of this imaginary river, the total time for the removal of all the sand will be one *sara*, and 300,000 *saras* equal one *mahākalpa*. (Incidentally, it takes 8,400,000 of these to complete the transmigration of a soul.) This is not the total time of the universe for it continues for infinitely longer.[33] Alternatively, space is also projected as time where the

[29] A *yojana* has been variously calculated and the range extends from two and a half to nine miles.

[30] *Saṃyutta Nikāya*, 2. 180–1.

[31] Ibid., 181–2.

[32] W. Norman Brown, *Man in the Universe*, Berkeley 1966, 77.

[33] A. L. Basham, *History and Doctrine of the Ājīvikas*, London 1951, 253–4.

measurement of the universe with a rope equals the distance which a male celestial being flies in six months at the speed of 2,057,152 *yojanas* in one blinking of the eye.[34] In such reckonings a human life-time would constitute a minuscule moment, described in fact as a dew drop on the tip of a blade of grass when the sun rises or the turning of the chariot wheel which turns by just one place on its rim.[35] Spatial descriptions of extended time are intended to suggest an infinity of time. But since the silk scarf would have disintegrated in the first hundred years or so, spatial descriptions amount to a negation of measurement. It is in this ultimate sense that the Mauryan emperor Aśoka refers to the continuation of his policies by his descendants and by posterity for a *kalpa*.[36] An infinity of time came to represent all of creation.

In Purāṇic cosmology, the *mahāyuga* is more manageable than the *kalpa* since it takes the figures from Manu, converts them to an equivalent in human years and the figures chosen continue to conform to a pattern. Each of the four *yugas* decreases in regulated length with an intermediate dawn and dusk. The Kṛta-yuga extends for 1,728,000 human years, which figure is divisible by 12. The Tretā-yuga decreases in length by a quarter and is 1,296,000 years, and is divisible by 9. The Dvāpara-yuga is reduced by a third and is 864,000 years in length and is divisible by 6. The Kali-yuga, is reduced by a half and is 432,000 years in length and is divisible by 3.[37] The names of the four ages are called after the throw of the four-sided dice, from best to worst. The connection with dice

[34] A. Ghosh (ed.), *Jaina Art and Architecture*, 3 vols., New Delhi 1974–5, 3, 519, n.2. The figure here is 2,857,152, which, it has been said, might be a typographical error since other sources carry 2,057,152.

[35] *Visuddhimagga*, 1. 231,238, quoted in A. K. Coomaraswamy, *Time and Eternity*, Ascona 1947.

[36] Fourth Major Rock Edict. J. Bloch, *Les Inscriptions d'Asoka*, 1950, 100. Fifth Major Rock Edict, Ibid., 102.

[37] *Viṣṇu Purāṇa* 1. 3. 11 ff; 6. 1. *Matsya Purāṇa*; 142 ff. In some texts the fourth age had been called *āskanda* or *tiṣya*. Kane, *History of Dharmaśāstra*, 3, 887.

introduces the element of chance into what may otherwise appear to be pre-ordained. Play at dice is opposed to a permanent accumulation of wealth and has a levelling effect, sometimes even circulating that which is scarce. Transactions of exchange tend to get neutralized as the game proceeds.[38] Was time seen as playing a similar role?

This construction of a time scale has many interesting facets. Orderliness of a mathematical kind was basic to the concept. The shortening of the length of each *yuga* is in descending arithmetical progression. The numbers have a mathematical link as in figures such as 60, 72, 84, 360, 1200, 432,000. The numbers also echo a variety of sources; 432,000 is said to be the number of the syllables in the *Ṛg Veda* and the number in the three Vedic texts is double that, 864,000.[39] It is unlikely that a precise syllable count was made of the *Vedas.* Were these numbers in turn picked up from other sources? In Mesopotamian schedules, apart from the use of the basic sexigesimal system, the final sums are multiples of the same integer which in India came to be associated with the sum of divine years in a cosmic cycle. The multiplication of 1200 by 360 yields 432,000. This was also the time period given for the pre-diluvian kings in Babylonian sources as recorded by Berossos, the Babylonian historian of the third century BC [40] During the previous centuries Achaemenid west Asia had encroached on north-western India and possibly the number 72, which was basic to Biblical and Babylonian chronology, became popular in Indian time calculations. From the Babylonian perspective too, some numerals such as 7,9,12,360 were seen as endowed with a special magical

[38] J. Woodburn, 'Egalitarian Societies', *Man*, n.s., 1982, 17, 431–51. Some later texts raise objections to gambling, presumably when the accumulation of wealth is not to be questioned. Baudhāyana, *Dharmasūtra*, 2, 15–16.

[39] *Śatapatha Brāhmaṇa*, 10. 4. 2. 22–5. Kane, 5, 1, 689–90.

[40] P. Schnabel, *Berossos und die Babylonisch-Hellenistische Literatur*, Leipzig 1923, 261–3. D. Pingree, "The Purāṇas and Jyotiḥśāstra: Astronomy", *Journal of the American Oriental Society*, 1990, 110, 2, 275.

potency and were therefore treated differently from figures in mathematics.[41] Yet these figures occur in astronomy and the similarities may not be altogether accidental. It would seem that such figures may have been travelling back and forth between India and west Asia as they continued to do into later centuries.

IV

The Authors

Numbers such as these were not unfamiliar in the calculations of astronomers at this time but there was not always a uniform agreement on the figures basic to calculations. One at least of the astronomers did not accept, for purposes of his own calculations, the unequal length of the four *yugas*. Āryabhaṭa in the fifth century AD was singled out even in later times as having argued in favour of four ages of equal length of 1,080,000 years.[42] A subsequent astronomer, Brahmagupta, disagreed with this and endorsed the alternative figures closer to the cosmological scheme. The cosmography of a flat earth was also rejected in favour of a sphere. In the mid-eighth century the astronomer Lalla refuted what he found unacceptable in Purāṇic texts.[43] Still later, Vaṭeśvara disagreed with Brahmagupta and supported Āryabhaṭa.[44] There appears to have been some divergence among astronomers as also between them and the authors of the *Purāṇas.*

What then was the nature of discourse among the authors of the *Purāṇas* constructing an imaginary cosmos and the astronomers after the mid-first millennium AD? Were the

[41] F. Cumont, *Astrology and Religion among Greeks and Romans,* New York 1912/1960 (rep), 18, 62.

[42] Alberuni, 1, 373–4.

[43] Lalla, *Śiṣyadhīvṛddhidatantra.* D. Pingree, 'The Purāṇas and Jyotiḥśāstra: Astronomy', *Journal of the American Oriental Society,* 1990, 110, 2, 274–80.

[44] S.N. Sen, 97.

paurānikas, using the immensity of the figures and resorting to mathematical patterns, attempting to intimidate those who listened to the recitation of these texts? Where the numerals were common to the *Purāṇas* and to astronomy, even if there was no logical connection between the two categories of knowledge, a claim to further authenticity on the part of the *paurānikas* would seem to be implicit. Was there an intellectual divergence among the authors of various categories of texts for, although they were all *brāhmaṇas*, they were trained differently and performed different functions? Although they belonged to the same *varṇa* there was within it a professional differentiation which had social dimensions. The mere fact of a brahmanical authorship of the various texts need not assume an identity of content and purpose, and there may well have been ideological differences.

Interestingly the incorporation of cosmic time is particularly emphasized in some texts, such as the *Mahābhārata* and certain *Purāṇas* which are believed to have originally had a link with bards. The later written versions of the texts are said to have been revised by the *brāhmaṇas*. The Bhṛgu *brāhmaṇas* are sometimes associated with this and they have a curiously ambivalent social position in the *brāhmaṇa varṇa*.[45] Were the authors of the *Purāṇas* unable to keep abreast of the astronomers and mathematicians who had incorporated Hellenistic and other systems into their theories? For example, Yavanarāja Sphujidhvaja states in the third century AD that in the previous century Yavaneśvara translated a Greek astrological text, now lost, into Sanskrit as the *Yavana-jātaka*. In the fourth century, Mīnarāja, who also refers to himself with the title of Yavanarāja, wrote the *Vṛddha-yavana-jātaka*. These texts are quoted by Indian astronomers.[46] It may be said

[45] V.S. Sukthankar, 'The Bhṛgus and the Bhārata: A Text-historical Study', *Annals of the Bhandarkar Oriental Research Institute*, 18, 1–76. F.E. Pargiter, *The Purāṇa Text of the Dynasties of the Kali Age*, Delhi 1975 (rep), 77 ff. R.P. Goldman, *Gods, Priests and Warriors*, New York 1977.

[46] D. Pingree, *The Yavanajātaka of Sphujidhvaja*, *I*, Cambridge, Mass. 1978. Introduction.

in passing that there is a virulent attack on the Yavanas, the people from the west, in a text with the curious title of *Yuga Purāṇa*, although interestingly, the expertise of the Yavanas in astronomy is conceded.[47] Varāhamihira states that although the Yavanas are *mlecchas*, and therefore outside the social pale, nevertheless, given their knowledge of astronomy, they are honoured as *ṛṣis*.[48] If there was a change from calculations based on the constellations and the moon to planetary and solar astronomy around AD 400, it may have also encouraged divergent thinking.

V

Time and the Decline of *Dharma*

The answers to some of these questions may also lie in the insistence on social and moral decline underlined in Purāṇic cosmological time. This was consistently endorsed as characteristic of change over the four ages. Sometimes the description of the *yugas* is merely a prelude to the lengthy statements on the reversal, from the brahmanical perspective, of norms and mores, which reversal characterizes the Kali age. The gradual decline of *dharma* is stated both directly and in symbols. The utopian conditions of the first age, also sometimes referred to as Satya, the age of Truth, diminish slowly until nothing of the utopia is left in the Kaliyuga. Thus in the first age people live to 400 years, never suffering from disease or from insecurity. By contrast, in the fourth age, life expectancy comes down to 100 years and the

[47] D.C. Sircar, *Studies in the Yuga Purāṇa and other Texts*, Delhi 1974. J.E. Mitchiner, *The Yuga Purāṇa*, Calcutta 1986.

[48] *Bṛhatsamhitā*, 2. 32. M. Ramakrishna Bhat (ed.), *Varāmihira's Bṛhatsamhitā*, Delhi 1981.

śūdras are in the ascendent.[49] In the Kṛta age men lived as long as they chose to and procreation did not require sexual activity, but in the Kali age marriage became necessary.[50] In another text life-expectancy drops from 30,000 in the Kṛta age to 100 years in the Kali age.[51] In the Jaina tradition the start of the cycle was evident by the tallness of humans, a man's height being six miles and the number of his ribs being 256. Gradually both the height and the number of ribs decreased until in the present era, life expectancy is down to 125, the number of ribs to 16 and the height to seven cubits (*hastas*, of about eighteen inches). And this will decrease further in the future.[52] Or there is the image of *dharma*, sometimes likened to a bull, which stands on four legs in the first age and drops a leg in each subsequent age, symbolizing the decline in moral and social order.[53] The present is invariably an age of evil when social mores are turned upside-down. This was in part the expected decline in the decreasing cycle where human actions would relate to the quality of the *yuga*.

It could also be interpreted as resentment at royal patronage to non-brahmanical ideologies, for the *brāhmaṇas* were not yet at the forefront as recipients of material prosperity. The Kaliyuga symbolizes the breaking down of caste ranking as a determining feature of social activities. Mention is made of *mleccha* rulers, corrupt *brāhmaṇas* and upstart *śūdras* taking on the airs of *brāhmaṇas* and performing priestly functions. Equally important, the subordination of women, so crucial to the continuance of caste, disintegrates and results particularly in sexual freedom for women.[54] This

[49] Manu 1.83. Kane, 3,244 ff; 892 ff. *Viṣṇu Purāṇa*, 6. 1 and 2. *Mahābhārata*, Vanaparvan, 148. 10ff ; 186. 23ff.

[50] *Mahābhārata*, Śāntiparvan, 200, 35 ff.

[51] *Aṅguttara Nikāya*, 4, 156.

[52] S. Stevenson. *The Heart of Jainism*, New Delhi 1970 (rep.), 273 ff.

[53] Manu 1. 81–2, 8, 16.

[54] *Viṣṇu Purāṇa*, 6. 1. 10 ff. *Mahābhārata*, Vanaparvan, 188. 10–93.

is unlikely as a description of an actual situation and the Kaliyuga is here being constructed as the antonym to an ideal brahmanical society. Historical evidence points to social change in the latter part of the first millennium AD but not of the kind envisaged in the description of the Kali age. For example, *brāhmaṇa* ascendency was established through extensive royal grants of land to a variety of *brāhmaṇas* but this did not lead to a rescinding of the picture of the Kali age. The idyllic community of the distant past is expected to return but in the equally distant future. But the *yugas* were not merely a measurement in time. Conflicting views among the authors of the texts setting out the norms could be sorted out by arguing that a particular interpretation, no longer current, was prevalent in the previous *yuga*.[55] Substantial changes in customary laws and rituals explained as Kalivarjaya are in effect related to problems arising from social change in the latter part of the first millenium AD.[56] The horrors of the Kaliyuga are recited repeatedly from this period onwards. The coming of the tenth *avatāra* of Viṣṇu, Kalkin — a name also associated with time — will usher in a new age. Kalkin will destroy the *melcchas*, the rulers and the heretics.[57] There is a touch of the messianic in the coming of Kalkin.

Slotted into this theory of the decline of *dharma* is also the notion of transmigration or metempsychosis — *karma* and *saṃsāra*. The cyclic notion is reinforced by the idea of transmigration, with the *ātman* or soul being constantly reborn. Much earlier, the *Upaniṣads* had tied together the notions of time, the planets and rebirth in the argument that after death the soul travels along two major paths — the *devayāna* or path of the gods and the *pitṛyāna* or path of the ancestors. Those who were free from rebirth took the former path which was associated with the sun and led the soul to the world of Brahmā and eternal life. Those who had to undergo

[55] Kane, 3, 865 ff.

[56] Ibid. 926 ff, 966 ff.

[57] *Viṣṇu Purāṇa*, 4. 24. 98. P.V. Kane, 3.923 ff.

rebirth took the path of the ancestors, associated with the moon, and eventually returned to earth.[58] Implicit in this notion are certain consequences. There is the inevitability of death with which time comes to an end. Religious beliefs attempt to reverse this inevitability by proposing rebirth through many lives, or, as in the Semitic religions, everlasting life in heaven or hell subsequent to Judgement Day. In either case, one cannot escape the consequences of one's actions. Therefore, if present action determines the future, then the past, present and future are inextricably linked.[59] This kind of thinking was in turn incorporated into horoscopy.[60]

The deterministic procession of time towards decline is arrested and challenged by the individual *karma* and this idea became even more significant with the notion that *bhakti* — devotion to and sharing in the grace of the deity — was an avenue of release from rebirth. It is at the human level that the immensity of time can be challenged for in its totality time is almost beyond human comprehension. There is a near dialectical relationship between the individuality of *karma* and the virtual inevitability of the time cycle. The decline in morality in the fourth age acts as a peg on which one can hang one's inability to change the course of events particularly if it points towards retrogression. But the four ages need not be perceived as enclosed units for it is said that a king's conduct characterizes the identity of the age and this ties ethics and social behaviour to time.[61] Ultimately the possibility of the return of the cycle provides the necessary optimism for continuing human action and also gives a meaning to human action in the past: it makes history necessary.

The change, implicit in each *yuga*, is so firmly emphasized that one may wonder how the idea that cyclic time did not

[58] *Bṛhadāranyaka Upaniṣad*, 6. 2. 15ff. *Chāndogya* 5. 10; 10. 1. 2; 4. 15.

[59] P.V. Kane, *History of Dharmaśāstra*, Poona 1946, 3, 923 ff. 5, 484 ff. Balslev.

[60] Kane, 5, 484ff. The sixth-century text, the *Bṛhajjātaka*, links horoscopy to *karma* and *punar janma*.

[61] Manu, 9. 301–2. *Mahābhārata*, Śāntiparvan, 70. 6.

conceive of change took root in modern views on the subject. Admittedly, in the existing *mahāyuga,* the notion of change in the Purāṇic version is towards decline and not towards progress although the conduct of the king can change this direction. The linking of a particular period of time with social change marks a difference between the Puranic cosmological time with its implications for human society, and time as conceived in astronomy. Jayasiṃha points to the decline of planetary motions as the *mahāyuga* progresses, but this may be seen as a different concept of decline from the Puranic.[62] The figures from astronomy are relatively value-free, arising out of computations of time. This difference is important to the relationship between time and history.

VI

Myth and History

The induction of cosmological time into the early *Purāṇas* raises the question of the relationship of myth to history and it is to this that I would now like to turn. It has been argued that myths narrate events in primordial, atemporal moments which constitute sacred time and differ from the continuous profane time of daily routines. Therefore, by narrating myths profane time is abolished.[63] The question then is whether this was true of the treatment of time in the *Purāṇas.* Although not stated directly, was there at least the suggestion that a differentiation was being perceived between different forms of time and the assessment of past events ? Was cosmological time seen as mythic time ? Was mythic time segregated

[62] D. Pingree: personal communication.

[63] Eliade, *Cosmos and History* : *the Myth of the Eternal Return,* 112 ff. 'Time and Eternity in Indian Thought', in *Man and Time,* Bollingen Series, xxx, 3.

from chronological time in narrating the past? Was this segregation seen as a mechanism for separating myth and history?

Among the *Purāṇas*, the *Viṣṇu Purāṇa* observes what is described as the ideal format in its five sections and one of the five provides an overview of the perceived past. This is the *vamśānucarita* which narrates the succession of those who ruled and can be divided into three distinct, although unequal, sections.[64] The narrative begins with the briefest reference back to the previous sections of the text which describe the genesis of the universe, giving details of creation, of time cycles as both the *mahāyugas* and the *manvantaras*, and of cosmography. The Manus are mentioned in passing, spanning immense cycles of time. They have no association with specific events nor do they indicate any particular social condition.

In the reign of the seventh Manu there occurs the great Flood from which Manu is saved by Viṣṇu in his fish incarnation, the *matsya-avatāra*.[65] Manu and the seven *ṛṣis* are placed in a boat and the boat is tied to the single horn of the fish (the incarnated Viṣṇu) and they go through the waters of the Flood and are lodged safely on the top of a mountain (in some texts, this is Mount Meru, the *axis mundi*). When the Flood subsides, creation starts anew. The story of the Flood is in many ways similar to the Mesopotamian story. The earliest version occurs in the *Śatapatha Brāhmaṇa* and may reflect a borrowing from west Asia where there are still earlier versions of the story.[66] The Flood acts as a time marker separating the period of the Manus from that of the *kṣatriya rājās* who followed. Floods have a dual symbolism of

[64] *Viṣṇu Purāṇa* 4. Romila Thapar, 'Genealogical Patterns as Perceptions of the Past', *Studies in History*, 1991, n.s., 7, 1, 1–36.

[65] This is narrated in great detail, for obvious reasons, in the opening chapters of the *Matsya Purāṇa*, but not in the *Viṣṇu Purāṇa*.

[66] *Śatapatha Brāhmaṇa*, 1. 8. 1. 1 ff. W.G. Lambert and A.R. Millard, *Atrahasis*, Oxford 1969.

water washing away that which is physically present as well as the silt deposited from the Flood providing a fresh beginning in the space which had been flooded.

In the next and second section of the chapter on succession, the measurement of time changes radically from the cyclic time associated with the Manus and the *manvantaras*, to reckoning time as generations through lengthy genealogies. Cosmological time appears to be now distanced from the lists of descent by the use of a time schedule seemingly more manageable in human terms. I would like to suggest that both the Flood and the change to reckoning in generational time through genealogies are mechanisms of demarcating myth in cosmological time from that which occupies the ambiguous area approaching history.

The listing of generations in the *Viṣṇu Purāṇa* begins with the description of Manu's progeny who are said to be the ancestors of the earliest *kṣatriyas*. Among them the most important are Ikṣvāku who initiates the Sūryavaṃśa or Solar lineage, and Iḍā or Ilā, whose androgynous form is suggested and from whose female self are descended another group of *kṣatriyas* identified as the Candravaṃśa or Lunar lineage. These two descent groups are also integrated into the two epics, for the heroes of the *Rāmāyaṇa* are of the Sūryavaṃśa and those of the *Mahābhārata* are of the Candravaṃśa. The association of the sun and the moon with these descent groups carries a rich symbolism which touches on many facets, but for our purposes here it is significant as a parallel to the calendars in use. Time reckoning in this section is characterized by the sequence of generations and is for all practical purposes an exercise in linear time, although a location within the *yuga* system forms the ultimate time frame.

The term used for a succession list of any kind or a genealogy is *vaṃśa*, derived from the name for bamboo. This is an appropriate image where each node marks a new generation of growth. This in itself would suggest linear time. Genealogies have a tentative beginning in the early chapters of the epics, but the construction of a narrative in genealogical form comes into its own in the early *Purāṇas.* This may be called a construction since it covers almost a hundred generations and such an immense genealogy could hardly have been an authentic record.[67] It is however possible that genealogies, not as authentic descent lists but as narratives of the past, existed in earlier centuries and were incorporated into and reorganized in the *Purāṇas.* Thus Megasthenes, the ambassador from the Hellenistic Seleucid kingdom in Iran, is quoted as saying that the Indians count kings over 153 (or 154 according to the later Roman historian, Pliny) generations or 6451 years and three months from the time of Alexander (in the fourth century BC.), going back to the earliest settlement which it is claimed was established by Bacchus.[68]

The genealogies in themselves are not invariably authentic but they incorporate patterns and narratives which are indicative of a recognition of particularities. For example, the Sūryavaṃśa pattern is the history of descent from father to eldest son alone, generally suggestive of primogeniture, whereas the Candravaṃśa often lists more than a single line of descent among brothers, suggestive perhaps of a segmentary lineage system. The genealogies are therefore not necessarily intended as historically accurate — and this would be evident from the variants in the name and position in the descent list among the different *Purāṇas* — but they do seem to be making a statement about how the past was perceived and these perceptions may be intended as the more authentic history.

The descent list of the Sūryavaṃśa peters out. The Candravaṃśa, purporting to record segmentary clans,

[67] F.E. Pargiter, *Ancient Indian Historical Tradition,* London 1922.

[68] Solin, 52. 5 ; Pliny, *Natural History,* 6. 21. 4–5. Arrian in the *Indika IX*, gives the figures of 153 generations, from Dionysus to Candragupta, and 6042 years. J.W. McCrindle, *Ancient India as Described by Megasthenes and Arrian,* London 1877, 115, 203.

continues to the grand finale of the *Mahābhārata* war in which virtually all the clans are directly or indirectly involved and few survive. The catastrophic war, described as the end of the glorious age of the *kṣatriyas,* becomes another time-marker. If the choice of a time marker is a signpost to the culture, it would seem appropriate that the *kṣatriya* clans would terminate their activities in a war. The keeping of genealogies and reckoning by generations, whether factual or fictive, are important to lineage-based societies where rank is determined by birth and such clans claim dominant social status.[69] Genealogical time becomes important to the process of legitimation. Earlier generations can be stretched back into a remote past or claims to heroic ancestry can be telescoped so as to be placed closer to the claimant.

That both the Flood and the *Mahābhārata* war were viewed as significant time-markers is indicated by the uncertainty as to where the start of the Kaliyuga should be placed.[70] The *Viṣṇu Purāṇa* states that the Kali age began after the war,[71] although some other texts place it earlier, thus eliminating a precise time. However, the start of the Kaliyuga in the *Viṣṇu Purāṇa* is located with reference to a constellation, thus implicitly suggesting a point in time. The astronomers, for reasons of facilitating calculations, worked out the date of the Kaliyuga as equivalent to 3102–1 BC. This was the date which came to be adopted in inscriptions and histories as well where precise dates were required.[72] But in the *Purāṇas* it was viewed more as the condition of society than as a precise point in time. Cosmological time did not debar other forms of time reckoning, perhaps more realistic and therefore liable to be subsumed in cosmological time.

[69] Romila Thapar, *From Lineage to State,* Delhi 1984.

[70] Kane, 5, 687.

[71] *Viṣṇu Purāṇa,* 4. 24. 104–7, 113. F.E. Pargiter, *The Puranic Texts of the Dynasties of the Kali Age,* Delhi 1975 (rep.), 61.

[72] Aihole inscription of Pulakeśin II, *Epigraphia Indica,* 6.7. This is a neat inclusion of the shorter Śaka era reckoning within the span starting with the Kaliyuga. Varāhamihira, *Bṛhatsamhitā,* 13, 3. J.F. Fleet, 'The Kaliyuga of 3102 BC', *Journal of the Royal Asiatic Society,* 1911, 479–96 and 675–98. Kalhaṇa, *Rājataraṅginī* 1. 51–6.

Subsequent to the *Mahābhārata* war, in the third section of the chapter on succession in the *Viṣṇu Purāṇa*, the narrative dramatically changes its tense from the past to the future and becomes a lengthy prediction of events. This would seem to be another example of pointing to historical change, through adopting a new category of time. What follows soon after is a listing of dynasties which is a change from the earlier lists of descent groups and within these dynasties the succession of rulers with, in some *Purāṇas*, their regnal years. Time periods and regnal years of the initial dynasties are obviously exaggerated but the lists gradually become more credible. The geneological form continues and the succession of dynasties as a new pattern of chronology is suggestive of linear time. The generational form is however limited to the names within the dynasty. Dynasties as such are generally not related to each other and in some cases it is specifically mentioned that the successor dynasty began as a *bhṛtya* or in the service of the earlier one.[73] The association with the Kaliyuga is less in terms of a point in time and more as an explanation of why, when the *kṣatriya* clans died out, it was possible not only for *śūdras* to rule — which at that time was contrary to the norms — but it was also possible later for kings to be from socially unacceptable groups, such as the *mlecchas* or those outside the social pale, the *vrātya-kṣatriyas* or degenerate *kṣatriyas* and the Śabaras and Pulindas who were forest dwellers and therefore regarded as primitive and beyond the boundaries of caste society. Prophesying history becomes a mechanism for using the past to lay claim to controlling the future. But the use of the future tense had its obvious limitation, namely, that the prophecy had to stop at the point when the text was composed, in this case towards the mid-first millennium AD.

Within the narrative of the chapter on succession in the *Viṣṇu Purāṇa* there is a demarcation of three periods based on various categories of time. The first is remote, that of the Manus and their large time cycles ; the second has a faint

[73] *Viṣṇu Purāṇa*, 4. 24. 43. Pargiter, *The Puranic Texts...* 38.

continuity from the first but focuses on a changed chronological pattern through genealogical or generational time; and finally, subsequent to the *Mahābhārata* war there follows a period of dynastic time reckoning. Cosmological time in this context, although all-encompassing, is nevertheless viewed as distant and possibly as mythical time. Dynastic time in effect takes the functional form of historical chronology. A distinction between myth and history, although not stated in these terms, appears to have been perceived. The coming of the Kaliyuga heralds a major change in time-reckoning. The forms in which time is depicted seem to be making a statement about historical change.

VII

Historical Time

But let us not forget that in the immensity of the time cycle we are still at the threshold of the Kaliyuga of 432,000 years. A more realistic kind of time reckoning was therefore also required. This drew on actual historical needs and is in some ways related to the last section of the chapter on succession in the *Viṣṇu Purāṇa*. Cosmological time did not debar other forms of time reckoning, even those perhaps with shorter spans and therefore liable to be subsumed in the compass of cosmological time. These may be viewed as fragmentary arcs within the cycle which take on the role of linear time. The dichotomy between cyclic and linear becomes increasingly vague.

An innovation of a new kind drawing on both astronomy and history provided another set of time markers and inaugurated a system of timereckoning which was distinctively different. This has curiously been overlooked by those insisting on early Indian time concepts being exclusively cyclic. The use of eras as well as dating by regnal years had gained currency, simultaneously with activity in astronomy and cosmology. This is particularly evident in documents concerning those in political authority. Regnal years go back to the earliest historical inscriptions, the edicts of the Mauryan emperor Aśoka, issued in the third century BC. Regnal years and eras point to time reckoning being based on a precise point in time and the starting point of the reckoning being known.

Linear time came to be used more extensively from the Christian era onwards in a variety of ways. Dynastic lists gradually came into circulation. Biographies of those in power, and especially kings, took as their time bracket the dynasty to which the subject of the biography belonged, relating him both to a description of origins and to early rulers, but focussed on the major activities of particular kings. The use of historical eras located kings and dynasties more firmly in time. The event or the person became a point in time and became stable within that tradition. The use of eras gained currency and this is particularly evident in documents emanating from those in authority.

The system of eras, according to some scholars, grew out of points in time invented to facilitate calculations in astronomy. The Kṛta era of 58 BC, also known as the Mālava era, and later, from the eighth century AD referred to as the Vikrama era, has been claimed as commemorating an historical event, although the suggestion has also been made that it may be associated with astronomy.[74] The term *saṁvatsara* came to be used for era. Other commonly used

[74] D.C. Sircar, *Indian Epigraphy*, Delhi 1965, 251 ff. F. Kielhorn, 'Examination of Questions Connected with the Vikrama Era,' *The Indian Antiquary*, 1891, 20, 397–414. If there is a link with astronomy, it may be suggested that Mālava may have been associated with Ujjain, the meridian for some calculations in astronomy. Both Bivar and Fussman have associated the Vikrama era with Azes I. A.D.H. Bivar, 'The Azes Era and the Indravarma Casket', *South Asian Archaeology, 1979*, Berlin 1981, 369–76. G. Fussman, 'Nouvelles Inscriptions Śaka: ère d'Eucratide, ère d'Azes, ère Vikrama, ère de Kaniṣka', *BEFEO*, 1980, 67, 1–43.

eras were the Śaka (AD 78), the Kalacuri Cedi (AD 247–8), the Gupta (AD 319–20) and so on. Subsequent to this there is a mushrooming of new eras all over the sub-continent.

The historical use of an era sometimes associated it with either an accession — such as the Gupta era — or with being a status symbol adding lustre to a reign — as in the case of the Cālukya-Vikrama era. At the functional level, eras introduced more precise dating in official documents. But this was not the only significance of using an era. More importantly, it helped separate cosmological time reckoning from the functional, although the former was not discarded. That the fashion for and computation of eras began from the use of methods influenced by Hellenistic astronomy may be one explanation, but it was also related to other changes which were conducive to the establishing of eras.

Dynasties are associated with monarchies and these in turn presuppose the emergence of a state system. The adoption of a short-spanned and more precise time reckoning associated with those in authority, was encouraged by the establishing of a state. This time reckoning, even when encompassed by the longer spans of cosmological time, introduces a precision which lends strength to the authority of the state. The need to maintain state records and official documents, not to mention texts legitimizing persons and institutions, tended to make the history of those in authority more evident. The time dimension of these was effectively linear. Elements of linear time in the context of early India have therefore a different origin from linear time in the Judaeo-Christian tradition, where it is linked to the sacred.

The use of historical eras may have been partially influenced by the parallel tradition of the Buddhists where major events came to be dated in the number of years from the *Mahāparinirvāṇa* or the passing away of the Buddha. The date for this, it was believed, was carefully recorded and after the removal of some discrepancies in late texts, most scholars, basing themselves on the sources in question, accepted 486 or 483 BC as the date of the death of the Buddha. Recently this date has been questioned and it is being suggested that the Buddha may have lived and died almost a century later.[75] What is significant, however, is that within particular Buddhist traditions there was a stable date. Perhaps because of this stable date, chronicles written by Buddhist monks, for example, display a sharper sense of time and relate all events to this date, which is associated with a historical person. Perhaps the historicity of the Buddha and the establishing of the *saṅgha* separated myth from history, although the narrative of individual events was often wrapped in myths. Buddhism maintained monastic institutions, the chronology and history of which were, in some cases, recorded when they became centres of power. Sectarian breakaways, of which there were many, could claim greater legitimacy if they placed themselves in relation to this history. Proselytizing ideologies claim legitimacy, both from myth and presumed history. There was also, for instance in the Sri Lankan Chronicles, such as the *Dīpavaṃsa* and the *Mahāvaṃsa*, a reconstruction of regnal years and events relating to the earliest narrative about the history of Sri Lanka, in order to corelate events in Sri Lanka with the biography of the Buddha. Later the history of the *saṅgha* was integrated with the political history of Sri Lanka and in its initial stages even with the rule of the Mauryas in India.[76] This became necessary because Aśoka came to be projected as legitimizing the sect of the Theravāda and the authors of these chronicles were Theravāda monks.

The adoption of historical eras or regnal years meant that official documents began to carry dates. Among these documents are inscriptions which are in effect the annals of

[75] H. Bechert (ed.), *The Dating of the Historical Buddha*, 2 vols., Gottingen 1991.

[76] L.S. Perera, 'The Pali Chronicles of Ceylon', in C.H. Philips, *Historians of India, Pakistan and Ceylon*, London 1961.

Indian history. Issued by individual rulers and by members of the ruling class in the main, they include votive records relating to grants and gifts as well as statements of events, especially those important to politics and administration. Some carry brief histories of the dynasty as a prelude to the specific action recorded. The date is precise and includes the era or the regnal year of the ruler, the season, month, fortnight and the day. It follows calendrical requirements for a date and this enables the calculation, for example, of its equivalence in the Gregorian calendar. Facility in the use of calendars would have required professional expertise. Hence the continuing importance of the astrologer, who, apart from horoscopy, sustained his authority by keeping track of both lunar and solar calendars.[77] The status of the astrologer in the earlier texts remained low even within the *brāhmaṇa varṇa* and he was excluded from *śrāddha* ceremonies, but interestingly, the later *Bṛhatsamhitā*, endorsing astrology, contradicts this and refers to the astrologer as the *sāmvatsara* and requires that he be honoured as the chief guest at a *śrāddha.*[78]

Precision in dating inscriptional documents became necessary because they were often official statements or legal charters. The recording of a precise moment requires a context and a location. Alternatively, depending on the nature of the grant, it may have been required to negate the effect of something inauspicious such as an eclipse. In such cases the precision in dating had to do with an astrologically appropriate moment. Despite the interest in horoscopes, history became more recognizable and in its use of time reckoning, it gradually sloughed off some of its earlier ritual context.

Apart from inscriptions, other categories of records such as biographies and dynastic and regional chronicles — the *caritas* and the *vaṃśāvalis* — articulated views on the past.

[77] Kane, 3, 126. D.C. Sircar, *Indian Epigraphy*, Delhi 1965, 227.

[78] Manu, 3. 162; 6. 50. Baudhāyana 2. 1. 2. 16. *Arthaśāstra*, 9. 4. 25–6. *Bṛhatsamhitā*, 2. 6 ; 2. 31, quoted in Y. Krishan.

These evolved into genres of literature and borrowed from the courtly literary style but their functions, as records and as legitimizing those in power were new and significant. Biographies, particularly of kings, took as their time bracket the dynasty to which the subject of the biography belonged. They focussed on what they assessed as the more significant events of the reign. Where authorship is specific, the recording of time also tends to be more specific. The composition and records of poets and bards, sometimes close to the court, but often closer to popular sentiment, were yet another form of legitimation, but could occasionally contest the official version of events.[79]

The *caritas* and *vaṃśāvalis* drew, when they chose to, on the *Purāṇas* but their view of the past was not identical to that of the *Purāṇas*.[80] Examples of such *caritas* are the *Harṣacarita* of Bānabhaṭa, the biography of the seventh century ruler Harṣavardhana, or Bilhaṇa's *Vikramānkadeva-carita* which focuses on Vikramāditya VI, an eleventh century Cālukya king.[81] Some of the lengthier inscriptions carried narratives of the dynasty and among these is the tenth century Khajuraho inscription set up by Dhaṅga for his father, Yaśovarman.[82] This is an official version of the origins and early history of the Candella dynasty. Two contested versions are known : one refers to their origins and caste status which is placed low and the other is an alternative view of the reign of one of the kings from the perspective of a popular ballad.[83] An example

[79] Romila Thapar, *Clan, Caste and Origin Myths in Early India*, Simla 1992.

[80] Romila Thapar, 'Society and Historical Consciousness: the *Itihāsa-Purāṇa* Tradition', in S. Bhattacharya and Romila Thapar (eds.), *Situating Indian History*, Delhi 1986, 353–83.

[81] For references to other such biographies, see V.S. Pathak, *Ancient Historians of India*, Bombay 1966. A.K. Warder, *An Introduction to Indian Historiography*, Bombay 1972.

[82] *Epigraphia Indica*, 1, 122.

[83] *Pṛthvirāj-rāso* by Candbardai refers to the low origin of the Candellas and is written from the point of view of their then enemies, the Cahamānas. The *Ālhākhaṇḍ* is a later epic which gives a very different picture of the reign of the Candella king, Paramardī, from that available in his own inscriptions.

of the more common form of the *vaṃśāvali* is the one from Chamba.[84]

These texts and inscriptions pertaining to past events frequently began with the origin myths of the dynasty as a preamble. Origin myths could go back to the time cycles of the Manus and relate to non-calendrical time but could also be set in the genealogical section of what I have called generational time. This serves to legitimize the founders of a dynasty by linking them with the heroes of Purāṇic ancestry. Some, however, may not resort to Purāṇic anc stry, although it tends to be brought in indirectly. By way of contrast, the narrative, as it continues in such texts, relates the succession of later rulers. This is set in a matrix of generations and of dynastic lists, emphasizes the unique event, and goes beyond the Purāṇic view of the past in, what I would like to suggest, were the major concerns perceived as important to historical change. These were primarily the recognition of the importance of acquiring caste status, the emergence of institutions linked to state formation and the establishing of new religious sects supportive of monarchy. Thus, in the Chamba *vaṃśāvali,* the origin myth merely links the earliest time with the heroes of Purāṇic ancestry. The subsequent narrative of the rulers of Chamba revolves around changes of many kinds, such as the claims to high status, the shifting of the capital to an area more conducive to revenue appropriation and administrative control, the making of grants, the introduction of Vaiṣṇavism, and so on. The chronology is what we would recognize as historical. Categories of time demarcate the earlier story from the later narrative. Such 'devices of temporal distancing' also provide indications of how the past was perceived.[85]

[84] J. Ph. Vogel, *Antiquities of Chamba State,* Calcutta 1911, 82 ff.
[85] Fabian, 31.

VIII

Eschatology

New chronological forms did not result in a new eschatology at the beginning and end of creation. For this, the cyclic theory continued to be the basis of cosmological time and for the larger time bracket the conditions of the Kaliyuga were referred to.[86] Elements of the eschatology of linear time do occur even within the broadly cyclic, but there is, for example, no single deity controlling time as in the Semitic religions. Time itself is sometimes projected as a deity. Time was a creator begetting heaven and earth, and that which was and that which shall be.[87] Time could be the ultimate cause.[88] The past, present and future are woven across space like warp and woof.[89] Time was imperishable and was said to encompass creation but since it was a deity it could also bring about destruction.[90] An even more evocative image describes time as *asya lokayantrasya sūtradhāraḥ*, literally, the string-holder/stage manager of this mechanism which is the universe, or that which regulates the universe.[91] However some elements of the eschatology seemed to have encouraged deviations. Among these may be noticed the variations in the structure of the cycle itself, as also the innovative idea of the coming of a saviour-figure who could intervene to change conditions and who assists in taking the cycle towards the next golden

[86] An interesting adaptation of this eschatology comes from Bali. A Balinese Hindu, Anandakusuma, asserted that the Kṛta age had recommenced in 1898. Among his reasons for saying so was that the progress of science culminating in the moon landing marked the kind of conditions which would initiate the Kṛta age. F.L. Bakker, *The Struggle of the Hindu Balinese Intellectuals*, Amsterdam 1993, 91.

[87] *Atharvaveda*, 19. 53, 1–12; 54, 1–5.

[88] *Śvetāśvatara Upaniṣad*, 1. 2. *Maitrī Upaniṣad*, 6. 15.

[89] *Bṛhadāraṇyaka Upaniṣad*, 3. 8. 3–4.

[90] *Bhagavad-gītā*, 11. 32.

[91] Bhartṛhari in *Vākyapadīya*, 3, 9, 3–5, quoted in W. Halbfass, *On Being and What There Is*, New York 1992, 205.

age. The coming of such a figure, it would seem, may not have been unrelated to the linear perceptions of time.

In Jaina cosmology, time is represented by a wheel with twelve spokes. The six ascending spokes (*utsarpiṇī*) span a period of virtue and harmony, though gradually changing, and the descending six (*avasarpiṇī*) refer to a period of increasing deterioration.[92] The two together constitute one rotation which is the equivalent of one *kalpa.* At the dawn of the Kṛta age, utopian conditions prevail. Humans are luminous and beautiful and are born as couples, giving birth to a fresh couple just before dying. The *kalpavṛkṣas* as wish-fulfilling trees satisfy all wants. There are no social distinctions, no persons in authority no sickness or poverty. At this time Bhāratavarṣa was called *bhogabhūmi,* an epithet which changed to *karmabhūmi,* when the decline implicit in time set in.[93]

In the Buddhist concept of the wheel of time, the four ages change but without an evident break. The golden age returns and is the commencement of another cycle. A series of such cycles would seem to take the shape of a spiral and if the spiral is stretched, it approximates a more linear form. Within the larger cyclic cosmology, generational time is invoked by listing the succession of the elders of the monasteries, often co-related with segments of dynastic history. This had a bearing on succession to high office, but was also important to property rights when the monasteries became landlords. Theravāda Buddhism, as it evolved in Sri Lanka, viewed the mission of the Buddha as a unique event. Northern Buddhism had a variant on this perception in its emphasis on the saviour figure.

The saviour-figure was that of the Buddha to come, the Buddha Maitreya or 'the friendly one'. As the last Buddha, his eventual coming is referred to in the early Buddhist texts,

[92] S. Stevenson, *The Heart of Jainism,* New Delhi 1970 (rep.), 272.

[93] *Paumacariyam,* 3. 37ff: 102. 126–132. K.R. Chandra, *A Critical Study of Paumacariyam,* Vaisali 1970, 318 ff.

but somewhat in passing.[94] Gradually the legend grew and it was said that when people became wicked and were given to violence, the Buddhist *dharma* on the decline, would be revived by Maitreya. Given the anarchy which followed this decline, people took to the forests and hid in the hills. The forest again becomes the retreat from the evils of life in the towns and villages. Ultimately, with the coming of the Buddha Maitreya, people would return and live once more in accordance with the *dharma.*[95] The past is pushed back by recalling the many Buddhas before Gautama and their long spans of time. Thus Dīpankara lived for 84,000 myriad lakhs of years a hundred thousand unaccountable *kalpas* ago. This is a timeless time and we have seen how time is negated in the spatial descriptions of the *kalpa.* The idea is firmed up by the mid-first millennium AD possibly because of the declining patronage to Buddhism among competing religions in some areas. The anticipation of a Buddha to come would shore up support for Buddhism. The Buddha Maitreya is associated with the upward movement of the wheel of time in the direction of the eventual return of the golden age. It is in effect a millennarian movement. So it is not surprising that the figures linked to the coming of the Buddha Maitreya were five hundred, one thousand or fifteen hundred years, from that of the Buddha. That Mahāyāna Buddhism in northern India was also in dialogue with Zoroastrianism, Christianity and Manichaeism could point to some rub off of millennarian ideas from these onto Buddhism. Visions of heaven and hell also became prominent in Mahāyāna Buddhist writing. Descriptions of one celestial paradise depict it as prosperous and fertile, inhabited by gods and men, and filled with fragrant flowers, singing birds and gem-trees bearing the seven gems, with lotuses which were a *yojana* in size and emitting rays, from each of which a Buddha emanated, and

[94] *Digha Nikāya,* 3. 75 ff.

[95] J. Legge, *The Travels of Fa-hien,* Oxford 1886, 110.

there were also vast rivers of fragrant waters — a scene of almost psychedelic glory.[96]

Millennarian and messianic ideas have more evident forms where the eschatology is linear, but they do not necessarily have to be rooted in prophetic-type religions, for the coming of the saviour can also be related to cyclic time concepts. A parallel to the Buddha Maitreya, though perhaps of a more messianic kind, was the tenth *avatāra* of Viṣṇu — Kalkin. In the *Viṣṇu Purāṇa,* the Kali age is associated with a reduction in the prevalence of *dharma,* a reversal of social norms and the exploitation by avaricious rulers of the people through taxes and other burdens. People will therefore flee to the mountains and live the life of food-gatherers. Forest dwellers had earlier, in the same chapter, been dismissed as being beyond the boundaries of caste society. However, in this case, those who had been members of a better society were reduced to a primitive existence. It is curious that this retreat of the population into subsistance seems to be the contrastive pre-condition to the return of the golden age, in both Buddhist and Brahmanical visions of the future.

The *Viṣṇu Purāṇa* states that the coming of Kalkin will occur towards the end of the Kaliyuga and will usher in the new cycle beginning with the age of virtue. He will destroy the *mlecchas,* the low-caste rulers and the heretics, and re-establish the authority of the *brāhmaṇas.*[97] He will of course be a *brāhmaṇa* himself ! The Kaliyuga is recognized as being different from other ages and requiring the constant intercession of Viṣṇu in various *avatāras.* The compassionate tone of the Buddha Maitreya story contrasts sharply with the strident voice predicting the coming of Kalkin. Perhaps the difference lay in the restoration of the Buddhist *dharma* being the primary purpose of the coming of Maitreya, whereas Kalkin's concern was also to restore power and wealth to the upper castes.

[96] *Sukhāvatīvyuha,* 15 ff. For a discussion of the rationale of the particular seven gems, see Xinru Liu, *Ancient India and Ancient China,* Delhi 1988, 53ff.

[97] *Viṣṇu Purāṇa* 4. 24. 98ff.

In all these eschatologies, the golden age is at the beginning of the cycle and in some it returns when the cycle is completed and the next one begins. Descriptions of these utopias do not suggest the need for effort and labour. Thus in a Buddhist text, it is said of the Uttara-Kurus that they claimed no possessions either of wealth or of women, nor did they need to cultivate the land, for ripened grain was always naturally available.[98] Elsewhere the earth itself was said to be edible, or there were wish-fulfilling trees which provided all needs. But when the decline set in and utopian conditions diminished, the requirement for labour arose. This is associated with conflict between people over the division of society into families and access to food and fields. There is a relationship between time and the necessity to labour.[99]

A story is related in Buddhist texts about the election of the Mahāsammata — the great elected one, who became necessary in a period of decline when men and women fought over the instituting of families, over food and over the ownership of fields. The situation of constant conflict was resolved by electing a protector, and contracting rights and obligations.[100] In the Brahmanical view of the earliest age, there was neither a king nor punishment, but gradually human passions destroyed its perfection.[101] The office of the *rājā* had to be created to control the deterioration of social conditions. Here the recognition of decline does not call for the people electing a ruler but the gods appointing one and there is a contractual agreement between the appointee and the people. Utopian times are characterized by an absence of labour. The necessity to labour comes in periods of decline. Yet this is not

[98] *Dīgha Nikāya*, 3. 199, 7.

[99] E.P. Thompson, looking at the question of time and labour in a very different context, makes the point that the change brought by industrialization and capitalism introduced a new time discipline in England which moved away from traditional time. 'Time, Work, Discipline and Industrial Capitalism', *Past and Present*, 1967, 38, 56–97.

[100] *Dīgha Nikāya*, 3. 85 ff.

[101] *Mahābhārata*, Śāntiparvan, 59. 13ff.

an absolute criteria for labour, especially where labour is also linked to moral values. Those who constructed these utopias were either *brāhmaṇas* or Buddhist and Jaina monks, none of whom were labouring men. In theory the Buddhist *bhikkhu* did labour but it was of a different kind since it centred on the concerns of the renouncer and renunciation ideally abandoned or reduced to a minimum both time and labour. But then, the elimination of the need to labour is characteristic of many utopias, including the Judaeo-Christian.

Judaeo-Christian eschatology propounded the initial paradise of the garden of Eden and the trajectory of time terminated with the paradise in heaven, at least for those fortunate enough to have a judgement in their favour. This was a rejection of the earlier cyclic theory of the ancient Greeks. Medieval Christian theology was averse to cyclical theories. Only the Greek concept of eternity with its endless duration of seamless time, enters Christian eschatology.[102] Yet curiously, in the modern transposing of linear time as an essential component of historical consciousness, the cyclic cosmology of the Greeks was segregated from their historical writing. In this case, cyclic time was not seen as negating history. Thus, a refusal of history through recourse to cyclic time was identified more frequently with colonial cultures.

This might explain the reluctance and even the dismissal of attempts to enquire into how these concepts of time were constructed, after the failure of the initial attempts to comprehend them. H.H. Wilson, among the more respected Indologists of the nineteenth century, commenting on the description of time in the *Viṣṇu Purāṇa*, makes a telling statement. 'It does not seem necessary to refer the invention (of time) to any astronomical computations or to any attempt to represent actual chronology.'[103]

Had the initial enquiry been pursued, the links between astronomical computations and the grand design of cyclic

[102] R. Sorabji, *Time, Creation and the Continuum*, London 1983, 98ff; 182ff.
[103] *Viṣṇu Purāṇa*, trans. H.H. Wilson, 22, n.4.

time as well as the more mundane time reckonings of historical chronology would have become more visible. The shading away of myth from history was also sometimes articulated in categories of time. The simultaneous use of different categories of time is symbolic of registering historical change and priorities in historical functioning. These differentiations, it seems to me, are significant, not merely because we in the twentieth century are analysing past concepts of time, but because there was a reason in the past for making these differentiations.

The characterizing of societies as using either cyclic or linear time is an inadequate explanation for the centrality or otherwise of history. Research, even into European history, has endorsed various categories of historical time and to that extent has distanced itself from the earlier single category. Time, as conceived in cosmology or eschatology, does not exclude the use of other categories of time and these can be simultaneous in the same society. It seems more appropriate to enquire into how a society uses a particular category and what is being intended by that use. Thus the statements which each form of time reckoning are making are not identical. The inclusion of cyclic time is not a characteristic of cultures which are historically stunted but an indication of historical complexity. This complexity is reflected in the perceptions of the past in pre-modern times, the premises of which were different from the writing of history today.

This attempt at an exploration of time and history is not just an exercise in intellectual curiosity. In questioning the presuppositions about societies and cultures as they have been conceptualized in the historiography of recent times, it becomes necessary to enquire into many facets of the past. I have tried to argue that even concepts of time in early India, as read by earlier scholars, need to be interpreted afresh. Our readings both of time and of history have undergone mutations. But the metaphor remains.

Bibliography

PRIMARY SOURCES

Alberuni. Sachau, E.C. (trans.), *Alberuni's India*, Delhi 1964 (reprint).

Ālhā-Khaṇḍa, Waterfield, W., *The Lay of Alha*, Gurgaon 1990 (reprint).

Aṅguttara-nikāya, Morris, R. and Hardy, E. (eds.), P.T.S., London 1976 (reprint).

Arrian, *Indika*, McCrindle, J.W. (trans.), *Ancient India as Described by Megasthenes and Arrian*, London 1877.

Atharva Veda Saṁhitā, Vishvabandhu (ed.), Hoshiarpur 1960–2.

Baudhāyana Dharma-sūtra, Hultzsch, E. (ed.), Leipzig 1884.

Bhagavad-gītā, Zaehner, R.C. (ed.), *The Bhagavad-gītā*, Oxford 1975 (reprint).

Bloch, J., *Les Inscriptions d'Asoka*, Paris 1950.

Chandbardai, *Pṛthvirājarāso*, Mohan Singh (ed.), Udaipur 1965.

Dīgha-nikāya, Rhys Davids, T.W. *et al.* (eds.), P.T.S., London 1975 (reprint).

Epigraphia Indica.

Fa-Hien. Legge J., *The Travels of Fâ-hien*, Oxford 1886.

Kalhaṇa, *Rājataraṅginī*, Stein, M.A. (ed.), London 1892; (trans.) London 1900.

Kauṭilīya, Arthaśāstra, Kangle, R.P. (ed. and trans.), University of Bombay, 1965.

Mahābhārata, Sukthankar, V.S. *et al.* (eds.), B.O.R.I., Poona 1933.

Manu Dharma Śāstra, Motwani, K. (ed.), Madras 1959 (trans.) Bühler, G., *The Laws of Manu*, Varanasi 1967 (reprint).

Matsya Purāṇa, Poona, Anandasram Sanskrit Series, 1907.

Paumacariyam, Jacobi, H., (ed.) Varanasi 1962.

Pliny, *Natural History*, London 1938.

Ṛg Veda Saṃhitā, Max Müller F. (ed.), Varanasi 1966 (reprint).

Saṃyutta-nikāya, Rhys Davids, C. and Woodward, F.L. (trans.), P.T.S., London 1918–30.

Śatapatha Brāhmaṇa, 5 vols., L.V.S. Press, Bombay 1940.

Upaniṣads. Radhakrishnan, S., (ed.) *The Principal Upaniṣads*, London 1953.

Varāhamihira, *Bṛhatsaṁhitā*, M. Ramakrishna Bhat (ed.), Varanasi 1981.

Viṣṇu Purāṇa, Gita Press, Gorakhpur, V.S. 1990.

Wilson, H.H. (trans.), *Vishnu Purana*, Calcutta 1961.

SECONDARY SOURCES

Articles

Bentley, J., 'Remarks on the Principal Eras and Dates of the Ancient Hindus', *Asiatic Researches*, 1808, vol. 8, 315ff.

———, 'On the Hindu System of Astronomy', *Asiatic Researches*, London 1809, vol. 8., 195ff.

Bivar, A. D. H., 'The Azes Era and the Indravarma Casket', *South Asian Archaeology, 1979*, Berlin 1981, pp. 369–76.

Cardona, G., 'A Path Still Taken: Some Early Indian Arguments', *Journal of the American Oriental Society*, New York, 1991, 3, 3, pp. 445–64.

Colebrooke, H., 'Hindu Astronomy', *Asiatic Journal*, 1826, 21, 360ff.

Davies, S., 'On the Indian Cycle of Sixty Years', *Asiatic Researches*, 1794, vol. 3, 289ff.

Eliade, M., 'Time and Eternity in Indian Thought', *Man in Time*, Princeton University, New Jersery, Bollinger series xxx, p. 3.

Fleet, J. F., 'The Kaliyuga of 3102 BC', *Journal of the Royal Asiatic Society of Great Britain and Ireland*, 1911, pp. 479–96, and 675–98.

Fussman, G., 'Nouvelles inscriptions Śaka: ère d'Eucratide, ère d'Azes, ère Vikrama, ère de Kaniṣka', *BEFEO*, 1980, 67, pp. 1–43.

Inden, R., 'Orientalist Construction of India', *Modern Asian Studies,* 1986, 20, 3, pp. 401–46.

Jones, William, 'The Third Discourse', *Asiatic Researches,* vol. 1, 1789, p. 354.

Kielhorn, F., 'Examination of Questions Connected with the Vikram Era', *The Indian Antiquary,* 1891, 20, pp. 397–414.

Krishan, Y., 'The Astronomical Revolution in India about AD 400 and its Implications', *Vishveshvaranand Indological Journal,* Hoshiarpur, 1977, 15, 2, pp. 265–84.

Nakamura, H., 'Time in Indian and Japanese Thought', in Fraser, J.T. (ed.), *The Voices of Time,* London, 1986.

Perera, L.H., 'The Pali Chronicles of Ceylon', in Philips, C.H., (ed.) *Historians of India, Pakistan and Ceylon,* London 1961.

Pingree, D., 'Astronomy and Astrology in India and Iran', *ISIS,* 1963, 54, 2, pp. 176, 229–46.

———, 'The Purāṇas and Jyotiḥśāstra: Astronomy', *Journal of the American Oriental Society,* 1990, 110, 2, p. 275.

Sen, S.N., 'Astronomy', in Bose, D.M. *et al.* (eds.), *A Concise History of Science in India,* New Delhi, 1971. p, 81.

Sukhthankar, V.S., 'The Bhṛgus and the Bhārata, a Text Historical Study', *Annals of the Bhandarkar Oriental Research Institute,* 18, pp. 1–76.

Thapar, Romila, 'Genealogical Patterns as Perceptions of the Past', *Studies in History,* 1971, N.S. 7,1, pp.1–36.

———, 'Society and Historical Consciousness: the Itihāsa-Purāṇa Tradition', in Bhattacharya, S. and Thapar, Romila (eds.), *Situating Indian History,* Delhi 1986, pp. 353–83.

Thompson, E.P., 'Time, Work, Discipline and Industrial Capitalism', *Past and Present,* 1967, 38, pp. 56–97.

Wilford, F., 'On the Chronology of the Hindus', *Asiatic Researches,* vol. 5, 1808, 241 ff.

Woodburn, J., 'Egalitarian Societies', *Man,* N.S. 1982, 17, pp. 431–51.

MONOGRAPHS

Bakker, F. L., *The struggles of the Hindu Balinese Intellectuals,* Amsterdam, 1993.

Balslev, A. N., *A Study of Time in Indian Philosophy*, Wiesbaden, 1983.

Basham, A. L., *The Wonder that Was India*, London 1954.

———, *History and Doctrine of the Ājīvikas*, London 1951.

Bechert, H. (ed.), *The Dating of the Historical Buddha*, 2 vols., Göttingen 1991.

Bhattacharya, S. and Thapar, Romila (eds.), *Situating Indian History*, Delhi 1986.

Bose, D. M. *et al.* (eds.), *A Concise History of Science in India*, New Delhi 1971.

Chandra, K.R., *A Critical Study of Paumacariyam*, Vaisali 1970.

Coomaraswamy, A.K., *Time and Eternity*, Ascona 1947.

Cumont, F., *Astrology and Religion among Greeks and Romans*, New York, 1960 (reprint).

Eliade, M., *Cosmos and History: the Myth of the Eternal Return*, New York 1959.

Fabian, J., *Time and the Other*, New York 1983.

Fraser, J.T., *The Voices of Time*, London 1986.

Ghosh, A. (ed.), *Jaina Art and Architecture*, 3 vols., New Delhi 1974–5.

Goldman, R.P., *Gods, Priests and Warriors*, New York 1977.

Halbfass, W., *On Being and What There Is*, New York 1977.

Kane, P.V., *History of Dharmaśāstra*, vols. 1–5, Poona 1958.

Lambert, W.G. and Millard, A.R., *Atrahasis*, Oxford 1969.

Liu Xinru, *Ancient India and Ancient China*, Delhi 1988.

Mandal, K. K., *A Comparative Study of the Concepts of Space and Time in Indian Thought*, Varanasi 1968.

Mill, James, *The History of British India*, vol. 1, London 1958, 5th ed.

Mitchiner, J.E., *The Yuga Purāṇa*, Delhi 1986.

Norman Brown, W., *Man in the Universe*, Berkeley 1966.

Pargiter, F.E., *The Purāna Texts of the Dynasties of the Kali Age*, Delhi 1975 (reprint).

———, *Ancient Indian Historical Tradition*, London 1922.

Pathak, V.S., *Ancient Historians of India*, Bombay 1966.

Philips, C.H., (ed.) *Historians of India, Pakistan and Ceylon*, London 1961.

Pingree, D., *Yavanajātaka of Sphujidhvaja*, Cambridge Mass., 1978.

———, *Jyotiḥśāstra*, Wiesbaden 1981.

Schnabel, P., *Berossos und die Babylonisch-Hellenistische Literatur*, Leipzig 1923.

Schwab, R., *La Renaissance Orientale*, Paris 1950.

Sircar, D.C., *Studies in the Yuga Purāṇa and Other Texts*, Delhi 1964.

———, *Indian Epigraphy*, Delhi 1965.

Sorabji, R., *Time, Creation and the Continuum*, London 1983.

Stevenson, S., *The Heart of Jainism*, Delhi 1970 (reprint).

Thapar, Romila, *Clans, Caste and Origin Myths in Early India*, Simla 1992.

———, *From Lineage to State*, Delhi 1984.

Toulmin, S. and Goodfield, J., *The Discovery of Time*, Harmondsworth 1967.

Vogel, J. Ph., *Antiquities of Chamba State*, Calcutta 1911.

Warder, A.K., *An Introduction to Indian Historiography*, Bombay 1972.

Index

Cultural Transaction and Early India

CULTURAL TRANSACTION AND EARLY INDIA: TRADITION AND PATRONAGE

CONTENTS

PREFACE

The two lectures which follow were given as the I. H. Qureishi Memorial Lectures for 1987 at St. Stephen's College, Delhi University, on 22 and 23 January 1987. I would like to thank my colleague Professor K. N. Panikkar for his comments on an earlier draft.

New Delhi
May 1987

Romila Thapar

1. TRADITION

A variety of beliefs about India's past have simmered over the last couple of hundred years. Some among them have come to be accepted as part of the country's cultural tradition and have been accorded the status of tradition. It may be argued that this happens when societies are searching for identity and the pronouncements of historians, particularly of cultural historians, come to be accepted as axioms. It becomes necessary therefore for historians to pause from time to time, to take stock as it were by asking whether what has come to be accepted as tradition deserves to be so accepted. This is what I propose to attempt in the two lectures. The change of focus becomes imperative either when there is new information on the past or when the process of interpreting the past undergoes change. It is primarily the latter which in this case suggests a re-assessment.

A consideration of cultural history would have to begin with an attempt at defining culture and this has been the subject of much discussion in recent decades. I can at best attempt a very brief summary.

The term culture itself has its own history. The primary meaning of culture is the cultivating of natural growth and by extension in recent times it has come to mean the cultivating of the human mind. Among historians of the eighteenth and nineteenth centuries culture and civilization became synonymous. The association of culture was however with superior social groups. The inadequacy of this limitation contributed towards the redefinition of the term in which it was extended to include all patterns of behaviour and ways of life. Culture therefore refers to behaviour patterns socially acquired and socially transmitted by means of symbols. It includes language, tradition, customs and institutions. It is in this wider sense that I am using the term.

Furthermore, culture in relation to tradition links the past to the present. It has therefore a historical context which is as significant as the cultural form itself.

The historical process is decisive to the definition of culture, yet the understanding of Indian culture is poorly served in this respect, for it is assumed that the historical process has a static interpretation and has remained broadly unchanged over the last century, or, that culture is a one-time event which has survived untampered with from the past to the present. From newspaper editors to prime ministers everyone pronounces on the civilization and culture of the Indian past, unblushingly unconcerned with their historical basis. There are now, at least among historians, new kinds of analyses of cultural institutions and forms. Cultural history and its analysis juxtaposes the form with those who create it and those who order its creation, and also attempts to see it as a social signal.

The continuity of culture is generally related to traditions which, in turn, are made up of cultural forms. Tradition is defined as the handing down of knowledge or the passing on of a doctrine or a technique. Cultural history implies looking analytically both at what goes into the making of a tradition as well as that which is interpreted by historians as tradition. We often assume that a form is handed down in an unchanging fashion and that what comes to us is its pristine form. However, the sheer act of handing on a tradition introduces change, and not every tradition is meticulously bonded by mnemonic or other devices to prevent interpolations or change. A tradition, therefore, has to be seen in its various phases. Even the concept of *paramparā*, which at one level appears to be frozen knowledge, reveals on investigation variations and change. Traditions which we today believe have long pedigrees may on an historical analysis be found to be an invention of yesterday. In other words, what we regard as tradition may well turn out to be our contemporary requirements fashioned by the way we wish to interpret the past. Interpretations of the past have also come to be treated as knowledge and are handed down as tradition. I would like to consider some of these interpretations in their historical context, for this may clarify their validity or otherwise to being regarded as tradition.

Let me illustrate these ideas with a few examples.

The disjuncture between normative values and social reality is often so evident that it is sometimes surprising to come across normative values being taken for descriptions of reality. But it is necessary to distinguish between the organization of external reality as a theory and the reality itself. Thus, the *dharmaśāstras*, the normative texts *par excellence*, inform us of the rules of *varṇa*. It is assumed that at least the members of the higher *varṇa* observe these rules. However, from the earliest times there are certain discrepancies. The Vedic texts refer to various important Vedic *brāhmaṇas* as *dāsīputraḥ,* being born of *dāsīs.*[1] Dīrghatamas, married a *dāsī* whom he is said to have found among strange people in the east, and she was mother to his son, the respected Kakṣīvant. Evidently these *brāhmaṇas* took the rule of exogamy literally and married far out. But equally intriguing is the origin of the compiler of the *Mahābhārata,* the learned Veda Vyāsa. His father, the *ṛṣi* Parāśara, became enamoured of a girl of a fisherman's community as she rowed him across the river. Despite her fishy odour he made his intentions clear. She resisted him at first, but finally accepted his advances when he promised that she would be rid of the odour of fish. The boat was enveloped in a discreet curtain of clouds and the now sweet-scented girl eventually gave birth to Veda Vyāsa. The ambiguity of his mother's origins are further complicated by the story that she had been an *apsarā's* daughter abandoned as a foundling among fisher folk.[2] And this becomes a stereotype among such origin myths, raising a host of questions regarding the treatment of identity.

How are we to interpret this? First of all, and certainly, that our ancestors had a sense of humour and were willing to invent stories about these lapses from the normative perspective of even those whom they revered—a quality which is difficult to find in contemporary India, for such stories would be unheard of today. But what is more important, and once we get past the symbolic meaning, is that origins obviously do not have to conform to normative rules and were possibly not very significant.

This is even more marked in the origin myths of a variety of royal families claiming *kṣatriya* status in the post-Gupta period.[3] Prior to the Gupta dynasty the *Purāṇas* refer to such families being of *brāhmaṇa* and even *śūdra* origin. Few in fact were *kṣatriya* in spite of the insistence of the normative texts on the *kṣatriya* origins of ruling families. The myths of many such families of the later period, as those of the Guhilla and Candella, make one suspect that the families may have been obscure and that they sought status through fabricated genealogies, linking them to the Sūryavaṃśa and Candravaṃśa lineages, which lineages seem also to have been an invention of a particular historical time.

[1] *Pañcaviṃśa Brāhmaṇa* 14.6.6; *Bṛhad-devatā*, 4.11–15; 21.15; *Ṛg Veda* 1.58

[2] *Mahābhārata*, Ādi parvan, 57.56.

[3] Romila Thapar, 'Genealogy as a Source of Social History', in *Ancient Indian Social History: Some Interpretations*, New Delhi 1978, pp. 326–60.

In shying away from coming to terms with this divergence, we blind ourselves to the possible flexibility of a society which, in certain situations, was probably as important a characteristic as the theoretical insistence on the minutae of rules of social behaviour. We thereby provide a simplistic explanation for a complex arrangement. The concession to the *brāhmaṇa* that he could marry into any *varṇa* was, in some ways, parallel to the incorporation of belief and ritual from a variety of sources in the making of religious sects—an incorporation which defies the forcing of what we call Hindu sects into a homogenous, uniform, clearly identifiable and ecclesiastically organized religious entity. This epitomizes a perspective different from that of the Judaeo-Christian and Islamic model.

But how are we to interpret high culture literature which mocks the *brāhmaṇa*? In the plays of Kālidāsa the *vidūṣaka*—the stereotype of companion or fool—is a *brāhmaṇa* not speaking Sanskrit and mocking the essence of brahmanism as contained in the *dharmaśāstras*. The normative texts, of course, do not carry even a hint of the *vidūṣaka* as a category of *brāhmaṇa*. Admittedly, in a literature intended for the royal court the foil to the king could only be a *brāhmaṇa*, since a member of another caste would amount to *lèse majestie*. But did he have to be such a non-brahmanical *brāhmaṇa* that even the king mocks the *brāhmaṇa* in him? Was this an ironic commentary on the *purohita* or on particular categories of *brāhmaṇa* elsewhere taken more seriously? So distinct a contravention of the norm can only point to the norm not being pervasive.

Talking of Kālidāsa, we assume that his version of the story of Śakuntalā was the one made familiar to people of all ages since the writing of the play. Yet Kālidāsa was himself taking an existing tradition and transforming it into something new and in keeping with his own time and place. There were two versions of the Śakuntalā story in circulation with two different audiences. The earlier version occurs in the *Mahābhārata*, where the origin myth of the founder of the Pūru lineage, Bharata, is recited.[4] The story begins with a massive hunt led by the *rājā* Duḥṣanta, where we are told that many families of tigers were laid low and many hundreds of deer killed. The hunt, as hunts in epic literature often are, is a war against nature, causing havoc and destruction all round. Arriving at the hermitage of Kaṇva, Duḥsanta is welcomed in the absence of the *ṛṣi* by Śakuntalā, who

[4] *Mahābhārata*, Ādi parvan, 63 ff.

happily converses with him without any reservation. When asked about her parentage she explains that she is the natural child of the *apsarā* Menakā and the *ṛṣi* Viśvāmitra and was left a foundling at the hermitage of Kaṇva. When Duḥṣanta, attracted by her beauty, proposes a *gāndharva* marriage, she replies in a spirited fashion that she will agree only on condition that her son is declared the *yuvarāja*, which condition Duḥṣanta accepts. A few years later she arrives at his court with their son Bharata. Although he recognizes her, Duḥṣanta pretends not to know her and, even as she argues her rights, he abuses her parents, referring to Menakā as a slut and to Viśvāmitra as a lecher, and dismisses her as a whore. Whereupon a celestial voice proclaims that the boy is in fact the child of Duḥṣanta. He then accepts both mother and son, maintaining that his earlier pretence was merely to ensure that the legitimacy of the child would be declared before his people. The story may well have been introduced as a form of genealogical latching on.

Kālidāsa introduces the sub-plot of the signet ring which drops off Śakuntalā's finger; and Duḥṣyanta (as the name occurs in Kālidāsa), loses his memory owing to a curse and does not remember the association with Śakuntalā until he sees the signet ring. In effect, the feel of the play is completely different from the epic version of the story.

Śakuntalā in the epic is a confident, high-spirited, assertive young woman who knows what she is about and is not going to be taken for a ride. In the play she is submissive, shy, reserved, perhaps even a little frightened and cowed down by her love for the king. She is the new subservient woman of upper caste courtly culture who is incapable of arguing in defence of her rights or objecting to the treatment by Duḥṣyanta. Kālidāsa has invested Śakuntalā with status. The king's major concern is the need for an heir, unlike in the epic where it is Śakuntalā who is anxious that her son be declared the *yuvarāja*. Today, we have accepted Kālidāsa's depiction of the submissive woman and have ignored the far more independent characterization of the epic version, in part at least, for reasons which have to do with attempts to justify the subservience of women with an appeal to what is regarded as 'our tradition'.

Even within the tradition, the image of Śakuntalā was not universally that of the Kālidāsa play. A larger number of people were familiar with the recitation of the *Mahābhārata* version and the epic character was better known. The heroine of the play would traditionally have had a limited audience.

The play focuses on the contrast between two backgrounds, that of the forest and the court. The hermitage, which in a sense mediates between the two, is set in a natural environment where social behaviour is in accordance with the gentleness of nature. The court is a structured background with little of nature intervening and is alien to the forest. This contrast is a repeated theme in early Indian writing. The dichotomy of the *grāma* and the *aranya* represent the two poles of the settlement and the wilderness, of order and disorder, of the known and the unknown.

Normative texts and creative literature differ in the handling of those who live in the hermitage. The normative curriculum refers, of course, only to males of the upper caste and requires a life cycle which covers the well-known four stages of studentship, householder, renouncer and ascetic. Written into this life cycle is the opposition of *gṛhastha* to *samnyāsa*, of householder to ascetic.[5] The brahmanical system insists on the fulfillment of the social obligations of a householder, that is, a gainful occupation and the procreation of a family, before renunciation can be thought of. In the Buddhist and Jaina systems renunciation or the entry to monkhood was open at any point in life. The brahmanical system reflects the fear that renunciation at an early age may upset the requirements of society and that the true value of renunciation comes after a socially fulfilled life. That the good *gṛhastha* also had many obligations towards the welfare of the *brāhmaṇas* should not be forgotten.

Generally, descriptions of the *āśrama* in creative literature do not depict a place of austere practices. They tend to be forest retreats set in sylvan surroundings with an emphasis on empathy with nature. That hermits had technically broken away from social obligations meant that they had no more to do with the *grāma* and were at one with the *aranya*. But somehow this did not preclude them from observing social regulations when required to do so.

Above all, through the act of renunciation and the practice of *yoga*, *tapasya* and *dhyāna*, the renouncer was believed to acquire supernormal powers. In the normative tradition renunciation was the prelude to asceticism and the means of achieving release from rebirth. The distance from society was intended to underline the need for isolation and contemplation in pursuit of this goal. In a sense it was a

[5] Romila Thapar, 'Householders and Renouncers in the Brahmanical and Buddhist Tradition', in T. N. Madan (ed.), *Way of Life*, New Delhi, 1982, pp. 273–98.

selfish act in as much as it was a-social. In effect, however, as is clear from descriptive passages referring to asceticism, the supernormal powers became an asset on which the power of the ascetic was based. It was this which enables the *ṛṣi* to acquire extra-sensory knowledge, to fly through the air, to destroy through a curse or to grant boons. In the non-normative texts the *ṛṣi* acquires the same powers as the gods, and frequently the gods fear the power of the *ṛṣi* and try to break it, as was done successfully in the case of Viśvāmitra by sending Menakā to seduce him. It would seem that at one level renunciation and the renouncer became an alternative avenue of authority in the popular mind which even kings had to accept.

This was not the power of religion, since the *ṛṣi* was not a religious functionary and was not concerned with priestly activities. At the root of his power lay the ability of the renouncer to break away from society and to contravene the normative rules of social behaviour. The case of the ascetic or *samnyāsi* was more extreme, since he had to have his death rituals performed before he could take up *samnyāsa* signifying a complete break with his house-holding functions. This may in part explain why the renouncer often emerged as the symbol of dissent and protest and came to be regarded as an alternative source of power, a symbolism which has been respected even in the Indian political movements of the twentieth century. The renouncer cannot be explained away in the simplistic formula of being a religious leader since he accumulates in himself a complex inter-relation of social signals.[6] As a source of alternative authority the renouncer is distinct from both priestly power and the coercive authority of the state. The socio-political role of the renouncer is, it seems to me, a characteristic feature of Indian civilization and requires a more thorough analysis. This would question the notion that Indian society has always been other-worldly because of the attraction of renunciation. Instead, it requires that we examine more analytically the many dimensions to the role of the renouncer in society.

The institutionalizing of renunciation developed early among the Buddhists, Jainas and a variety of non-brahmanical sects referred to as Śramaṇas. Individual salvation, it was argued, was more easily obtained through renunciation and joining the *saṅgha* or Order—a parallel or alternative society demanding the termination of social

[6] Romila Thapar, 'Renunciation: the making of a Counter-Culture?' in *Ancient Indian Social History: Some Interpretations*, New Delhi, 1978, pp. 63–104.

obligations at a personal level. But few of these renouncers cut themselves off completely. Most lived in the proximity of settlements, for it was enjoined upon the lay follower that he had to support monks with alms and gifts. Such acts would earn merit for the lay follower, and this accumulation of merit would assist him in his own salvation. The obligation to support the renouncer not only strengthened the *saṅgha* as an institution but also created a sense of community among lay followers. This sense of community was a contrast to the idea of *varṇāśramadharma*. *Varṇa* was the apparatus of segregation and of cordoning off groups. Buddhist social thought was more inclusive in that it cut across caste segments, and in worship and belief, at least, referred to a more universal ethic applicable to almost all. It was a community essentially of monks extended to lay followers, but not separated into castes. This sense of community may have had something to do with the aggressive hostility meted out to Buddhists and Jainas by various sects of what we have come to call the Hindu religion.

This hostility may account for the virtual weeding out of the alternative texts and perspectives, namely, those not in agreement with the brahmanical tradition, from what we now regard as our cultural heritage. Soon after the time when the secular epic the *Rāmāyaṇa* had been converted into sacred Vaiṣṇava literature by the Bhārgava *brāhmaṇas* and the hero Rāma had been recorded as an *avatāra* of Viṣṇu, a Jaina poet, Vimalasūri, in the early centuries A.D. wrote his version of the *Rāmāyaṇa* in Prākrit, the *Paumacariyam*. It is the first of a number of Jaina versions of the *Rāmāyaṇa*, and the persistence with which the theme of what they referred to as the true *Rāmāyaṇa* was taken up, suggests that the Jaina authors had something significant to say. Vimalasūri states specifically that his is the true version as against that of the *brāhmaṇas* which is a collection of falsehoods. The broad outlines of the story are similar, but there is a significantly different treatment of Rāvaṇa and the *rākṣasas*. It is clearly stated that the *rākṣasas* are not demons and that the word is linked to the root *rakṣ*, to protect. Rāvaṇa was neither ten-headed nor a meat-eating fiend, and all that has been said about him by foolish poets—*mukhakukavi*—is untrue.

Rāvaṇa is an ardent Jaina and a protector of Jaina shrines. Being an adept at ascetic practices, he has the ability to fly and is therefore called *ākāśamārgi*. His relationship with Sītā is sensitively portrayed as that of a man genuinely fond of her and upset by her rejection of him.

The austerity of exile is frequently punctuated by prosperous villages, beautiful cities and royal palaces. The theme of exile in all epic literature seeks to legitimize the association of various geographical places with the heroes of the epic. That there is a Rāma-kuṇḍ, Sītā-kuṇḍ and Pāṇḍava-lena in almost every part of the Indian subcontinent is not because the exiled heroes actually visited these areas, but because in later times, when the epics were appropriated as sacred literature in these areas, there was a desire to link local geography to the events of the epic. The theme of exile or wandering is a stereotype of epic literature and happily permits of this kind of association.

A striking difference in the *Paumacariyam* is the absence of the need to uphold the *varṇāśramadharma* and the status of the *brāhmaṇa*. Here the *brāhmaṇas* are the heretics and the preachers of false doctrines who acquired their status through fraud. The most respected social group other than princes are merchants, although maximum reverence is naturally given to the Jaina *munis*. Finally, both Daśaratha and Rāma renounce the world and the Jaina ethic triumphs over the *kṣatriya* ethic.

In many ways the *Paumacariyam* is the mirror image of the Vālmīki *Rāmāyaṇa* and a comparative study of the two would be most illuminating. Yet the *Paumacariyam* is dismissed as being a biased Jaina account, as though the Vālmīki version is unbiased. But the value of the *Paumacariyam* is that it presents an alternative picture growing out of an alternative system, even if it is an alternative system which has been successfully eroded from what we call our tradition.

I have already mentioned that, in creating a tradition we sometimes select from the past those normative values which may have a contemporary appeal but which may even be contrary to historical actuality. The insistence on the tradition of religious tolerance and non-violence as characteristic of Hinduism, which is built on a selection of normative values emphasizing *ahiṃsā*, is not borne out by the historical evidence. The theory is so deeply ingrained among most Indians that there is a failure to see the reverse of it even when it stares them in the face. The extremity of intolerance implicit in the notion of untouchability was glossed over by regarding it as a function of society and caste. The fact of this intolerance is now conceded so casually, that the concession is almost beginning to lose meaning. Apart from this, we also need to look at more direct examples of religious persecution. Curiously, even when historians have referred to such activities as indications of intolerance and persecution,[7] there has been a firm refusal on the part of popular opinion to concede that Hindu sects did indulge in religious persecution.

The persecution of Buddhists in Kashmir is referred to by Hsüan Tsang, but, lest it be thought that he being a Chinese Buddhist monk was prejudiced, the testimony of Kalhaṇa in the *Rājataraṅgiṇī* should be more acceptable. Hsüan Tsang refers to the atrocities of Mihirakula against the Buddhists both in Punjab and in Kashmir in the sixth century A.D. Hsüan Tsang may well have been exaggerating when he lists the destruction of 1,600 Buddhist *stūpas* and *saṅghārāmas* and the killing of many thousands of Buddhist monks and lay-followers.[8] Kalhaṇa gives an even fuller account of the king killing innocent people by the hundreds.[9] This is often dismissed by attributing the anti-Buddhist actions of Mihirakula to his being a Hūna. But it should not be forgotten that he was also an ardent Śaiva and gave grants of land in the form of *agrahāras* to the *brāhmaṇas*. In the words of Kalhaṇa: 'Brahmans from Gandhāra resembling himself in their habits and verily themselves the lowest of the twice-born accepted *agrahāras* from him.' It is possible that the recently discovered *stūpa* at Sanghol in Punjab, where sculpted railings were found in the vicinity of a *stūpa* dismantled and packed away, indicates this persecution of the Buddhists. Kalhaṇa writes of an earlier persecution of Buddhists in Kashmir and the wilful destruction of a *vihāra*, again by a Śaivite king. But on this occasion the king repented and built a new monastery for the Buddhist monks.

Courtly literature, particularly plays written after the seventh century A.D., is replete with invective against Buddhist and Jaina monks who are depicted as morally depraved, dishonest and altogether what one might call the scum of the earth. Mahendravarman's *Maṭṭa-vilāsa*, a farce, is amongst the earliest plays. In the *Mudrārākṣasa* of Viśākhadatta, a constant refrain states that it is inauspicious to see a Jaina monk. The *Prabodha-candrodaya* of Kṛṣṇa Miśra, a drama of the eleventh century, dwells on the theme of a Kapālika converting a Jaina and a Buddhist monk to Śaivism by offering them wine and women, both of which they are said to hanker after. In the Śaiva temples at Khajuraho, Jaina monks, especially of the *digambara* sect,

[7] e.g. K. A. Nilakantha Sastri, *The Cholas*, Madras 1955, pp. 636, 645.

[8] *Si-yu-ki*- I. 168, 171.

[9] *Rājataraṅgiṇī*, I 289–307.

are depicted in the worst possible erotic poses.[10] Such references and depictions do not amount to persecution but reflect a contemptuous attitude towards Jaina and Buddhist monks which they would doubtless have found very galling, particularly as they occur in the literature and art of aristocratic groups. The depiction of monks and ascetics as debauched may have been due to the court's contempt for a variety of ascetics, some of whom were associated with socially unacceptable practices. Such depictions in courtly literature may also have been an attempt to play down the authority associated with renouncers and ascetics in the popular mind. But it is significant that the Buddhists and Jainas are more commonly made the subject of attack.

Evidence on the persecution of Jainas by Śaiva sects comes from a variety of sources. The earliest known cave temple originally dedicated by the Jainas in Tirunelveli district was, subsequently in the seventh century, converted into a Śaiva temple.[11] This was not a case of appropriating the temple and gradually changing it. Quite clearly, the Jaina images were either destroyed or erased, sometimes only partially, and fresh Śaivite images carved in the same place. In the case of the partially erased sculpture it is possible to recognize traces of the original. Where the image is totally gouged out the desecration is visible.

The Śaiva saint Jñāna Sambander is attributed with having converted the Pāṇḍya ruler from Jainism to Śaivism, whereupon it is said that eight thousand Jainas were impaled by the king. This episode is represented in painting and sculpture in medieval temples and is enacted to this day in some Śiva temples during their annual festival. In later times, royal patrons made attempts to appease the Jainas by building Jaina, Śaiva and Vaiṣṇava temples in close proximity. But in these areas the Jaina temples soon fell into disrepair whilst the other flourished.

Such activities were not restricted to a particular area. The Jaina temples of Karnataka went through a traumatic experience at the hands of the Lingāyatas or Vīraśaivas in the early second millennium A.D.[12]

[10] D. Desai, 'Placement and Significance of Erotic Sculptures at Khajuraho' in Michael Meister (ed.) *Discourses on Siva*, Bombay 1984, pp. 143–55.

[11] K. Vellaivaranan, *The First Seven Tirumunis*, Annamalai 1972, pp. 143–4; K. R. Srinivasan, 'South India', in A. Ghosh (ed.), *Jaina Art and Architecture*, Vol. II, New Delhi 1975; R. Champakalakshmi, 'Religious Conflict in the Tamil Country', *Journal of the Epigraphical Society of India*, Vol. IV, 1978.

[12] P. B. Desai, *Jainism in South India*, pp. 82–3, 101–2, 24.

This would explain in part why some Jaina texts have pejorative references to Basava, who founded the Vīraśaiva sect. The Jaina temples at Lakkuṇḍi were located in the proximity of an affluent *agrahāra* and the Vaiṣṇava *brāhmaṇas* accepted Mahāvīra as an incarnation of Brahmā. Later, however, one of the temples was converted into a Śaiva temple. At Huli, the temple of the five Jinas was converted into a *pañcaliṅgeśvara* Śaivite temple, the five *liṅgas* replacing the five Jina images in the *sancta*.[13] Some other Jaina temples suffered the same fate. An inscription at Ablur in Dharwar eulogizes attacks on Jaina temples as retaliation for Jaina opposition to Śaivite worship.[14] Sculpted panels at this site depict the smashing of Jaina images. In the fourteenth century the harassment of Jainas was so acute that they had to appeal for protection to the ruling power at Vijayanagara.

Inscriptions of the sixteenth century from the Srisailam area of Andhra Pradesh record the pride taken by Vīrasaiva chiefs in beheading *svetāmbara* Jainas.[15] The local records of this area refer to the frequent persecution of the Jainas. In Gujarat, Jainism flourished during the reign of Kumārapāla, but his successor persecuted the Jainas and destroyed their temples.[16] However, Jainism was so well-established here that periodical persecution did not really shake it.

My purpose in drawing attention to the Śaivite persecution of Buddhists and Jainas is not an attempt at being provocative. We have here a major historical problem which requires detailed investigation. The desire to portray tolerance and non-violence as the eternal values of the Hindu tradition has led to the pushing aside of such evidence. That there were mutual intellectual borrowings in certain philosophical schools should not prevent us from seeing the reality on the ground. If there were cases of diverse religious sects co-existing, there were also situations of antagonism. The evidence of persecution raises the question of the degree to which such activities on the part of various religious groups were seen as a way of claiming ascendancy and power.

A related question is whether the Hindus as a community were

[13] M. A. Dhaky, personal communication. See also James Burgess, Report of the First Season's operations in the Belgam and Kaladgi Districts, Jan. to May 1874, *ASWI*, No. 1, reprint Varanasi 1971, p. 12.

[14] *Epigraphia Indica*, V. p. 237.

[15] P. B. Desai, *Jainism in South India*.

[16] S. B. Deo, 'Expansion of Jainism', in A. Ghosh (ed.), *Jain Art and Architecture*, Vol. II.

aware of or perpetrated this hostility, or whether it was perpetrated only by a segment of the Hindu community, substantially the Śaivas. An historical evaluation of such persecutions would be required to ascertain the sects involved and their social affinities. If only certain segments of society, whether castes or sects, were involved, the effect of these on other segments would be worth inquiring into, as also the influence of religious militancy on the segment itself. Would these actions have had an impact on the values associated with the Hindu community, assuming, of course, that there was at this time the consciousness of a single Hindu community? The argument put forward in recent times that the Buddhists, Jainas and a variety of Hindu sects were all part of the compendium religion we call Hinduism has also contributed to these animosities being dismissed as minor sectarian rivalries, whereas the evidence points to a different assessment.

It is historically important to know why this persecution of the Buddhists and Jainas occurred in particular by the Śaivas. I can only offer a few comments. At the religious level, it may have had to do with asceticism. Was Śiva seen as the ascetic *par excellence* and the patron deity of ascetics, and were Buddhist and Jaina monks seen as imposters? Did Buddhist and Jaina monks find the worship of the *lingam* offensive owing to the puritanism inherent in both these systems? Yet the Tantric versions of these systems conceded to practices and ideas which were opposed to puritanism. If the hostility related only to religious differences, then it should have surfaced earlier in time. It is interesting that it begins about the middle of the first millennium A.D. and gains force through the centuries until Buddhism eventually fled the country and Jainism was effectively limited to a few pockets. The persecution predates the coming of Islam to these areas, so that the convenient excuse that Islamic persecution caused the decline of these religions is not applicable.

The rise of Śaiva and Vaiṣṇava sects was often tied to *bhakti*, and in the peninsula some sections of these sects were sometimes the agencies of intolerance. Was the relationship between the devotee and his deity so intense that it led to an inability to tolerate other forms of religious expression? *Bhakti* teachers appealed to professional groups which gradually became socially significant—not necessarily by rising in the social scale, but by mobilizing themselves as social entities. The social organization of these religious groups differed. Whereas the Buddhists and Jainas built upon a sense of community incorporating a universalizing ethic, Vaiṣṇava and Śaiva sects tended to be more narrowly demarcated. In a sense some of the contemporary Śaiva and Vaiṣṇava sects which emerged in the peninsula were protest movements articulating a new social identity, and this may have led to conflict. But this argument would not, of course, apply to the persecution of Buddhists in Kashmir. Here it appears to have been a confrontation between the Śramaṇas and the *brāhmaṇas,* drawing on a long history of earlier animosities and where the ruling groups were also involved. The hostility would have had to do with competition for royal patronage, apart from other factors. In the case of hostility between the Vīraśaivas and the Jainas it would seem that, among other things, it resulted from competition for commercial power and patronage and the hostilities were between social groups, with an appeal to the State for protection. By the late first millennium A.D. the Buddhists in eastern India, and the Jainas in Gujarat and the peninsula, had large monastic estates, or else the monasteries were financed from the revenue of a large number of villages assigned to them by royalty. Some of the hostility, therefore, may have arisen over the control of property. The Jainas in the peninsula were certainly a socially dominant group in competition with other similar groups. The recognition and analysis of intolerant behaviour would tell us something about the way in which social groups perceived each other.

I have been emphasizing Śaiva hostility, which is not to suggest that the Vaiṣṇavas were altogether partial to Buddhists and Jainas. But there seem to be fewer examples of persecution by the Vaiṣṇavas. This, too, requires an explanation. An obvious explanation is that the *avatāra* theory of Vaiṣṇavism made it an assimilative religion except, of course, that the incorporation of a cult was generally after it had been emasculated. Thus, the Buddha in some late texts came to be treated as an *avatāra* of Viṣṇu. The underlying strength of this religious induction was that the *avatāra* was a-historical, in other words, the historicity of the *avatāra* and his being located in space and time was irrelevant to the religious process. This was, of course, in striking contrast to the historicity of the founders of various Vaiṣṇava sects. Unlike contemporary Hindu movements today, which seek to find birth-places and historicity for the *avatāras* of Viṣṇu and even drag in archaeology in the attempt to prove this, such searches were of little concern to the majority of the Vaiṣṇavas in the past. It becomes pertinent, therefore, to inquire into the question of the period of history when the need for historicity enters belief in the *avatāras*, and why.

The persecution of Buddhists and Jainas was not a principal concern with all Hindu sects; nevertheless it was socially important enough to be recorded by some. If there had been a Hindu community with an all-India identity, it would have been aware of the intolerance of some of its constituents and pronounced upon it. That this intolerance is not characteristic of the entire community does not suggest the tolerance of Hindus, but, rather, that the consciousness of community determined by a religious identity, based on certain essential uniformities and cutting across segmental differences, may not have been prevalent.

The term 'Hindu' is used for the first time in Arabic sources referring to the inhabitants of the subcontinent across the Indus. For them it simply meant the indigenous. It does not appear to have been appropriated by those who constitute what we today call the Hindu community until very much later. The historical context suggests that it did not connote a specific identity but was intended to include those who were neither Muslim nor Christian. It would be worth investigating whether historically the label 'Hindu' became a convenient umbrella under which to include a large number of segments which lay outside the more identifiable followers of Islam and Christianity. In the case of Islam and Christianity the religious identity cut across caste and sectarian concerns. There was no such clear-cut religious identity among what have been called Hindu castes and sects where the caste and sectarian identity was primary. Perhaps it would be more appropriate to see the latter as separate communities. The putting together of these latter groups into what came to be seen as the Hindu community was however important to the process of nation-building in recent times.

The religious identity among groups which had constituted what has come to be called the Hindus was earlier a series of sectarian identities rather than one of a universalizing kind. Such an identity would require close and effective communication if action as a community was at stake. Even at the levels of the political elite, and given their use of a common language, Sanskrit, there appears to have been little communication. During the years when Rajendra Cola was campaigning in the south and the east, Mahmud of Ghazni was attacking the temple towns of north-western India. One would expect that this onslaught on Hinduism, as it is described today, would have found some reference in the court of one who was then the greatest Hindu king. However, such reflections are absent. What is equally curious is that the Kashmiri poet Bilhaṇa, the biographer of the

Cālukya king, Vikramāditya VI mentions in the concluding canto of the *Vikramānka-deva-carita* that he visited Somanātha, and goes on to make disparaging remarks about the local Gujaratis but makes no mention of the attack on the temple by Mahmud: and this biography was written about three generations after the attack. Are we not, then, perhaps exaggerating or being imprecise when we talk today about the existence of an all-India Hindu community during those times? There appear, instead, to have been a number of segments largely determined by caste, custom, language and region; and only at certain levels were religious identities recognizable as being similar. For the rest, caste identities probably were more significant and the religious belief systems and actions of particular castes may have had some common features. There was certainly geographical mobility among *brāhmaṇas* and a certain degree of universality among them too, but this was not a Hindu identity in the sense of enveloping people at all levels in all sects. Śankarācārya, for instance, organized a Śaivite *brāhmaṇa* identity which was only a segment of and did not include the totality of what is today called a Hindu identity. Even the observance of *varṇa-aśrama-dharma* remained a normative aspiration. Differences of language, customary law and worship kept the segments segregated.

It is important to differentiate between common civilizational symbols, which are recognized over an area, and the consciousness of a community acting towards common social and religious goals. Whereas the former was evident in India the latter appears not to have been so. It is also worth examining the possibly different role of the inter-relation between religion and society in such a caste and sect-based system. Historians have long looked at religions in India, whether indigenous or imported, from the perspective of the teachings of the texts. If religion in the past has to be properly understood, this obviously has to be related to the practice and perceptions of the religious groups. Tolerance and persecution has to do with such perceptions. It is worth noticing, for example, that in the early encounter between religious sects in India and Islam, Muslims were rarely referred to as such. The terms used were either ethnic—Turuṣka/Turk, or geographical—Yavana/West Asian, or the more generalized *mleccha*, meaning impure and covering a wide range of non-Muslims as well. This is a very different perception of 'the other' from what we have tried to make of it by postulating a society divided into Hindus and Muslims.

The Hindu community as an all-India phenomenon identifying

itself as a large community encompassing all aspects of 'Hindu' belief and worship appears to have been a development of recent centuries. The notion may well have been encouraged not only by the adoption of the label 'Hindu', but also by the use of this label by Orientalist scholarship, which attempted to format Hinduism as an historically evolved religion along the lines of Christianity, and by the demands of political representation as they emerged in the nineteenth century. Here the term Hindu connotes effectively the capturing and claiming of almost all religious belief and practice other than that associated with Islam and Christianity. It bunches together a range of religious sects, some so antithetical to each other that it is difficult to accept them under one label. This perhaps also explains the ease with which that pre-eminent institution, the Ramakrishna Mission, can claim to be both Hindu and non-Hindu.

For such a diverse community to create a uniform cultural tradition for itself can become an exercise in juggling with history. Traditions are not self-created: they are consciously chosen, and the choice from the past is enormous. We tend, therefore, to choose that which suits our present needs. The choice has its own logic and we are perhaps not fully aware of the directions which such choices may take. If we are to understand the role of religion in the Indian society of earlier times we may have to move away from the paradigm of Hinduism and the other religions in India as projected in the colonial period. There has to be an awareness of social relations actually experienced and the representation of these by particular social groups. In the search for a cultural tradition Hindus turn to normative texts and the brahmanical tradition as the exemplars from the past. This has the advantage that it acts as a kind of all-purpose Sanskritization. But it excludes a large range of both valuable and essential cultural experience. Complex societies have competing value systems and attempts are made by the more established to delete ideologies of protest or of divergent values, as I have tried to show. The awareness of the historical context of a cultural form or an ideological supposition may help us understand that cultural forms change their function over time, both through the internal development of the form and through the imprint of external factors. In other words, cultural forms are embedded in social realities and when we consciously choose a cultural form we should be aware of this reality. It is only then that the choice becomes intelligible.

In this lecture I have attempted to show that we have a variety of beliefs about India's past which have been projected as part of our cultural traditions. We speak of a well-regulated society characterized in all cases by an observance of caste rules, but we pay less attention to instances where these rules were not observed. The latter would go contrary to the tradition, but would provide insights into nuances of social dispositions and perhaps foster a variant tradition about the functioning of society. We see the tradition of renunciation largely as a search for individual salvation with an emphasis on the value of other-worldliness, but miss out the importance of the seemingly contradictory role of the renouncer as a figure of authority in society. We insist on the tradition of tolerance and non-violence as an essential feature of Hindu practice and, by neglecting the evidence to the contrary, diminish our understanding of the religious and social inter-relations of a major part of India's cultural past. This aspect would be further illuminated if we had a more precise historical view of at least the concept of community, instead of assuming its existence in a particular form from earlier times. Communities in contemporary India, be they Hindu, Muslim, Sikh, Christian or whatever, seek legitimacy by asserting a long history for their existence. This claim relates closely to our understanding of a secular society in the present. A more precise comprehension of the community in Indian history would clarify some of the problems of the present day as well. Our understanding of all these institutions from the past is closely related to our perceptions of ourselves in the present. It is imperative therefore that historical legitimacy should not be given arbitrarily without first ascertaining its historical viability.

2. PATRONAGE

In the previous lecture I tried to relate the notion of what we accept as cultural traditions to the historical process within which they have to be viewed. I would now like to take up a few cultural symbols which have conventionally gone into the making of what we regard as some of India's cultural traditions, and look more closely at the levels of meaning which inhere to such symbols. This category of cultural symbols presupposes the creator of the form and the person for whom it is created: a relationship which is founded on the notion of an exchange between the two. It is not an equal exchange, for it often involves that which is tangible with that which is intangible. The exchange hinges on the question of patronage, which is central to the continuity of cultural symbols in society. It also introduces the social manifestations of the symbol.

When we refer to the Indian cultural inheritance we tend to focus on forms of expression, whether it be the crafts, poetry, architecture, values or whatever, and frequently forget the exchange relationships which were crucial to these forms and which imbued them with a social function without which they may not have survived. By social function I do not mean merely the mundane use of an object or form, but rather its multiple role within society. Its survival is inherently tied to the historical process since the cultural symbol changes in accordance with historical change and is rarely static either in form or in social function. We tend today to treat cultural symbols from the past as if they existed in a vacuum, unrelated to space and time and pick out and isolate them in accordance with our contemporary definitions of past culture as well as our present needs. But even traditions are not self-created: they are socially controlled, both in their making as well as in the selection from them of what is required for contemporary purposes. It seems to me, then, that in order to understand the cultural symbol and its role in a tradition, we need to explore more fully the relationship of exchange or patronage involved in the fashioning of the cultural form and its social reference points. If I am not discussing the act of creativity here it is not because I find it unimportant, but because my emphasis for the moment is on different matters.

The definition of patronage is popularly treated as a restricted one: the wealth given by a person of superior status to an artist to enable the latter to produce a work of art. But the act of patronage is neither so restricted nor so simple. It implies a variety of social categories which participate in the making of the cultural object; implicit also is the understanding of the institution which is created from the act of patronage and has social manifestations. It becomes the legitimizer of the patron and, in addition, to a possible role of authority, may take on other social roles. Not least of all is the consideration of the audience to which the act of patronage is directed, which may operate as the arbiter of the patronage in question. Patronage therefore can act as a cultural catalyst..

Let me illustrate this.

I would like to begin with the most simple and most direct example of what might be called man-to-man patronage. I am referring to the *dāna-stuti* hymns of the *Ṛg Veda*.[1] A bard composed a hymn in praise of his patron who was often the chief of a clan. The occasion for this was often a successful cattle raid against a neighbouring chief or tribe in which the chief and his followers captured a large number of cattle and, preferably, a few herders as well. The occasion was of central importance to a society and economy where a cattle raid was one of the two ways of increasing a herd—the other being breeding. The newly acquired herd was distributed among the clansmen, with doubtless the chief keeping a major share. From this wealth he rewarded the bard who had composed the *stuti* or the eulogy on the chief. And as reward the bard received lavish gifts of head of cattle and horse, gold, chariots and slave-girls. Hence the seeming man-to-man relationship.

But this relationship had a wider dimension. The bard argued that it was his invocation to the deities which resulted in a victorious raid, and this, together with the eulogy, required a reward from the chief. The gift from the chief was thus his due reward. In the eyes of society the status of the chief was further enhanced by the eulogy. The *stuti* was not only the *rājā*'s claim to fame but it reiterated his right to be a *rājā*. In the act of gift-giving a transference of wealth took place between the chief and the bard which, in a society based on reciprocal economic relations, was a significant act. Not least, such bards claimed that they had bestowed immortality on the chief, and how right they were, for we now know of the existence of these *rājās* largely from the

As for example, *Ṛg Veda*, 8.5; 6.27; 8.46; 10.93; 8.1; 1.126; 10.107.

dāna-stuti hymns. Those chiefs who were magnanimous in their gifts were held by the bards as models and it was suggested that other chiefs should follow their example

This nexus between bard and chief receives social sanction and becomes rooted in society. It is incarnated repeatedly when society changes and is germane to the multiplicity of *praśasti*s or eulogies in later times, although the form undergoes a mutation. The briefest but most fulsome in praise occur in inscriptions from the Gupta period onwards, with the most famous of the early ones being on Samudragupta. More elaborate forms occur in the biographies of kings referred to as the *carita* literature. The biography of Harṣavardhana, the *Harṣa-carita* of Bāṇa, and the later *Vikramānka-deva-carita* of Bilhaṇa whose patron was the Cālukya king Vikramāditya VI, come to mind as better examples of this genre. The *praśasti*s were not concerned primarily with recording factual evidence but were involved in the same matters which have been mentioned earlier. The eulogy legitimized the status of the ruler, and this was particularly necessary where the rule of primogeniture had been broken; it underlined the expectations from a just king; it bestowed immortality on the ruler, as is evident from cases where the poet was specially invited to compose the *praśasti*; it recognized the role of poets as part of the royal entourage. Such texts were not meant to be taken literally. In effect, they give us an elaborate view of the courtly culture much prized at that time.

Buried in them, however, was also the genealogical element central to those making claims to status. In a society where status was ostensibly conditioned by birth, it was necessary to claim the highest lineage connections. These were provided to families that had risen politically by genealogists whose authority in relation to their patron was substantial. The eulogy became the rhetoric of this relationship. Since he passed judgement on a man of high status, the bard acquired an independent authority and was regarded as inviolate, and could, if he chose, become the articulator of dissent. His pronouncements on the legitimacy of the king placed him in a sense outside the hierarchy of caste. Thus, in some states of Rajasthan, if he disapproved of the action of the king, the bard would proclaim that he wished to fast unto death—what was called a *dharnā*—and, if he died, the guilt for his death would rest on the king. The king would, in fact, be guilty of the death of his legitimizer. The social reference of the bard in such situations was therefore more than a mere poet composing eulogies. The *praśasti* was not merely a courtly gesture or the creation of a new literary genre, for it carries many other meanings and assumptions. The author was integral to social and political articulation.

I have so far referred to the cultural form as manifest in primarily non-tangible ways. *Stuti*s and *praśasti*s were largely compositions to be recited and heard, even when they were recorded in writing. I would like to turn to another kind of cultural idiom, the three dimensional form of monuments which are visible on the physical landscape. Monuments from the past are generally regarded as architectural forms encapsulating aesthetic formulae and religious statements and are today evaluated and discussed largely in these terms. But implicit in monuments is a gamut of meanings which need to be made more explicit if the monument is to be fully understood. I would like to take as an example the *stūpa* as a cultural symbol, but, for reasons which I hope will become evident, limit the discussion to the *stūpa*s at Sanchi, Bharhut and Amaravati.[2] The *stūpa* begins as a small commemorative tumulus or one enshrining relics. At this point its social function is limited. However, the change of patronage also changes the scope not only of its aesthetic and religious symbolism but incorporates a range of social statements which give it a meaning additional to that of its original form.

We are so accustomed to giving dynastic labels to everything from the past that, for a long time, such monuments have been described as Śuṅga or Sātavāhana art. Yet the dynasties of the Śuṅgas and the Sātavāhanas were only marginally involved, if at all, with these monuments. The patrons were the communities of traders, artisans, guilds of craftsmen, small-scale landowners—the *seṭṭhigahapati* families—and monks and nuns. Mention is made of guilds of ivory-carvers and corn dealers, of weavers, potters, perfumers, bead-makers, garland-makers, timber merchants, cloak-makers, blacksmiths, masons and builders.[3] Only a smattering of families from royalty or high political and administrative office are listed. Fortunately, these monuments are studded with votive inscriptions—the pious records of those who contributed towards their construction. Examples of this category of patronage are available from the second century B.C. to the fourth century A.D. In some cases this form of patronage becomes unique where the craftsmen who actually work on the object of patronage are themselves the patrons, as in the case of the ivory-

[2] J. Marshall and A. Foucher, *Monuments of Sanchi*, Vols. I–III, Calcutta, 1940.

[3] *Epigraphia Indica*, V. Lüders List of Inscriptions. See inscriptions from Bharhut and Amaravati.

carvers' guild from Vidiśā who sculpted part of the gateways at Sanchi. The themes depicted at these sites were commensurate with the life and aspirations of these social groups. Not surprisingly, stories from the *Jātaka* literature are frequently illustrated.

The link with earlier forms of patronage is at one level the act of gift-giving or *dāna*, although the context of the gift is different in each case. The gift in the earlier system was given by one person to another, not necessarily in a personal capacity, since it was often determined by the status and function of the two persons concerned. Community patronage, which is what distinguishes the particular *stūpa* architecture discussed here, was largely a collection of individual gifts brought together through a religious identity and a more loosely defined social identity. The gift was made initially at least for personal reasons and not because of the requirements of status or function. This possibly changed over time. Donation involved an exchange of a gift (*dāna*) in return for merit (*puṇya*). The gift was a gift of a collectivity but at the same time its record was personalized. The gift went towards the building of a religious institution, the Buddhist *saṅgha*. In the earlier system the patron and the recipient had a reciprocal dependence and the objects exchanged tended to be inalienable. In the case of a gift to the Buddhist *saṅgha* it took the form of wealth or labour, both of which were alienable, and the relation between the donor and the *saṅgha* was voluntary. The significant difference here was the creation of a more tangible cultural form, which became the nucleus of a more complex social institution. Artisans as patrons reflect social mobilization in a period of social change with possibilities of upward mobility. Such patronage points, therefore, to the respect given to artisans, at least by urban society. In contrast to this, the *dharmaśāstra*s rate artisans as socially low. Artisan guilds and even financiers' guilds became a feature of the urban landscape during this time. The hereditary recruitment to the guild and endogamous marriage encouraged the conversion of a guild into a *jāti*. Guild donations were, therefore, potentially caste donations, but obviously extending over more than one caste. Some of these artisans and guilds were doubtless also seeking both status and publicity by recording their donations, quite apart from merit. The ivory-carvers' guild which sculpted the gateway at Sanchi may well have achieved renown, and may have been the same which carved some of the exquisite ivory panels so reminiscent of the Sanchi gateway, which found their way to the city of Begram in Afghanistan, a royal centre of the Kuṣāṇas.

Donations were both specific to a monastery as in the case of Kanheri, Karle, Bedsa and the other numerous rock-cut monasteries of the Deccan, as well as more generalized for the benefit of the community, as at the *stūpas* at Sanchi, Bharhut and Amaravati. In the former, the spectacular *caitya* halls are often surrounded by contrastingly bare monastic cells. Both *stūpa* and monastery encapsulated the power of the *saṅgha* as an institution, and the *stūpa* became its recognized symbol. The sacred structure with its casket of relics was demarcated from profane space by a railing with elaborately sculpted gateways. Contributions towards the construction of the railings and the adorning of gateways was an act of piety involving the entire community of believers. The *saṅgha*, consisting of a body or renouncers, was regarded as an alternative source of authority which governed both social and religious life. When those in political authority were patrons of the building of the *stūpa* they were seeking legitimation from the *saṅgha* apart from their personal piety. When the community as such helped build the *stūpa* it was seeking the protection of this alternative authority as well as invoking it. Monuments therefore were never merely religious or artistic edifices with functions limited to the performance of ritual. Inevitably, there were also levels of authority written into the symbolic understanding of the monument. Such authority was almost tangible where the monument supported a religious institution. Possibly, this may in part account for their vulnerability to attacks from competing religious sects.

The votive inscriptions provide evidence on the wide networks of geographical contacts, indicating yet another dimension to the concept of a Buddhist community. Donors belonged to various parts of the Deccan, although local donations were of course high in number. The location of the monuments along trade routes would point to urban connections or with market centres. Some donations at Karle near Poona came from Buddhist Yavana traders from Afghanistan, and possibly even Egypt as part of the Roman trade with the west coast of India. The extensive geographical net was drawn together by the appeal to a community of common belief, ritual and religious identity.

Other kinds of links were also known. Members of a royal family invested money in a guild, the interest of which went towards financing some aspect of the Buddhist *saṅgha*. Here a different kind of nexus is established which still draws on patronage but of a less obvious kind and brings together royalty, commercial interests and the *saṅgha*. In this case the gift plays a dual role—as donation as well as investment.

One of the more striking aspects of these donations is the number of women donors. Donations from queens and women of the royal family are, of course, known from the early phases of many Buddhist sites. Since it had to include more than a single religious sect, royal patronage, being in theory above the competition for patronage, seems in the early period to have handled the division along gender lines. Where kings presided over brahman *yajñas* their wives and sisters made donations to Buddhist monuments.

What are however far more notable are the donations of ordinary women to the building and adornment of *stūpas* and *caityas*. These come in larger numbers from the families of small-scale landowners, traders and artisans. In the case of donations of land the names of the women are listed as part of a family. But more generally contributions are linked to individual names. Sometimes the donations are made by husband and wife. On other occasions by a mother and son or by sisters, but many are just the names of single women. What is even more interesting is that almost half the women who have recorded their donations individually were nuns, and, indeed, even among male donors large numbers of monks are listed. This raises a host of questions. Did these women share in rights to the family property? In the case of a single woman making a donation, was this part of her *stri-dhana*, the wealth given to her by her mother and over which she in theory had complete control? It seems curious that such records are more frequent in Buddhist and Jaina contexts than in those of other religious sects. The over-ruling of the Buddha's objections to an order of nuns was apparently an act of great foresight. It seems that women had a distinctly better status in the so-called heterodox sects than in brahmanism. Such women clearly did not regard Sītā as their role model, nor do they appear to have paid much attention to the injunctions of the Manu *Dharmaśāstra* requiring women in every stage of life to be subservient to men. Of course, the association of women with this kind of donation, suggestive of a particular status, is prevalent during a specific time and in relation to a specific objective.

Community patronage of this kind began to decline from the mid-first millennium A.D. I have used the term community in the context of the Buddhist *stūpa* and this may require some explanation. Those that donate to the *stūpa* belong by and large to castes spread across the social spectrum, although the majority belonged to the middle levels. The donations collected for the creation and embellishment of the *stūpa* represent a religious community and there are a large number of small donations. There were also other Buddhist monuments built substantially from royal donations, and these would not be included in the category of community patronage, although they were similar in architectural form. The sense of community among the Buddhists saw them as participating in an identity which drew on a uniformly recognized religious practice and belief historically evolved and cutting across segmental differences. This is not to suggest that there were no sectarian differences within Buddhism. But the sects within Buddhism related themselves to a common historically evolved religion, to differences of interpretation of the original teaching, and to the preceding forms of religious practice. Such sects are dissimilar to the sects within Hinduism, many of which have diverse origins, do not necessarily relate to the same set of historical events and some of which repudiated the very texts regarded by others as the foundation of their religion. Even in this case, however, the question which needs to be investigated is whether the Buddhist community, as evident from the votive inscriptions discussed, continued to have the same identity in later periods and in relation to other parts of the country. Possibly this sense of community was tied to particular historical circumstances and, as was often the case with such self-perceptions, may well itself have undergone a change.

In contrast to this Buddhist sense of community, a guild of silk weavers also built a temple to Sūrya in central India, but contributions were collected from only one guild, even though its members were no longer professionally confined to silk weaving.[4] In this case, the notion of community is more limited. It neither includes other guilds nor other worshippers of Sūrya. Royal and aristocratic patronage gradually came to predominate and supersede community patronage. This is noticeable even in the western Deccan at Ellora and Ajanta. The importance of the *stūpa* as a symbol seems to give way slowly to *caitya* halls and *viharās*. The new patronage, being very substantial, enabled the maintenance of large monasteries. It was this, again, which became the pattern in eastern India, with Nalanda financed by the endowment of a hundred if not two hundred villages, and other monastic centres such as Vikramaśila and Paharpura equally well off. The smaller collections made by traders and artisans were giving way to the lavish endowments of royalty. The focus shifted to strengthening

[4] Mandasor Inscription. J. F. Fleet, *Corpus Inscriptionum Indicarum*, Vol. III, pp. 79ff.

the monastic establishment. The *sangha* therefore, had now to function to a greater extent than before as a landowner and a propertied institution. As such, it came into competition with other religious institutions which were also receiving endowments from royalty, namely, the temples of various Hindu sects.

The genesis of the temple appears to have been a small shrine-room housing an image as the nucleus of a cult. This is suggested by one of the earliest examples of the Gupta period located in the shadow of the Sanchi *stūpa*. The single room acquired adjoining structures. With the conversion of a cult into a sect with a following, and the patronage of local political authority also thrown in, the small shrine evolved into the complex structure associated with Hindu temples. The temple comes to dominate the landscape when it takes the form of a structure as determined by architects, builders and craftsmen—the *sūtradhāra*, *sthāpati* and *śilpin*. As with the *stūpa*, it is initially an architectural form built to identify a place of worship. But from the moment of its expansion it takes on the qualities of a social symbol and, in many cases, a very complicated one.

The Simhachalam temple in the Vishakhapatanam district of Andhra Pradesh is one such example.[5] Its history and function is by no means unique, nor is it the largest of temples. It is merely one among many others in the country, and its evolution follows a pattern which, in its broad outline, is repeated elsewhere in the late first and early second millennium A.D. It arose in the proximity of Buddhist structures and is said to be located at the site of one. A number of Hindu temples have Buddhist sites lurking in their foundations. The earliest votive inscription of the eleventh century is that of a merchant. But in the subsequent five centuries merchant donations are few, and the five hundred and odd inscriptions on its walls recording donations are largely of members of royal families of the various dynasties which ruled in the area, their ministers and commanders—the *mahāpātra*s and *senāpati*s—their officers and their feudatories, a different clientele from those of the Buddhist *stūpa*s of the Deccan. The eleventh century temple was destroyed in the thirteenth century and even its inscribed stones were used as building material for the new temple at the site. Thus, some of the earlier records were built casually into the walls of the new temple and are lost to us. The district saw a fast turn-over of political authorities, the Cālukya-Colas, Eastern Gaṅgas, Kākatīyas,

[5] K. Sundaram, *The Simhachalam Temple*, Waltair, 1969.

Gajapatis, Vijayanagara and eventually the Sultans of Golconda in the late sixteenth century. Dynastic changes are evident not only from the votive inscriptions but also from the mixture of architectural styles from Orissa, Telengana and South India, and from the iconographical features of the wide ranging images with mutations tied both to sculptural injunction and local beliefs.

A complaint was taken to the Sultan of Golconda that Muslim soldiers had vandalized the temple. The Sultan sent an officer to sort out the matter and make endowments for the *brāhmaṇas* attached to the temple and reactivate it. In the late eighteenth century there were a series of Maratha raids in the area and it is not clear from the records whether the temple was safe from them. There is a conspicuous absence of any Maratha donations.

In the nineteenth century parts of the earlier thirteenth century soft-stone structures began to decay and damaged the temple, requiring extensive repairs. Local opinion now insists that these repairs were required because the temple was damaged by 'the Muslims'.

The central shrine room houses a curious image of Varāha-Narasimha Viṣṇu. The image was originally a Śiva-liṅgam. But, after an extended visit from Rāmānuja, the temple was converted to Vaiṣṇavism. The *sthala-purāṇa* of the temple relates the story that he ordered the existing lingam to be cut and sculpted to the form of Viṣṇu Narasimha. Halfway through this process the icon began to bleed and, in great fear, the sculptors appealed to Rāmānuja, who then ordered them to stop their work. Hence it remains an incomplete image, and when it is covered with sandal-paste, as it is most of the time, it continues to look like a *lingam*.

The thirteenth-century temple boasted of a vestibule, a porch, an assembly-hall, a *nāṭya maṇḍapam* and a variety of halls for special festivals, not to mention a surround of shrines to subsidiary deities. The treasury where the substantial jewels of the deities were kept adjoined the temple, and beyond the outer courtyard were the temple tanks, the gardens and the structures which housed the vehicles of the deity.

Donations to the temple endowed it with extensive assets. The large acreages of arable land were leased out to tenants. Revenue had to be collected from these, as also from the villages which the temple received as endowments. In some instances, this revenue permitted the temple to act as a bank—not only for rural credit but also to finance trading guilds. The daily offerings of cash and jewels had to be registered. All this required a large number of functionaries. The head of the temple was given the appropriate title of *bhoga parīkṣā* and he was both the religious head as well as the superintendent or *adhikāri* of the administration of the temple. The rituals were performed by a body of priests and mention is made of thirty *brāhmaṇas* in this category. The assistants who helped them with the ritual were distinct from the pandits and the *adhyāpakas* who recited the purāṇic and epic texts. Their number had reached fifty-two in the nineteenth century. Lower down the social scale were the musicians, torch bearers and the *devadāsīs*, and of the latter mention is made of one hundred in the thirteenth century. The administration of the temple had a separate hierarchy of office-bearers, including the treasurer/*bhaṇḍāri*, accountants/*śrikarnams*, goldsmiths, stonemasons, carpenters and iron smiths, as also those employed as attendants and palanquin bearers, sweepers and cleaners, elephant keepers, *śūdras* who cultivated the flower gardens as well as herdsmen from the tribe of the Boyas to tend the many thousand head of cattle and sheep owned by the temple. Religious and administrative offices were hereditary and incumbents were paid with endowments of land or a share of the offerings.

The temple was, in fact, a large estate employing hundreds of people in various capacities. Not surprisingly, the ritual treated the chief deity as a dominant landowner in a *jajmani* system. The economic assets were held in the name of the deity and the employees performed services for the deity. The social hierarchy was perhaps more easily maintained in a system of service relationships. Power was enhanced where the temple authorities not only collected taxes but also exercised judicial rights. Additional income came in at the time of fairs and festivals and from pilgrims. The temple was often the major agricultural entrepreneur of the region, bringing new land under cultivation. Commerce was also encouraged, not only by the markets catering to pilgrims from various places, but also by traders bringing in exotic items, such as perfumes, musk, rosewater and camphor to be used in ritual.

The temple, therefore, represented a continuum of functional and symbolic meanings. For some it was the cosmic body of the deity or the cosmic form of the universe. Its architecture and sculpture were the articulation of theories on aesthetics and iconography. The music and dance of the *devadāsīs* were integrated into musicology and, at another level, the *devadāsīs* were regarded as sacred concubines. The *maṭhas* attached to the temple for training priests developed into centres of sectarian activity as well as centres for formal education and debate. The recitation of the epics, *purāṇa*, *kathā* and *kāvya* to audiences of pilgrims and devotees assisted the process of interaction and the assimilation of the 'high' culture with the local culture. For the devotee the temple was a sanctified place of worship. For the king it was both a place of worship and a source of legitimation. This led to successive rulers from a variety of dynasties recording a donation on the temple walls. It became a nucleus of loyalty to the king, and this was particularly necessary where there was a fast change of fortunes among royal families. As a nucleus of loyalty it would draw not only on the institution but also on the networks of devotees and pilgrims. And who with any political sense does not know that the loyalty of local factions is of the utmost importance in building a political base? So great was the need for this political base that a military outpost was established at the temple as early as the eleventh century.

The state saw the temple as a revenue collecting institution as well, and, even if the revenue did not come to the state, the amount was so large nevertheless and the management of cash and endowments so complex that it required some state supervision. The Gaṅga dynasty therefore established a high-ranking officer—the *Kaliṅga parīkṣā*—to supervize the fiscal and administrative work of the temple functionaries and act as a liaison between the temple and its royal patrons. It has thus been argued that the temple became a political outpost of the Gaṅgas.

Inscriptions on a temple wall are legal documents recording the property rights and administrative functioning of the temple. The recording of donations from royalty and from officers of the upper levels of administration was as much symbolic of their political supremacy as of their religious identity. The temple as an institution was a recipient of a transfer of wealth, and this exchange in the form of patronage established a reciprocal relationship between those who ruled and required legitimation to rule and those who provided the legitimation and were supported financially by their patrons. This was in a sense a more complicated projection of the rather simple relationship which I referred to at the start of the lecture, namely, that between the bard and the chief via the *dānastuti*. Whether the form was that of the eulogy or the *stūpa* or the temple, in each case it was the act of patronage which was germinal to the creation of a form and a set of relationships.

A temple was more than a place of worship. It was an institution and, as such, paralleled the *saṅgha* and acquired a status similar to that of the dominant property owners of the time. It could house a deity who on occasion would be regarded as the suzerain overlord by the reigning king and thus acted as a further source of legitimacy. The Gaṅgas are known to refer to themselves as the feudatories—*rauta*—of Jagannath at Puri. Temple ritual imitated the daily routine of the royal household and the deity was treated at least as a feudal chief if not the overlord. As an institution, and through the services it required, it integrated a hierarchy of castes from *brāhmaṇas* to *śūdras* with each one assigned its duties related as closely as possible to the normative rules of the *dharmaśāstra* texts. Possibly, only in the institution of the temple were the normative texts sought to be literally applied. It also reiterated strongly the segregation advised by the normative texts and prohibited the untouchables entry to its sacred precincts.

The temple was a recognized social institution which sought, however, a special sanction for protection as a sacred centre. Such a sanction was generally conceded. But on occasion it was not. When a king was in a political or financial crisis he might loot the temples: a case in point being the king of Kashmir, Harṣadeva, who in the eleventh century faced an economic crisis and decided to despoil the temples in his kingdom in order to obtain their abundant wealth. He appointed a special officer, the *devotpāṭana-nāyaka*, to do so.[6] Alternatively, the richer temples became the target for greedy Turks and Afghans who seized their wealth. In other instances, where the acquisition of wealth had less priority, the attack on the temple may well have been for religious reasons or else arising out of social or political hostility, as possibly in the case of the Vīraśaivas, or of Aurangzeb. In such cases religion is used to validate a variety of causes. Inevitably for the historian, the temple is more than just a place with a religious identity, and when temples are attacked the reasons can be manifold. The transformation of the original, simple *deva-griha* housing the deity, which was the genesis of the temple, into what was often called the *prāsāda* or palace touched many levels of social, political and economic existence other than the obviously religious. What may be functionally religious can have other functions as well which supersede the sect and speak to the society.

I have discussed three distinct cultural categories—the *praśasti* or eulogy, the *stūpa* and the temple. These are frequently referred to

[6] *Rājataraṅginī*, VII, 1081–1095.

when we speak today of India's cultural heritage from the past. I have tried to suggest that, common to them all, is the interaction between the creator of the cultural idiom and the patron, that the idiom itself is not independent of this relationship, but that in this process an institution is born which has a wide social relevance. By institution I do not mean only a public organization, but an integrated, organized behaviour-pattern through which social control is exercised. This comes to include the recognition of a social reference point which evolves out of the existence of the form, but may not originally have been envisaged as part of the form. The bard or the poet is seemingly only concerned with the *rājā*, but his composition as a *praśasti* becomes a cultural form. This, in turn, reflects on the role of the bard in relation to the *rājā*, and also fixes certain functions of the bard in society where the bard becomes the legitimizer of the king but can, also, for this reason, articulate a protest against the king. The trader and the artisan are concerned with the *saṅgha*, but both the *stūpa* and the nature of donations to it impinge on a large range of social concerns, involving the status of the donor as well as the function of the *saṅgha* in society, which function changes when the donors change. I have tried to show that it gives expression to a range of actual articulation which goes beyond just the aesthetic or religious appeal of the *stūpa* or *caitya*. A king donates wealth for a temple built by an architect. From this is born a parallel institution to existing ones, with a multiplicity of social roles. The temple has a horizontal nexus with its patrons which is based on a relatively equal exchange of wealth for legitimation and the social recognition of piety. But it also has a vertical nexus with those who keep it going, which endorses and legitimizes a hierarchy of unequal status and dependence, as well as an inequality of social access to the goods and services of the temple. The temple, therefore, has also to be seen as an institution, as was the *saṅgha* earlier, and has to be assessed as a social and political statement apart from its religious function. In each case a new cultural idiom is created, a new cultural signal. But our recognition, comprehension and acceptance of this signal should go beyond the creator and the patron, and should include a recognition of its social reference point. In our present-day recognition of the idiom we frequently neglect the institution which it gives rise to and interpret the signal in too narrow a way. An understanding of the signal involves more than just an appreciation of its religious or aesthetic form.

In the three examples which I have discussed, patronage in each case picks up a seminal form and develops it almost to the point of losing the original. It encapsulates within it a relationship of exchange, which not only relates the patron to the object of patronage but introduces a further relationship between the object and society. This relationship has many manifestations and often goes beyond what may originally have been the purpose of the object.

Each of these three examples also supports three distinct notions of authority which were prevalent in the Indian past and which, it has been argued, are among its civilizational symbols. The eulogy focuses on political authority. The *stūpa* draws on the institution of *bhikkhus* or renouncers who, on joining the order, discontinued their normal social obligations but created an alternative society. The temple symbolizes the authority of the priestly function. These notions of authority were distinct, but there was some overlap in the practice of this authority: the bard had in part a status similar to that of the renouncer in as much as he was often seen as outside the normal hierarchy of caste and, at the same time, evolved a ritual which gave him a special sanction: the alternative society of the renouncer gave rise to a kind of moral authority which could impinge on social behaviour and political action: the priest drew strength from investing political authority with elements of divinity and used the sanction of ritual and worship to control social action. These were civilizational symbols whose outer forms varied somewhat when dynasties changed or new religions were introduced or when new kinds of political action were required. But the message of the symbol rather than its literal form constituted a continuity in Indian history. Such symbols reach out to many manifestations of social and individual life. To confine them to merely the aesthetic or the religious or the purely formal is to fail to comprehend them in their totality.

I have tried to show that a cultural form has its own history and that its mutation is related to changing historical contexts. To see it as part of a historical continuum provides nuances which introduce a variety of insights into the form. I have given only a partial view of such insights. Added to this, the redefinition of the concept of culture encourages an emphasis on the social context in which a cultural form is placed. This provides fresh perspectives and reinforces the significance of the historical process to the understanding of cultural traditions and symbols.

The keepers and recorders of the past are in greater demand when groups, communities and societies are searching for identities. For each of these there are critical points in time when, for various reasons, identities have to be clarified, sharpened and given a direction. Cultural identities may seem innocuous, but more often than not, are equally strongly motivated as other identities, since, in effect, they incorporate social behaviour and actions. Groups in society select and propagate those cultural symbols which they can control.

Our selection of cultural forms today has been inevitably conditioned by the historical experience of the last two centuries. The projection was based on an image of an ideal society closely observing normative texts. The cultural traditions so selected emphasized upper-caste values, other-worldliness, religious tolerance and a rather simplistic notion of a community, all of which were taken back to an early past. The current re-assertion of cultural identities directed towards the needs of nation-building requires of us a deeper analysis of cultural traditions and symbols. It is not sufficient that we echo and re-echo what has been said in the past few decades. This becomes particularly relevant when culture as defined in a narrow sense is sought to be made the basis of a national identity.

Let me, then, repeat that we should be aware of the cultural traditions which we are creating and what goes into the making of a tradition: that normative values have to be juxtaposed with social reality if we are to understand the contribution of each; that the study of alternative traditions will provide us with a clearer image even of what we regard as established traditions and the manner in which they relate to others; that the selection of symbols which are constituted into a tradition are seldom random and generally have a purpose which should not go unnoticed; that such cultural symbols are not solely aesthetic forms or religious forms but have a social reference point.

The continuity of culture, therefore, cannot be viewed merely as some kind of mystic communication from one generation to another, where the people involved are mute recipients. When cultural traditions seek legitimacy from history, thereby imprinting themselves on the perception of the present, and are used as building blocks in the construction of contemporary identities, then the voice of the historian has perforce to be heard.

Index

From Lineage to State

FROM LINEAGE TO STATE

Social Formations in the Mid-First Millennium B.C. in the Ganga Valley

Foreword

The Krishna Bharadwaj memorial lectures, of which this monograph is the first, were instituted in honour of the founder of the Centre for Economic Studies and Planning, Jawaharlal Nehru University, who was until her untimely death in March 1992 at the age of fifty-six, its seniormost professor and intellectual leader. It is her intellect which fashioned the nature and content of its academic programmes, it was her vision which shaped its *modus operandi*, and her values which determined its ambience.

What was noteworthy about Krishna Bharadwaj's leadership of the Centre, however, sprang not merely from her academic excellence or her sense of dedication. These are, necessary qualities required of anyone venturing upon the task of setting up a good academic centre. But they are not enough. What Krishna Bharadwaj possessed was the complete conviction that the academic centre of which she was a part could be as good as any in the world — a conviction which is rare in India these days.

But her conviction was not a matter of mere braggadocio. She considered two conditions absolutely necessary for making this conviction a reality and strove hard to achieve them. The first was a process of continuous collective self-evaluation which she enjoined upon all her colleagues, and which had to be based on an awareness of what was happening elsewhere. Whenever she travelled, whether it was abroad or within the country for a seminar, she made it a point, upon her return, to discuss with her colleagues what 'they' were doing 'there', what 'we' should be doing 'here', what 'our' strengths and weaknesses were relative to 'theirs', and so on.

The second condition, according to her, was that we had to evolve a research-cum-teaching agenda *of our own*. No centre in India could flourish, by international standards, merely by mimicking what was happening abroad, merely by showing proficiency in solving problems which were posed abroad. The problems had to be rooted in the social reality of our own country, and the effort to grapple with them had to be, very consciously, located within the intellectual endeavour of our country. This conviction of hers was in apparent contradiction with her own intellectual preoccupations. A theorist by inclination, an ardent follower of classical political economy, inspired by the work of Piero Sraffa, a leading member of an international group of theoretical economists occupied in developing a critique of neo-classical economics, she could scarcely be considered as being engaged in problems thrown up by the Indian economy.

But the contradiction was only apparent. She was neither an empiricist, nor a votary of Indian 'exceptionalism', not even a believer in the view that there was something transcendental about the Indian specificity. Her emphasis on taking up problems rooted in the Indian social reality was not a plea for turning one's back upon theory or theoretical struggles. On the contrary, her plea for investigating *our* real problems was simultaneously a plea for a richer theory, a theory with a body to it, one which is all the more powerful because it has been used for investigating real problems facing economies like ours. And she considered academic centres only in countries like ours capable of developing this richer theory, because it is *our* problems which had been hitherto excluded from the ken of 'mainstream' economics.

In her own work she attempted this synthesis of theory with concrete investigations of problems of economies like ours. To what extent she succeeded, to what extent her output was based on a genuine synthesis, as opposed to representing an ensemble of insightful theoretical work and insightful work on development economics, remains a matter which future research will unravel. But this belief in synthesis underlay her conception of what the teaching and research programme of the Centre should be. The Centre, she felt, could progress towards this synthesis only if the intellectual training it imparted was complete in at least three respects: it had to combine rigorous theory with rigorous history; it had to provide alternative theoretical perspectives, i.e. students had to be well-versed in the Classical, the Marxian, the Walrasian, and the Keynesian perspectives (she completely rejected the Schumpeterian notion of 'progress' in economic theory culminating in the Walrasian equilibrium); and it had to instil in them an awareness of the connectedness of disciplines.

A striking feature of Jawaharlal Nehru University from its very inception was its emphasis on interdisciplinarity. Krishna Bharadwaj, while reiterating this emphasis, insisted that true inter-disciplinarity was not synonymous with 'the pauper's broth of eclecticism' but arose out of a solid grounding in a particular discipline. The idea was not to produce jacks-of-all-trades who were masters of none, but rather to produce *masters* of particular trades whose mastery derived precisely from the fact that they were also familiar with other trades.

This was to be sure an ambitious programme; it placed a heavy burden on both teacher and student. But it was also an exciting programme. In Krishna Bharadwaj's Centre, as indeed in the university as a whole in the early 1970s, one could not escape the feeling that something fantastic was being tried out. Whatever the success of the experiment, it was not *dreary*. And the experiment, too, while it may not have measured up to Krishna Bharadwaj's rigorous standards, was far from being unsuccessful: distinguished visiting scholars have confessed that when they first set foot in the university they were astounded that a place like this could exist anywhere in the world.

Krishna Bharadwaj was very much a part of the heroic age of the university. In honouring her memory through these lectures, the Centre of Economic Studies and Planning does not merely honour its founder, and express in a ritualistic fashion a nostalgia for a bygone era. It emphatically reiterates its commitment to the assumptions which Krishna Bharadwaj worked on. Times have changed; but these changes, while making the task of realizing the vision implicit in these assumptions more difficult, have not invalidated the assumptions. We live in a more difficult world, but our vision and our commitment remain unimpaired.

Indeed the conception of these lectures derives precisely from these assumptions. Each year, an outstanding scholar belonging to a particular discipline, who nonetheless has a degree of familiarity with and empathy towards other disciplines, who can communicate to a wider university audience certain ideas belonging to the frontiers of his or her own discipline and based on his or her own research work, will be invited to speak. These lectures, needless to say, are not confined to economics; they represent a project with the primary objective of bringing some intellectual excitement, initially to the campus and subsequently through their publication to a wider audience; and above all they constitute an experiment.

Krishna Bharadwaj, I am sure, would have been happy with all three features.

Prabhat Patnaik

Centre for Economic Studies and Planning
Jawaharlal Nehru University

CONTENTS

FROM LINEAGE TO STATE

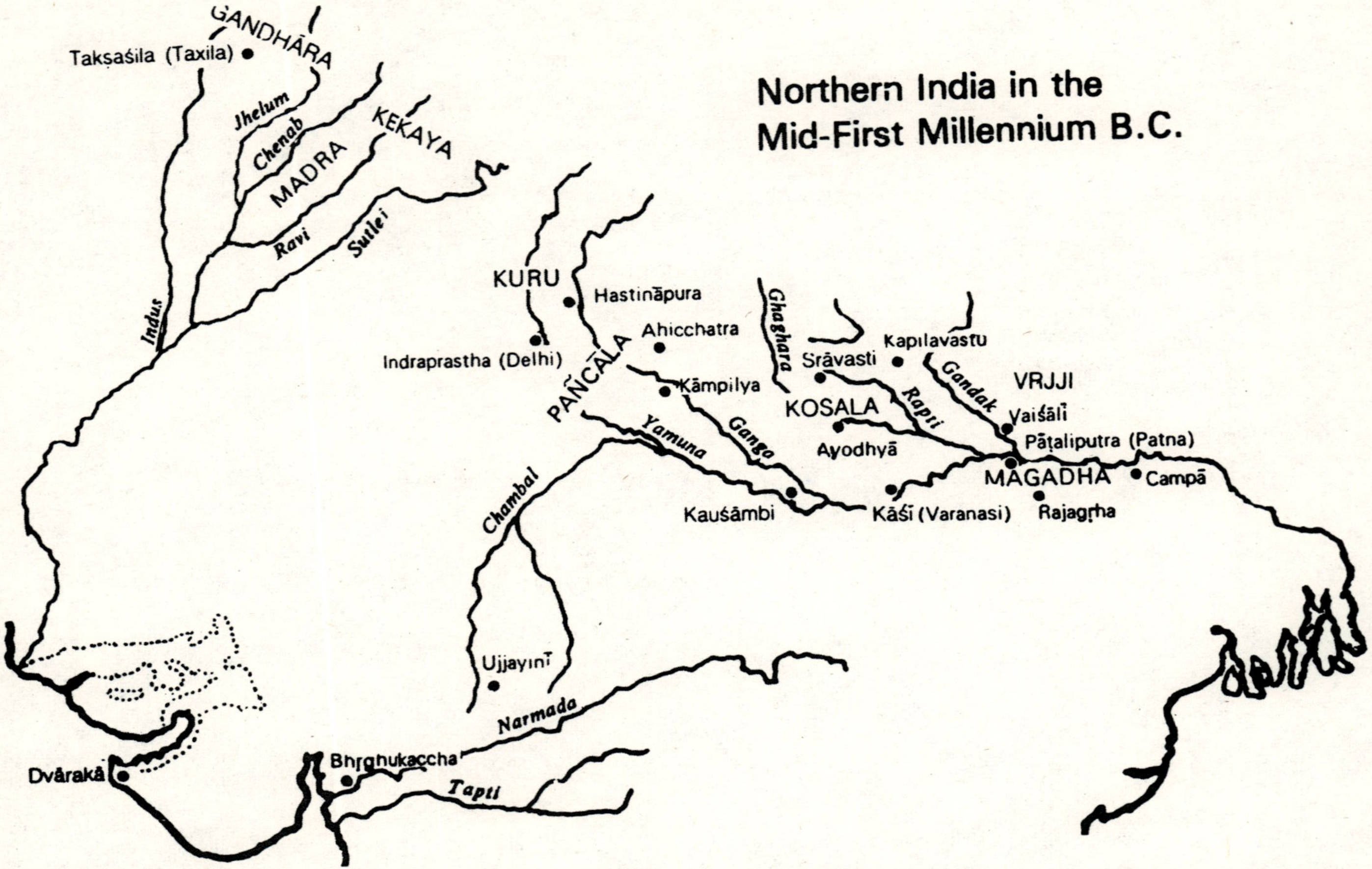

Northern India in the Mid-First Millennium B.C.

I PRELIMINARIES

Theories on the earliest formation of states in India have been few and generally simplistic. There is none of the conceptual richness which characterizes the discussion on state formation in Africa or Meso-America, partly perhaps because the latter have drawn on ideas relating to the early state among political anthropologists. This poverty of theory on the early Indian state has also been in part due to an abiding obsession with a single image, that of Oriental Despotism: an image projected initially by British administrators and historians and which did not even find its counterpoint, as did many other images from the same source, in the more radical writings of this century.[1] The equally generalized Marxist concern with the Asiatic Mode of Production,[2] in the face of contrary empirical evidence, continued to be enthusiastically projected. The labours of Indian Marxists who have tried to show its inapplicability[3] have often been brushed aside, particularly by those who are interested in it as a theoretical concept. The nature of the Indian state became a favourite subject with those historians who were influenced by Indian nationalism. Studies on the political institutions of early India assumed the existence of the concept of the state but rarely analysed the process by which state formation came about. The concern was substantially with proving the importance of republics, democratic forms and constitutional monarchy or with projecting a monolithic, unitary state virtually from its inception,[4] thereby providing ammunition for the

[1] Romila Thapar, *The Past and Prejudice*, New Delhi, 1975.

[2] Lawrance Krader, *The Asiatic Mode of Production*, Assen, 1975.

[3] Such as the papers by Irfan Habib and S. Naqvi in *Science and Human Progress*, Bombay, 1974. See also, Bipan Chandra, 'Karl Marx: his theories of Asian societies and colonial rule' in Marion O'Callaghan (ed.), *Sociological Theories: Race and Colonialism*, UNESCO 1980, p. 383 ff; cf. P. Anderson, *Lineages of the Absolutist State*, London, 1974.

[4] N. N. Law, *Aspects of Ancient Indian Polity*, Oxford, 1921; U.N. Ghoshal, *A History of Hindu Political Theories*, Calcutta, 1923; K. P. Jayaswal, *Hindu Polity*, Bangalore, 1943 (first edition 1924); A. S. Altekár, *State and Government in Ancient India*, Banaras, 1949.

nationalist ideology. In the last couple of decades a few attempts have been made to describe the difference between the non-state situation and the emergence of the state.[5] These studies can be followed up with a more detailed analysis of the formation of the state. That the latter would have a bearing on even the late forms of the state in India is evident from the most recent studies of some Indian states.[6]

The emergence of a state marks a qualitative change in the history of a society since it arises out of and initiates a series of interrelated changes at many levels. The transition from an absence of states to state systems in the mid-first millennium B.C (the earliest historical period for which there is sufficient literary evidence), has generally been treated as a sudden change. Ṛg Vedic society has been described as a tribal society and that of the later Vedic period as one of state-based kingdoms, the transition having occurred during the period from the late second to the early first millennium B.C. This has sometimes been assumed on the basis of the conquest theory[7] of the rise of the state, which argues that after the supposed conquest of the area by the Aryans when they gained control over the indigenous society, the state almost automatically came into existence. Where the theory of internal stratification[8] and diversification has been applied in preference to the conquest theory, it has been argued that class stratification is reflected in the caste structure with the *kṣatriyas* forming the ruling class and the *viś* constituting the peasantry. In this situation the increasing power of the former led to the emergence of states.

One of the problems in examining the nature of social stratification in early India has been the rather casual and imprecise translations of indigenous terms into English. The influence of European history on nineteenth century Indologists has generated a tendency to use parallels from European society and particularly feudal England, in translating terms relating to socio-economic forms even in literature as early as that of Vedic times, as for example the

[5] R. S. Sharma, *Aspects of Political Ideas and Institutions in Ancient India*, Delhi, 1968 (first edition 1959); C. Drekmeier, *Kingship and Community in Early India*, Berkeley, 1962.

[6] H. Kulke, *Jagannātha-Kult und Gajapati Königtum*, Wiesbaden, 1979; B. Stein, *Peasant State and Society in Medieval South India*, Delhi, 1980.

[7] F. Oppenheimer, *The State*, New York, 1914.

[8] R. H. Lowie, *Primitive Society*, New York, 1920, p. 380 ff.; H. H. Gerth and C. W. Mills, *From Max Weber*, London, 1947, p. 252 ff.

uniform translation of *viś* as peasantry and *śūdra* as serf.[9] The assumption was that *rājanyas/kṣatriyas* were nobles and barons and *śūdras* were serfs.[10] This has resulted in some confusion in attempts at defining exactly when a peasant economy came into existence in northern India. If the *viś* represented the peasantry in Vedic times then various other features which co-exist with a peasant economy should also be present, but this as we shall see, is not the case. The establishment of a peasant economy is also crucial to many theories regarding the origins of the state and the prime movers towards state formation.

Stratification has been viewed as a precondition to the emergence of the state since stratified groups become involved in internal conflicts, require contracts for agreements or result in the evolution of a powerful élite. The prerequisites for stratification are however under debate.[11]

Thus, the theory of stratification is applied in the concept of the Asiatic Mode of Production by arguing that village communities consisting of peasant agriculturalists in the main had a communal land tenure and the state intervened and appropriated the surplus. Here despotism and the irrigation system are secondary traits. Where it is argued that the state owned the land and organized agriculture through settlements of cultivators, there class opposition would be absent.[12]

The most influential theory on the nature of the early Indian state and one which has held the field for many decades is that of Oriental Despotism with its variants and among these the Asiatic Mode of Production. Briefly summarized, the discussion on the state in pre-modern India assumes a static situation until the colonial period, the only change being from clan systems to the socie-

[9] A. A. Macdonell and A. B. Keith, *Vedic Index of Names and Subjects*, vol. II, Delhi, 1967, pp. 389 ff., 202 ff. (fst. ed. 1912).

[10] This is a major weakness even in the recent and otherwise excellent translation of the Critical Edition of the *Mahābhārata* by J. A. van Buitenen (Chicago, 1973). The translator states that he took the terms from the *Vedic Index* and confesses that 'the choice probably was a mistake'. *Journal of Asian Studies*, XXXV, May 1976, no. 3, p. 471.

[11] E. R. Service, 'Classical and Modern Theories of the Origin of Government', in R. Cohen and E. Service (eds.), *Origins of the State*, Philadelphia, 1978. Also H. T. Wright, 'Towards an Explanation of the Origin of the State', in the same publication.

[12] H. J. M. Claessen and P. Skalnik, 'The Early State: Theories and Hypotheses', in H. J. M. Claessen and P. Skalnik, *The Early State*, The Hague, 1978, p. 1 ff.

ty being engulfed by the despotic state, a change believed to have occurred in antiquity.[13] The state was characterized by its ownership of the land with an absence of private property in land, by a despotic king extracting revenue from the village communities which were otherwise autonomous and autarchic except that production being purely agricultural was dependent on irrigation facilities controlled by the state through a hierarchy of officials who also collected the revenue. In such a situation towns were administrative centres, there being an absence of commerce. The only commodities produced were for royal or courtly consumption. The village community although autonomous within itself was nevertheless totally subservient to the state.

Recently a variant on the Asiatic Mode of Production has been suggested with data relating to the Inca state in Peru and its environs.[14] The pre-Inca situation was one in which land was owned communally by clans, was redistributed periodically between extended families who worked it but did not own it and labour was in the form of communal labour with the villagers acting in co-operation. The Incas conquered these clans and declared that all land was the property of the state and some of it was declared crown land. The rest of the land was worked by the members of the clan but as forced labour. The clans lost their rights over the land in terms of ownership but continued to have rights of possession and use, and production therefore remained communal in spite of a changed mode of production. The Inca state maintained some of the earlier customs of providing food, drink and seed to the cultivators in a seeming attempt to suggest that the earlier system still prevailed. There was also an administrative organization to control the clans. The operational base to the Inca system was that labour was now involved in conquest and defence, irrigation, enlargement of the area of cultivation and in the cult of the

[13] K. Marx and F. Engels, *On Colonialism*, Moscow, 1968; P. Anderson, *Lineages of the Absolutist State*, London, 1974; R.A.L.H. Gunawardana, 'The analysis of pre-colonial social formation in Asia in the writings of Karl Marx', *Indian Historical Review*, 1976, II. no. 2, p. 365 ff.; D. Thorner, 'Marx on India and the Asiatic Mode of Production', in *Contributions to Indian Sociology*, 1966, no. 9; Bipan Chandra, 'Karl Marx; his theories of Asian Societies and Colonial Rule', in Marion O'Callaghan (ed.), *Sociological Theories: Race and Colonialism*, UNESCO, Paris, p. 383 ff.

[14] M. Godelier, *Perspectives in Marxist Anthropology*, Cambridge, 1977, p. 186 ff.

ancestors and construction of monuments. Projects involving large numbers of people as manpower followed after the establishment of the state. The state in such a system was the collective landlord and therefore the superior community. Kinship relations as ties in production were destroyed as was the earlier social formation.

The centrality of irrigation systems has been picked up by other commentators arguing for technology as a major variable.[15] The managerial function behind irrigation systems, particularly in the organization of labour and maintenance of control, is seen as germinal to the idea of the state. Control over irrigation does not necessarily imply despotism[16] but does provide a source of power, although the relationship of irrigation to environment, soil, cropping patterns and calendric foci would have to be considered before a correlation can be established. The managerial functions in such a situation became the pre-conditions to the state.

If irrigation systems are seen as a causative factor then the ecological context has also to be discussed for, apart from managerial functions, those with access to good agricultural land would tend to accumulate power. But the nature of control in early societies would vary, where nomadic groups were sometimes known to overpower sedentary agriculturalists. In a situation of evironmental circumscription where, for instance, prime agricultural land is surrounded by poor quality land, sedentary cultivating groups may prefer to come under the hegemony of the surrounding nomadic groups rather than migrate from good agricultural land.[17] The resulting tension may have led towards the formation of a state. Migration would also become difficult in the proximity of areas unfavourable for resources. The emergence of a proto-state in such ecological relationships has been suggested in the case of nomadic groups in juxtaposition with agriculturalists in Baluchistan, where the leading family of the pastoralists becomes the focus of power and the settled agriculturalists are the source of wealth and labour.[18] Such a symbiotic relationship may have

[15] J.H. Steward, *Theory of Culture Change*, Urbana, 1955.

[16] E. and R. C. Hunt, 'Irrigation, Conflict and Politics: A Mexican Case', in R. Cohen and E. Service (eds.), *Origins of the State*.

[17] R. L. Carneiro, 'A Theory of the Origin of the State', in *Science*, 1970, 169, pp. 733-8. Also, 'Political Expansion as an Expression of the Principle of Competitive Exclusion', in R. Cohen and E. Service, *Origins of the State*.

[18] B. Spooner, 'Politics, Kinship and Ecology in S.E. Persia', *Ethnology*, 1969, i, pp. 139-52; P. C. Salzman, 'The Proto-State in Iranian Baluchistan', in Cohen and Service, *Origins of the State*.

characterized the declining Harappan culture and the advent of the Aryan speaking peoples in north-western India in the second millennium B.C.

Population growth and social circumscription are described as primary factors towards state formation where surplus can only be produced under coercion and population growth creates the need to produce and control surplus.[19] This theory does not however examine the reasons leading to population growth. Some significance has also been given to population pressure creating tensions which become accentuated when there is a conflict between communal and private ownership, particularly in societies undergoing such change.[20] Such tension is sometimes diffused by groups migrating to new settlements. Here authority tends to accrue to the founding groups who become the holders of property with preferential access to resources.[21] The coming about of the state can also be seen as an integrative process in which a variety of factors conducive to conflicts are sought to be settled and controlled.[22] Where there is a possibility of groups in conflict being able to migrate, there this fission would prevent conflict as well as make it unnecessary for the mechanism of a state to control conflict.

Increasing social and cultural heterogeneity can also lead to social stratification and a tendency towards centralized political control. In the process of stratification and the building up of a hierarchy, marriage alliances are of some importance. Endogamous alliances strengthened a small group with potential and actual power. Exogamous marriages were more suitable for the assimilation of new groups. Differentiation in status is then wrapped up in legitimation which often derives sanction from religious beliefs and ritual in early societies. Legitimation increases the distance between those of high status and commoners. Sacral kingship is an aspect of this distance and is in turn tied to beliefs concerning the welfare and prosperity of a society being symbolized in that of the individual regarded as the chief.

[19] K. V. Flannery, 'The Cultural Evolution of Civilisations', in *Annual Review of Ecology and Systematics*, 1972, 3, pp. 399-426.

[20] M. H. Fried, *The Evolution of Political Society*, New York, 1967.

[21] R. Cohen, 'The Political System', in R. Naroll and R. Cohen, *A Handbook of Method in Cultural Anthropology*, New York, 1970, pp. 484-99.

[22] E. R. Service, *Origins of the State and Civilisation: The Process of Cultural Evolution*, New York, 1975; R. Cohen, 'The Political System', in R. Naroll and R. Cohen (eds.), *Handbook of Method in Cultural Anthropology*, New York, 1971.

In the elaboration of social stratification as a force in state formation others have emphasized the role of urban centres and trade,[23] where trade is generally confined to, or at least reinforces the status of the wealthy, both in terms of actual wealth as well as in terms of trading in goods which are regarded as special and difficult to come by.

These theories point to the analysis of state formation being a complex process in which a range of factors may be crucial and may apply differentially to varying situations. As such there can be no single factor which causes the change, although certainly some would be more central than others. The logical extension of this argument would also be that the forms taken by the state once it had come into being would vary in accordance with the nature of its origin. This allows of the possibility of a variation in the types of early states. These would in turn influence to some extent the typologies of state systems prevalent in different areas and periods of time. A distinction has also to be maintained between primary state formation with which the present study is concerned and secondary state formation which relates more closely to later typologies of states and their control over lineage or proto-state societies.

The investigation of pre-state forms has been much debated in recent decades. Differences between bands, ranked societies, stratified societies, chiefships and state systems have been elaborated upon, as for instance in the writings of Morton Fried. To this may be added the perceptive work of Karl Polanyi[24] which, even if unacceptable as a total paradigm, does nevertheless provide some insights which are very pertinent to the analysis of early historical societies. There has also been considerable discussion on the concept of what has been called the lineage mode of production, proposed by Emmanuel Terray[25] and Pierre-Philippe Rey,[26]

[23] R. McC. Adams, *The Evolution of Urban Society*, Chicago, 1966.

[24] K. Polanyi, *Dahomey and the Slave Trade*, Seattle, 1966; K. Polyani, *et al.*, *Trade and Market in the Early Empires*, Glencoe, 1957; K. Polanyi, *The Great Transformation*, Boston, 1957.

[25] E. Terray, *Marxism and 'Primitive' Societies*, New York, 1972; M. Bloch (ed.), *Marxist Analyses and Social Anthropology*, ASA Studies 2, London, 1975.

[26] P. P. Rey, 'Class Contradiction in Lineage Societies', in *Critique of Anthropology*, 1979, 4, nos. 13 & 14, pp. 41-60; 'The Lineage Mode of Production', *Critique of Anthropology*, Spring 1975, no 3., pp. 27-79.

and commented upon by Maurice Godelier[27] ano Claude Meillassoux.[28] Another useful study of the lineage system relates to data from ancient Polynesia.[29] In attempting to re-examine the process of state formation in northern India in the mid-first millennium B.C. the arguments derive from some of the implicit questions posed in these studies. This does not mean however that the present work is in agreement with the theories put forward by these studies and in fact on some points there is not only divergence but disagreement. Nevertheless, within the broad framework of the discussion on stratification and lineage systems, it was felt that the characteristics of the lineage system do appear to be recognizable in much of what we know of Vedic society.

A lineage has been defined as a corporate group of unilineal kin with a formalized system of authority.[30] It has rights and duties and accepts genealogical relationships as the binding factor. It can be divided into smaller groups or segments. Several unilineal descent groups go to make up a clan which traces its origin to an actual or mythical founding ancestor. The basic unit in such a system is the extended family based on a three or four generation lineage controlled by the eldest male who represents it on both ritual and political occasions. The constituents of the family and its relations with the descent group are based on the system of marriage alliances, involving both the circulation of women and the exchange of wealth associated with it, residence patterns, and rights relating to the wealth produced by the family as an independent unit as well as in its relationship with the clan. Such rights in property are determined by settlements in new territory, inheritance orders and acquisition of wealth. The family has clearly defined rights on pasture-lands, livestock and cultivated land. These are frequently rights of usage determined by rules rather than ownership. The optimum size of the lineage is determined by environment and economy. The jural community takes decisions and is constituted from the dominant authentic lineage segments. Ritual occasions are

[27] M. Godelier, 'The Appropriation of Nature', ibid., *Perspectives in Marxist Anthropology*, Cambridge, 1977.

[28] C. Meillassoux, 'Historical Modalities of the Exploitation and Over-exploitation of Labour', in *Critique of Anthropology*, Summer 1979, vol. 4, nos. 13 and 14, pp. 7-16. 'From Reproduction to Production', *Economy and Society*, 1972, vol. 1, no. 1, pp. 93-105;

[29] I. Goldman, *Ancient Polynesian Society*, Chicago, 1970.

[30] J. Middleton and D. Tait, *Tribes without Rulers*, London, 1964.

marked by sacrifices offered to a cult object where the congregation is often the descent group of the lineage. In the lineage mode of production[31] the jural community has some control over production and its inherent exploitative tendencies differentiate it from the more egalitarian bands and ranked society. Exploitation takes the form of those in authority claiming power on the basis of kin connections and wealth and excluding those who are unrelated. This exclusion could be expressed in non-kin groups labouring for the others. In such a system the produce, whether acquired through labour or from raids, is divided on the basis of redistribution in which voluntary tribute and gift-giving plays a central role. Kinship relations have a genealogical base and at the same time are a unit of production in accordance with lineages, segments and extended families. In a clear separation between élite groups and commoners, kinship constitutes a charter for establishing the authority of the ruling lineage through genealogical connections. Rituals reinforce the system, particularly initiation rituals and the public worship of ancestors.[32] Myths of origin become significant in emphasizing the separate and special nature of the élite. Heterogenous groups are knit together through their dependence on the ruling clan. Political stability often lies in the open frontier which makes migration possible so that tensions within the clans can be eased by the migration of some. Territorial sovereignty or the delineation of boundaries do not play a central role. Lineage becomes the legal sanction and regulates the activities of its members. The chief therefore acts through and in relation to a lineage and not as an individual. Traditional history would also take the form of a history and exposition of the lineages which is essentially a charter of legitimation, often in the form of precedents and guidelines.

In contrast to lineage systems the establishment of a state points to a different kind of society. A state registers the evidence of a political authority functioning within a territorial limit, and delegating its powers to functionaries. This is financed by an income collected by those who contribute regularly on an impersonal basis to its maintenance and acts as an instrument for integrating social segments identified not merely by ritual roles but also by economic functions.[33] These four attributes are essential but their

[31] Terray, *Marxism and 'Primitive' Societies*.

[32] E. V. Winans, *Shambala*, Berkeley, 1962

[33] L. Krader, *Formation of the State*, New Jersey, 1968; 'The State in History', in *Studies in History*, forthcoming.

importance in a particular situation may vary and their application need not be equal in every instance. A state has further been defined as a collection of specialized agencies and institutions both formal and non-formal which help in maintaining an order of stratification. Hierarchy is as acceptable as is differential access to basic resources. The hierarchical groups may be defined as classes in which the opposition lies between those who labour and those who enjoy the fruits of the labour and the resultant surplus. A conflict between these groups would be one condition for the emergence of the state and implies that other forms of authority have become ineffective. Obedience to officials is a necessary characteristic and this is not tied by bonds of kinship. The state has an obligation to defend its citizens and its territory, implying an identification of its citizens over others and a monopoly over the use of force. The jurisdiction of the state is defined in terms of its sovereignty over a fixed territory and membership is therefore determined by residence or birthright in a territory.[34] The state establishes and maintains its sovereignty both externally and internally, the former by protecting the territory from aggression and the latter by the promulgation of laws. The observance of customary rules is gradually formalized, often resulting in the codification of laws. Taxes are regulated and collected, and become a permanent part of the income of the state. Censuses of the population are sought to be maintained since these would be crucial, among other things, to the systematic collection of taxes. The state establishes and maintains sovereignty both in external relations and internally: the former through military strength and the latter through legitimacy, power, the control of groups involved in production and the organization of taxes and a treasury.[35] It has also been argued that the emergence of a civil society, an essential prerequisite for a state, is characterized by a differentiation between public tax and private rent.[36] The maintenance of law and order is preferably to the exclusion of individual actions and is at the effective level in the hands of the ruling groups, who also have preferential access to strategic goods and services.

The state regulates social relations in a society which is divided

[34] S. F. Nadel, *A Black Byzantium*, London, 1942.

[35] Fried, *Evolution of Political Society*, p. 235 ff.

[36] Krader, *Formation of the State*.

into the rulers and the ruled.[37] The main administrative function is to keep the balance between those who hold office and those who aspire to it and is concerned with people as a reference point. The community passes its surplus product to the state through its administrative hierarchy. A distinction is maintained between communal lands and state lands. When necessary, extra economic coercion can be used to obtain the surplus. The state controls succession to high office and provides avenues for upward mobility to a few. In its ideological function it justifies social divisions, supports powerful religious systems where they are of use to the state, maintains the coherence of heterogeneity, for instance by insisting on a common official language or by trying to inculcate a common cultural idiom.

The state therefore is differentiated from government and also, in turn, from society. The functions of the state are performed through the government in which the process of policy-making is crucial and is the concern of political élites.[38] Policy is usually in support of those interests which stem from privileged groups who have access to rights over land and over ideology in the form of religion, shared interests leading to the formation of an interest group. The privileged group in addition to controlling resources is often one with either the favour of the king or else a following of kinsmen, clients or professionals which makes the group important. The tension between the privileged and the unprivileged can either lead to the overthrow of the former by the latter where the existing political structure would have to be overthrown or more often, to attempts by the latter to enter the ranks of the former. This would result in the new group being accommodated as part of the élite, either directly or through some fictionalized relationship.

Centralization of power depends on the ability of the government to interfere in society. One area where this may be limited is the sphere of law where the prevalence of customary law may restrict the application of a code determined by government. The degree of control exercised by the government over office-holders would also determine the degree of interference. Where appointments are made by the government and holders are liable to

[37] P. Skalnik, 'The Early State as a Process', in Claessen and Skalnik, *The Early State*, p. 597 ff.

[38] P. Lloyd, 'The Political Structure of African Kingdoms: an Exploratory Model', in *Political Systems and the Distribution of Power*, ASA Monographs 2, London, 1965.

transfer, the power of the state would be greater than institutions managed by local patrons and magnates over whom the state has nominal control. This in turn relates to the question of the composition of political élites. In early societies it is rarely open to all. It is conditioned by the power of the royal lineage; the rights in land of privileged groups, particularly rights to waste land; the degree to which the group can manipulate physical force; and the degree to which the individual has any alternative to maladministration other than migration. Factors which can lead to a change in the political system revolve around democratic processes, conquest, extensive trade and the decline of a political élite.

In this study an attempt is made to examine four different situations: the Ṛg Vedic and Later Vedic societies of the Indo-Gangetic watershed and the western Ganga valley as well as the *gaṇa-saṅgha* system and the emergence of monarchies in the middle Gaṅga valley. In both regions there is evidence of a change in the direction towards state formation. In the fomer it tends to be stymied but in the latter it reaches fruition. There is greater similarity in the first two societies than in the second two. The Later Vedic society evolves out of the Ṛg Vedic; but the *gaṇa-saṅgha* and the monarchical states are in a sense political bipolarities. Thus it becomes necessary to investigate the variations in polities rather than to assume that since they belong to an early period they must be similar. In drawing out the dissimilarities the emphasis may inadvertently be placed on sharp contrasts, such as that of the importance of ritual in some pre-state systems and that of contract in a state system. Such counterposing may clarify the argument but it has to be recognized at the same time that in early societies there is a considerable intermeshing and accommodating of contrasts which can often hide the nature of change. In attempting to show the contrast between the lineage and the state system it should not be assumed that this contrast was familiar to contemporary observers, or that it was as sharp as is postulated in a theoretical analysis.

The areas and types of states under discussion were not the only examples of state formation during this period. The territories of Kamboja and Gandhāra (the latter with its capital at Taxila) are mentioned among the early *janapada*s as also those in the Punjab, western India and central India. The western and middle Ganga valley have been selected not merely because there is maximum data on these areas for an analysis of the process of state formation and because they are contiguous areas and therefore useful to a comparative study but also because these areas provide the prelude to the emergence of the complex state system of the Nandas and Mauryas. Not surprisingly this region is also regarded as the most important in the ancient Indian historical tradition. Similarly there was a wide geographical distribution of the *gaṇa-saṅghas* or chiefships which were also located in the Punjab and western and central India, and were contemporary with those in the middle Ganga valley. This study is limited to the latter for much the same reasons as those for the territories which were to evolve into kingdoms.

The earliest evidence on social formations locate this activity in north-western India and gradually the major portion of the sources confine themselves to what has come to be called *madhya-deśa*, or the middle region. The Vedic texts which provide this evidence are the *Ṛg Veda* and what is generally termed the Later Vedic Literature (i.e., the *Sāma, Yajur* and *Atharva Veda*s together with their associated texts the *Upaniṣad*s, *Aranyaka*s and *Brāhmaṇa*s). The date of these texts remains somewhat uncertain and controversial. The *Ṛg Veda* is believed to be of earlier origin than the others but even in this the tenth *maṇḍala* (book) is later and some scholars would also include the first *maṇḍala* as of late origin. Similarly, there are parts of the *Atharva Veda* which are believed to be earlier than the rest of the text. The suggested date for the earlier sections of the *Ṛg Veda* would be sometime between the latter part of the second millennium and the early first millennium B.C. The Later Vedic Literature is dated closer to the mid-first millennium B.C. ranging from the eighth to the sixth centuries. The two epics, the *Mahābhārata* and the *Rāmāyaṇa* are quite evidently compiled at various periods and even the Critical Editions of both, admirable as they are, have not been able to prune the texts to the original or approximate epics. They were edited until as late as the mid-first millennium A.D. but sections of the texts would relate to earlier societies, possibly going back to the early first millennium B.C. and perhaps to some even earlier memories.[39]

Subsequent to this, in what may be regarded as the period of the early state, the sources used consist of the *sūtra* literature, especial-

[39] Romila Thapar, 'The Historian and the Epic', in *Annals of the Bhandarkar Oriental Research Institute*, Poona, 1979, LX, pp. 199-213; Romila Thapar, *Exile and the Kingdom: Some Thoughts on the Rāmāyaṇa*, Bangalore, 1978.

ly the *Gṛhya* and *Dharma-sūtras*, the more important among the latter being those of Baudhāyana, Gautama and Āpastamba. The grammar of Pāṇini, the *Aṣṭādhyāyi,* is generally dated to the fifth, though some would prefer the early fourth century B.C. The Buddhist Pāli Canon is widely used for this period in spite of its imprecise chronology although some attempts have been made at a chronological stratification.[40] Among the Buddhist texts, sections of the *Dīgha, Majjhima, Sañyutta* and *Aṅguttara Nikāya*s are early. The *Vinaya Piṭaka* and the *Jātaka*s are later, some parts of which possibly date to the Mauryan period. The *Jātaka* literature is more difficult to date as the verses in it are believed to be of early origin. The above sources which provide the evidence for the *gaṇa-saṅgha* chiefships and the early forms of the state in the kingdoms of Kośala and Magadha relate in the main to the middle Ganga valley and date to the latter half of the first millennium B.C. These sources are therefore later than the corpus of Vedic literature Jaina sources have not been brought into the discussion since, valuable as they are, their chronology remains as yet even more obscure. Attempts to date the *Arthaśāstra* of Kauṭilya remain elusive although its time bracket is that of the Mauryan and post-Mauryan period, i.e. from the fourth century B.C. to the third A.D.[41] The *Viṣṇu Purāṇa* dates to the Gupta period or the mid-first millennium A.D. Purāṇic sources and the *Viṣṇu Purāṇa* in particular are central to the structure of genealogies because although they were composed many centuries after the purported events, they are not only based on an oral tradition but they constitute the core of the early historical tradition. Genealogical data from Vedic sources tends to be very limited. The Purāṇic data, even if deliberately inflated, is nevertheless regarded as the literature which preserves the past. The chronological stratification of literary texts, particularly those which arise out of religious needs or come to serve a religious function and which have been preserved as part of an oral tradition before being edited and recorded in writing, do present multiple problems in providing data on precise points of historical and social change. Because of the difficulty in assigning an exact chronology to the sources it is impossi-

[40] G. C. Pande, *Studies in the Origins of Buddhism*, Delhi, 1957.

[41] R.P. Kangle, *The Kauṭilīya Arthaśāstra*, pt. III, Bombay, 1965; T.R. Trautmann, *Kauṭilya and the Arthaśāstra*, Leiden, 1971

ble to be precise or dogmatic as to when particular changes took place, except in a rather general way. Consequently the major significance of these sources lies more in their indication of the nature of the trends of change which they delineate rather than in a precise dating of the change.

The geographical background to these sources is in some cases a little easier to define than their chronology. Most of the texts included in the category of Later Vedic Literature relate to the western Gaṅgā valley (the Kuru-Pañcāla region) but some among them, such as the *Śatapatha Brāhmaṇa,* seem also to have included north Bihar and others are thought to have been familiar with western India and Gujarat. Pāṇini's grammar probably relates more closely to north-western India but nevertheless has references to the Ganga valley. There is a controversy as to whether the *Dharma-sūtra* of Baudhāyana may not have been written in south India. Buddhist literature is more firmly confined to the middle Ganga valley (eastern Uttar Pradesh and Bihar) with Śrāvasti and Rājagṛha providing the two focal urban centres. However, later interpolations into these texts could have had their provenance in central India or the north-west or even further afield. The archaeological data discussed for these regions covers northern Rajasthan, the Indo-Gangetic watershed extending to present-day Punjab and the northern half of Haryana, the Ganga-Yamuna *doāb* ('the land between two rivers', generally referred to as the Doāb), and its eastern fringe in present-day Uttar Pradesh, as well as the middle Ganga valley, demarcated by a somewhat lower elevation than the western Ganga valley, and consisting of eastern Uttar Pradesh and northern Bihar.

The main theme of this study is to suggest that the Vedic period saw a change from the lineage system (most closely represented by the data of the *Ṛg Veda*) to a combined lineage and householding economy (as suggested by the Later Vedic texts); that in the post-Vedic period the sharper stratification of the chiefdoms of the middle Ganga valley was in part a continuation of the lineage system but in effect also germinal to the tendencies encouraging state formation and therefore these *gaṇa-saṅghas* were both a contrast to, as well as in some ways the pointers to the kingdoms of Kośala and Magadha which saw the emergence of a peasant economy and subsequently commerce

It is not our intention here to argue that the model of the lineage system developed by anthropologists exactly fits the picture of

Vedic society. It is used more in the nature of a general theory helpful in reconstructing the past and trying to prise from the data something more than just a descriptive narrative. The householding economy (a term borrowed from Polanyi), and which has been suggested as part of the Vedic lineage system would probably be unacceptable to many who are familiar with the lineage system from other sources, but its possibility in this specific case seems plausible; and this particularly where its association with the lineage system eventually leads to the weakening of the latter and the emergence of a peasant economy. A certain degree of hopefully creative speculation has gone into this analysis.

The use of the term 'lineage society' is preferable to 'tribal society' which is what has been used in the past for Ṛg Vedic society. Tribal society in the Indian context is ambiguous and includes a range of cultures from stone-age hunters and gatherers to peasant cultivators. Lineage society as defined here narrows the connotation somewhat and is perhaps more precise. This term also emphasizes the centrality of lineage in all its aspects which is of the essence in such a society, particularly in relation to power and access to resources, whereas 'tribe' remains vague on this point.[42] Significantly there are fewer references to individual chiefs in the Vedic sources and more frequent ones to lineages, thus indicating that power was still based on legitimacy through lineage.

In the Indian situation lineage society gave shape and form to caste structure. Lineage elements such as kinship and marriage rules are important to caste. When differing forms of stratification begin to emerge an attempt is made through the *varṇa* framework to draw them together into a holistic theory of social functioning. In the later stage the occupational groups employed in production, the *śudras*, are added on as a fourth category but denied a lineage form, so that their exclusion is made explicit. At the same time their origin as a group is determined by occupation and locality and this marks a major difference in the *varṇa* system itself. When lineage-based societies gave way to state formation, the socio-economic changes reflected in the transition are also reflected in the structure of caste with the emergence of what is seemingly a duality between ritual status and actual status. The continuance of *varṇa* is in a sense the continuance of an aspect of lineage society and of

[42] A. Béteille, 'On the concept of tribe', *International Social Science Journal*, 1980, vol. XXXII, no. 4, pp. 825-8; M. Fried, *The Evolution of Political Society*, pp. 154-74.

ritual status. The latter becomes the survival of the lineage system and is most clearly articulated on ritual occasions. Economic status arises from new changes and has to be adjusted to ritual status. The latter is strengthened in those situations where the two statuses coincide.

The study of the early forms of the state is particularly relevant for Indian history since the process of state formation was a continuing one throughout the centuries with new areas being brought into state systems. It has been said that there was a pathological fear of anarchy defined as the absence of a king: it can be argued that it was not the fear of anarchy but the justification for the continual process of state formation which was being emphasized. The emergence of the state in any of the regions of the Indian subcontinent was not a uniform change affecting the entire region but very often was initially limited to small nucleii. A study of the earliest forms therefore may provide a pattern which was either repeated or modified or reorganized in later periods, but of which the constituents would remain substantially the same. Apart from the early form taken by the state it is equally relevant to analyse the pre-state form and examine the condition from which the state emerged, as these pre-state forms are also met with in later periods in areas adjoining the major states.

State formation has its own interest for the historian. But an attempt is being made in this study to relate the early Indian historical tradition to phases of historical change which correspond to the transition from lineage to state systems. The *itihāsa-purāṇa* tradition embedded fragmentarily in Vedic literature and the epics and more substantially in the *Purāṇa*s, such as the *Viṣṇu Purāṇa* and later texts, has often been dismissed as a fanciful rendering of the past, since it does not conform to the recognized models of historical writing. It is being argued here that the failure to recognize the format of this tradition, derives mainly from the inability of modern historians to perceive the essentials of this tradition in the context of the earlier society which can perhaps be better defined if viewed in terms of a lineage society and its mutation in time to a state system. In other words, the *itihāsa-purāṇa* tradition is seeking to record such a change but the record becomes legible, as it were, only when viewed in terms of its relations to particular social formations. The linking of the historical tradition with historical change will be attempted in the fourth chapter. By way of contrast the Buddhist handling of the historical tradition takes on its own distinctive form and although the constituent elements are present, their articulation relates even more closely to historical change and their form is more easily recognizable. A detailed discussion of these historical changes therefore becomes the preface to comprehending the meaning of the *itihāsa-purāṇa* tradition. The continuity of the form of the early historical tradition may also be explained by the continuing process of state-formation, particularly in those areas which are characterized by an earlier lineage society.

II LINEAGE SOCIETY

The archaeology of the Indo-Gangetic divide and the western Ganga valley indicates that the settlement of this area goes back to the second millennium B.C. The upper Doāb in particular receives the stragglers of the Late Harappan culture and is the hub of a possibly unrelated people of the Ochre-Colour Pottery culture. Ultimately the much more impressive sites of the Painted Grey Ware[1] culture come to dominate the region. This culture seems to have spread from northern Rajasthan and southern Punjab in the late second millennium B.C. into the western Ganga valley with a heavier settlement in the upper Doāb. Recent excavations in the Beas-Sutlej *doāb* indicate an overlap between the Late Harappan[2] and the Painted Grey Ware Cultures which, if correct would point to some continuity of Harappan traditions, albeit indirect and probably dilute, into the first millennium B.C.

The changing of river courses in southern Punjab and northern Rajasthan where the Painted Grey Ware is found in abundance, may have necessitated a movement south-eastwards to avoid the ensuing ecological uncertainties.[3] Sometimes the sites are located

[1] V. Tripathi, *The Painted Grey Ware*, Delhi, 1976.

[2] J.P. Joshi, 'Interlocking of Late Harappan Culture and Painted Grey Ware Culture in the Light of Recent Excavations', *Man and Environment*, 1978, vol. I pp. 100-3.

[3] R.C. Raikes, 'Kalibangan: death from natural causes', in *Antiquity*, 1968, 42, pp. 286-91; Suraj Bhan, 'The Sequence and spread of pre-historic cultures in the upper Sarasvati basin', in A. Ghosh and D.P. Agrawal, *Radio-Carbon and Indian Archaeology*, Bombay, 1972, p. 252 ff.; Suraj Bhan, 'Excavation at Mitathal 1968 (Hissar)', *Journal of Haryana Studies*, 1969, I, January no.1, pp. 1-15.; H.T. Lambrick, *Sind: A General Introduction*. Hyderabad 1964; Gurdip Singh, *et al.*, 'Late Quarternary History of Vegetation and Climate of the Rajasthan Desert, India'. *Philosphical Transactions of the Royal Society of London*, 1974, 267, no. 889, pp. 467-501.; B. Ghose, Amalkar and Z. Husain, 'The Lost Courses of Sarasvati River in the Great Indian Desert: new evidence from Landstat Imagery', *The Geographical Journal*, 1979, 145, pt 3, pp. 446-51.; *idem*, 'Comparative Role of the Aravalli and Himalayan River Systems in the Fluvial Sedimentation of the Rajasthan Desert', *Man and Environment*, 1980, IV, pp. 8-12.; Suraj Bhan, *Excavation at Mithathal (1980) and other Explorations in the Sutlej-Yamuna Divide*, Kurukshetra, 1975.; Suraj Bhan and J.G. Shaffer, 'New Discoveries in Northern Haryana', *Man and Environment*, 1978, II, pp. 59-68.; K.N. Dikshit, 'Exploration along the Right Bank of River Sutlej in Punjab', *Journal of*

on dry river beds suggesting hydraulic changes. The Sutlej, described in post-Vedic sources as the river with a hundred channels has been known constantly to change its course. The Sarasvatī, the river of many pools, disappeared into the desert near Sirsa leaving only traces of its original bed. It has been argued that a change in the course of the Yamuna drew off the waters of the Sarasvatī and other rivers of the Indo-Gangetic divide. Added to this is the possibility of climatic changes with increasing aridity in northern Rajasthan.[4] Given the increase in the size of sites of the Painted Grey Ware, it is equally plausible that there was a demographic rise which led to a search, in a literal sense, for fresh fields and pastures new. The argument that a profusion of closely spaced settlements may point to shifting cultivation requiring new sites every few years would probably not apply in this case since the archaeological evidence suggests a more sophisticated agricultural activity. The Painted Grey Ware culture marks an assertive society, richer than its immediate predecessors. There is evidence of pastoralism and agriculture with the noticeable presence of a new animal, the horse, and with minimal use of iron (almost restricted to weapons) in the early part of the first millennium B.C. The finely made, wheel-thrown grey pottery with its floral and geometric designs provided a further distinction to the culture.

The *Ṛg Veda* refers to various tribes settled in the region between the Indus, the rivers of the Punjab and the now extinct Sarvasvatī, an area described in the text as the *sapta sindhavaḥ*.[5] The major concentration of settlements from archeological data points to the lower *doābs* of the Punjab and it is possible that the text may have been referring to the five rivers at their points of confluence rather than to their upper reaches. The Sarasvatī is described as eventually joining the ocean,[6] which it has since ceased to do, if it ever did. The possibility of hydraulic changes in this area would date to the latter half of the second millennium B.C., a date which would not conflict with the generally accepted chronology for much of the *Ṛg Veda*. Hydraulic changes in northern Rajasthan and the watershed may

History, 1967, 45, pt II, pp. 561-68.; C. Ramaswamy, 'Monsoon over the Indus Valley during the Harappan Period', *Nature*, 1968, 217, pp. 628-9.

[4] Gurdip Singh, 'The Indus Valley Culture', *Archaeology and Physical Anthropology in Oceania*, 1971, vol. 6, no.2., pp. 177-89.

[5] VIII. 24.27 ; VIII. 96; IV. 28.1; See also III. 23.4.; X. 75; VII. 95; II. 41. 16; VI. 61.

[6] *Vedic Index*, II. p. 434. This is Roth's reading. The verses cited carry no reference to its going to the Ocean.

well have required migrations of a scale such as are suggested in the movement of the Bharatas and the Purus from southern Punjab and northern Rajasthan to Haryana and the upper Doāb or the wanderings of the Yadus to Mathura and Saurashtra. Desiccation and changes in river courses would have caused major population movements.

Ṛg Vedic society was essentially pastoral. This did not preclude agriculture although agrarian activities are more frequently described in the later section of the text. The pastoralists may well have controlled the agricultural niches without being economically dependent on them, particularly if the cultivated areas were worked by people other than those who belonged to the pastoral clans. The society of the Ganga-Yamuna Doāb as reflected in the Later Vedic texts was more dependent on agriculture although cattle-rearing remained a significant activity. Historically the west bank of the Yamuna has been associated with continuing pastoralism whereas the Doāb itself became prime agricultural land fairly early. Sedentary settlements become characteristic of the increasing emphasis on agriculture, although here again the change was evidently not rapid. Settlements in the Doāb would have had to adjust with the smaller settlements of earlier populations indicated by the Ochre Colour Pottery and the Copper Hoard cultures,[7] which may well have been assimilated by the more dominant culture. The existence of earlier agricultural communities in the region may have formed the nucleii of the larger communities as is suggested by the evidence from those sites where settlements of the Ochre Colour Pottery culture are succeeded by the Painted Grey Ware. It is not surprising then that both the Kurus and the Pañcālas are in origin confederations of earlier clans some of which were known to the *Ṛg Veda*. Neither the Kurus nor the Pañcālas as such are referred to in the *Ṛg Veda*. Whereas the Kurus emerged after the confederation of the Pūrus and the Bharatas in the main, the Pañcālas, as the name suggests, were an amalgam of five clans.[8] It would be reasonable to ex-

[7] B and R. Allchin, *The Birth of Indian Civilisation*, Harmondsworth, 1966, p. 200 ff. The Copper Hoard culture which seems to have had its provenance in the middle Ganga valley but the artefacts of which are found in large numbers in the Doāb, remains controversial since some archaeologists associate it with the Ochre Colour Pottery culture on the basis of its having been found with this pottery at a few sites, but others regard it as a distinct culture which cannot be precisely dated because the copper objects are found in caches and rarely in excavations.

[8] *Śat. Brāh.* XIII. 5.4.7 ; *-āla* as a termination is difficult to explain as an Indo-Aryan root. But it is worth noting that in Proto-Dravidian *āḷ* has a distinct meaning

pect that this confederation was the result of a re-alignment arising out of new settlements and some degree of conquest and subordination. In the case of the Kurus it is the Pūru lineage which is listed as the dominant one.[9] The subordination was not necessarily of non-aryans by aryans (whoever the latter may have been!) but equally of various weak clans by the strong, all or whom could have called themselves aryans. The emergence of what came to be identified as the Kuru-Pañcāla region was clearly important as it is called *madhya-deśa* and *āryavarta*, the land of the *ārya*s in later tradition,[10] and is regarded as the epitome of *āryan* society. However, the assimilation of earlier populations would also have resulted in the inclusion (in later texts and rituals) of earlier traditions surviving among indigenous groups.

The pastoralism of Ṛg Vedic society made livestock breeding, and more specially, cattle herding the major activity. Pastoralism is dependent on assured grazing grounds and the ability to accumulate and increase the herd, this being the primary source of wealth. It required what the *Ṛg Veda* describes as 'meadows rich in grass'.[11] Its political implications demanded that grazing grounds be demarcated and a constant watch kept to exclude trespassers. The accumulation of cattle, *gāviṣṭhi*, comes through breeding as well as capturing other herds.[12] Cattle raids are therefore a form of acquiring fresh stock and the same word is used for such raids. The winner of cows, *gojit*, is an epithet for hero.[13] The Kuru-Pañcāla *rājā*s we are told, raided in the season when the dew falls.[14] Inevitably the worst enemies are the Paṇis, given to cattle lifting.[15] Cattle raiding is often accompanied by the capture of herders who are often enslaved. Leadership in this situation requires the ability to protect not only the herd, since cattle are the chief form of wealth, but also one's clan, and to defend the claim to ownership of cattle and control over the grazing ground or *vraja*. Hence the synonyms

which would suit the present context. *DED* 341 *āl* refers to one who rules or controls. *DED* 342 gives āḷ the connotation of a man or hero. Pañcāla could therefore mean the five chiefs, as a confederacy, provided one can accept a bilingual and therefore a mixed form of Indo-Aryan and Proto-Dravidian.

[9] F.E. Pargiter, *Ancient Indian Historical Tradition*, London, 1922.

[10] *Ait. Brāh.* VIII. 14: *Kauṣitiki Up.* IV. 1.; *Manu* II. 17-74.

[11] I. 42.8.

[12] *Ṛg V.* VIII. 86.2.

[13] *Ṛg V.* 3.47.4; 5.63.5; 6.31.3.

[14] *Tait. Brāh.* I. 8.4.1.

[15] *Ṛg. V.* II. 24.6-7; *Vedic Index*, I. 471

of *gopa, gopati* and *janasya gopati* for the *rājā*,[16] as against the later terms *nṛpati* and *nareśvara*,[17] the lord of the herd eventually giving way to the lord of men. Leadership in the context of cattle raids and protection also became the incentive for winning loyalties and establishing the rights of lineages.

Grazing lands are liable to change since the same pastures may not remain constant year after year and cattle herders have to be mobile. Since the economy is dependent on the increase of the herd, identification with land plays a peripheral role and the search for pastures remains crucial. Thus the Pūrus are earlier said to be settled along the grassy banks of the Sarasvatī,[18] but later become the core of the Kuru lineage in the Ganga-Yamuna *doāb*.

Wealth is frequently computed in heads of cattle and in this the cow has a special status. The *gomat* is the man of wealth.[19] The cow is a unit of value, a man's life being calculated to be worth a hundred cows (*śatadeya*). It gains religious sanctity and is sacrified on the more auspicious occasions.[20] It acquires the sanction of a totem animal in that its flesh is eaten on specified occasions in association with rituals,[21] or equally specially when welcoming a guest. The condemnation of the arbitrary killing of cows would point to their ritual importance.[22] Wealth is also computed in heads of horse, crucial to cattle raids and migrations. The horse too acquires religious sanction but less so than the cow. Its sacrifice is symbolic of fertility and power but its flesh is not eaten. The horse appears to have been more valuable than the cow.[23] In the enumeration of wealth the numbers of cattle are invariably much larger than those of horses. The latter is not ritually sacrificed in the same number as cattle. This may well have to do with the necessity of importing horses into India. Apart from the north-western borders the Indian ecology was not generally conducive to breeding horses of quality.

[16] *Ṛg. V.* III 43.5; IX. 35.5; 97.34; X. 67.8; *Ait. Brāh.* VIII. 12.17; *Śat Brāh.* II. 6.4.2. ff. R. S. Sharma, 'Forms of Property in the Early Portions of the *Ṛg Veda'*, P of I.H.C., 1973, pp. 94-101; 'From Gopati to Bhupati', in *Studies in History*, July-Dec. 1980, II, no. 2, pp. 1-11.

[17] *Ṛg. V.* II. 1.1; IV. 20.1; VII. 69.1 ; X. 44.2-3; *Atharvaveda*, V. 18.1.

[18] *Ṛg V.* VII. 96.2.; IV. 38.

[19] *Ṛg V.* IX. 107.9.

[20] *Ṛg V.* II. 7.5; VI. 16.47 ; X. 91.14 ; X, 169.3 ; *Atharvaveda*, X. 10.

[21] *Vedic Index*, I. p. 10 ; *Ait. Brāh.* I. 15 ; *Tait. Brāh.* II. 17.11.1 ; *Śat. Brāh.* III. 4.1.2 ; *Apa. G.S.* VIII. 22.3-11

[22] *Atharvaveda*, XII. 4.38,53 ; 5. 36-9.

[23] *Ṛg. V.* I. 83.1 ; IV. 32.17 ; V. 4.11 .

The *rājā* or chief was the successful leader of a raid and by extension, of a battle.[24] The booty thus acquired was distributed among the clan, but the distribution was already unequal. Some of it was retained by the *rājā*, but a substantial amount was also claimed by priestly families on the grounds that their rituals ensured success in battle and they were the bestowers of praise and therefore of immortality on the hero. The heroic ideal, apart from bravery, included generosity in gift-giving and thus, implicitly, access to wealth. The *dāna-stuti* hymns of the *Ṛg Veda*[25] refer to the established heroes as gift-givers in extravagant terms. Cattle, horses, gold, chariots and female slaves are said to have been bestowed in their hundreds and thousands on enthusiastic bards and priests. The wealth is as mobile as the chiefs from whom it comes and its recipients. The figures may be exaggerated but wealth was distributed at least among the families of the priests and the chiefs, a redistribution which increasingly neglected the rest of the clan. The ability to conduct a successful raid was in part motivated by the capacity to acquire wealth in order that it be distributed or even destroyed in a potlatch type ceremony; this is reflected in increasing references to the bestowal of wealth on ritual occasions, particularly to priests.[26]

The reciprocal relationship between chief and priest undergoes its first change in the period after that of the *Ṛg Veda* as is reflected in the other Vedic texts. Pastoralism, even in the earlier period did not exclude agriculture but the balance between the two gradually shifted in favour of agriculture. The more elaborate ceremonial sacrifices of the later period such as the *rājasūya* include offerings made of grain together with milk, *ghī* and animals.[27] Plough agriculture is referred to in the *Ṛg Veda*,[28] generally in the later *maṇḍalas*, but curiously some of the major agricultural implements carry names which are linguistically non-Aryan, such as *lāṅgala*.[29] That there were sedentary agriculturalists in this region prior to the Ṛg Vedic period is evident from archaeology. The Asuras for exam-

[24] *Ṛg. V.* I. 116.21 ; VI. 32.3.

[25] *Vedic Index*, I. p. 336; II. p. 82.

[26] Romila Thapar, '*Dāna* and *Dakṣinā* as forms of Exchange', in *Ancient Indian Social History : some interpretations*, New Delhi, 1978, p. 105 ff.

[27] Ibid.

[28] I. 23.15; X. 34.13; X. 117.; X. 101.3; a hymn addressed to the *kṣetrapati* in IV. 57 is believed to be late although included in the early section of the text. E.W. Hopkins, 'Pragathikani', *JAOS* 1896, 17, p. 84.

[29] Romila Thapar, 'The Study of Society in Ancient India', in *AISH*, p. 211.

ple are said to have had a correct knowledge of the seasons for agricultural activities.[30] The subordination of such groups to pastorally based power is not unknown and could be explained in terms of environmental circumscription, where, in favourable areas cultivators prefer not to migrate when encroached upon by pastoralists.[31] Alternatively, the close proximity of herders to agriculturalists may well have led to a symbiotic relationship of mutual dependence. Thus herders might graze their animals on the stubble of fields or be provided with fodder in return for protection. Such agriculturalists would then accept the authority of the herder chiefs without necessarily being conquered by them. At the individual level this would require a relationship simultaneously drawing on notions of alienness and friendship which is perhaps what is reflected in the complex meaning of the word *ari*. Such symbiotic relationships could encourage circuits of exchange of a simple and direct kind, should the herders practise transhumance. They would also presuppose a situation of bilingualism should the two groups be speaking different languages. It has been suggested that the presence of non-Aryan features, particularly Proto-Dravidian and Austro-Asiatic, in Vedic Sanskrit may have resulted from situations of bilingualism between speakers of Indo-Aryan and other languages.[32]

The migration into the Doāb carries few references to the conquest of or battles against local populations. Most of the celebrated battles were among the major clans and conflicts involved claims to territorial control and rights of succession to these territories. Apart from the famous *dāśarājña*[33] when the Bharatas fought against a confederacy of ten clans, the best known of which were the group of five, the Pūru, Druhyu, Anu, Turvaśa and Yakṣa/Yadu; the Bharatas were also involved in battles against the well-established *dāsa* chief Śambara and raids against the cattle-lifting Paṇis.[34] The Turvaśa and the Yadu fought against the Bharata Divodāsa and were defeated by his son Sudās,[35] the Sriñjayas were victorious against[36] the Turvaśa and Vṛṣivant as also

[30] *Śat. Brāh.* I. 6.1.2-4.

[31] R.L. Carneiro, 'A Theory of the Origin of the State', in *Science*, 1970, 169, pp. 733-8.

[32] M.M. Deshpande and P.E. Hook, *Aryan and Non-Aryan in India*, Michigan Papers on South and South-east Asia, no. 14, 1978, Ann Arbor, 1979.

[33] *Ṛg V.* VII. 83; VII. 18.

[34] *Ṛg V.* I. 51.6; II. 19.6; VII. 8.4. [35] *Ṛg V.* VII. 18. [36] *Ṛg V.* VI. 27.7.

against the Bharatas and the Satvant.[37] Such references come from the *Ṛg Veda* or refer to earlier events in the later texts and the location of such hostilities was in areas to the north-west of the Doāb and prior to the migration into the Doāb. There appears to have been systematic settlement on the new lands with the indigenous population either being absorbed, or being pushed to the margins of the settlement. Such settlements would have been clearings in the monsoon forests which covered the Ganga valley at the time. The proximity of the forests is always present in the consciousness of the settlers as is evident from the contrasting images of *grāma* and *aranya,* where the forest is the place of exile, of demons and *rākṣasas*, but also where the hermitages of *ṛṣis* were situated. The latter were in a sense the vanguard of the new society and the hermitages could act as the nucleii of new settlements. This might also explain why there was such hostility towards these hermitages from those who regarded the forests as their hunting grounds.[38]

The story of Pṛthu Vainya, the first righteous ruler according to tradition, is pertinent in that Niṣāda, the original chief created by the *ṛṣis*, whose name becomes synonymous with hunting and gathering tribes, is expelled to the forest to become a hunter and gatherer. Pṛthu Vainya who is created subsequently introduces cattle-rearing and the plough, an action for which the grateful earth goddess Pṛthivī bestowes her name on him.[39] The entire process would not have been too difficult for those acquainted with the superior technology of iron weapons, with the horse and chariot, and no longer pastoralists but familiar also with the advantages of agriculture That land was now recognized as an item of wealth is evident from its ownership being vested in the clan. The *rājā* Viśvakarma Bhauvana was rebuked by the earth, Pṛthivī, when he tried to make a grant of land and it is also stated that the *rājan* cannot settle people on land without the consent of the clans (*viś*).[40] There is no reference to the sale of land in the Vedic texts.

In the initial stages of settled agriculture pastoralism retained its importance. Apart from the milk provided by cattle, the grazing of cattle in fallow fields resulted in the manuring of these fields not to

[37] *Śat. Brāh.* XIII. 5.4 11; *Ait. Brāh.* II. 25; *Vedic Index*, I., p. 64 ff. R.S. Sharma, *Śūdras in Ancient India*, 2nd ed., Delhi, 1980. p. 17.

[38] Romila Thapar, *Exile and the Kingdom: some thoughts on the Rāmāyaṇa*, Bangalore, 1978. See also *Ṛg V.* x. 146. 1-3.

[39] *Atharvaveda*, VIII. 10.24; *Viṣṇu Purāṇa* I. 13. Romila Thapar, Origin Myths and the Early Indian Historical Tradition', in *AISH*, p. 294 ff.

[40] *Ait. Brāh.* VIII. 21.8; *Śat. Brāh.* XIII. 7.1.15.

mention the use of cattle in providing power for traction. This was known to the earlier people of the *Ṛg Veda*[41] and doubtless intensified as agriculture began to take precedence over pastoralism. Not only does agriculture become more important than cattle rearing in the Doāb but it may also have been the utopian land yielding two crops a year. Reference is made in later sources to harvests of barley in summer and rice in autumn and to the best fields yielding two crops.[42] It has recently been argued from archaeological evidence that double cropping in the Doāb appears to have been regular at this time.[43] Whether it was a system of double cropping or one of rotation remains uncertain, but of the increasing importance of agriculture there can be no doubt. The *Ṛg Veda* refers to the cultivation of *yava* (barley).[44] The later texts mention *vṛhi* (rice).[45] The cultivation of both was possible in the lower Doāb, as for example at Atranjikhera (Etah Distrct). The sites from which rice remains are available are located in the more elevated areas of the Doāb and its environs, and this was clearly not wet rice cultivation. Since it was grown in rotation with barley and wheat its cultivation was neither as labour intensive nor as demanding of irrigation as was the cultivation of rice in the middle Ganga valley. It is equally possible that some of the rice was not locally cultivated but brought from the area to the east of the upper Doāb where it was more widely grown and where wheat and barley played a lesser role. In the later texts there are references to heavy ploughs drawn by anywhere between six to twenty-four oxen,[46] which would be indicative of the heavier wetter soil east of the Doāb. The *Ṛg Veda* mentions wells and doubtless these were used for irrigation as well in the watershed area and the western Ganga valley.[47] Given the obsession with the theme of release of waters in the frequent references to the conflict between Indra and Vṛtra, it is tempting to think that agriculture was primarily dependent on rainfall.

The gradual transition to agriculture made an impact, perhaps indirectly, on other aspects of Vedic life. Among these was the

[41] *Ṛg V.* I. 161.10; IV. 57.4-8; X. 102.8.

[42] *Strabo* XV. 1.13 and 20, quoting Megasthenes of the late fourth century B.C.

[43] K.A. Chaudhuri, *Ancient Agriculture and Forestry in Northern India*, Bombay, 1977.

[44] *Vedic Index*, II., p. 187

[45] *Vājasaneyi Saṃhita* XVIII. 12.

[46] *Atharvaveda* VI. 91.1; *Śat. Brāh.* VII. 2.2.6; *Kaṭhaka Saṃhita* XV. 2.

[47] X. 101. 5-7; I. 105.17.

pattern of change in different sections of society. The vedic *jana* (tribe) incorporated a number of *viś* (clans). These may in origin have been more egalitarian but by the time of the *Ṛg Veda* were bifurcated into the *viś* and the *rājanya*, the latter constituting the ruling families. The description of the *rājanya* even in the Later Vedic literature depicts him as sporting a bow, shooting arrows with accuracy, running chariot races, drinking *surā* and being in effect the epitome of the hero. It was from among these families that the *rājā* was chosen. In one place it is said that those who successfully complete the *aśvamedha* sacifice will share in *rāṣṭra* and become *rājā*s worthy of consecration whereas those who fail to do so will remain members of the *rājanya* and the *viś*.[48] The original relationship between the *viś* and the *rājanya* must have been close.

The bifurcation of Ṛg Vedic times suggests a division into the senior lineages of the *rājanya*s and the lesser, junior or cadet lineages which continued to be called *viś*. Clan lands were held in common by both lineages but worked by the lesser lineage, since the permission of the *viś* was necessary before the *rājā* could settle people on the land. The clans were the original settlers which is the literal meaning of the word *viś* and when land was converted to agricultural use or agricultural land was incorporated into the territory over which the *viś* claimed usage, it belonged jointly to the *viś*. In the past *viś* has been translated as peasantry.[49] This has led to some ambiguity in determining the beginnings of a peasant economy in the Gaṅga valley. ('Peasant economy' is here differentiated from 'peasant society' since the former entails specific obligations and dues which may be absent in the latter where the emphasis is on the presence of cultivators.) That *viś* means a clan is generally accepted and it is used as such for *dāsa*s and *ārya*s. The *viśpati* is in some contexts the chief of the clan and in others the head of the household.[50] Rights on land were probably of usage since ownership is not recorded. The demarcation and measurements of fields mentioned in the late books of the *Ṛg Veda*[51] may well have been lineage and family allotments rather than indications of ownership. Pastoral land raises no problems, remaining common to the village as *vraja* and most animal grazing took place on waste land and forest, of which there was plenty at

[48] *Śat. Brāh.* XIII. 4.2.17.

[49] E.g. R.S. Sharma, 'Class Formation and its Material Basis in the Upper Gangetic Basin, *c.* 1000-500 B.C.', *IHR*, July 1975, II, no. 1., p. 1 ff.

[50] *Atharvaveda*: IV. 5.6; IV. 22.3; *Tait. Sam.* II. 3.1.3.; *Ṛg V.* VII. 55.5

[51] I. 110.5.

that time. The allocation of holdings was probably made by lots; hence the symbolic significance of dicing and its association with wealth. Cultivation could also have been carried out by rotation with no claims to ownership.

The bifurcation of clans into those of higher status and others is not unusal. It often comes about through a claim to differentiation between elder sons and younger sons or the ability of some to lead in cattle-raids, to protect the clan, to establish new settlements as also through the control of alliances with other clans. In the Ṛg Vedic case there was a distinction between the chariot-riding warriors who were pre-eminently the guardians and protectors of the *viś* and the latter who were more sedentary and were the producers of both pastoral and agricultural items. The *viś* as the junior lineage provided prestations, informally extracted on special occasions, to the *rājanya*s who redistributed these among a limited group with *dāna* and *dakṣinā* given to *brāhmaṇas* and bards and oblations offered at the *yajña* rituals. The link between the *rājanya* and the *viś*, suggesting an earlier, closer relationship, is referred to obliquely, for example in the statement that the *kṣatra* and the *viś* might eat from the same vessel,[52] which in a society placing a high value on commensality was a substantial statement of relatively equal status. It is also said that the *kṣatra* is created out of the *viś*, the analogy being to *soma* the ritual drink which when purified leaves the substance for the more common inebriant, *surā*.[53] A comparison is also made then in terms of one being *soma* and the other various plants or of Varuna and the Maruts or Indra and the Maruts or Yama and the Pitṛs.[54] It is interesting that these comparisons are to superior and inferior statuses in the same species. Had the *viś* in origin been commoners with no lineage status or links with *rājanya*s it is unlikely that so much effort would have gone into stating the obvious, that the *viś* was inferior to the *rājanya* and the less powerful.[55] That some awareness of the earlier relationship of common origins persisted is indirectly suggested by the statement that those who seek to equate the two produce chaos.[56] The *rājanya*s as the senior lineages doubtless kept a larger share of the booty from raids but as long as the wealth came from pastoralism in the main it had a relatively more equitable distribution. The relationship between the *rājanya*

[52] *Śat. Brāh.* IV. 3.3.15

[53] *Śat. Brāh.* XII. 7.3.8.

[54] Ibid., III. 3.2.8.; II. 5.2.27.; VII. 1.1.4.

[55] Ibid., XIII. 2.2.15, 2.9.6.

[56] Ibid. V. 1.3.3.; XII. 7.3.15; V. 3.4.11.

and the *viś* in the *Ṛg Veda* is not as distant as it was to become in the Later Vedic period. The *viś* brought its prestations in the form of *bali* to the *rājā* or the chief[57] and the relationship is a subordinate one since the *rājā* is generally chosen by other *rājā*s and the *viś* is essentially the provider of tribute. It is this which sustains the families of the *rājanya*s, together of course with the booty from raids.

Within the broad framework of this dual division there is a further expansion of both those who utilized this wealth and those who produced it. The redistribution expanded from the *rājanya*s to include the priests who legitimized them through the performance of rituals. This in turn required a larger amount of wealth and when booty could not provide enough then the *viś* had to increase its agricultural output. Sacrificial rituals drew off a large proportion of extra wealth and in this process the status of the *rājanya* was not only ensured but gradually raised through priestly legitimation and eventual association with deities. The redistribution at the sacrificial ritual became a fee for the priest. The *viś* was involved as the provider of items to be used as oblations and as the gifts bestowed by the *rājanya* on the *brāhmaṇa*. The *rājanya* of the *Ṛg Veda* was gradually replaced by the *kṣatriya* of the later Vedic period, the term deriving from *kṣatra* meaning power. The power was based on a greater control over the *jana* and its territory which is partly expressed by the territory being named after the *kṣatriya* lineage; to this was added the increasing investment of the ruling chief with attributes to deities by the *brāhmaṇas* as also the demands made by the *kṣatriya* on the *viś*. The latter is succinctly summarized in the sentiment that the *yajamāna* ensures cattle to the *vaiśya* which leads to the subordination of the *vaiśya*, and the *kṣatriya* then requires that the *vaiśya* bring out what he has stored away.[58] That the demands were met was because the *kṣatriya* led the settlement in new lands and protected those already in existence. The advantage of an increasing emphasis on agriculture was that wealth could be augmented without resorting to many cattle raids and this was encouraged by the *kṣatriya*s asserting their superiority. Cattle raids did not cease but began to play a more marginal role in the access to wealth.

The distance between the *kṣatriya* and the *viś* brought about a certain tension and ultimately took the form of the *kṣatriya* claim-

[57] *Ṛg V*. x. 173.6.

[58] *Śat. Brāh*. I. 3.3. 15.

ing more rights of appropriation and the *viś* being reduced to subordination.[59] The tension between the two is indicated in remarks such as, the *kṣatra* eats the *viś*,[60] the simile being that of the deer eating grain, or the repeated reference to the *rājā* as the *viśāmattā*,[61] 'the eater of the *viś*' and the *kṣatriya* being more powerful than the *viś*. The *viś* sets apart a share for the *kṣatriya*,[62] the latter having a share in whatever belongs to the former; suggestive of the germinal idea of what later became a tax and where terms for taxes in later periods such as *bhāga* (a share) and *bali* (a voluntary tribute) can be traced back to these times. In all accounts the *viś* is made obedient to the *kṣatriya*. Despite the distancing between the *kṣatriya* and the *viś* there is no ritual and social exclusion as there was with the *śūdra*s who were not even allowed to enter the sacrificial enclosure (*śālā*) to which only *brāhmaṇas*, *rājanya*s and *vaiśya*s had access.[63] But the *vaiśya* was treading a tight rope for those with wealth could associate with senior lineages whereas those who were impoverished were doubtless treated on par with the *śūdra*s. The difference begins to be evident in occasional statements, for on the whole the *viś* was still included in with the *brāhmaṇas* and the *kṣatriyas*.

The necessity for the *viś* to increase their production to meet these new needs was met partly by new settlements and more land coming under cultivation and partly by incorporating the services of those who were outside the lineage system and could be employed. In this situation the *śūdra*s and *dāsa*s would be the ones available for such work. This ultimately brought about a householding economy in which the extended family constituted the household and employed labour in a series of service relationships. The overall lineage structure did not require a radical change since the flow of wealth still pertained essentially to the requirements of prestations which were consumed in sacrificial rituals and gift-giving. The word for wealth, *rayi* has its origin in the root **rā*, to give.[64] The prestations made by the *viś* to the *kṣatriya*s and the labour provided by the *śūdra*s was a sufficient basis for stratification although the maintenance of stratification

[59] *Tait. Saṃ.* v. 4.6-7.; I. 8.11-12; *Śat. Brāh.* VIII. 7.1.12; X.4.3.22; XII.7.3.15.

[60] *Ait. Brāh.* VIII. 12.17; *Śat. Brāh.* VIII. 7.1.2.; VIII. 7.2.2.; IX. 4.3.5.

[61] *Ait. Brāh.* VIII. 17.; *Śat. Brāh.* III. 3.2.8.

[62] *Śat. Brāh.* IX. 1.1.25.; IX. 1.1.18.

[63] *Śat. Brāh.* III. 1.1.9.

[64] *Ṛg V.* I. 96.7.; *Nirukta* IV. 17.; S. Varma, *The Etymologies of Yaska*, Hoshiarpur, 1953, p. 51.

did not require the machinery of a state, the importance of lineage still being central and adequate for asserting authority. It is perhaps in this context that the *viś* and the *prajā* are said to go down before the *kṣatriya*.[65] *Prajā* is a new concept and presumably includes the non-kin groups as well as the non-lineage groups such as the *śūdras*. A further exclusion of the *viś* from their original status lies in the statement that the *viś* cannot eat the offerings at the sacrifice.[66]

A group of clans constituted a *jana* and the territory where they settled was referred to as the *janapada*, literally where the tribe places its feet. Since the economy of the *jana* included hunting and pastoralism, large forested areas adjoined the settlements and could even carry the name of the *jana*, as for example, the Kuru-vana. Actual control over territory was limited to smaller areas of cultivated land. As long as the settlements were comparatively small (as is suggested by archaeological evidence), lineage authority was sufficient as a mechanism of control. This is in part indicated by the fact of the *janapadas* being named after the *kṣatriya* lineages which had established their control in the area. Thus apart from the Kuru and Pañcāla, mention is made of Kekaya, Madra, Matsya, among others.

The *ksatriya* lineages claimed control over the territory of the *janapada* but the notion of a well-defined territory was uncertain at this time. The boundaries between *janapadas* tend to be topographical features such as forests, rivers and streams and hills. Territory was seen as the clearly indentifiable settlements and the more liminal areas of forests and waste land between settlements. The term which in the post-Vedic period is used for territory, *rāṣṭra*, is mentioned at this time, but its meaning does not seem to be that of a well-defined area over which absolute control is claimed. *Rāṣṭra* from the root **rāj*, to shine, is used more in the sense of realm, sphere or authority. Both in the *Ṛg Veda* and later Vedic texts it is the sustaining of the *rāṣṭra, rāṣṭrabhṛt*, which is crucial.[67] In the reference to the *rāṣṭrabhṛt* oblations the idea of nourishing is further endorsed by the oblations being of *ghi* (clarified butter).[68] This would hardly suggest territory in a literal sense. It is also stated that the *rājās* are the *rāṣṭrabhṛt* and because of their association with the deities they are permitted by the gods to offer

[65] *Śat. Brāh.* III. 9.3.7. [66] Ibid., II. 5.2.24. [67] *Ṛg V.* X. 173
[68] Śat. Brāh. IX. 4.1.1. 13.

the *rāṣṭrabhṛt* oblations. Even more important is the statement that only he becomes a *rājā* who is allowed by other *rājā*s to assume the title. This suggests a strengthening of the demarcation between lineages to which the *rājā*s belonged and the lower status lineages which played little or no role in the choice of the *rājā*.

There is some controversy as to whether the *rājā* was elected by the clans or was the choice of a more select group. In one hymn of the *Ṛg Veda* it is clear that those who chose the *rājā* are distinct from the *viś*.[69] The nature of the bifurcation between the senior and junior lineages would support the former selecting the *rājā* if only to further curb the power of the *viś*. The demand of *bali* would have been weakened if the *viś* had the right to elect a *rājā*. The *Śatapatha Brāhmaṇa* asserts that ruling power and social distinction are attached to a single person and multiplicity is the characteristic of the clan.[70] Yet in another hymn of the *Ṛg Veda*, again of a late section of the collection, there is a reference to the *viś* chosing a *rājā*.[71] Possibly this was the earlier custom which was later discontinued when the *rājanyas* became more powerful.

The ṭitle *rājā* has frequently been translated as king rather than chief. In many cases the later meaning of the term is applied to these early sources. Yet even in later periods the connotation of *rājā* has varied from landholder to king. The office of *rājā* in the Vedic sources was primarily that of a leader in battle and the protector of the settlements. This is evident both from the functions of the office and the association of *rājā* with Indra. Gradually the notion of the *rājā* as the nourisher and as the symbol of prosperity and fertility took precedence and the deities associated with the office were suitably enlarged. Reference to *rājā*s as in an assembly[72] would suggest members of the *rājanya* lineages or an assembly of chiefs. Later references even when the role of the *rājā* had changed still occur, often in the plural, and suggest persons belonging to a superior social group rather than individual kings, for example, the *rājā*s sharing the wealth among themselves and offering a sixteenth share at the *yajña* or the prayer for the prosperity of the *rājā*s.[73] It was at these assemblies that one among the *rājā*s was chosen to preside and to protect. The office was not hereditary to begin with and the choice and the consecration of the *rājā* would have occurred with every vacancy. It is curious that of the many

[69] *Ṛg V.* x. 173.1.

[70] *Śat. Brāh.* IX. 3.1.13-14.; IX. 4.3.10.

[71] *Ṛg V.* x. 124.8.

[72] Ibid, x. 97.

[73] *Atharvaveda* ii. 6.4.; *Tait. Sam.* v. 7.4.3.; *Vāj. Sam.* 18.48.

close associates listed as the *ratnins*, there is no mention of any heir-apparent as would be expected in a system of kingship with hereditary succession. In the later Vedic period the consecration of the *rājā* became more elaborate with claims to *kṣatra* and consecration became an avenue to power. Claims to sovereignty and increasing demands of prestations were sought to be justified through consecration rituals. The absolute, secular authority associated with kingship appears to be absent in these sources and the income from prestations is poured into the rituals and given to those who perform the rituals. This also led to the greater inter-dependence of the *kṣatriya* and the *brāhmaṇa*, a relationship which is pointed to in the *Śatapatha Brāhmaṇa*. It is said that the *brāhmaṇa* was the god Mitra and therefore the conceiver and the *kṣatriya* was Varuṇa the doer. At first they were separate and thus undermined each other's power. Then Varuṇa called for unity with Mitra and conceded pre-eminence to him, after which both prospered.[74] Thus the *kṣatriya* must always have a *brāhmaṇa* (the reverse is too obvious and is left unsaid!). In the absence of both the hereditary principle and primogeniture the consecratory rituals had special significance to legitimation. In the search for power, consecration became the hallmark of the *rājā* backed by senior lineages of the *kṣatriyas* and the cultivation of land was left to the householding families of the *viś*.

The inclusion of the householding system in the lineage structure was probably a marginal change to begin with. Gradually it became the thin end of the wedge which was partially responsible for erosion of the lineage system with the eventual arrival of the notion of private ownership of land and of the development of commerce as more than just exchange. The significance of non-kin labour in the householding economy can be seen at the point where in some areas lineage society underwent a change and the householding economy emerged but in a different framework incorporating a peasant economy and commerce.

Initially the householding system was probably common to both the *rājanyas* and the *viś*. Hence the *gṛhapati* or the head of the household could be from either and is mentioned with respect in the texts. In the late sections of the *Ṛg Veda* and in the *Atharva Veda* the *gṛhapati* appears to be of the higher lineage since the term is brought in when describing the nuptials of the daughter of *Sūrya* the sun-god.[75] Elsewhere in the *Ṛg Veda* Agni is called the *gṛhapati*

[74] *Śat. Brāh.* IV. 1.4.1 ff.

[75] *Ṛg V.* X. 85.; *Atharvaveda*, XIV. 1 and 2.

and the sacred household fire is the *gārhapatya*.[76] That the *gṛhapati*s are associated with wealth is indicated by a hymn in which Pūṣan is urged to make them generous in their gifts.[77] In the later Vedic literature there are references to *gṛhapati*s and *yajamāna*s which suggest *kṣatriya*s but do not preclude *vaiśya*s. The principal ritual role of the *gṛhapati* was that of the *yajamāna* (he who orders the sacrifice) and it is possible to trace the growing importance of the *gṛhapati* through the rituals. The *vaiśya gṛhapati* occurs in the later Vedic literature but more often in the context of the *grāmaṇī*. It is said that all *vaiśya*s wish to become *grāmaṇī*s, probably because *grāmaṇī*s were thought to be wealthy.[78] That the *grāmaṇī* was from the *viś* is clear from the ceremony when the *rājā* visits the home of the *grāmaṇī* and offers oblations to the Maruts and it is said that the Maruts are the *viś*, a connection which is frequently mentioned, and that the *grāmaṇī* is also the *viś*.[79] The *grāmaṇī* was among the lineage heads and important families of the *viś* who had both power and wealth. Their wealth did not come from prestations but was produced by their own efforts, its abundance dependent on an economy which may be termed householding.

With the increasing shift to agriculture and the decreasing interest in pastoralism the role of the *rājanya*s as chariot-riding chiefs carrying out cattle raids and bringing in booty was not as conducive to producing wealth as it had been earlier. When the *rājanya*s were converted into *kṣatriya*s and they acquired power and became the hub of the redistributive system they came to depend more on the agricultural activities of the *viś* and the prestations which the *viś* could provide. Since numerically the *kṣatriya*s as chiefs would have been considerably smaller than the members of the *viś* such a dependence was not impossible. Gradually therefore the householding economy came to be associated with the lineages of the *viś* rather than with those of the *kṣatriya*s. In a more sedentary phase the household became the unit of agricultural production and doubtless began to claim permanent usage over the land which it worked and in which it invested its labour, a permanency which was acceded to by the community when it saw that it was necessary to agriculture and that it ensured a predictability in prestations. With the weakening of clan control over agriculture and probably more so in new areas of settlement the permanency of

[76] *Ṛg V.* I. 12.6.; I. 36.5.; I. 60.4.; VI. 48.8.
[77] Ibid., VI. 53.2
[78] *Tait. Sam.* II. 5.4.4.
[79] *Śat. Brāh.* V. 3.1.6.

usage was likely ultimately to be transmuted into family ownership. This was probably aided by a greater concern on the part of the *kṣatriya* lineages with demanding prestations than on asserting ownership over clan lands. Prestations were stored in the *kṣatriya* household for consumption in rituals, for using in gift-giving and to furnish the basis for the generous hospitality expected of the *kṣatriya* household. However the storage seems to have been short-lived as the references to such 'treasuries' are few and far between.[80] The households of the *viś* also began to maintain a minimal storage in cases where the *gṛhapati*s of the *viś* are described as *yajamāna*s. The eventual emergence of the *gṛhapati* as a social category was in relationship to the *viś*. When *viś* is replaced by *vaiśya* it suggests an altered status, the clan element decreasing and the individual status becoming more apparent. At this stage the *śūdra* is also mentioned more frequently and a distinction made between the *vaiśya* and the *śūdra,* as in the famous passage which states that the *vaiśya* can be oppressed but the *śūdra* can be beaten or slain.[81] This raises the question of whether the actual cultivation was done by the *vaiśya*s or the *śūdra*s.

The cultivator in the technical sense of the word was the *kīnāśa* of the *Ṛg Veda*[82] and is referred to as the *karṣaka/kassaka, kṣetraka* and *śūdra* in post-Vedic literature. *Vaiśya* is not used for the cultivator although the *vaiśya* may have derived his wealth from agriculture. The explanation for this may lie in the need to differentiate between three categories of cultivators: the primitive cultivator, the cultivator in a system which has been called the householding economy and the cultivator in a peasant economy. Primitive cultivation is almost limited to swidden and subsistance agriculture and is outside our context. In the second category the household is the unit of production and consumption based on agriculture and livestock breeding. In borrowing the term 'householding' from Polanyi[83] an attempt is made here to use it with reference to a pre-state society. Although in the Vedic period

[80] *Ṛg. V.* x. 97.6.; x. 191.; *Atharvaveda* III. 29.1.

[81] *Ait. Brāh.* VII. 29.4.

[82] IV. 57.8. *Kīnāśa* in later texts has an ambiguous meaning. The general sense is that of a cultivator who may not own the land he cultivates and is therefore better translated as a ploughman working for a wage and dependent on the owner. B.N.S. Yadav, 'The Kali Age and the Social Transition', *IHR*, 1978-9, v., nos. 1 and 2, pp. 37-8. Ṛg Vedic references to *kṣetra* suggest cultivated land or just land rather than individual holdings (I. 100.18.; I. 33.15.; III. 31.15; V. 45.9; X. 85.4; X. 91.6).

[83] K. Polanyi, *Dahomey and the Slave Trade*, p. 70 ff.

householding does not emerge as an independent social formation in the terms in which Polanyi describes it, certain attributes of the form can however be usefully extracted from Polanyi's model and can perhaps elucidate Vedic data.

Polanyi describes the household as consisting of agnatically related men and their families claiming membership of a patrilineal lineage. The household as a unit is often made up of smaller houses functioning as an entity. Inheritance remains within the kin group and alienation of neither house nor land is permitted. The cult of the ancestor is the focus of the household and is maintained by hereditary priests. To this may be added other features: the household utilizes family labour as well as some specialists—herders and craftsmen for example—who are not kinsmen and are more in the nature of retainers except that they are not paid a wage but maintained by the household and paid in kind. Presumably such labour could be extended to cultivators helping in the fields. Slaves would be attached to the families of chiefs and they would be mainly domestic slaves. The household consumes much of what it produces but the excess is taken by those to whom it is politically subordinate in the form of prestations and gifts. This system is marked by the absence of two factors which distinguish it from a peasant economy. Firstly the family exercises rights over the land which it cultivates and there are no tenants since cultivation is carried out by family labour and by those who are attached to the household in various occupational capacities. Secondly there is no regular contractual payment of rent or tax to the political authority or to the state since it does not presuppose the existence of a state. The point at which taxes start to be paid by the household is also the point at which cultivation through membership of a landowning lineage weakens and individual ownership is asserted, even though lineage ties would still be respected and often seen to be effective.

The *viś* was by now characterized by the householding system, with the *gṛhapati* as the patriarchal head, commanding both family labour and that of *śūdra*s and *dāsa*s. Neither of the latter were helots and could well have been impoverished members of the *dāsa-varṇa*, their subordination arising as much from their being aliens outside the lineages as from their impoverishment. It is difficult to describe the *śūdra*s or the *dāsa*s as helots in the strict sense as there were clans of each which co-existed with the *ārya*s and some of the chiefs of these clans are described as wealthy or are spoken of with respect in the earlier texts. In time however the terms *śūdra* and *dāsa* came to be used for those performing labour services. The interchangeability of *ārya* and *dāsa* status in the post-Vedic period and the fact that an *ārya* could become a *dāsa* for a temporary period precludes a system of helotage.

The mention of *bali, bhāga* and *śūlka* has been interpreted as reference to taxes of various kinds. But none of these were collected at a specified time and regularly, nor were they of a precisely defined amount and there is no mention of specific occupational groups from whom they were collected or of designated persons who made the collection. All these conditions were fulfilled in the post-Vedic period when taxes were collected and these terms were used as terms for taxes. In Vedic literature their connotation would appear to differ. The *balihṛt* is clearly the tribute paid by a conquered tribe in one instance.[84] More frequently *bali* is a generalized offering made by the *viś* and may better be translated as tribute or a prestation rather than tax.[85] If there was any seasonality associated with the *bali* then it related to the performance of rituals or occasions of consecration. It may in origin have been the tribute of a defeated tribe but came to be extended to offerings brought by subordinate groups to those in authority. Terms such as *balihṛt* and *balikṛt*[86] can be rendered as the bearers and providers of tribute rather than as tax-paying groups, as in the case of the reference to the *vaiśya* as the *balikṛt*. This is further clarified by the request to the gods to distribute the wealth thus collected.[87] *Bali* therefore remained a prestation. *Bhāga* in the sense of share relates to the distribution of spoils after a raid or the division of prestations on ritual occasions. Its origins may be traced to the offering of the first fruits as a token to the sanctity of the chief, an idea which is known to other early societies.[88] It is connected with *bhāgadugha* which because of the word *dugha* (milking) can be interpreted as the collector of the share or in the association of *bhāgadugha* with Pūṣan, the distributor.[89] The share of the chief is not stipulated and this is in contrast to the later

[84] *Ṛg V.* VII. 6.5.

[85] E.g. *Ṛg V.* I. 70.5.; V. 1.10. See also J. Gonda, *Ancient Indian Kingship ...*, Leiden, 1969, pp. 12-13.

[86] *Ṛg V.* VII. 6.5.; X. 173.6.; *Ait. Brāh.* VII. 29.

[87] *Atharvaveda*, III. 4.2-3.

[88] Goldman, *Ancient Polynesian Society*, p. 509; cf. *Śat. Brāh.* V. 2.3.9.

[89] *Tait. Sam.* I. 8.9.2; *Kāṭhaka Sam.* XV. 4; *Tait. Brāh.* I. 7.3.5; III. 4.8.1. *Śat. Brāh.* I. 1.2.17; V. 3.1.9.

period when it is said that the king is to receive one-sixth of the share as a wage for protecting the people,[90] and still later when in the post-Mauryan period the designation *ṣaḍbhāgin* (the receiver of one-sixth share) comes to be used for the king.[91] The term *śulka* in the *Ṛg Veda* does not mean a tax but is used in the sense of a measure of value and in the *Atharvaveda* the context is generally that of the weak paying a price to the strong.[92] In the *dharma-śāstra*s of the post-Vedic period and in Pāṇini there is the meaning of a tax but also the meaning of a nuptial gift or dower, suggesting that it might have been used for bride-price or dowry.[93] This meaning could well have gone back to the Vedic Period when such gifts were a part of marriage alliances. The words *bali, bhāga and śulka* do change their meaning from tribute, distribution and price (in the sense of value) in the *Ṛg Veda* to forms of taxes and dues in the later *dharma-śāstra* literature. Whether they meant the former or the latter in the intermediate period of the later Vedic texts would depend largely on the context of their occurence and the context suggests the greater likelihood of the former meaning. The change of meaning carried with it a major change in the relations between the chief and the clan. From voluntary giving with a pattern of mutual honouring it changed to compulsory giving with a pattern of unequal reciprocity. As long as status was based on genealogy the inequality was symbolic, when it was based on land it became substantial.[94].

The *vaiśya* as the *gṛhapati* was the source of wealth for the *kṣatriya* and the *brāhmaṇa* through prestations for the *kṣatriya*, and through *dakṣiṇā* as well as the items consumed in the course of the sacrificial rituals, for *brāhmaṇas*:[95] hence the statement that *vaiśyas* can be oppressed, presumably to extract further wealth.[96] The *vaiśya* was beholden to the *kṣatriya* for protection as well as the provision of lands to settle and cultivate. The prestations necessary for the sacrificial ritual precluded a completely self-sufficient village economy and established links across lineage segments and consequently a circuit of villages as well. With the disintegration of

[90] *Baudhāyana* D.S. I. 10.18.1.

[91] *Arthaśāstra* II. 15; *Viṣnu D.Śā.* III. 22.

[92] *Ṛg V.* VII. 82.6; VIII. 1.5; *Atharvaveda*, III. 29.3; III. 4.3; *Śat. Brāh.* XI. 2.6.14 qv.; *Vedic Index*, II, p. 387.

[93] Pāṇini, IV. 3.75.

[94] Goldman, *Ancient Polynesian Society*, p. 509.

[95] *Śat. Brāh.* IV. 4.2.15; IV. 6.9.3-5; IV. 6.9.25; XI. 8.4.1 ff; XII. 1.1.1 ff.

[96] *Ait. Brāh.* VII. 29.4.

clan holdings, the *gṛhapati* who had earlier cultivated lands held jointly gradually came to exercise ownership, though perhaps still as the head of the family, over land cultivated by the family, since the *Dharma-sūtras* in the subsequent period invest him with the right to bequeath property to his eldest son or divide it among his sons.[97] The transition from clan ownership to family holdings was probably accelerated when clan settlements became more scattered in new clearings together with the establishment of the economic viability of the household as a unit. In such a situation voluntary prestations were perhaps less forthcoming and the need for protection in new areas was paid for by a regular contribution which was to assume the character of a tax in the post-Vedic period. This became feasible when, with the intensification of plough agriculture, such an economic surplus was possible. Ultimately, in the post-Vedic period the decline of the householding economy would lead to the rise of peasant tenures in which the *śūdras* were to emerge as the major peasant group. This change is reflected in the statement in a *Gṛhya-sūtra* that the *gṛhapati* should have his fields ploughed, suggesting thereby not only the working of the land by another[98] but possibly also the individual ownership of land since the *gṛhapati* is not described as a member of a lineage.

The changing relationships wrought by agriculture and the new settlements in the western Ganga valley would also have required some readjustments within the *viś*. Those who were able to establish a household and farm would have aspired to *gṛhapati* status and constituted a part of what came to be the *vaiśya varṇa*. Others reduced to the condition of labourers and artisans would have moved increasingly to the edges of society to finally become part of the larger population of *śūdras*. At a still further remove, *dāsa* came more frequently to mean a slave. Most references suggest domestic slavery as in the case of the hundreds and thousands of slaves employed in the household of Yuddhiṣṭhira and who are listed as part of his wealth staked in the game of dice.[99] The figures are almost certainly exaggerated, for the functions which they performed would not have required such excessively large numbers.

These developments resulted in a series of contrasting status stratifications which were sought to be arranged into a system through the scheme of *varṇa*. The earlier texts speak of an *ārya-varṇa* and a *dāsa-varṇa*, suggesting a dual division.[100] The words

[97] *Baudhāyana D.S.* II. 2.3.2 ff.

[98] *Aśvalāyana G.S.* II. 10.3.

[99] Sabhā Parvan, 46 ff

[100] *Ṛg V.* I. 104.2; III. 34.9; II. 12.4.

are traced to *arya* and *dāha* in Iranian sources and *ārya* connotes a man of wealth and possessions,[101] a frequent association in Vedic sources too. A contemporary lexicon explains it as an owner or master[102] and Pāṇini glosses it with the statement, *aryaḥ svāmi vaiśyayoḥ*,[103] the wealth of the *vaiśya*s being an indication. The *dāha* of the early Iranian becomes *dasa* in Vedic texts and means 'a male, man, a hero', in much the same sense as *manuṣa*. This is often the meaning of the names taken by tribal groups.[104] Tacitus refers to the Arios and the Dahas settled along the Indus river.[105] (That *ārya* was a term of respect is clear from Buddhist sources where *bhikkhu*s are often addressed as *ārya* and where the *ārya* and the *dāsa* are juxtaposed to mean master and slave, especially with reference to lands beyond the Indus.[106]) The dichotomy is expressed in Vedic sources by regarding the *dāsa-varṇa* as of a different symbolic colour. In the *Ṛg Veda* they are associated with wealth, walled settlements, and with darkness or blackness.[107] But they were apparently not a helot group or slaves since their wealthier members are mentioned by name. These were evidently people of some substance and *dāsa* chiefs such as Balbūtha and Tarukṣa are eulogized by *brāhmaṇas* for their munificence or else, as Śambara, are feared for their strength.[108] Some *dāsa* chiefs are so powerful that Indra is said to have battled against them.[109] The *viś* of the *dāsa* are referred to in the *Ṛg Veda*,[110] indicating that they were distinct and separate. Possibly the *dāsas* of the *Ṛg Veda* were agricultural communities

[101] H.W. Bailey, 'Iranian *Arya* and *Daha*', *Transactions of the Philological Society*, 1959, p. 71 ff.

[102] *Naighantaka* 2.6.

[103] III. 1.103.

[104] Curiously the area inhabited by the *daha/dāsa* being the Indus valley would suggest an earlier nomenclature which I have argued elsewhere applied to this region and that is Makan. This in Proto-Dravidian would convey the same meaning of a man, or hero or male. The name Suvīra is also indicative of the same meaning, being used for this region in a still later period and occurs frequently as Sindhu-Suvīra. Romila Thapar, 'A Possible Identification of Meluhha, Dilmun and Makan', *JESHO*, 1975, XVIII, pt 1, p. 30 ff.

[105] *Annales* 10-11.

[106] *Maj. Nik.* II. 144-50; *Samantapāsādikā* II., p. 238.

[107] II. 12.4; 20.8; III. 12.6; IV., 16.13. 30.13; VIII. 40.6; X. 69.5-6; *Atharvaveda*, VII, 90.1-2. Blackness is also associated with the *asuras* and the *rākṣasas* and was probably symbolic of all those who were not speakers of Indo-Aryan.

[108] *Ṛg V.* VI. 31.4; VII 99.5; *Ṛg V.* VIII. 32, 40 and 46; *Chand. Up.* IV. 2.1-5; *Vedic Index*, II. p. 355.

[109] *Ṛg V.* I. 51.5-6, 103.8, 104.2; V. 30; VI. 20.7.

[110] II. 11.4; IV. 28.4; VI. 25.2.

of the Late Harappan or post-Harappan cultures of the area, perhaps even of the agricultural niches scattered in the region. That the word eventually came to mean 'slave' may initially have had more to do with the hostility towards them than with their actual subordination. The *Dasyu*[111] are noted for their variant religious beliefs and customs which the *ārya*s saw as the negation of their own and which appear to have been the chief distinguishing characteristic. The assimilation of these groups was facilitated by their being given subordinate status. Reference to *ārya-kṛita* in later texts indicate a status to which a person can be restored after having been a *dāsa*.[112] *Varṇa* was to become a system of putting together the structure of the society and the colour symbolism was retained. The four *varṇa*s were latter associated with the colours white, yellow, red and black.[113] In the dual division of *ārya* and *dāsa*, the *ārya* was distinguished by wealth and status. The *ārya*s would be those who either belonged to the senior or to the cadet lineages (*rājanya*s and the *viś*) as well as those who were included in the circuit of prestations and redistribution, that is, the *brāhmaṇas*. The *dāsa*s were excluded from this circuit even when they were wealthy enough to bestow gifts on the *brāhmaṇas*. With the sharpening of stratification and the beginnings of professional specialization, the constituents of the *ārya*s were more clearly demarcated into *brāhmaṇa*, *kṣatriya* and *vaiśya*, with the *śūdras* incorporating an amorphous group of excluded clans and low status professions. The former described as *dvija* or twice born (the second birth being initiation) in later texts deepens the demarcation and underlines the connection between initiation and lineage customs.

Another contrast of a more broadly cultural kind but going back to Iranian sources was that between the *deva*s and the *asura*s. Among the Iranians the *deva*s were hostile and the *ahura/asura* god-like. In Vedic sources both are described as the progeny of Prajāpati[114] and the *asura*s in some cases are treated with respect but eventually come to represent evil, hostile forces. The *asura*s though feared are depicted as the more sophisticated of the two. They lived in permanent habitations whereas the *deva*s moved about in carts.[115] They were acquainted with the right seasons for

[111] *Vedic Index*, I. p. 347; *Ṛg V.* I. 33.4; I. 51.8; VII. 6.3.

[112] Pāṇini IV. 1.30; *Arthaśāstra* III. 13. In the *Ṛg V.* VI. 22.10 the *dāsas* and *āryas* are jointly invoked.

[113] *Aśvalāyana G.S.* II. 8.6-8: cf. *Rg. V.* X. 20.9. The Licchavi clans are distinguished by a difference in colour but not skin pigmentation. *Mahāvagga* VI. 30.3-4.

[114] *Śat. Brāh.* I. 5.3.2; I.7.2.22; II. 2.2.8; VI. 6.2.11.

[115] Ibid. VI. 8.1. 1-2.

agricultural activities[116] and associated with wheel-thrown pottery.[117] The *asura* form of marriage involved a bride-price[118] and they performed regular burial rites.[119] The magical power of the *asuras*, perhaps a subtle concession to their superiority, which plays a role in the narrative of the *Mahābhārata*, is mentioned in the *Ṛg Veda* in association with the bringing of rain.[120] The ambiguity towards the *asuras* revolving around common origins, power and hostility, remains a constant feature in Vedic literature.[121]

To this list may be added a further social duality, recorded only in later Vedic literature.This essentially linguistic distinction to begin with, between the *ārya* and the *mleccha,* separating the speakers of Indo-Aryan from others, takes on a social connotation as well, with *mleccha* meaning a barbarian or one outside the pale and ritually impure.[122] The recognition of basic differences in these dualities of *deva-asura* and *ārya-mleccha* is an indication of the recognition of heterogeneity and the need to juxtapose the differences within a working system.

The integration of groups through particular forms of kinship was a parallel process and is more often referred to in the concept of the *gotra*, literally meaning a stockade for cows, which was used to identify descent groups among the high status *varṇas*. Initially it appears in more frequent association with the *brāhmaṇas* and was to remain essential to *brāhmaṇa* identity. Later sources mention certain *kṣatriyas* (such as the Andhaka-Vṛṣṇi, Śākyas and Licchavis) using *gotra* identities. But among them it was more a means of differentiating between families within the clan than for wider social identification. The *gotra* was an exogamous clan where exogamy was emphasized in the prohibition on marrying *sagotras*, and marrying those related upto seven generations on the father's side and five on the mother's. The latter would preclude cross-cousin marriage, so a special exception had to be made in case of *brāhmaṇas*

[116] Ibid. I.6.1.2-4 [117] *Tait. Brah.* ii. 2.9.5: *Maitrāyani Saṃhitā* I. 8.3.

[118] *Yajñavalkya Smṛti* III. 61; Manu III. 31.

[119] *Śat. Brāh.* XIII. 8.1.1. *Chāndogya Upaniṣad* 8.8.5. [120] V. 63.3.

[121] A curious reference to the bull *asura*, Vṛṣṇa, in the *Ṛg Veda*, III. 38.4 calls to mind the bull as a clan name which occurs so frequently in early Indian tradition in the form of Vṛṣṇi, Vṛṣabha, Ṛṣabha, not to mention the frequeny of the bull on the Harappan seals.

[122] *Śat. Brāh.* III. 2.1.23. Romila Thapar, 'The Image of the Barbarian in Early India', in *AISH*, p. 152 ff.

[123] E. Senart, *Le Mahāvastu*, I, pp. 283-361, *Pāṇini* I. 2.65 ff.

from the south.[124] The exogamous basis of the *gotra* system doubtless facilitated the induction of outsiders of high or appropriate status; the insistance on marrying out meant the necessity of bestowing equal status on new groups and inducting such groups into the *varṇa*. This is reflected in the increase in the number of brahmanical *gotras* from seven to eighteen and forty-nine, and many more by the end of the first millennium A.D. Doubtless the increase was partly due to segmentation among the main *gotras*, although this generally took the form of a new *gaṇa* or *pravara*, a new sub-group. More likely this was also the result of co-option of new groups. This might account in part for *brāhmaṇas* of non-*brāhmaṇa* ancestry. The counterpart to exogamy was that inheritence of property was open only to members of the same *gotra*.

For the *kṣatriyas* to adopt the *gotra* system was something of an anomaly since they were identified by lineage or *vaṃśa*, preferred endogamy and are known to have made cross-cousin marriages as well as to have married into collateral lineages. There is a greater frequency of variation in the actual types of marriages among *kṣatriyas*. The classic example would be the implications of marriage alliances in the three generations of Pāṇḍavas from Pāṇḍu to his sons and grandsons who subscribe to endogamy, fraternal polyandry and cross-cousin marriage, but all among lineages claiming *kṣatriya* status. Within the *vaṃśa* there was a differentiation between the senior lineages and the rest as is interestingly demonstrated by the story of Yayāti and the interchange of status between his eldest and youngest sons, Yadu and Pūru;[125] the inheritance having gone to the youngest, it became necessary to justify this action. Endogamy among the *kṣatriya vaṃśas* was doubtless encouraged because land rights were vested in kinship links and birth. In the initial transition to agriculture, genealogical links would have acted as a means of narrowing access to status and resources; genealogies of increasing depth in later sources would perhaps point to wider mobilization, particularly among the Candravaṃśa lineages which tend to follow a segmentary pattern. There is evidence of a fairly widespread movement of peoples not only from the watershed to the Ganga valley, but also into the Vindhyan region. The assimilation of local populations must certainly have been part of the reason for the frequency of breaking away or

[124] *Baudhāyana* D.S., I. 1.2.1 ff.

[125] *Mahābhārata*, Ādi Parvan, 71 ff; cf. Udyoga Parvan 104.121 and 147.3-13.

a fissioning off from the main lineage, although migrations were also a form of easing tension and establishing new settlements.

The nuclear unit in such a society was the *kula*, the family, and a group of such families made up the *grāma* or village. *Grāma* by extension therefore also referred to a community. In some instances it conveyed the meaning of a body of men.[126] It was therefore a larger unit than the *kula* but smaller than the *viś*. The term *grāmaṇī* used for a village headman in many sources was also at this stage the chief of an aggregate of families or of a community settled in the same place. The larger unit *viś* or clan is recorded even among the *dāsa*. It counted in turn towards the identity of the tribe or *jana*. The word *jana* carries the notion of people as well as growth and fecundity.[127] A characteristic phrase of this literature is *pañca-janāḥ*, the precise meaning of which remains elusive.[128] It has been suggested that it may refer to five specific tribes whose eponymous ancestors are the founders of the clans, namely Yadu, Turvaśa, Druhyu, Anu and Pūru, or that it may symbolize the totality of the people, the image deriving from the five fingers of the hand.[129] The notion of the *pañca-janāḥ* seems to have been basic to the pattern of one of the two major *kṣatriya* lineages, that of the Aila or Candravaṃśa as given in the *Purāṇa*s and the *Mahābhārata*.[130] The main lineages are described as descended from the five sons of Yayāti of which the Paurava and the Yādava are the most important and the descent lines close with the victory of the five sons of Pāṇḍu at the Kurukṣetra battle. At crucial points of geographical diffusion, the genealogies list a pattern of five brothers such as the reference to the five sons of Uparicara establishing themselves along the southern bank of the Yamuna as far as Magadha[131] or the five sons of Bali establishing themselves in eastern India.[132] At one level the concept of the *Pañca-janāḥ* could have referred to all the clans, but at another level it carried a

[126] *V.I.*, I., p. 245 ff.

[127] Minoro Hara, 'A Note on the Sanskrit Word Jana', *Pratidānam*, The Hague, 1968, p. 256 ff.

[128] *Vedic Index*, I, p. 269; II., pp. 466-7. D.D. Kosambi, 'The Vedic "Five Tribes"', *JAOS*, 1967, 87, pp. 33-9. Yāska's *Nirukta* III. 8.8.; IV. 23.1, explains it as the five categories of *pitṛ*, *gāndharva*, *deva*, *asura* and *rākṣasa*.

[129] *Ṛg V.* I. 108.8; W.P. Lehman, 'Linguistic Structure as Diacritic Evidence on Proto-Culture', in G. Cardona *et al.*, *Indo-European and Indo-Europeans*, Pennsylvania, 1970.

[130] *Viṣṇu Purāṇa* IV. 10 ff.

[131] *Mahābhārata*, Ādi Parvan 57.

[132] *Viṣṇu Purāṇa* IV. 18.

symbolism which remains obscure.[133] If it is to be interpreted as the symbol of the totality then its derivation would probably be from the notion of the four on all sides and the one in the centre, thus reflecting the idea of the four quarters as well.

The *kula, viś* and *jana* was a spatial distribution moving in widening circles from the nucleus to the rim. A vertical hierarchy was also evident in the *jana* with the distinction between the *rājanya* and the *viś*, where the *rājanya* was increasingly identified with the senior lineages aspiring to power and the *viś* represented the lesser lineages. Among the *rājanya* were those who had been consecrated as chiefs.[134] The *rājanyas* had access to power, *kṣatra,* and came to be called *kṣatriyas*, and the gradual displacement of the term *rājanya* by *kṣatriya* would indicate the emergence of a new focus of power among the ruling clans. The etymology of *rājā* remains uncertain and the later view that it derived from the verb 'to please' is unacceptable. The roots **raj,* **rañj,* **riñj*, suggest the connotation of the verb 'to glow' or 'to shine'. This could be extended to mean the one who shines and is resplendent and therefore the chief.[135] It has also been suggested that the Indo-European root **reg̃* for *rex* in Latin indicates the one who leads, directs, follows what is right or proceeds in a line,[136] a meaning which would suit the idea of a head of a lineage. The increasing emphasis on the special status of the *rājanya/kṣatriya* had its counter-weight in the declining status of the lineages of the *viś*. The *viś* perhaps consoled themselves through a control of the householding economy in which they continued to have access to wealth as the *gṛhapatis*. Nevertheless the wealth of the *rājanya* was considerably greater since he was the recipient of prestations and

[133] Echoes of the idea seem to continue in the later concept of the *pañca-vīra* or five heroes of the Vṛṣṇis, a segment of the Yādavas. The five heroes were eventually worshipped as part of a cult in Saurashtra, southern Rajasthan and Mathura. The Tamil tradition of the Aimperumvelir, the five great *vel* chiefs is also curious, particularly as the Velir claim to be of Yādava descent. The notion of five constituting a unit is often found in the Indian subcontinent. The sacrificial ritual in the *Śat. Brāh.* involves five animals, listed as man, horse, bull, ram and he-goat, and the *gṛhastha* is required to perform five *yajñas* during the day, etc.

[134] This is evident from even later references to the *gaṇa–saṅgha* system as in Pāṇini VI. 2.34.

[135] Yāska, *Nirukta*, II. 3. This presents a parallel with the Proto-Dravidian *vel*. DED 4562 and 4524 would suggest a homophone meaning the chief and the resplendent one.

[136] E. Benveniste. *Indo-European Language and Society*, London, 1973, pp. 311-12.

doubtless also took a substantial share of the booty. Although much of this wealth went into the *yajña*s some of it would certainly have been temporarily stored since the *rājanya* was expected to use it to make gifts on frequent occasions.

The emergence of the *kṣatriya* was linked to clan rights over land as well as to the sanction given to the new status by the *brāhmaṇa*. In the definition of the *ārya*, three groups are mentioned, the *brāhmaṇa*, *kṣatriya* and *viś*. Whether or not one subscribes to the theory of the tripartite function in viewing the relationship between the three,[137] or to the definition of these three which such a function assumes, it is clear that an attempt is made to link them. But gradually, this link is broken when the *vaiśya* is more often included with the *śūdra* and the two are regarded as of lower status than the *brāhmaṇa* and the *kṣatriya*. Kinship links between the *brāhmaṇa* and the *kṣatriya* are occasionally conceded but the formal systems remain quite distinct. The ranking order between *brāhmaṇa* and *kṣatriya* is ambivalent to begin with where the former is dependent on the latter for *dāna* and *dakṣinā* and the latter requires that his power be legitimized by the former.[138] In any case the two are superior to the rest of the community, a superiority which is clearly expressed in the formula that the *vaiśya* and the *śūdra* should be enclosed by the *brāhmaṇa* and the *kṣatriya* at the sacrifice in order to make the former submissive.[139] Even in burning wealth, so characteristic of the *yajña* ritual, the decision to do so is controlled by those who had access to the maximum wealth—the *kṣatriya* and the *brāhmaṇa*. The redistribution of wealth was therefore curtailed by the requirement of reciprocity between the *ksatriya* and the *brāhmaṇa* where the reciprocal relationship enhanced the status of each. The *kṣatriya* provided the *brāhmaṇa* with what was essentially a sacrificial fee disguised as it may have been in ritual gift-giving. The *brāhmaṇa* not only bestowed legitimation on the *kṣatriya* but also gave him access to special skills and knowledge intermeshed with the ritual which inevitably augmented the power of the *kṣatriya*.

[137] G. Dumezil, *Mythe et Épopée*, I and II, Paris, 1968, 1971; *Flamen-Brahman*, Paris, 1935.

[138] Later sources mention *kṣatriya*s moving to brahmanhood such as the Kāṇvas who were of the Ajamīḍha lineage. *Viṣṇu Purāṇa* IV. 19; Garga who was a Bharata, ibid.; Mudgala of the Candravaṃśa lineage, *Bhāgavata Purāṇa* IX. 21; and Harita of the Sūryavaṃśa, *Viṣṇu Purāṇa* IV. 3.

[139] *Śat. Brāh.* VI. 4.4.13.

In addition to the first three the other distinctive unit included in the overall definition of a caste society was the *śūdra*, associated with servility in the earlier texts. The *śūdra*s were described in the later *Dharma-sūtra*s as including *sankīrna* or mixed *jātis*. Each *jāti* was born out of a hypergamous (*anuloma*) or a hypogamous (*pratiloma*) marriage from among the three *dvija* or upper castes, *brāhmaṇa*, *kṣatriya* and *vaiśya* or their progeny. The number of *jāti*s could theoretically increase on each new intercaste marriage but in effect the increase occured whenever there were major changes in which new social groups and professions were established. The *śūdra* as a *varṇa* was clearly a category added onto the original structure at a time when artisans and cultivators had to be accommodated and when alien groups were assimilated into caste society and had to be assigned varying statuses. That the concept of the *sankīrna-jāti* was a later attempt at explaining a *de facto* situation is evident from the divergence in the texts regarding the particular combinations of castes producing *śūdra* offspring.[140] The elimination of kin-body in the case of *śūdras*, by assigning them only the status of their parents, was a means of excluding them by denying them a lineage connection. In a strongly lineage-oriented society this would in itself place them outside the social pale. The occasional substitution of *śūdra* and *dāsa* would suggest that many of the groups included in the *śūdra* category may have earlier been *dāsa*s prior to the technical meaning of the word as slave. Etymologically *śūdra* could have been derived from *kṣudra* meaning small. Both these are known to have been the names of particular peoples at some stage. Latin sources mention the Oxydrakoi and the Sudracae and Sodroi as tribes of north-west India.[141] The Kṣudraka are linked with the powerful Mālava (the Malli/Malloi of the Greeks) almost as a compound to mean the small and the big. Mention is also made of the *gaṇa*s of the Śūdras and the Ābhīras dwelling on the Sarasvatī[142] The sense of smallness was worked into that of lowliness, indicated in a statement that the *śūdra* is the servant of another, he can be made to work at the will of his master and even be beaten,[143] a sentiment endorsed in the later *dharma-śāstra*s as well. The denial of a lineage and the insistence on mixed caste origins, if not the word *śūdra* itself, would

[140] Manu, x. 1-73 discusses the origins of various *samkīrna jātis* of *śūdras*.

[141] *Curtius Rufus* ix. 4; cf. *Mahābhārata*, Sabhā Parvan 48.14.

[142] *Mahābhārata*, Sabhā Parvan 29.9.

[143] A. Sharma, 'An Analysis of the Epithets applied to the Sūdras in Aitareya Brāhmaṇa vii. 29.4', *JESHO*, Oct. 1975, xviii, pt 3, pp. 300-18.

also point to the members of this group coming from a floating population of those who had fallen out of lineage ties and were available to serve whomever could provide them with a livelihood. As such the labour of the *śūdra* was to become an important factor in eventually augmenting the wealth of those whom they served.

Distance between the *dvija* and the *śūdra* was also maintained through the notion of pollution. This was to influence yet another category that, designated by the adjective *vrātya* or degraded, applied to degradation from the three upper castes, resulting from the non-observance of the required rituals. Thus *vrātya-kṣatriya*s was to become a useful category in which to place those who were politically powerful but were obviously not *kṣatriya*s in the true sense. The ultimate in distance and separation was of course the untouchable who is referred to in the later period. Purity and pollution, central to the question of ritual status was expressed in terms of bodily contact, through ceremonies relating to rites of passage; through touch, the one among the five senses which was crucial in this matter; through food taboos and through sex by the regulation of marriage relations.

The theoretical construct of caste society was not the simple unfolding of a class society, nor the mechanical measurement of ritual status. It was an attempt at inter-locking a series of social units based on diverse rules of functioning but all in the context of a lineage system. At least three formal structures were to evolve from this genesis: the exogamous *brāhmaṇa gotras*, the preference for endogamy of the *kṣatriya*s and the *śūdra jāti*s identified by parental status in which lineage is negligible. The differentiation therefore includes the widest possible lineage system, the out-going *gotra*, as well as the narrowest social unit, the *śūdra jāti*. In its initial phase the notion of *varṇa* attempted to construct a complete social framework using differentiated lineage systems demarcated by distinctive kinship forms. Variations in marriage rules are sometimes indications of status where higher-status groups prefer exogamy and lower status groups endogamy. Descent however lies at the heart of status.[144] At the theoretical level this would be one condition for working out a hierarchy, although the emphasis lies in each unit constituting its own method of comprehending lineage. Added to this was the notion of ritual status which was made explicit in the idea of purity and pollution where the hierarchy goes

[144] Goldman, *Ancient Polynesian Society*, p. 418 ff

from the purest to the most polluting, and where, in an exchange of services, those not actively involved in production would claim higher status on the basis of intangible authority seeking justification from religious sanction through the performance of rituals. Yet implicit in this hierarchy is the attempt to define and limit the access of each group to economic resources by the gradually increasing insistence on occupational functions, accompanied by the channelizing and redistribution of wealth being limited to the castes claiming ownership of clan resources and higher ritual status. That the attempt was not entirely successful, would be suggested by economic stratification also taking place within each of these vertical *varṇa* groups. There are impoverished *brāhmaṇas*[145] and there are wealthy *śūdras*.[146] The inequality implicit in the process of an exchange of services was to the advantage of those who were dominant, who had access to resources and used these to claim higher status. In terms of economic status the wealthier *brāhmaṇa*, the *rājanyas* and the *gṛhapatis* among the *viś* would constitute the upper level, their wealth being comparable. The initial attempt therefore in the *varṇa* scheme was not to reflect a class system but a lineage system and seek to integrate and reflect the reality of a lineage system. When eventually the lineage system declined, the structure of caste society also underwent a change, even though it carried with it elements of the lineage system.

With ritual status as a criterion of hierarchy, it was relatively easier to induct groups into higher *varṇas*. *Brāhmaṇas* of *kṣatriya* origin are met with in the earlier sections of many genealogies and may even reflect common origins in some cases. What are equally evident are *brāhmaṇas* of non-Aryan origin. Agastya and Vasiṣṭha are said to have been born from jars.[147] Kavaṣa Ailūṣa, the Ṛg Vedic seer appears to have been a *dāsiputraḥ* as was the well-known Kakṣīvant.[148] These may have been *dāsa* families of some standing who could have been profitably inducted into the *brāhmaṇa varṇa*. The associations of the early *brāhmaṇa gotras* are barely in conformity with orthodox tradition considering that the Bhṛgus were priests to the *daitya* kings,[149] and Pulastya was the ancestor of the *rākṣasas*.[150] Induction would also have been easier through

[145] *Ṛg V.* I. 105.7 ff.
[146] *Śat. Brāh.* V. 3.2.2; *Pañcaviṃśa Brah.* VI. 1.11.
[147] *Ṛg V.* VII. 33.10-1
[148] *Vedic Index*, I. p. 143, 366, II. 259.
[149] Pargiter, *Ancient Indian Historical Tradition*, pp. 197, 307.
[150] Ibid. p. 241.

exogamy. In later periods it was maintained that the *gotra* system was prevalent only among *brāhmaṇas*,[151] although it is conceded that *kṣatriyas* could take the *gotra* of their *purohitas*.[152] In the case of the *kṣatriyas*, recruitment to the *varṇa* meant latching onto one of the two major genealogies, Sūryavaṃśa or Candravaṃśa, which was done with considerable facility in the first millennium A.D., when low status chiefs acquired power and aspired to the best lineage links.[153] Within the *varṇa* however it often took economic reality to guarantee tangible status.

At the core of the *jana* the substantial division was the bifurcation of the *kṣatriya* and the *viś*. In the initial structure of the *varṇa* system, both the *brāhmaṇa* and the *śūdra* could have been, as it were, addenda. As priests attached to the clans, the ancestry of the *brāhmaṇas* went back to the shamans, mantics and seers of earlier times (the *vipras* and the *ṛṣis*), to which were added the reciters of hymns and the living manuals on rituals. The latter may have required co-option of priests from the indigenous cultures since the continuance of ancient rituals is strongly endorsed. The more priestly function of the *brāhmaṇa* comes into its own in the rituals of the Later Vedic texts. His special status is underlined by his privilege of being allowed to consume the remains of the sacrifice and this included the flesh of the sacrificed animal.[154] In the analysis of rituals, elements of earlier cultures may be seen to have survived.[155] It has been argued that the notion of purity and pollution may have been a survival of Harappan times. If Harappan society was ruled by an aristocracy claiming power through ritual and religion then it would be tempting to suggest that the *brāhmaṇa-śūdra* dichotomy went back to Harappan times, constituting the equivalent of an *ārya* and *dāsa varṇa* and into which the *jana* with its dual division of *kṣatriya* and *viś* intruded, and had to be accommodated. This is not to suggest that there was a continuity from Harappan times, but that some elements of an earlier culture can be recognized as part of the new lineage system.

[151] Medatithi commenting on Manu III. 5 maintains that the *gotra* and *pravara* system was prevalent among the *brāhmaṇas* alone and quotes the *Aśvalāyana Śrauta Sūtra* I. 3 in support (P.V. Kane, *History of Dharmaśāstra*, II. 1, p. 493).

[152] *Apastamba Śrauta Sūtra* 24.10.11-12

[153] Romila Thapar, 'Social Mobility in Ancient India with Special Reference to Elite groups', in *AISH*, p. 122 ff.

[154] *Vedic Index*, II, p. 83; *Ait. Brāh.* VII. 26; *Śat. Brāh.* III. 4.1.2; VII. 5.2.37-42.

[155] Romila Thapar, 'The Archaeological Background to the Agnicayana Ritual', in F. Staal(ed.), *Agni*, Vol.I., Berkeley, 1982

The *varṇa* framework therefore was visualized as a structure for the integration of varying sub-systems rather than merely a reflection of the socio-economic hierarchy. This would account for the seeming changelessness of the rules of social functioning, although within each sub-system change was clearly registered. That the *varṇa* system was a consciously worked out structure by the mid-first millennium B.C. is apparent from the late hymn added onto the *Ṛg Veda*, the *puruṣasūkta*,[156] in which the origin of the four *varṇa*s from the body of Prajāpati is described: the symbolism being that of separate limbs performing different functions but co-ordinated in the unit of the body and listed in hierarchical order. The tying in of this description to a ritual event was perhaps an implicit emphasis on *varṇa* relating increasingly to ritual status.

Not only was the stratification rationalized in the concept of *varṇa*, but the function of each group was more clearly defined. The *brāhmaṇa* was now less of the seer and more of the expert on ritual. The more elaborate rituals such as the consecration sacrifices for the *rājā*s required an array of trained professional priests. The more simple *gṛhya* (domestic) rituals described in the *Gṛhya-sūtra*s, mainly concerned with rites of passage, required a single *brāhmaṇa* in most cases. The increasing importance of both categories of rituals emphasized not only the political role of the *brāhmaṇa* as a source of legitimization for chiefs but also as the authority and sanction of cultural identity in relation to the *gṛhapati*s, as also for the assimilation of new groups. The emphasis on *vāc* and *mantra*, the correct recitation of the right formula required meticulous training and memorizing with a comprehension of the language of the texts, which in turn became a criterion of *ārya* - hood together with the observance of *varṇa* rules. The Kuru-Pañcala region was noted for the excellence of the language and the relative purity of the rituals, suggesting that it was in this area and this period that the norms were decided upon—a time and a place which had already seen a considerable assimilation of varying groups of people and observances. Many of the people further away such as those in the *janapada*s of the Punjab and the middle Ganga valley are castigated for having discarded the rituals,[157] a rebuke which had more to do with other changes in these areas.

The importance of political authority is highlighted in the substitution of *rājanya* by *kṣatriya*. The context of the *rājanya* was

[156] *Ṛg V.* x. 97.

[157] *Atharvaveda* v. 22.14; *Baudhāyana* D.S., I. 1.2.13 ff.

essentially status within the lineage. *Kṣatra* implied temporal authority and power which was based less on being a successful leader in battle and more on the tangible power of laying claim to sovereignty over territory, demanding prestations and also symbolizing ownership over clan lands. The status of the chief had been hedged around by his relationship to various clan-gatherings. Among these were the *gaṇa, vidatha, sabhā, samiti* and *pariṣad*, some of which, as nomenclatures at least, survived into later periods although their functions changed.

The *gaṇa* is identified by the name of a common ancestor and is also reflected in the *gotra* system in which sub-groups are referred to by *gaṇa*s. That it was at some stage a clan would seem evident from terms such as *gaṇapati, gaṇeśa* and *gaṇasya rājā*, which were synonyms for *rājā*.[158] It may have been a special body of selected members who held equal status and formed a peer group, as is suggested by the *kṣatriya gaṇa*s of later sources, and by the compound of *gaṇa-sangha*s for chiefdoms.[159] It may have been a cattle raiding peer group in origin since the leader is associated with cattle raids.[160]

The *vidatha* as its name suggests was probably a ritual occasion on which the distribution and sharing of wealth took place, among other things.[161] Booty being a major source of wealth, the *vidatha* would also be linked with cattle raids and heroic exploits.[162] The distribution doubtless had to carry the sanction of *brāhmaṇas* as well as their inclusion as recipients, hence their presence at these gatherings.[163] Sāyana's gloss that the *vidatha* be equated with the *yajña*[164] would be expected in a system where redistribution or exchange of wealth was a ritual occasion. This in turn would explain the need for Indra-Mitra-Varuna being the presiding deities of the *vidatha*.[165] That the *vidatha* declines in the later Vedic period would reinforce its original function as the ritual occasion for the redistribution of wealth for, when other forms of economic redistribution became prevalent, the *vidatha* would have become

[158] *Ṛg V.* II. 23.1; *Ait. Brāh.* I. 21.
[159] *Vāyu Purāṇa* 88.4-5; 86.3; 94.51-2.
[160] *Ṛg V.* VI. 59.7; IX. 76.2.; III. 47.4.
[161] *Ṛg V.* II. 1.4; III. 38.5-6; VII. 40.1; *Atharvaveda* I. 13.4.; *Vedic Index*, II, p. 296. cf., ṚV. X. 11.8.
[162] *Ṛg V.* II. 1.16; I. 56.2.
[163] *Ṛg V.* X. 91.2-9
[164] R.S. Sharma, *Aspects of Political Ideas and Institutions in Ancient India*, p. 85 ff.
[165] J.P. Sharma, *Republics in Ancient India*, London, 1968, p. 72.

redundant. Although it has been argued that the *vidatha* was a folk assembly, a view which has been strongly opposed,[166] it was nevertheless of some consequence to Ṛg Vedic society judging by the frequency of reference to it. If it was an occasion for the distribution of wealth, then even its being a kin gathering rather than a folk assembly would be in keeping with such a function.

Indo-European cognates for *sabhā* mean the assembly of the kinsfolk which would make its membership exclusive.[167] In later periods the *sabhā* becomes an advisory body assisting the king. The association of the *sabhā* with gambling may have had antecedents in the division of grazing lands and arable lands by lot.[168] This would of course be a different function from sharing booty. This is indirectly supported at the symbolic level in the Sabhā Parvan of the *Mahābhārata*. The Pāṇḍavas lose their wealth and power in a game of dice which is held in the *sabhā* which was an assembly of kinsmen who not only witness the throw of dice but also discuss the question raised by Draupadi regarding the legal validity of Yudhiṣṭhira placing her as a stake when he himself had lost his freedom.

Dicing is not merely indicative of a weakness for gambling. The names used for the dice and the throws are heavily imbued with symbolic meaning. Dicing is not only associated with the *sabhā*, the most respected of the assemblies, but the one who throws the dice is on occasion referred to as the *sabhā-sthānu*,[169] literally, the pillar of the assembly hall. This gives dicing far greater importance than mere entertainment. Its significance may have derived from a time when the throw of dice determined the division of wealth. This can only be inferred from the frequent association of dicing with wealth and the notional significance of dicing with rituals conferring and legitimizing power. The inclusion of a simulated game of dice as part of the ritual of the *agnyādheya* and *rājasūya* sacrifices[170] would again point to its symbolic importance. Possibly lots were also transferred from one person to another by a throw of dice, an echo of which can be heard in the events of the Sabhā Parvan. Thus

[166] R.S. Sharma, 'Vidatha: The Earliest Folk Assembly of the Indo-Aryans', *JBRS* 1952, xxxvii, pts 3-4, pp. 429-48; J.P. Sharma, *Republics in Ancient India*, p. 62 ff.

[167] cf. *RV* II. 24.13; VII 1.4; *Atharvaveda*, XIX. 55.6; XII. 1.56; VIII. 10.5; XX. 128.1.

[168] *Rg. V.* X. 71.10; *Atharvaveda* VII. 12.3.

[169] *Vedic Index*, II., p. 426.

[170] *Vedic Index*, I., p. 2; G. Held, *The Mahabharata: an ethnological study*, London, 1935.

the association of wealth and loss of wealth with gambling need not be taken in a literal sense but may refer to a more complex activity involving an exchange of wealth conditioned by a throw of dice. The stake was referred to as *dhana,*[171] generally meaning wealth and rarely, booty. The earlier texts refer to *vibhīdaka* nuts used as dice and since these cannot carry numbers, a computation must have been essential to gambling.[172] Later there are references to throws—Kṛta, Tretā, Dvāpara and Abhibhū or Kali—which suggest numbered surfaces of dice reading four, three, two and one. These terms are ultimately transferred to the division of the *mahā-yuga* into four *yuga*s or periods of cosmic time, thus linking the throw of dice with time and fate. The association of a share or distribution of wealth with the notion of fate is also evident in the use of terms such as *bhāga* and *bhāgya.*

The terms *sabhā* and *samiti* occur more frequently in the late books of the *Ṛg Veda* and in the later Vedic literature. In the *Atharvaveda* they often occur together.[173] There is also an association of the *rājā*s (in the plural) with these assemblies suggesting that they were the gathering points of the senior lineages, those of the *rājanya*s. The infrequency of the presence of the *viś* in these assemblies may reflect its declining status. The presence of the *rājā*s did not preclude the selection of one among them as the presiding *rājā.*[174] The *samiti* appears to have been a more open assembly than the *sabhā. The pariṣad* is mentioned even less frequently and appears to have had an even smaller membership.[175] If its later function is any clue to its origins then it may have been a body of specialized advisers, although such a body may not have been particularly relevant to the political needs of the time.

To the extent that some were plenary assemblies, and some limited to the *rājanya*s, they were essentially occasions for reiterating hierarchy and order; consultation was more a ritual function than an administrative necessity as it was to become in later periods. Over time, some of these gatherings declined in importance whilst others increased and even changed their function. To maintain that in the Vedic period different tribes used different forms of assembly is not indicated by the evidence as the gatherings are not

[171] *Vedic Index*, I., p. 388
[172] Ibid. p. 2 ff.
[173] *Atharvaveda* VII. 12.1; VIII. 10.5-11; XII. 1.56. *cf. RV.* IX. 92.6; X. 97.6.
[174] *Ṛg V.* X. 124.8, 166.4, 173.1; *Atharvaveda* I. 9.3; III. 4; IV. 22
[175] *Ṛg V.* III. 33. 7.

differentiated in accordance with tribes.[176] What is certainly feasible is that some types of assembly were more central to the functioning of certain tribes than others.

Sharing of wealth was an intrinsic part of raids providing booty. Cattle-herding and agriculture provided the items required for the performance of rituals. The redistribution and consumption of this wealth was channelled through separate acitivities. Booty from raids was shared by general consent in the assemblies where the larger shares presumably went to the chief who led the raid as well as to the priest who had invoked the deities and who would be doubly blessed if he was also to perform the role of the bard eulogizing the chief, as he often did in the *dāna-stuti* hymns of the *Ṛg-Veda*. This would serve to reinforce the status of the *kṣatriya* and the *brāhmaṇa* and further demarcate them from the lesser lineage of the *viś*. The wider distribution among other members of the *viś* who had participated in the raid was doubtless conducted in the assembly so that it would not be an arbitrary division. A decline in inter-tribal raids would lead to a corresponding decline in those assemblies where the wealth from such raids was allocated to the clan of those who were successful in the raid. The wealth listed in the *dāna-stuti* hymns, primarily cattle, horses, chariots, gold and slave girls were all items which could have been picked up in a raid. Wealth obtained from herding and agriculture consisted of objects offered as prestations at the ritual of sacrifice and therefore included the best animals of the herd, milk, *ghī*, grain, cakes and the like. The offering of these items had to be induced from the *viś* and the ritual occasion provided the incentive to part with wealth. The redistributive aspect lay not only in the gifts made to the priests but also in the sacrificing of the animals and the burning up of the other items as part of the prayer for the well-being of the *yajamāna* and the *viś*. The destruction of wealth in this fashion was a method of underlining the status of the *yajamāna* (either a chief or a *gṛhapati*) but at the same time, a subtle means of preventing the *yajamāna* trom amassing excessive wealth.

The specific and precise functions of each of the assemblies remains unclear. With a changing social system the interlocking of functions and overlapping between them also changed and varied. The curb on the concentration of power in the hands of the *rājā* was not a legal formality, but was born out of a society in which power was not completely restricted to a few. With the narrowing

[176] J.P. Sharma, *Republics in Ancient India*, p. 15. ff.

of kinship rights on land and an increase in prestation requirements, the more exclusive gatherings of kinsmen such as the *sabhā* became channels for the concentration of power and the more open assemblies were further diffused. The selection of the chief which was validated in the assemblies gradually gave way to more emphasis on succession being legitimized through ritual consecration by the priest.[177] The nature of these assemblies indicates that they relate to stratified societies and not to egalitarian clans.

The retinue of the *rājā* moves in inverse proportion to the concentration of power in his hands and includes widening circles of representation. This is reflected in his relationship with the *ratnins*,[178] a term frequently translated as 'recipients of treasure' but originally meaning 'recipients of a gift'. The list varies slightly from text to text but generally includes the *purohita, rājanya*, chief wife, favourite wife, discarded wife, *senāni, sūta, grāmaṇī, kṣattar, saṃgrahītar, bhāgadugha* and *akṣavāpa*. Some texts include the *go-nikartana* which has been taken to mean a slayer of cows or a butcher and by extension probably a huntsman. In the course of the *rājasūya* ritual the *rājā* goes to the home of each and there offers an oblation to a particular deity. The deity is generally one that is associated with the function of the *ratnin* and relates to either protection, fertility and the evil eye or wealth and its distribution. This procedure is referred to as the *ratna-havis* and symbolizes the *rājā* making a gift to the *ratnins*. In a society characterized by the system of gift-giving this would be seen not merely as a symbol of the status of the *ratnins* but also as a sign of the *rājā*'s dependence on them. It is for this reason that they are referred to as the makers of the *rājā*. (The post-Vedic concept of the *ratnāni* reflects a reaching back to the idea of the *ratnins* since it consists of the seven elements which are said to constitute the 'treasures' of the king : the wife, the minister, the general, the wheel, the elephant, the horse and the jewel. The inclusion of the latter four suggests a distancing of the king from his subjects, where each object provides an abstract concept associated with kingship.)

The *ratnins* are the support to the *rājā*'s office both at the symbolic and functional level. The *purohita* at this early stage rode in the *rājā*'s chariot and recited the appropriate *mantras* for his safety

[177] *Śat. Brāh.* v. 3.3.12; *Ait. Brāh.* viii. 5 ff; *Tait. Brāh.* i. 7.51 ff; *Pañcaviṃśa Brāh.* xviii. 8 ff.

[178] *Vedic Index*, ii, pp. 199-201

and well-being.[179] His role as domestic priest to the royal household evolved with the coming of monarchy. The *rājanya* was clearly an important member of the clan. The inclusion of the wives points to fertility rituals, the avoidance of the evil eye from the discarded wife and marriage alliances. The latter would be particularly important in a ritual such as the *rājasūya* where even if the *rājā* had made fresh alliances through marriage, the earlier links had to be restated. The rest of the twelve would be members of the *rājā*'s entourage but with a wider concern with economic and political functions. The *sūta* (bard) remained close to the *rājā* and ensured his immortality in the land of the living. As *saṃgrahītar* the charioteer had responsibility for the well-being of the *rājā*. In one of the variant lists the significance of the chariot is further emphasized by the inclusion of the *takṣa-rathakārau* (carpenter and chariotmaker) amongst the twelve.[180] The *senāni* as a designation was used in later times for the commander of the army. In this context the latter probably refers more to the head of a troop since there is no reference to any regularly constituted army or to professional soldiers. Raids and battles seemed to have been the business of members of the *viś*.[181] The *kṣattar* is taken as the door-keeper or as one who distributes. The *bhāgadugha* and the *akṣavāpa* were both involved in distributive functions in the lineage system. The emphasis in this group is on the centrality of the *rājā* in his chariot, presumably symbolic of the cattle raid and of skirmishes highlighting his role as protector; of the dependence on fertility for prosperity; and of the persons involved in the procedure relating to the distribution of wealth. The twelve *ratnins* represent the sanction of a wider circle but they remain essentially within the orbit of clan functioning. The extent to which they were regular office-bearers is limited since there is little reference to the periodic assesment and collection of taxes or to a separate armed force. It was however from the germinal functions of this group that the designations for some of the later offices were adopted. The *rājā* at this point remains the 'eater of the *viś*; the *viśāmattā*[182] and the *bhāgadugha*[183] assists him in this activity. Thus the *rājā* was surrounded by persons performing specific functions and some of them were even in a sense his retainers but there was no adminstrative machinery and no

[179] Gonda, *Ancient Indian Kingship* ..., London, 1969, p. 65 ff.

[180] *Maitrāyanī Sam.* II. 6.5; IV. 3.8; *Śat. Brāh.* V. 3.1.1 ff; V. 4.4.7; *Tait. Brāh.* I. 7.3.1 ff; *Tait. Sam.* I. 8.9.1 ff.

[181] *Śat. Brāh.* V. 4.3.8.

[182] *Śat. Brāh.* VIII. 7.1.2, 7.2.2.

[183] *Śat. Brāh.* I. 1.2.17, V. 3.1.9; *Tait Brāh.* I. 7.3.5; *Tait. Sam.* I. 8.9.2.

system of delegating powers. The existence of the *ratnins* would point to two significant developments. One was the emergence of a group of non-kinsmen who ultimately took on the character of retainers to the *rājā* and who could contribute to the accumulation of power in the office of the *rājā*. It is also suggestive of a relationship between the *rājā* and others not based on kinship but on reciprocity.

Underlying the concept of *kṣatra* is that of *rājya*, temporal authority which is demarcated from sacred authority, and this is firmly stated at the time of the consecration when it is said that the *rājā* has authority over the people, *prajā*, but the *brāhmaṇs* accept only the authority of the deity Soma.[184] Yet the actual relationship between sacred and temporal authority was one of interdependence. Various categories of *rājya* are listed of which the most eminent is "the chief of the gathering" or the *sāmrājya*.[185] This is often translated as 'empire', but a more realistic rendering would be to regard it as a high status among *rājās* (chiefs) and with the increasing tendency for clans to confederate, the status of *samrāj* would become inevitable. As a corrective to the assumption that the *rājā* held excessive power it is well to keep in mind that the same chiefs who are associated with the performance of the consecration rituals as part of their claim to *sāmrājya* were also the ones who carried out their raids in the dewy season and received a share of the booty.

Exalted titles such as *samrāj, virāj, parameṣṭha, ādipati* and so on are scattered throughout the texts and should not perhaps be taken too literally. The various ceremonies performed by the *rājā*s were in the nature of *saṃskāra*s, purification rituals and ceremonies for imbuing the *yajamāna* with power. These rituals were said to place the *rājā* in the proximity of the gods and gradually the *rājā* came to be accepted as divinely appointed. The gods were eligible to titles incorporating sovereignty, paramountcy and overlordship, and as a consequence of these ceremonies the *rājā* also felt himself eligible for such titles. Thus the attributes of Indra and of the chief of the clan tended to merge and the one was seen in light of the other. Divine appointment drew the chief towards kingship but this was still short of claims to divinity. The latter became more common in the period after the rise of the monarchical state. The analogy with the gods also underlined the role of the *rājā* as the nourisher and the protector and protection was so

[184] *Śat. Brāh.* v. 3.3.12.

[185] *Ṛg V.* III. 55.7, 56.5; IV. 7.1; V. 63.5; VI. 7.1; VI. 27.8; VIII. 19.32; VIII. 42.1.

important that it was equated with discipline and the avoidance of chaos.

It is stated that a people without a *rājā*, was a condition of anarchy.[186] The fear of anarchy is frequently alluded to which is not surprising in a society moving towards complex stratification. The *rājā* was in many ways the economic and political pivot of the lineage system. He integrated the control over territory with access to available resources as also production where productivity was a measure of the chief's efficiency. His position is symbolized in the linkage between the well-being of the clan and the physical well-being of the chief. This focus on the chief led to additional attributes associated with him. Not least among these was a connection with the gods and even if he was not himself regarded as divine, the insistence that the gods had intervened in his selection marked him out as a special person. This was not occasioned by a mere fancy for proximity to the gods, but the exigencies of an increasingly heterogeneous society demanded a category of persons who could be invested with authority. To concentrate power in one family could also have been the solution to tensions and hostility among the clans. In situations of migration to new areas, leadership plays an important part. Migration itself would help to stabilize political power by channelizing the potential for conflict into fission, provided settlements in new areas were attractive and did not involve constant battling against powerful previous inhabitants. A mechanism for assimilating such populations would allow migration to act as a safety-valve which prevented a major change towards state formation. The continual proliferation of such a system could have been checked by an obstruction to fission which would possibly have forced the change.

With the gradual concentration of power in the families of chiefs, there followed other changes which were eventually to move in the direction of encouraging the emergence of kingship. It is not easy to locate the point of change but the tendencies were clear. Election and selection was superseded by attempts at hereditary claims[187] as is evident from the genealogies, admittedly shallow in the early stages, as for example that of Sudās.[188] Genealogies of greater depth occur in the *Mahābhārata, Rāmāyaṇa* and *Purāṇas*, and were compiled in a later period. The gradual emphasis on primogeniture safeguarded succession within the lineage. The link

[186] *Ait. Brāh.* I. 14.6; *Tait. Brāh.* I. 5.9.1 ff.

[187] *Ṛg V.* x. 33.4.

[188] *Vedic Index*, II, p. 454

between the *brāhmaṇa* and the *kṣatriya* became stronger with the latter exchanging legitimation for gifts, *dāna*[189] Implicit in this relationship was the idea that those who invest the *rājā* with divinity or legitimize him are alone permitted to remove him.[190] This was a far cry from the elected chief or legitimacy being based on kinship rights. The latter were still important but subject to brahmanical approval as is evident from the story of the wicked *rājā* Veṇa whom the *brāhmaṇas* had finally to strike down with stalks of the sacred *kuśa* grass.[191] Another important concession was the investment of the *rājā* with the right to punish (*daṇḍa*) and to make him exempt from punishment.[192] This was the necessary concomitant to his being made responsible for maintainance of law and order. However these aspects are not especially highlighted until the subsequent period.

Notions of divinity associated with the office of the *rājā* guaranteed the eventual transition to kingship. This restricted eligibility for the status of *rājā* to families already associated with the office. Earlier ideas of the well-being of the community being directly related to the health and well-being of the chief were reinforced at the rituals, particularly those focusing on rejuvenation, such as the *vājapeya*. Physical deformities of any kind invalidated claims to rulership and could create a crisis over succession. The blindness of Dhṛtrāṣṭra and the skin ailment of Pāṇḍu precluded both from uncontested succession and introduced the complication over the inheritance of the realm of the Kurus which had finally to be sorted out through a war. The sacerdotal status of the *rājā* also bestowed on him certain essential powers, necessary for the prosperity and fecundity of the kingdom, as for example, that of bringing rain. The king as 'rainmaker' is a widespread idea in many societies and its prevalence in the Indian tradition is recorded in a number of instances when drought accompanies the rule of an unrighteous *rājā* who has to be removed or goes voluntarily into exile before the rain falls again.[193]

The major sacrificial rituals such as the *rājasūya, aśvamedha, vājapeya,* became occasions for the consumption of wealth in lengthy ceremonies, some extending over many months. These were

[189] Romila Thapar, '*Dāna* and *Dakṣinā* as forms of Exchange', in *AISH*, p. 105 ff.

[190] *Śat.. Brah*, v.3.3.12.

[191] *Mahābhārata*, Śānti Parvan, 59.115; *Viṣṇu Purāṇa* I. 13.

[192] *Śat. Brāh*. v. 4.4.7.

[193] The story of Devāpi in some versions combines the disqualification of a physical ailment with legitimacy associated with drought and rain. *Ṛg V*. x. 98; *Nirukta* II. 10: *Bṛhaddevatā* VII. 148 ff; *Viṣṇu Purāṇa* IV. 20.

accompanied by lavish libations of milk and *ghī*, offerings of grain in various forms and the sacrifice of the choicest animals of the herd. The *yajña* took on some of the characteristics of the potlatch in literally burning up all this wealth. The redistribution of wealth through gift-giving on such occasions was primarily from the *kṣatriya yajamāna* to the *brāhmaṇa* priests. The change from animal herding to agriculture is reflected in the objects included as *dāna* and *dakṣinā* where heads of animals gradually gave way to preparations of grain and eventually to land. Only gold remains constant. The need for extensive consecration rituals would suggest that initially the position of the *rājā* as a superior among other *rājā*s was not so secure and required validation. If the *rājā* was selected to be the chief then he would not only have to prove himself but would also have to be invested with the requisite powers which would demarcate him from other *rājanya*s. This was prior to the assumption of such a status through the system of hereditary kingship. It is interesting that of the two families, it is the Pāṇḍavas establishing themselves at the new centre at Indraprastha who perform the *rājasūya* and not the well-entrenched Kauravas at Hastināpura.

Gift-giving served to reinforce social status and reciprocity between the dominant groups. The notion of obligation was seen as the priest performing services for the *rājā* and in return receiving gifts. Since in every case the gift was an object of considerable material value and therefore crucial to the livelihood of priests who had no other means of material support, it is ostensibly symbolic but in effect a fee.[194] Gift-giving was not restricted to an exchange between *kṣatriyas* and *brāhmaṇas*. At the *rājasūya* sacrifice for example, initially gifts are brought by other chiefs as prestations to the *yajamāna*, the *rājasūya* of Yuddhiṣṭhira being such an occasion.[195] The chiefs vye with each other in making valuable gifts, partly because the value of the gift reinforces their status and partly because it is expected that when they in turn perform the *rājasūya* a still more valuable gift will be returned.

Spectacular sacrifices involving the resources of the *rājā* were not the only occasions for gifting or redistributing wealth. Periodic sacrifices relating to changing seasons or to phases of the moon were part of the regular calender of observances among those of high status.[196] Social obligations were also sources of economic

[194] Romila Thapar, '*Dāna* and *Dakṣinā*'.

[195] *Mahābhārata*, Sabhā Parvan, 30 ff.

[196] *Śat. Brāh.* I. 6.3.36; II. 5.2.48.; *Tait. Sam.* I. 6.10.33.

distribution. The *saṃskāra* rituals of the *Gṛhya-sūtras*, and the domestic rituals enjoined upon every *gṛhapati*, were to be counted among such occasions both in expending wealth as part of the ritual and in prestations to the *brāhmaṇas*. In addition, expiatory *prāyaścitta*[197] ceremonies became a regular requirement, particularly for those who travelled to areas beyond the pale, such as the *mleccha-deśa* of the Punjab and of the middle Ganga valley—areas which were looked upon as polluting, where the *yajña* rituals were not meticulously observed.

Food and feeding both for the living and the dead in the form of feasts and *śrāddhas* came to acquire central importance in the definition of prosperity. Hospitality and generosity even at the level of the *gṛhapati* were taken for granted. There are elaborate rules for the treatment of guests and the food fit to be served to guests.[198] These domestic rituals drew on the resources of the *gṛhapati*'s household and the wealth consumed was not booty from raids but the produce from cattle-rearing and cultivation carried out by the household. If a *gṛhapati* had obeyed the injunctions and observed each ritual as required by the *Gṛhya-sūtras* it is likely that he would have been left with little to invest in other activities.

The *yajña* was a ritual occasion and one of major religious significance. But embedded in this and equally important was that a precondition to these rituals was the availability of an economic surplus which was consumed in the ceremony and in gift-giving. Wealth was destroyed rather than put to alternative use or invested. Even the gifts to the *brāhmaṇas* had limited potential for creating a changed situation. The wealth was primarily provided by the *gṛhapati* in the form of tribute to the *rājā* and this was doubtless the reason for the statement that the *kṣatra* eats the *viś*. A successful raid or a victory in battle would also bring in booty which would contribute to the conspicuous consumption required in the *yajña*. Hence the heroic potentiality of the *rājā* was still of some consequence. The *dig-vijaya* or conquest of the four directions carried out by the Pāṇḍava brothers was an integral part of the *rājasūya* not only in terms of status and a declaration of political domination, but also to provide some of the necessities for the ritual. Tribute was the substitute for booty.

The burning of wealth through rituals was not just an irrational action, since the notion of long-term accumulation of wealth was

[197] *Śat. Brāh.* I. 1.4.9; XII. 4.1.6; *Atharvaveda*. V. 22.

[198] *Atharvaveda* IX. 6.3; *Śat. Brāh.* VII. 3.2.1; *Tait. Upaniṣad* I. 11.2.

absent at this time. The burning of wealth was part of what might be called a prestige economy. Some degree of economic redistribution took place in an indirect, restricted and ritualistic manner but was nevertheless noticeable since we are told that the *rājā* consumes the wealthy in the same way as fire consumes the forest.[199] The consumption of wealth on ritual occasions was a statement of status and political power. There was a sense of reciprocity with the gods who were the ultimate recipients of the wealth and were believed to bestow wealth on those who offered lavish sacrifices. The change in the political meaning of the ritual is evident in the changing form of the *aśvamedha* sacrifice. Whereas in the *Ṛg Veda* it is a relatively small affair aimed at conquering foes and acquiring prosperity, in the later Vedic texts it becomes an activity of political supremacy where the claim to the subjugation of others is a sequence to the initial ritual and is also a means of legitimizing control over new territories.[200] Echoes of the earlier society are maintained in the *yajña*s in the simulated chariot-races, cattle-raids and games of dice, all of which are an essential part of the ritual. The sacrificial ritual enhanced the status of the *yajamāna* and the priest who performed it. The benefits of the latter were doubtless part of the reason why some *brāhmaṇ*s came to be called very wealthy (*mahāśāla*). Temporal and sacral power is also symbolized in the relationship between the *rājā* and the *purohita*. The latter, at most merely the domestic priest of the chief's family, eventually becomes a formal office with the advent of kingship.

The destruction of wealth in the ritual placed severe limitations on these chiefdoms, limitations which acted as an obstacle to the easy transition to a state system. The establishment of a state system would require among other things either the weakening of such ritual prestations and channelling wealth in other directions or the generation of additional wealth to finance alternative activities. The *yajña* rituals were questioned but only by those who were searching for a path to salvation. The discourses in the *Upaniṣad*s and *Āranyaka*s questioned the efficacy of *yajña*s but posited an opting out of society through renunciation rather than an alternative channelling of wealth. Renunciation in itself was of some, though limited, consequence to the stimulation of social change through possible changes in the *yajña* ritual. When renunciation was tied to

[199] *Ṛg V.* I. 65.4.

[200] *Ṛg V.* III. 53.11; *Śat. Brāh.* XIIIth *kāṇḍa*; *Tait. Saṃ.* VII. 4.16; *Taittirīya Brah.* VIII. 1.1.1 *ff.*

a monastic community and this in turn was linked to lay support, then its role as a social catalyst began to take on serious dimensions.

The lineage system as it developed in the western Ganga valley resulted in a condition which might be called an arrested development of the state. The state was not by passed but the lineage system did not develop into a state in this area during this period. Certain trends inclined towards the emergence of a state but others remained impediments. There was a consciousness of territory and an identity with territory. The chief was required to integrate territory with resources and with economic production and distribution, a role which concentrated attention on him. Access to larger resources came about with intensified agriculture and a demographic rise leading to the extension of agriculture. But the increase in resources was not sufficient to finance a state system. The concentration of powers in the hands of the *rājā* raised his status and effective control, but at the same time, lesser chiefs were not his appointees and were chiefs in their own right. There was minimal delegation of authority.

The unity of society and internal harmony was sought through the *varṇa* structure. There were no formal procedures for legal action and redress of wrong was linked to social pressures and expiatory rituals. External protection was highlighted in the office of the *rājā* with some indirect attempt to sanction his control over physical force in the close association of the *senānī* with his immediate retinue, as well as the tradition of leadership in battle being a prerequisite for the office. There were multiple prestations to support elaborate rituals maintaining the status of both the *rājā* and sacred authority but there was no systematic method of collecting an income to finance the institutions of a state, much of the wealth being consumed in the prestigious rituals.

The continuity of some elements of the lineage system was possible for various reasons. It was a successful mechanism for incorporating a diversity of ethnic and cultural groups where each group maintained its identity in a relationship of juxtaposition to each other. This probably accounts for the extensive segmenting off in the genealogy of the Candravaṃśi *kṣatriya*s the geographical reach of which included northern, western and central India. The working out of the *varṇa* structure at this stage was not the codification of a new social formation but an elaboration of the lineage system in a way enabling its use as a framework within which social change could be registered and up to a point confined. Where land was easily available the system could reproduce itself through fission rather than have to undergo a change of form to accommodate the need for further resources or meet the pressure of numbers. Again, where land was easily cultivable without major co-operative organization and agriculture was reinforced by a strong pastoral base, the lineage system would serve the function of cohering groups without their having to subordinate themselves to a state. The western Ganga valley being favourable to such conditions did not require the major changes which were necessary in the middle Ganga valley. If the suggestion that agricultural niches were left relatively undisturbed in the Ṛg Vedic period and that there were no major agrarian innovations from the second to the early first millennium B.C. is acceptable, then there would have been no substantial technological change in the agrarian system requiring new mechanisms of control. The use of iron does not seem to have influenced agricultural technology until the middle of the first millennium B.C. Its major impact in the earlier phase was to facilitate the clearing of land to a marginal extent, but much more significantly in its use in weaponry.[201] If the *kṛṣṇa ayas* of the Vedic texts is taken as iron, which is very possible, the use of iron would have been mainly in the making of arrow-heads, spear-heads, knives, etc. This would undoubtedly have been the monopoly of the *rājās* in their role as protectors. Clearing by burning was evidently possible in the Doāb as is described in the burning of the Khāṇḍava-Vaṇa in order to establish the settlement at Indraprastha.[202] Iron technology was to become more necessary in the clearing of the marshlands and monsoon forests of the middle Ganga valley.

In the western Ganga valley the resources were neither sufficient to finance the institutions required for the establishment of a state nor were they directed towards the creation of such institutions. Archaeological evidence from the Painted Grey Ware culture points to the size of these communities (although larger and more numerous than previous settlements), being smaller than those of the subsequent period, that of the Northern Black Polished Ware. Territory was not seen merely as an area over which a *jana* had political control, for the territorial dimensions of marriage alliances were far wider, particularly for the *kṣatriya* caste. Like

[201] R. Pleiner, 'The Problem of the Beginning Iron Age in India', *Acta Praehistorica et Archaeologica*, 1971, 2, pp. 5-36.

[202] *Mahābhārata*, Ādi Parvan, 199. 25 ff; 214-19.

lineage, *varṇa* was a mechanism for assimilation but reflected a stratified society. The experience in the Kuru-Pañcāla area, as evident from Vedic literature and archaeology, appears to have been one of developing methods of accommodating diverse groups into a workable system based on control by lineage. The importance of the lineage base is reflected in the description of the Kuru-Pañcāla as among the *rājaśabdopajīvinaḥ* ('taking the title of *rājā*s', a term generally applied to chiefdoms), a statement which occurs in a text as late as the *Arthaśāstra*.[203] What is even more interesting is that the reference to the Kuru-Pañcāla comes in the section of the text which deals with the policy of a monarchy towards the *gaṇa-saṅgha*s or chiefdoms. The Kuru and the Pañcālas are listed among the pre-eminent of the *gaṇa-sangha*s, those of the Licchavis and Vṛjjis, as one category of the variants within that system. This would tend to question the description of the Kuru and Pañcāla *janapada*s being full-fledged monarchies in the Vedic period. The relatively shallow descent groups of Vedic literature and the continual segmenting off of the Candravaṁśa lineages would point to the feasibility of migration as a method of easing tension rather than the necessity of evolving a system of control through the state. The migration eastwards to the middle Ganga valley presented a different ecological scene and one in which the lineage system and the role of the *gṛhapati* both underwent a change, and particularly so with trade impinging as a new factor. In this new situation the *kṣatriya* claimed greater power and prestations were incarnated as taxes. The prising out of the state therefore took place in the region adjoining the western Ganga valley and under changed circumstances.

[203] XI. 1.5.

III. THE TRANSITION TO STATE

The *Śatapatha Brāhmaṇa* describes a migration from the Sarasvatī to the middle Ganga valley in the Story of Videgha Māthava who travels east but pauses at the river Sadānīra (? Gandak).[1] The land across the river is described as uncultivated and marshy because, 'it had not been tasted by Agni Vaiśvānara'. It became fit for settlement after Agni had crossed the river and this in turn became the boundary between the Kośalas and Videhas, both descendents of Māthava. The middle Ganga valley comes into historical focus with the migration and settlement of people along two routes. The northern route followed the foothills of the Himalaya and appears to be the one taken by Videgha Māthava; the second followed the south bank of the Yamuna and the Ganga at the base of the Vindhyan outcrops. Both routes ran along the elevated areas fringing the plain which were doubtless ecologically more familiar to those coming from the western Ganga valley, since the middle Ganga valley lies at a lower elevation and was probably even more densely forested and certainly given to large areas of marshland. The northern route turned south following the rivers, particularly the Gandak which joined the Ganga at a point not too far from Pāṭaliputra (Patna) where it also met the southern route.

Vedic literature has less to say about the middle Ganga valley which largely comprised lands beyond the pale, the *mleccha-deśa* of the Vedic sources. Much of the evidence for events in this area comes from Buddhist literature. Some comparative data, particularly on the functioning of the *gaṇa-saṅgha* chiefships, is available in the *Aṣṭādhyāyi* of Pāṇini, which often corroborates the statements from the Buddhist sources, even though Pāṇini was referring to *gaṇa-saṅgha*s in various parts of northern India and less specifically to the middle Ganga valley. There is a distinction between the types of *gaṇa-saṅgha*s described in the two sources. Those referred to by Pāṇini as spread over northern and western India such as the Madra, Andhaka-Vṛṣṇi, Kṣudraka and Mālava,[2] appear to be chiefships well before the emergence of the state

[1] I. 4.1. 14-17.

[2] Pāṇini, IV. 2.131; VI. 2.34; IV. 2.45 and the Kāśikā.

whereas those of the middle Ganga valley such as the Vṛjjis contain the rudiments of what were to become the essential characteristics of the state. Among the latter *gaṇa-saṅghas*, some were a single clan unit such as the Śākyas, Koliyas and Mallas located on the edge of the Himalayan *terai*. Others were confederacies of clans among which the pre-eminent was the Vṛjji of whom the Licchavis were the most important. The Vṛjji confederacy with its centre at Vaiśāli was a major political power, opposed to the expansion of Magadha. Monarchy with all its accoutrements is first established in Kośala and Magadha, although other areas such as Gandhāra, Kāśī (Varanasi district) and Kauśāmbi (Allahabad district) also provide indications of the evolution of monarchical systems.

The archaeological picture for the middle Ganga valley remains hazy for the second millennium B.C. and would require further excavation for clarification.[3] Neolithic-Chalcolithic sites occur in the Mirzapur and Varanasi districts as well as in the Saran and Gaya districts, suggesting that the early settlements lay between the northern edge of the plateau and the Ganga. This was geographically an area of attraction with a good drainage and therefore not given to marshland. It formed part of the southern route skirting the Ganga valley. The Neolithic settlements would point to an earlier population prior to the Black-and-red Ware cultures similar to those from western and central India. Painted Grey Ware occurs at Śrāvasti (Seth-Maheth in eastern U.P.) part of Kośala, indicating links with the western Ganga valley along the northern route as well as at Kauśāmbi and the Ganga-Yamuna confluence, indicating settlement along the Vindhyan outcrops. The main cultures prior to urbanization are those of the Black-and-red Ware pottery, the sites of which seem to follow the southern route and then spread northwards into the middle Ganga valley. They are located along the rivers and more frequently near inter-fluvial confluences which were also the optimum catchment areas. The pottery ranges from crude to refined, and

3 The data for this summary comes from *Indian Archaeology — a Review*, with particular reference to the section on the Explorations and Excavations in Uttar Pradesh and Bihar. In addition, A.S. Altekar and V. Misra, *Report on Kumrahar Excavations 1951-55*, Patna, 1959; A.K. Narain and T.N. Roy, *The Excavations at Prahladpur*, Benaras, 1968; A.K. Narain and T.N. Roy, *Excavations at Rajghat*, Benaras, 1976; B.P. Sinha and B.S. Verma, 'Preliminary Report of Chirand Excavations for the year 1969', *Patna University Journal*, July 1978, 23, no. 3, p. 97 ff; G.R. Sharma, *The Excavation at Kauśāmbi 1957-9*, Allahabad, 1960, p. 45 ff.

if it can be related to other Black-and-red Ware ceramics then its provenance might be western India with an extension eastwards south of the Yamuna and through central India. Its occurrence in the middle Ganga valley would be later in time and dates to the first half of the first millennium B.C.[4] That it is a precondition to urbanization, is suggested by the fact that it registers a demographic increase, shows in its late phases an acquaintance with iron technology and provides evidence of early cultivation of rice.

If ceramic industries can be taken as indications of cultural variation then the people of the Black-and-red Ware were culturally different although not entirely unrelated to those who dominated the western Ganga valley.[5] The Northern Black Polished Ware dating to about the sixth century B.C. marks a qualitative change. Its provenance is associated with the areas on both sides of the Ganga between Varanasi and Patna, which was also an area of concentration for the preceding Black-and-red Ware culture. The Northern Black Polished Ware is indicative of a more complex and sophisticated culture with some characteristics of urban living. The important sites are located at places which, from the literary sources, are known to have been urban centres. A confirmation of the archaeological processes towards urbanization in this area can only be ascertained after careful horizontal excavations which have still to be carried out.

The middle Ganga valley was a comparatively new ecological situation for the settlers, whether those of the Painted Grey Ware or of the Black-and-red Ware cultures, particularly with rice cultivation becoming the major agricultural activity. A domesticated variety of rice (*Oryza Sativa*) from neolithic settlements dating to the sixth millennium B.C. is claimed for sites in the Belan valley south of Allahabad.[6] Such cultivation would be essentially through scattering or at most in its more developed form, of the upland rice system, and organizationally different therefore from intensive wet rice cultivation which was to become characteristic of the middle Ganga plains. Nevertheless the presence of rice in the neolithic context permits the postulation of a gradual transition from one kind of cultivation to the other over a long period. Rice

[4] D.P. Agrawal and S. Kusumgar,' *Prehistoric Chronology and Radio-Carbon Dating in India*, New Delhi, 1974, p. 138.

[5] Romila Thapar, 'Purāṇic Lineages and Archaelogical Cultures', in *AISH*, p. 240 ff.

[6] G.R. Sharma, *The Beginnings of Agriculture*, Allahabad, 1980. pp. 22-3

grown by scattering or other less labour-intensive methods produces a low yield per unit of land. Where rice cultivation is being considered as one of the factors towards social change, the reference would be to wide-scale cultivation for purposes of more than subsistence harvests.

The clearing of land along the more elevated *terai* or at the base of the Vindhyan outcrops was still possible by burning. In the plains the land was more marshy and here iron technology would have been of greater use in cutting trees. The clearing of marshland was in any case more labour intensive and would have required a demographic increase.[7] River confluences, where many of the early settlements are located, would have sustained a larger population because they tend to be more fertile and these settlements may well have provided the labour. The yield of rice is higher per acre than of wheat; rice cultivation could therefore have supported a larger number of people. The demographic rise in the Northern Black Polished Ware period suggested by the increase in the size of settlements and their frequency would have required bigger yields to feed the growth in the population.

Kośala, in north-eastern Uttar Pradesh, was suitable for both barley and rice,but the wetness of adjoining north Bihar posed problems for the cultivation of barley. Its high temperatures and humidity made it ideal for rice cultivation. The wide flood plains of north Bihar, wider than those of the upper Doāb, provided good rice lands as also the banks of the *jhil*s (the semi-permanent lakes) and *chaur*s (the chain of temporary lakes formed during the rainy season), giving a marshland character to the landscape.[8] Buddhist texts[9] describe rice and its varieties with as much detail as the Ṛg Vedic hymns describe cows.

The cultivation of rice[10] required a new orientation to agri-

[7] E. Boserup, *The Conditions of Agricultural Growth*, London, 1965; M.R. Haswell, *The Economics of Subsistance Agriculture*, London, 1967.

[8] O.H.K. Spate, *India and Pakistan*, London, 1964, p. 515. R.L. Singh argues that substantial areas of the *bhangar* (old alluvium) were also suitable for rice cultivation (*Regional Geography*, Varanasi, 1971, p. 204, 5a).

[9] Buddhist texts differentiate between the ordinary variety or *vrīhi* and the fine quality grain, *śāli*. Among the latter were the *raktaśāli*, *kalamāśāli*, *mahāśāli* and *gandhaśāli*. H.N. Jha, *The Licchavis*, Varanasi, 1970, p. 33, n. 6; cf. V.S. Agrawal, *India as Known to Panini*, Varanasi, 1963, pp. 204-6.

[10] R.L.M. Ghose, *et al.*, *Rice in India*, ICAR, New Delhi, 1960; *The IRRI Reporter*, 5/75, Nov. 1975. The discussion on rice in the middle Ganga valley relates not to the type of rice cultivation which was known to the western Ganga valley at places such as Hastināpur, Atranjikhera and Noh, but rather to the large-scale and

cultural activity. Where it was unaided by irrigation the cultivation of rice meant single crop agriculture using the summer monsoon rains. There being only one major monsoon in this area, the crop was sown at the start of the monsoon and harvested before the onset of winter. A predominantly single crop system made it necessary to produce a substantial excess at each harvest, to be stored and used during the fallow season. There was a need therefore to considerably increase the yield of the single crop. This required more land to be brought under cultivation, more labour on the fields and in addition the construction of irrigation systems such as embankments, channels, tanks, to ensure a constant supply of water should there be drought — the water requirement of rice being larger than of any other crop of similar duration. Irrigation could be used both to supplement rainfall and to cultivate a second crop. The major form of irrigation remains the building of *bandhas* across small streams converting them into tanks. These are temporary and have to be carefully maintained. Canals are either taken off rivers or more frequently are inundation cuts. This appears to have been the general form of irrigation in earlier times as well. There is little evidence to show that construction of large reservoirs with sluices and water control in this area was undertaken as there is in some other rice growing areas.[11] The sources do however speak of tanks in the vicinity of Vaiśāli[12] and even though they seem to be small in size they may have been used for irrigation. Similarly, mention is made of tanks in Ayodhyā.[13] There is comparatively less reference to wells. Channels taken off rivers and *bandhas* are also mentioned as forms of irrigation and had to be maintained by constant clearing. This did not however require any large-scale state apparatus for maintenance of hydraulic machinery. It did require the use of slaves and labourers as is related in the story of the conflict between the Śākyas and the Koliyas[14] on the division of irrigation

widespread cultivation of rice as the single major crop and its impact on food-production and on the land-man ratio.

[11] The most impressive example being that of ancient Sri Lanka (R.L. Brohier, *Ancient Irrigation Works in Ceylon*, Colombo, 1934).

[12] Krishna Deva and V. Misra, *Vaiśāli Excavations 1950*, Vaiśāli, 1961; D.P.P.N. II., p. 943.

[13] *Rāmāyaṇa* II. 94.37. In verse 39, Rāma specifically inquires from Bharata whether there are sources of water for irrigation other than rainfall.

[14] *Kunāla Jataka*, London, 1970, p. 1 ff; *Dhammapada* VI. 80; X. 145. These texts are of course not contemporary with the Buddha but they do reflect the continuity of some ideas and the preservation of a perspective on the recent past.

water taken off the Rohinī river which separated their fields. Even in later periods, although irrigation works were encouraged by the state they were effectively constructed and maintained by local bodies of a private nature. The preparation of the field in the 'puddling process' is facilitated by the use of an iron plough-share in the continual reploughing of the land under water.[15] The use of iron plough-shares for this period and region has not as yet been attested to from archaeological sources but there is the mention of the term *ayovikāra kuśi*[16] which has been taken to mean an iron plough-share and there are descriptions of deep ploughing. Wet rice cultivation, the highest yielding form of rice cultivation in the lowlands of the middle Ganga valley does not permit of rotation with any other dry land crop and legume is the main crop after the rice harvest. Apart from irrigation aids providing a further harvest, yields could be increased by extending the area under cultivation, and this method appears to have been used judging by the references to cultivated land in large units of measurement. Irrigation is not so frequently or emphatically described as is the size of the areas under cultivation. Areas with access to upland rice such as the Himalayan foothills,[17] (*terai*), where a number of *gaṇa-saṅgha* chiefships were located, would have had the advantage of more than one crop per year, but a yield per unit of land which was lower than that of a comparable area of lowland wet rice.

That irrigation was a significant variable in social change does not necessarily imply a link between irrigation and despotism but rather suggests a relation between water control and the sources of power among ruling élites.[18] As has been pointed out, irrigation is in any case not an independent factor and is dependent on ecology, crops, land size, climate, water-balance, soil and the actual mechanisms of obtaining, transporting and storing water in addition to calendric activities. Rights over water are not monolithic but they tend to go together with those who have access to other resources as well. There is also a difference between irrigation systems which function more efficiently under a centralized authority and those which are better in a decentralized system.

[15] *The IRRI Reporter*, 5/75. Nov. 1975.

[16] Pāṇini IV. 1.42; V. 4.58-9 *Sutta-Nipāta*, 81 ff.

[17] This was referred to as *nivāra*, generally translated as wild rice. Pāṇini III. 3.48; R. Mehta, *Pre-Buddhist India*, Bombay, 1939, p. 190.

[18] E. Hurt and R.C. Hunt, 'Irrigation, Conflict and Politics: A Mexican Case', in R. Cohen and E.R. Service (eds.), *Origin of the State*, pp. 69-124.

Where land, labour and irrigation was made available the production of a surplus was feasible and this could support a larger population or intensify the social base of stratification. There are references to the *dāsa-karmakaras* (slaves and labourers) in the fields of the *rāja-kulas* (the land-owning *kṣatriya* clans)[19] and there is evidence of economic disparities among social strata. The dual stratification of *dāsa-karmakaras* employed by the *rāja-kulas*, with an absence of *gṛhapatis* (or *gahapatis* as they are called in Pāli texts), in the *gaṇa-saṅghas* is prior to private ownership. *Gahapatis* are occasionally mentioned in the sources relating to the *gaṇa-saṅghas* but rarely as agriculturalists. (*Gahapatis* are more evident in the monarchies of the middle Ganga valley). There is therefore a sharper stratification between the *kṣatriyas* and the *non-kṣatriyas*. In the middle Ganga valley, in contrast to the western Ganga valley, the use of land and irrigation in itself required not only intensive labour but the organization of labour on lines of cooperative interaction. In areas other than those of the *gaṇa-saṅghas*, although the major part of the produce was still household production, nevertheless the household unit was in competition with the larger clan holdings. Initially the latter seem to have been the richer and had the greater potential. With the increase in the size of effective holdings, a hierarchy of control over the resources and their working became necessary since there was more than a single resource-base and the interlinking of these required a co-ordinating group invested with authority. It would seem that the rich *gṛhapatis* were noticeably richer and this would have made for greater stratification. The survival of the *gaṇa-saṅgha* system in the heart of the rice-lands as evident from the Vṛji confederacy, would point to the efficiency of the larger clan holdings being able to provide the wealth required for the continuation of the system. However, in competition with the peasant and commercial economies as they emerged in the middle Ganga valley the clan holdings could not survive and finally went under.

The association of livelihood (*vṛitti*) was essentially with agriculture although other activites began to assume importance. The unit of settlement remained the *grāma*/village[20] and villages were classified according to size and predominant activity (*gonisādinivittho gāma, nalakāra gāma, lonakāra gāma*).[21] Land

19 *Kunāla Jātaka; Aṅg. Nik.* I. 128, 206; II. 205; *Dīg. Nik.* I. 60; 141.
20 Pāṇini VII. 3.14.
21 *PED*, p. 84; *Maj. Nik.* II. 206; *Aṅg. Nik.* II. 182; *Mahāvagga* VI. 33.4.

was classified as *ūṣara* (waste land, especially that which was saline), *gocara/vraja/ghoṣṭha* (pasture land) and *karṣa* (cultivated land).[22] The last-named is also described as *sītya* (furrowed) and *halya* (ploughed).[23] Separate holdings in the form of fields are mentioned as also the measurement and enclosure of these.[24] Terms such as *khetta* and *vatthu* are used to mean a field and a farm.

To argue that the technical feasibility of a surplus was sufficient to start a chain reaction which automatically led to state formation would be too mechanical an interpretation of the change. Surplus is in any case not an event but a process, as it has been rightly suggested.[25] The form of control is as important as the existence of the surplus, as is also the direction towards which it is channelled. In this not only is the contrast with the western Ganga valley an indication but there is also the variation between the *gaṇa-saṅgha* chiefdoms and the kingdoms in the middle Ganga valley. The preconditions were similar and yet the state system evolved more clearly under the aegis of a monarchical form. A comparison between the *gaṇa-saṅgha*s and the monarchies may serve to indicate the features which were crucial to the establishment of the state and which seem to relate to the control of economic resources and the form of political authority.

Migration into the middle Ganga valley was motivated not merely by a search for new land. Other possible causes could be a demographic growth which, if the land could not support the increased numbers or if there was no technological change to sustain the population, would be reason enough for tension and hostility within the initial group and would encourage migration to new areas. The movement eastwards may have been the result of a process of fission, so common in lineage systems. This is suggested, in the frequent theme of the segmenting off or fissioning among the *kṣatriya* clans as described in Buddhist sources.[26] Members of a *rāja-kula* family migrate to new areas, often from Varanasi northwards towards the Himalaya, and establish a new *janapada*. Such is the origin of the Śākyas, the Koliyas and the Licchavis.

Kṣatriya lineages with their ruling clans claimed the ownership of cultivated land. Territory was named after the *kṣatriya* lineage

[22] Pāṇini V. 2.107; V. 2.18; III. 3.119. *Kauśika-sūtra* 24.2; *Gobhila G.S.* II. 1.4.

[23] Pāṇini IV. 4.91 and 97.

[24] *Dīg.Nik.* I. 5; *Baudhāyana D.S.* III. 2.2.

[25] R. McC. Adams, *The Evolution of Urban Society,* Chicago, 1966.

[26] Romila Thapar, 'Origin Myths and the Early Indian Historical Tradition', *AISH*, p. 294 *ff.* ; *Dīg. Nik* I. 92 ff; *Sumangalavilāsinī* I. p. 260 ff; Papañca Sūdanī, I. 258

although it included categories of labour not related through kinship with the lineage. Possibly at the earliest stage the land had been cultivated by the clan, who claimed ownership over it but later began to employ labour when the size of the holdings was too large for a single family to manage. Since the land was held jointly by the clan and the right to ownership was based on birth, the produce as wealth was probably distributed among its members following certain rules of procedure. (The *Vinaya* texts not only refer to the distribution of food in the monastery but also discuss the ethics of how and what is to be distributed.[27] This may have been an adaptation from *gaṇa-saṅgha* procedures, given that food collected as alms would be the equivalent of wealth for a monk, quite apart from the symbolic role of food *vis-à-vis varṇa* regulations.)[28]

The *gaṇa-saṅgha* (or assemblies of a *kṣatriya gaṇa*) as a lineage system registers two important changes as compared to the Vedic lineage system. Possibly because in the middle Ganga valley they seem to have been chronologically later and the founders of the *gaṇa-saṅgha*s are often described as younger members of the established *kṣatriya* lineages, the fact of the *kṣatriya* lineages owning the land is clearly indicated. They have little use for prestations and the rituals are marginal, but the claim to land-ownership on the basis of birth into the lineage is established. Secondly, there is a noticeable absence of junior lineages. There is a demarcation between *kṣatriya* lineages as owners and the various non-kin groups who worked on the land as their employees and slaves. Production therefore was directly controlled by the *kṣatriya* families. Individual ownership is known to the Buddhist theory of the state, but the evidence on the *gaṇa-sanghas* suggests a joint ownership of land since it is referred to in the name of the *kṣatriya* **lineage**.

The middle Ganga valley had no uniform political system, since some *janapada*s supported kings and others retained the *gaṇa-sangha* system. That in some cases kingship is said to have been replaced by the *gaṇa-saṅgha* system points to the tenuousness of the idea of kingship or alternatively and more likely the misinterpretation of the term ***rājā***, literally a chief, but assumed to be a king by modern commentators. The *gaṇa-saṅgha* system, variously rendered by modern historians as republics and oligarchies, can perhaps be more precisely described by the terms chiefships or

[27] *Cullavagga* IV. 4.1 ff.

[28] Romila Thapar, 'Renunciation: the Making of a Counter-Culture?', *AISH*, p. 63 ff.

chiefdoms, where the ruling clans were differentiated from non-*kṣatriyas*. The members of the ruling clans are also referred to as the *rājās*, *rāja-kulas* or consecrated *kṣatriyas (abhiṣikta vaṁśyāḥ kṣatriyas)*.[29] Thus the Mallas had many *rājās*[30], the Vṛjji confederacy boasted of seven thousand seven hundred and seven,[31] and the Cedis had sixty thousand.[32] Every household had its head or *rājā* and the *saṅgha* is characterized by the use of the title of *rājā*s or what is described as *rājaśabdopajīvinaḥ*.[33] Within the *rāja-kula*s status was equal[34] although a distinction was made between the older (*vṛddha*) and the younger (*yuvan*) generation.[35] Decisions were taken by voting.[36] The *gaṇa*s had their own symbols[37] which doubtless were used on punch-marked coins. Categories of *gaṇa-saṅghas* are listed as *pūga*,[38] *vrāta*,[39] and *śreṇī*.[40]

Chiefdoms are characterized by a central leadership legitimized on the basis of birth. Genealogies, whether actual or fictionalized, are therefore of considerable importance and ancestry becomes crucial. The difference between the rulers and the ruled is initially that between certain descent groups having access to power and others who are excluded and among whom are the non-kin groups, generally providers of labour.[41] This last category could consist of local people conquered by the lineages who settle on their land or else could be captives or labouring groups brought from elsewhere. The *jana* name was to apply only to those who were descendents of the ruling *kṣatriya* lineage and not to the *dāsa-bhṛitaka* (the slaves and hired labourers).[42] That the social demarcation is sharp is reflected in the later story of how the king of Kośala. Pasenadi's son by a Śākya *dāsi* was not recognized as being of equal status by the Śakya *kṣatriya*s even though he became the king and the Śākyas accepted the suzerainty of Kośala.[43] In the conflict

[29] Kāśikā on Pāṇini VI. 2. 34; IV. 1.137.

[30] *Maj. Nik.* I. 231; *Dīg. Nik.* III. 207; II. 165ff.

[31] *Mahāvagga* VIII. 1.1.; the same figure is repeated in late texts such as the Tibetan *Dulva*, W.W. Rockhill, *Life of Buddha*, London, 1907, p. 62.

[32] *Cetiya Jātaka* no. 422.

[33] *Mahābhārata*, Sabhā Parvan 14.2 refers to, *grihe grihe hi rājānaḥ*; *Arthaśāstra* XI. 1. 5.

[34] *Mahābhārata*, Śānti Parvan, 108.30.

[35] Pāṇini I. 2.65; IV. 1. 162-3; *Dīg. Nik.* III. 74 emphasizes veneration of elders.

[36] Pāṇini IV. 4.93. [37] Ibid., IV. 3.127 [38] Ibid., V. 3.112.

[39] Ibid., V. 3.113. [40] Ibid. II. 1. 59

[41] Patañjali II. 269 on Pāṇini IV. 1.168. [42] *Kātyāyana* IV. 1.168. 2-3.

[43] *Bhadda-sāla Jātaka* no. 465; *Dhammapadaṭṭhakathā* I. 339 ff.

between the Śākyas and the Koliyas over the distribution of the irrigation water of the Rohinī river, the quarrel breaks out among the *dāsa-karmakaras* on both sides, but the actual fighting takes place among the members of the *rāja-kula*[44] since it becomes a matter of prestige and the *khattiyas* alone could defend their honour.

Since power was retained through birth, marriages tended to be made among those of equal status, sometimes within the lineage in the form of cross-cousin marriages. It has been argued that such references derive from the fact that these texts were collated and edited and revised in Ceylon and south India where cross-cousin marriages prevail and were not part of the original social system of the middle Ganga valley.[45] However, the cross-cousin marriage connections of the Śākyas occur even in the texts from the northern tradition of Buddhism.[46] Furthermore, cross-cousin marriage often prevails in areas where it is necessary to keep property inheritance intact within a small group and this would be suitable to a system of chiefdoms where the link between property and lineage rights was very close. Inequality is, as it were, hereditary, since lineages are given a rank which is determined by the best property going to the higher lineages.

The maintenance of high status sometimes requires marriage with a close kin as a mark of differentiation and references to sibling marriages are common as symbolic forms in the origin myths of the Śākyas, Koliyas and Licchavis.[47] This could also symbolize the purity of lineage, the ultimate source of descent being a single set of parents. The mutually supportive role of the mother's brother and the sister's son is referred to in the context of familial responsibility and inheritance and the mother's brother is the most important kinsman outside the household.[48] Even in the *Dharma-sūtras*, the kinsmen to whom the *madhuparka* (the oblation of honour, as it were), can be given, apart from the bridegroom, are the mother's brother and the father-in-law.[49] (Was this to ensure equal respect for agnatic and affinal relations or was the inclusion of the latter two an indication of their being identical in a cross-cousin marriage?)

[44] Introduction, *Kunāla Jātaka* No.536

[45] T.R. Trautmann, 'Cross Cousin Marriage in Ancient North India', in T.R. Trautmann (ed.), *Kinship and History in South Asia*, Michigan, 1974, p. 61 ff.

[46] S. Beal, *Romantic History of Buddha*, London, 1907, p. 18 ff.

[47] Romila Thapar, 'Origin Myths and the Early Indian Historical Tradition', *AISH*, p. 294 ff.

[48] N. Wagle, *Society at the time of the Buddha*, p. 92 ff.

[49] *Baudhāyana D.S.* II. 3.6.36.

The chief had a retinue of followers, often the younger members of the family, who performed the functions of a rudimentary administration. The administration of the Licchavis was looked upon with admiration by the Buddha,[50] and was more than rudimentary. There were said to be 7707 *rajas* resident at Vaiśāli, the capital of the Vṛjji confederacy.[51] These wère the heads of the *rāja-kula* families who were eligible to sit in the Vṛjji assembly which met in the assembly hall (*santhagāra*). The figure is nominal and exaggerated but the Vṛjji assembly would in any case have been large since it was a confederacy of eight clans. Procedures for the functioning of the Buddhist Saṅgha are thought to be based on those followed in the *gaṇa-saṅghas*. The assembly elected one person among them to preside. The *gaṇa-rājā* or *pramukha* was assisted by an *upa-rājā*. Regularly assigned seats and a committee suggest a ranking within the *gaṇa*.[52] A quorum was necessary[53] and voting by proxy was permitted. The resolution before the *gaṇa* was moved, discussed, had three readings and was finally put to vote.[54] Later commentaries refer to an elaborate judicial procedure which sounds more ideal than actual, in which a case could move through six levels of appeal before coming to the president of the assembly as the final appeal.[55] Mention is also made of officers such as the *senāpati* and the *bhāṇḍagārika*,[56] responsible to the *gaṇa*, reflecting a specialization in function arising out of military and fiscal needs. However there is no mention of a standing army (although the Vṛjjians are described as powerful)[57] nor of any periodic assessment and collection of revenue. These sources further refer to a toll on visitors coming to Vaiśāli which was paid at the gates and there is a reference to taxes paid by traders including *kṣatriya* members of the *gaṇa-saṅgha*.[58] Presumably if the land was held in common by the lineage there would be no occasion for the payment of land or agricultural taxes. There are references to *bhojakas* and *amaccas* (*amātyas*) suggesting some delegation of administrative control.[59] Doubtless such offices were in the hands of the *kṣatriya rāja-kulas*. This did not preclude them from inviting non-kin persons of high status from outside the *janapada* who were also appointed to some

[50] *Dīg. Nik.* II. 73 ff.
[51] *Mahāvagga* VIII. 1.1.1.; *Ekapaṇṇa Jātaka* no. 149.
[52] *Cullavagga* XII. 2.7.
[53] *Mahāvagga* IX. 4.1; I. 31.2; VIII. 24.6.
[54] Ibid., IX. 3.1 ff.
[55] *Sumaṅgalavilāsinī* II. p. 59.
[56] *Sumaṅgalavilāsinī* II. p. 673; *Nigrodha Jāt.* No. 445; *Suttanipāta* 556.
[57] *Dīgha Nikāya* II. 72
[58] *Sumaṅgalavilāsinī* II. p. 564 ff.
[59] *Kunāla Jātaka*, no. 536; *Dīgha Nikāya* I. 136; III. 64.

office.[60] However, these references come either from texts of a later period, or, are more frequently mentioned in the context of kingdoms superseding chiefships.

In the *gaṇa-sanghas* of the Ganga valley power still lay with the lineage as also the ownership of essential wealth and there is an absence of the collection of taxes by a superordinate agency. Such a system may be regarded as being a point in the process of state formation, an incipient state, or what Fried has called a stratified society.[61] Where the distinction between the non-state and the state is presented not in absolute terms but along a continuum, there the *gaṇa-saṅgha* system of the Vṛjjis would be a point along such a continuum, closer to state formation than, for example, the *gaṇa-saṅgha* system of the Vṛṣṇis of western India.

There is an oft-quoted passage from the *Mahāparinibbāna-sutta* where the Buddha maintains that the unity of the Buddhist *saṅgha* will survive as long as, among other things, it has frequent and formal assemblies, maintains concord, acts in accordance with the *Vinaya* (the discipline ordained for monk and monastery), and honours the elders.[62] This has been taken as an oblique reference to the functioning of the Vṛjjian *gaṇa-saṅgha* which is similarly advised in the preceding section.[63] The dependence on unanimity of decisions and distribution of wealth made harmonious relations an essential factor. .Discord was a constant possibility in the *gaṇa-saṅgha* system and the resultant fission would be outside the control of the system. In such cases the dissenting group would branch off and found new settlements in fresh areas, provided virgin land was available. Origin myths of the major chiefdoms refer to the exiling of younger members of a *rāja-kula* family as the starting point of a new settlement. The cause for discord is not stated, but as it is the younger generation which migrates and the new *janapada* does not register any major change as compared to the original, it can be surmised that a change in the system was not what was being demanded. Segmenting off provides the possibility of repeating the pattern elsewhere and thus relieving the pressure on the original group. Possibly some members of the *rāja-kula* were exiled when the original *janapada* was on the verge of becoming a monarchy and power was being captured by a single segment of the lineage. The frequency of groups branching off meant a continually expanding frontier and encroachments into forests and waste land. This

[60] *Sumangalavilāsinī* II. p. 522-4; I. p. 267; Rockhill, *The Life of Buddha*, p. 63 ff.

[61] *The Evolution of Political Society*, p. 185 ff.

[62] *Dīg. Nik.* II. 76.

[63] *Dīg. Nik.* II. 74.

in one sense stabilized the political situation and at the same time eased the tension arising from demographic and other pressures, but did not encourage major internal changes in the original *janapada*.

It was probably in the process of fission and segmenting off, and the settling of new lands that slavery became important. The rapid clearing of forest or waste land would be facilitated by the use of hired labourers to which the *rāja-kula* were already accustomed. If the indigenous populations of the new areas were enslaved, they would tend to take on the characteristics of helots where the slaves formed a distinct class and were born into it. There is however no direct reference to helotage. That the *dāsa-bhṛtaka* or *dāsa-karmakara* working on the land are often referred to as a compound term suggests that helotage was not what was meant. The *dāsa* are not identified as a particular ethnic or tribal group or even constituting a separate community by this time. The *karmakara/bhṛtaka* was in any case a labourer working for a wage and therefore theoretically free. It seems more likely that indigenous populations were put to work on the land but not in a condition of helotage. There is also a more frequent mention of domestic slaves in larger numbers.

It can be argued that unlike the Greek peninsula where, because of its topography, agriculture had perforce to be intensified with multi-cropping in which the use of slave labour became a necessity, in the middle Ganga valley because of rice cultivation, the opening up of new land in the extension of agriculture was a more effective form of obtaining larger yields. The relative expense of buying a slave was certainly high later in the first millennium B.C. when the cost of a slave was a hundred *kahapanas/kārṣāpaṇas* and that of a pair of oxen was twenty-four.[64] The same sources refer to a labourer earning anywhere between 1.5 and 4 *māṣakas* per day where one *masaka* was the equivalent of one-sixteenth of a *kahapana*.[65] It may therefore have been cheaper to have hired a labourer to work in the fields than to buy a slave, given that the extra labour required on a farm was seasonal and that in many cases wages could be paid in kind.[66] The high expense of slaves may have been because, unlike the Greek system, not all prisoners of war could be enslaved. The distinction between *ārya* and *dāsa* would

[64] *Nanda Jātaka* no. 39; *Gāmaṇi-caṇḍa Jātaka* no. 257.

[65] *Sutano Jātaka* no. 398.

[66] *Sunakha Jātaka* no. 242; *Amba Jātaka* no. 474; *Taṇḍulanāli Jātaka* no. 5.

have to be maintained. If there was an availability of labourers, slaves would not be necessary to production and would remain an item of luxury. This may explain the high incidence of domestic slavery. Slaves are said to be acquired through predatory raids,[67] judicial punishment[68] or are born as such to slave women employed by a family. The lack of growth of a slave base had to do with the ascription of *śūdra* status to the peasant and artisan and the fact that caste rules kept the *śūdra* subordinated to the point where his labour could be exploited and justification found for this. Another source of slavery, debt-bondage, being technically limited to a specific period discouraged permanent enslavement. Household slaves ranged from hewers of wood and carriers of water to the more accomplished cooks, nurses, dancing girls and concubines.[69] Slaves were often a part of the dowry of wealthy young women.[70] The total number of slaves both in production and domestic work does not seem to exceed the non-slave population as happened in Athens during the same period. The figures mentioned for domestic slaves are far larger than those of slaves employed in agriculture and craft production.[71] The use of the compound *dāsa-bhṛtaka* or *dāsa-karmakara* makes it difficult to compute a percentage, unless the compound is interpreted as *dāsa* being an epithet describing the condition of the labourers — a reading which is not generally accepted. The relatively high price of slaves would also have tended to reduce their purchase in large numbers for production and there is no evidence of slave markets suggesting the conversion of slaves into a commodity. It would seem that slavery was not the crucial variable as was the functioning of the *śūdra*. Although the preconditions for slavery were to emerge in the private ownership of land with a sufficient concentration in some hands to need extra familial labour as a permanent work force and in the development of production for markets requiring a similar labour force,[72] there was nevertheless an availability of labour through the *śūdra* category which made the acquisition of labour force from elsewhere marginal. The *bhṛtaka/karmakara* in the compound *dāsa-bhṛtaka* would be of *śūdra* status. The *bhṛtaka* and *karmakara* were those employed on wages (*bhṛti*) but as unskilled

[67] *Cullanārada Jātaka* no. 477.

[68] *Kulāvaka Jātaka* no. 31.

[69] D.R. Chanana, *Slavery in Ancient India,* New Delhi, 1960 p. 45.

[70] *Nimi Jātaka* no. 541; *Nānacchanda Jātaka* no. 289; *Uraga Jātaka* no. 354.

[71] D.R. Chanana, *Slavery in Ancient India,* p. 110 ff.

[72] M.I. Finley, *Ancient Slavery and Modern Ideology,* London, 1980, p. 73 ff.

labour.[73] The wages of skilled workmen — *śilpins* — are referred to as *vetana*.[74] The term for hired labourers was either derived from the period for which a labourer was employed as for example, *māsika* or monthly, or from the amount of wages which a labourer happened to be paid as for example, *pañcaka* or five.[75] The description from a somewhat later period of the rich *gahapati* Meṇḍaka's household provides a range of categories employed and the *dāsa*, whether working in the house or in the fields, is one among a number of others.[76] Whereas the others receive salaries in cash or in kind, the *dāsa* is the recipient only of food.

Members of the *rāja-kula*s are sometimes identified by their *gotta/gotra*. Thus the Śākyas are of the Gautama *gotra* and the Mallas and Licchavis of Vasiṣṭha.[77] Some are described as high, *ukkaṭṭha gotta* and some as low, *hīna*.[78] This may reflect an earlier period when both *brāhmaṇas* and *kṣatriyas* claimed descent from the same stock, reminiscent of the *brahma-kṣatra* group from the genealogical sources. Alternatively *kṣatriya* lineages may have associated themselves with the higher ranking *brāhmaṇa gotras* for acquisition of status. That the *brāhmaṇas* do not object to this would point to its being an acceptable custom.

Varṇa in Buddhist sources is listed differently with the *khattiyas/kṣatriya* as the highest followed by the *brāhmaṇa*, *vessa/vaiśya* and *sudda/śūdra* and the *caṇḍāla* as a frequent synonym for untouchable.[79] Equally often the list runs *khattiya, brahmaṇa* and *gahapati*[80] which seems to be a more realistic ordering of the socio-economic groups rather than that of ritual rank. The pre-eminence given to the *kṣatriya* would in itself suggest that the ritual ordering was absent in the Buddhist system, which is not surprising considering that brahmanical ritual was unacceptable to Buddhists and other followers of what have come to be called 'heterodox sects' — Nirgranthas (Jainas), Ājīvikas and varieties of Cārvāka and Lokāyata sects. All the three high status *varṇas*, —

[73] Pāṇini, III. 2.22.; I. 3.36. [74] Ibid., IV. 4.12. [75] Ibid., V. 1.80; V. 1.56.

[76] N. Wagle, *Society at the Time of the Buddha*, p. 153, *Mahāvagga* VI. 34.

[77] *Dīg. Nik.* II. 51 and 158. It has been argued that Gotama with reference to the Buddha is a personal name and not a *gotra*. D.D. Kosambi, 'Brahman Clans', *JAOS*, 1953, 73, pp. 202-8.

[78] In a division of high and low *Gotras*, the Gautama, Maudgalyāyana, Kātyāyana and Vaṣiṣṭha are considered high, whereas the Bharadvāja are low. *Suttavibhaṅga*, II. 1.2.2.

[79] *Dīg. Nik.* I. 97–107. [80] Ibid., II. 85. 109.

khattiya, brāhmaṇa and *gahapati* — are said to have as their aim the acquisition of wealth and wisdom.[81] The first does this through power to dominate territory; the second acquires it through Vedic learning and the fruit of the sacrifice which he conducts and the third through a craft and the result of his labour.

Varṇa as a system of social status and organization seems to be absent in the *gaṇa-saṅgha* areas. The lineage system in such areas is different from that in the western Ganga valley. Sacrificial rituals on a large scale played no role, whether religious or economic, and this made the *brāhmaṇa varṇa* redundant and altered the nature of the economy and the pattern of control. The emphasis was more on the availability and organization of labour and these societies were characterized by a demarcation into two broad groups, those who owned the land and those who worked on the land. The recognition of this demarcation made the *śūdra varṇa* unnecessary since the *dāsa-karmakara* were in effect performing the functions of the *śūdra*. In the absence of a householding system labour was provided by non-kin groups so that the changing status of the clan or *viś* is not recorded. Only the landowning families carry the label of *kṣatriya* and this differs from the definition of *kṣatriya* as it emerges in the western Ganga valley. Since the ritual status or *varṇa* is not given priority in these societies (the references to it in Buddhist sources relating generally to monarchical states), it is inevitably the *jāti* status which comes to be treated as the social reality.

Jāti is characterized by a dual distinction, that of the high and the low.[82] These are sometimes symbolized in the colours white and black with a range of shades in between.[83] The *khattiya* and the *brāhmaṇa* invariably belong to the *ukkuttha, ucca* or high *jāti* and and the *sudda* and *caṇḍāla* to the *hīna, nicca* or low *jāti*. The *vessa* is not invariably among the high as was the case with the brahmanical *dvija* unless the *gahapati* is seen to replace the *vaiśya*. It would seem that the notion of *jāti* or endogamous groups was being extended to other *varṇa*s, and to this extent *jāti* appears to have a different meaning in Buddhist sources from that in the *Dharmasūtras*. Endogamy would have conflicted with the exogamous *gotra* systems unless both *gotra* and *jāti* were being more flexibly and less rigidly interpreted to mean an adherence to marriage rules relevant to family and kinship. Significantly, it is said that these are impor-

[81] *Aṅg. Nik.* III. 363.
[82] Ibid., I. 162; *Suttavibhaṅga* II.1.2.2 ff.
[83] *Aṅg. Nik.* III. 383.

tant at marriage.[84] The emphasis on *gotra* and *jāti* would also point to the numerical increase of groups included within each *varṇa*; a growth of some complexity and size which could only be identified by indicating the boundaries of endogamous and exogamous alliances.

The unit which appears to be even more central to the lineage system at this time was *ñāti*, which has been rendered as the extended kin group.[85] Thus whereas the Licchavis, Bullis, Mallas, Koliyas and Śākyas all claimed relics of the Buddha on his death in view of their being fellow *khattiyyas*, the Śākyas alone were the *ñāti* of the Buddha.[86] Both *gahapatis* and monks make claims on their respective *ñātis* for support. In a kin-oriented society, the *ñāti* would be the crucial unit, lineages being ranked on the basis of *ñāti* connections. The *ñāti* was an agnatic group and the *ñātaka* was the affinal group. Decisions of the *ñāti* had a strong social sanction, for a Malla states that he finds the Buddha's teaching unacceptable but since his *ñāti* has decided to honour the Buddha he is also joining in.[87] The social nucleus in this society is therefore much more closely integrated with the kin group and the lineage and less so with ranking based on *varṇa*. It was doubtless this together with the rejection of Vedic rituals which made the area into a *mleccha-deśa* in brahmanical eyes. The dual stratification of high and low was more evident than other differentiations. The three upper groups are often demarcated by economic wealth. The *khattiya* as a term is said to derive from *khatta* and signifies having possessions, or alternatively from *kheta*, as the lord of the fields.[88] The economic status of the *brāhmaṇa* is emphasized in the references to the *brāhmaṇas* having been given grants of land. These are primarily in the kingdoms of Kāśi, Kośala and Magadha and *brāhmaṇa gahapatis* living in *brāhmaṇa gramas* are referred to.[89] The grants of land are so large that the epithet *mahāśāla*,[90] wealthy, is applied to these *brāhmaṇas*. In one case a Bharadvāj *brāhmaṇa* has so much land that he requires five hundred ploughs to cultivate it.[91] Some *brāhmaṇas* are described as rich, and living in fortified palaces manned by armed guards.[92] The granting of cultivable land to

[84] *Dīg. Nik.* I. 99.

[85] Wagle, *Society at the time of the Buddha*, p. 127 ff; Agrawala, *India as Known to Panini*, p. 95.

[86] *Dīg. Nik.* II. 165 ff

[87] *Mahāvagga* VI. 36.2.

[88] *Dīg. Nik.* III. 93.

[89] *Maj. Nik.* II. 141-2; *Dīg. Nik.* I. 111-12.

[90] *Saṁ. Nik.* I. 175.

[91] Ibid. I. 172.

[92] *Dīg. Nik.* I. 104-5.

brāhmaṇas reflects not only the primacy of land as an item of wealth in contrast to the earlier grants of cattle and gold, but also a further weakening of the idea of land being held jointly by the clan and indicates that the householding economy was seen as the more normal condition in these areas, encouraging in turn the private ownership of land. Since the epigraphic evidence on the granting of land to *brāhmaṇas, brahmadeya*, is absent until the early centuries A.D., these descriptions could perhaps be interpolations of a later period. Yet the association of land with *brāhmaṇas* becomes more common at this time, and it is probable that in the process of establishing kingdoms those who performed the legitimizing rituals for the new kings may well have been given grants of land, seeing that land was now the most valuable form of wealth in the middle Ganga valley. References to *brāhmaṇas* in the Buddhist sources occur more frequently in the context of kingdoms (and particularly of Kośala and Magadha) than in the *gaṇa-saṅghas*, perhaps because Vedic ritual was generally absent in the latter areas. That some of the *Dharma-sūtras* disapproved of *brāhmaṇas* living by cattle rearing, agriculture and serving the king[93] does not seem to have bothered the *mahāśālā brāhmaṇas* who did just that. When the Buddha addresses such *brāhmaṇa* landowners he refers to them as *gahapatis.*[94] The same sources which speak of the very wealthy *brāhmaṇas* also refer to some impoverished *brāhmaṇas* in professions which would normally have been prohibited to them by the *Dharma-sūtras.*[95] The wealth of the *brāhmaṇa* according to the *Dharma-śāstras* was said to come from *dāna* and this was theoretically the only source of income permitted to him as he was not expected to practise a profession. The logical consequence of this was that the *brāhmaṇa* should not be taxed, a view which is strongly reiterated in the *Dharma-śāstras.*[96] If all *brāhmaṇas* were exempt from tax then presumably even those who worked for a living at some profession would try and claim the exemption.

The substitution of *gahapati* for *vaiśya* points to the final disintegration of the original *viś*. The *gahapati* is not only the head of the household but is often also the landowner[97] deriving his land through the breaking up of the lineage held lands into family

[93] *Baudhāyana D.S.* I. 5.10.24, 28.

[94] *Maj. Nik.* I. 400 ff

[95] *Sam. Nik.* I. 170-71; *Gagga Jātaka* no. 155; *Somadatta Jātaka* no. 211, cf. *Āpastamba* II. 5.10.4 ff; *Gautama* VII. 8-21.

[96] *Manu* VII. 133-6.

[97] Wagle, *Society at the time of the Buddha*, pp. 151-2.

ownership. The *gahapati's* household extended over three or four generations and included kinsfolk as well as a range of servants and slaves. In the *Dharma-sūtras* the occupation of the *gṛhapati* consisting of cattle herding, cultivation and trade is associated with the *vaiśya* of the later *Dharma-śāstras* who constitutes the economic backbone of society together with the *śūdra*. Buddhist sources define the *kulapati* as having access to the same three occupations.[98] The household also seems to have produced some of its basic requirements. There are references to what may have been the production of cloth in each household.[99] Doubtless most of this was for self-consumption but some may have gone towards the building up of exchange in the *nigama* or market. Gradually the householding economy may have sought links with groups of craftsmen *(grāmaśilpin)*[100] and thus built up an exchange nexus.

References to *gahapatis* include men of wealth who may be associated with professions such as carpentry, medicine, etc., but have links with land and property,[101] or else have changed from agriculture to a diversity of professions characterized by a lucrative income. That the term had an intrinsic link with the *gṛhapati* of Vedic times is evident from the interpretation given by the Buddha to the concept of the sacred domestic fire, *gahapati-aggi*,[102] which is not used for *saṃskāra* rituals but symbolizes the supervision of household well-being. This was the parallel to the Vedic *gārhapatya-agni* which the householder received from his father and transmitted to his descendents.

Associated with the status of the *gahapati* were the *kuṭumbika* and the *gāminī. The kuṭumbika* was again the head of a family and a man of property who, in the *Jātaka* literature, is associated either with a rich landowner who is often said to be collecting his dues, or with commerce and usuary.[103] An element of moneylending in rural areas is also associated with *kuṭumbika* but probably this again refers to a later period.[104] *Gāmiṇī* derived from the *grāmaṇī* of the earlier period refers to the head of a band or professional group or the head of a village, presumably in the capacity of the chief of a

[98] *Aṅg. Nik.* III. 281.

[99] *Āpastamba G.S.* IV. 10.10.

[100] Pāṇini VI. 2.62; V. 4.95. Pāṇini differentiates between those who work for daily wages at the homes of their employers and those who were paid at piece-rate.

[101] *Aṅg. Nik.* I. 229; III. 391.

[102] *Aṅg. Nik.* IV. 45; *Dīg Nik.* III. 217. cf. Pāṇini IV. 4.90.

[103] *Succaja Jātaka* no. 320; *Satapatta Jātaka* no. 279; *Kakkaṭa Jātaka* no. 266.

[104] *Sālaka Jātaka* no. 249; *Takkala Jātaka* no. 446.

group settled in a village.[105] The section of the Buddhist texts addressed to the *gāmiṇīs* includes professions such as soldiers, elephant and horse-trainers, and stage managers. Authority in the village was sometimes vested in the *gāminī* who was also on occasion associated with the *nigama*,[106] a larger settlement with some degree of exchange and market functions.

The *gahapati* is also met with in the *nigama*.[107] In one case, the name of the town, Āpaṇa meaning a place of exchange or a shop, indicates the origin of the town.[108] It is possible that the origin of some of the *nigamas* may also be traced to villages specializing in particular craftsmen such as potters, carpenters and salt makers,[109] which may have become small specialized markets and later more general market centres. A corroboration of the *nigama* as a market town is available from numismatic evidence where a series of early coins carry the legend *'negama'*[110] suggesting that they were issued by a *nigama*. In the context of very large cities the word has also been interpreted as the ward or section of a city[111] where professionals working in a particular craft would live and work, again indicating some commercial connections. The market was the gathering point for rural produce and could also be tapped by merchants locating resources. As such it would have impinged on village economy, particularly where production was specialized. The phrase, *gāme va nigame*[112] is frequently used suggesting a distinction between the village and the *nigama* and also linking the latter to a rural nexus.

The existence of the *nigama* may also have been the base to the rise of some towns. A distinction has to be made between the city as a political centre and one which combined both political and commercial functions. There is a difference in the ethos of towns which were primarily political centres such as Hastināpur, Indraprastha,

[105] *Saṁ. Nik.* IV. 305 ff.
[106] *Saṁ. Nik.* IV. 309 ff.
[107] A Ghosh, *The City in Early Historical India*, Simla, 1973, p. 46.
[108] Pāṇini III. 3.119; *Maj. Nik.* I. 359.
[109] R. Mehta, *Pre-Buddhist India*, p. 213.
[110] J. Allan, *A Catalogue of the Coins of Ancient India*, London, 1967, pp. CXXVI-VIII, CXXX: The word *negamā* in Pali or *naigāmah* in Sanskrit most likely refers to the market or mercantile area of the city. A. Cunningham, *A.S.R.* XIV, p. 20. Epigraphically the coins date to a later period, Mauryan and post-Mauryan, but the sense of the word remains the same.
[111] Wagle, *Society at the time of the Buddha*, p. 22.
[112] *PED*, p. 249.

Ahicchatra and Ayodhyā and those which combine political with commercial functions, such as Śrāvasti, Kauśāmbi, Vaiśāli and Rājagṛha. The former are the locations of palaces and courts, the hub of political activity, to which was added in later periods when taxes were collected, the redistributive mechanism of a collecting agency and a distributing agency which provided a modicum of public services — not forgetting the all-important *dāna* to religious groups. Palaces are however yet to be found in the excavations of the early political capitals and this is perhaps due to the transition to monarchy being weak at this time. Admittedly the absence of horizontal excavations may be a partial explanation. Kauśāmbi has revealed a palace complex although its date remains somewhat controversial.[113] There is a striking absence of monumental public buildings in the early towns of the Ganga valley. Even in the Mauryan period, Pāṭaliputra alone was associated with impressive buildings. It is not until the wealth from external trade pours in during the post-Mauryan period that the cities of northern India are embellished with monuments. Towns which combined the functions of commercial centres with political capitals are distinguished by a more evident activity on the part of merchants and traders and sometimes included a sector which was regarded as the *nigama*. In the early progression towards urbanization there is little indication of towns growing around religious monuments or ceremonial centres. Neither the Vedic religion nor the early phases of Buddhism and Jainism had monuments of any size or places of pilgrimage other than cult spots. The growth of urban centres may also have been quicker in the middle Ganga valley since the nucleii of the *gaṇa-saṅghas* were the settlements occupied by members of the *rāja-kula*. Since they did not live on their lands but rather in a nucleated group there was a greater potential for the transition of such settlements into towns.

The term *pura*[114] was often employed for towns and originally meant a walled settlement or a locality. Fortifications were associated with political centres which were either the residence of the *rājā* and his entourage or of the families of the *rāja-kulas* in the *gaṇa-saṅgha* system. The fortification enclosed the urban settlement and separated it from the surrounding areas or its umland, thus demarcating the urban from the rural. But this separation was by no means absolute since the links between the two remained

[113] G.R. Sharma, *The Excavations at Kauśāmbi*, 1957-59, Allahabad, 1960.

[114] Pāṇini IV. 2.122.

strong. Fortifications also served to segregate excluded social groups such as the *caṇḍālas* who lived in villages in the vicinity. Early fortifications may have been in the nature of mud ramparts, with more elaborate structures belonging to the Mauryan and post-Mauryan period.[115] *Nagara* was the common term for a town and *mahānagara* used more frequently in the middle Ganga valley was the city.[116] Buddhist origin myths describing the emergence of the *janapadas* associate the earliest phase not only with the settlement of a lineage segment but also an urban centre.[117] Whereas in brahmanical sources, names of cities are often said to derive from names of kings, in Buddhist literature the names are associated with *ṛṣis*, plants and animals, as in Kapilavastu and Koliyanagara.

The rise of the city as a commercial centre in addition to being a political centre is linked closely to the emergence of trading groups and professions connected with trade. It is from the ranks of the *gahapatis* that the traders evolve.[118] In the *Dharma-sūtras* the association of trade is with the *vaiśyas* whose source of wealth is listed as the triple occupation of cattle-rearing, agriculture and trade, listed it would seem almost in order of historical change from *viś* to *vaiśya*. Clearly not all *vaiśyas* would have the surplus wealth to invest in trade and many would have continued to be cattle breeders and agriculturalists. The *grāmiṇī* is described as a *vaiśya* and the *grāmiṇī* would certainly be a *gahapati*. The *Gṛhyā-sūtras* prescribe the rites to be performed for success in trade, the *pāṇyasiddhi*.[119] Occasionally there is mention of members of *kṣatriya* families taking to trade and generally it is the younger sons.[120] In Buddhist sources the *gahapati* often computes his wealth in terms of grain as well as of coined money as in the case of the *gahapati* Meṇḍaka.[121] The image of the *kāma-dhenu* (wish-fulfilling cow) gives way to that of the self-replenishing grain measure. The *gahapati* is both the symbol of wealth and of the tax-payer.

In the middle Ganga valley in areas other than Magadha, Kośala and Kāśi the major sacrificial rituals played a marginal role judging by the infrequency with which they are mentioned. The weakening of the brahmanical orthodoxy would doubtless have released the

[115] A. Ghosh, *The City in Early Historical India*, p. 62 ff.

[116] Pāṇini IV. 2.142 and the Kāśikā, VI. 2.89.

[117] Romila Thapar, 'Origin Myths and the Early Indian Historical Tradition', *AISH*, p. 294 ff.

[118] *Ang Nik*. I. 116-17; IV. 282-3.

[119] *Hiranyakeśi G.S.* I. 1.4.8.

[120] As for example the *Ghaṭa Jātaka* no. 454.

[121] *Mahāvagga* VI. 34.

gahapati from ritual prestations and enabled him to use his wealth in a more generalized exchange. The economic fetters of the *yajña* in which wealth was consumed were now reduced and in some areas, were absent. With access to greater wealth in the middle Ganga valley through changes in agricultural production of various kinds, the *gahapati* would have used only a part of his wealth for ritual prestations. The other equally important aspect of the *yajña* which was the bestowal of status on the *yajamāna* and the reciprocity between the *yajamāna* and the *brāhmaṇa* could be acquired in some areas at least by a different mechanism, that of amassing wealth and making donations to the Buddhist *saṅgha* This had as much legitimacy in many parts of the middle Ganga valley as did the *yajña* in the western Ganga valley. Although the *gahapati*s are more frequently associated with the kingdoms, nevertheless the proximity and inter-links between the kingdoms and the *gaṇa-saṅgha*s in this area would have weakened the influence of orthodoxy. Many of them appear to have been lay-followers of the Buddhist and Jaina sects which made it possible for them to use their wealth in forms other than the *yajña*. It is not unexpected that brahmanical sources are generally not very sympathetic to those who live in cities.[122] The *gahapati*, liberated from ritual prestations and lineage limitations, could be said to have emerged with a more clearly defined economic function.

That the trader was a person claiming considerable respect from society, in spite of the disapproval of trade as an occupation for the upper two *varṇa*s in much of brahmanical literature, is evident from the word used for the trader, *śreṣṭhin* and its Pāli form, *seṭṭhi*, meaning, 'a person having the best'. *Śreṣṭhin* is used in a general sense in the later Vedic texts,[123] but it acquires a specific meaning in the Pāli texts. *Śreṣṭhin* is curiously, absent from Pāṇini who uses terms such as *vāṇija*[124] and *āḍya* and the word may therefore have been more current in Buddhist usage and in the middle Ganga valley. The use of *śreṣṭhin* probably originated from the link with the *gahapati* rather than with commerce *per se* or with the *varṇa* ranking of the *vaiśya* and was substantiated by the esteem given to merchants and traders in Buddhist sources. Trade is described as a

[122] *Baudhāyana D.S.* II. 3.6. 33.

[123] *Atharvaveda* I. 9.3; *Ait. Brah.* III. 30.3; *Tait. Brah.* III. 1.4.10.

[124] III. 3.52; VI. 2.13. In the *Rg. V., vaṇij* suggests 'wanderers', I. 112.11; V. 45.6.

high status occupation, *ukkaṭṭha-kammam.*[125] The term *seṭṭhi-gahapati* is used for those whose wealth is measured in large sums of money. Banking was to become a separate and important profession. The *seṭṭhi-gahapati*s had close ties with existing groups of high status and the trader was not therefore an alien in society.

Among other factors associated with wider social changes some of which led towards urbanization, the gradual utilization of iron can be cited as one of the increasingly noticeable technological changes. As a technology[126] it is recorded for the early half of the first millennium B.C. (with sporadic occurrences earlier) but the quantity of artefacts found and their function in non-military activities initally remains small. If *kṛṣṇa-ayas* refers to iron then doubtless its use was known and the skill of the technology was familiar, but the location of iron was distant. This might account for the paucity of iron finds and the fact that they are mainly weapons at this time. The location of ores was limited in the Ganga valley to south Bihar, and haematite-bearing soil although more widespread, was nevertheless still confined to the middle reaches of the Ganga. The extensive use of iron would have had to wait until the metal workers could tap these resources. The occurrence of iron in central India may point less to local deposits and more to contact with the Ganga valley sources. This uneven distribution encourages a circuit of exchange and in this process the metal can even be used as a medium of exchange. The greater efficiency of the weapons — iron arrow-heads, spear-heads, knives and blades would doubtless have appealed to the *kṣatriya rājās*. The social status of the blacksmiths is kept low partially because they were an itinerant group and therefore suspect in the eyes of sedentary peoples and partially to prevent them from using their skill in the new technology for acquiring power. The more specialized skill required for iron working also required a dependence on smiths and the uneven location of iron required smiths to be peripatetic. Iron technology therefore helped in preventing the emergence of self-sufficient villages.

The importance of iron technology is not merely that it introduces a change in the use of metals but that when the use of iron

[125] *Suttavibhanga* II. 1.2.1.

[126] R. Pleiner, 'The Problem of the Beginning Iron Age in India,' *Acta Praehistorica et Archaeologica*, 1971, pp. 5-36; D.K. Chakrabarty, 'The beginning of iron in India', *Antiquity*, 1976, 50, pp. 114-24; 'Distribution of Iron Ores and Archaeological Evidence of Early Iron in India', *JESHO*, 1977, xx. pt 2, pp. 166-85. G.R. Sharma, *Excavations at Kauśāmbi 1957-59*, Allahabad, p. 45 ff.

artefacts becomes more widespread the pace of change as compared to other metal technologies is accelerated. Its major significance at this time lies in its impact in the middle Ganga valley. Even if the direct evidence for the extensive use of iron at an early date is not very substantial, the indirect evidence would suggest that it had some impact. The Northern Black Polished Ware may have resulted from a high firing temperature which was made possible by the higher temperatures required for smelting iron as compared to copper. Further, the particular polished and shining quality of the pottery may derive from the presence of iron in the soil. The provenance of this particular pottery in the area between Patna and Varanasi, is in the vicinity of the iron mines of south Bihar and local haematite bearing soils. There is sporadic evidence of iron working in south Bihar and it is likely that initially the technology was in the hands of itinerant smiths (as it is largely even to this day in the servicing of many rural areas and more widely prior to the arrival of manufactured steel and iron goods). The routes of the itinerant smiths may have built up a circuit of trade connecting local levels of production.[127] An itinerant trade in salt may have played a similar role, the major salt mines being in the Punjab. Local circuits of trade linked the villages, *grāma*s, with the local market centres, *nigama*s, and these in turn with the towns, *nagara*s, the commodities in circulation being largely items of basic consumption. Some, such as metals and salt, would then enter into the larger circuits of trade which linked the *nagara*s with each other, a qualitatively different trade from the local circuits and where commerce was handled by the *gahapati*s and later the *seṭṭhi*s. This trade required investments of large amounts and close contact among the traders. Some of these contacts went back to earlier links between political centres and, with the growth of commerce, took on the character of commercial links.

The major routes (outside the local circuit) also linked the political centres. These links may originally have been forged through marriage alliances such as in the marriages between Gāndhārī and Dhṛtrāṣtra, Kaikeyi and Daśaratha. The *janapada*s to which they belonged — Gandhāra, Kuru, Kekeya and Kośala — were linked along the northern route, the *uttarapatha*. With the

[127] D.D. Kosambi, *An Introduction to the Study of Indian History*, Bombay 1956, pp. 11, 91.

growth of trade some of these political centres acquired commercial importance as well and in some cases the latter was to become the chief focus of activity. Thus Taxila in Gandhāra retained its commercial importance since it had access to west Asia, particularly after the sixth century B.C. when it lay on the eastern edge of the Achaemenid empire. Hastināpura met with disaster when the Ganga flooded the town and its inhabitants are said to have migrated to Kauśāmbi (near Allahabad). It was reoccupied in the mid-first millennium but never attained the status of other towns in the middle Ganga valley. Among these were the *mahānagaras* mentioned in Buddhist sources[128] — Śrāvastī (the capital of Kośala in the Buddhist period) seems to have replaced the Ayodhyā of the *Rāmāyaṇa*, possibly because the latter was too far south and therefore not on the main route running closer to the foothills, although Sāketa remains a major city on the route from Kośala to Kauśāmbi, thereby giving Kośala the advantage of two major cities; Rājagṛha the capital of Magadha commanding the fertile tract between the Ganga and the eastern outcrops of the plateau; Campā the capital of Aṅga (the Bhagalpur region of Bihar) and an active river port on the Ganga controlling trade going east; Kāśī, the centre of the kingdom of the same name and close to the confluence of the Ganga and the Gomati; Kauśāmbi near the confluence of the Ganga and the Yamuna with access to the route southwards through the Vindhyas. All these cities are characterized by their location on major routes or on rivers which were used as routes.[129] Most of these towns were also situated at the meeting point of two ecological zones. The early importance of the route from northern India along the foothills and then southwards following the Gandak, the *uttarapatha*, is indicated by its having been used by Bhīma, Arjuna and Kṛṣṇa when they travelled from Hastināpur to Rājagṛha in order to challenge Jarāsandha of Magadha.[130] The significance of the control over river traffic which grew in importance over time and superseded the *uttarapatha* is demonstrated in the rise of Pāṭaligrāma, as it was called in this period, to Pāṭaliputra, the capital of the Mauryan empire, located

[128] *Dīg. Nik.* II. 146; The term *mahānagara* especially in relation to the Ganga Valley is also used by Pāṇini in VI. 2.89.

[129] It is perhaps worth remembering at this point that until the railway network was established river traffic was of great importance in the Ganga valley and the siting of places was often in relation to river traffic. O.H.K. Spate, *India and Pakistan,* p. 558.

[130] *Mahābhārata*, Sabhā Parvan, 18. 26-30.

as it is, near the confluence of the major rivers of the Ganga valley. In a sense the rivers provided a wider circuit of exchange. The capitals of the *gaṇa-saṅgha*s such as Kapilavastu, Koliyanagara, Kuśinagara, Pāvā, are described as important towns but do not have the status of *mahānagara*s. Even Vaiśāli which controlled an important segment of the *uttarapatha* is not consistently listed as a *mahānagara*. In at least two cases, capitals which were political centres were shifted to locations on important commercial routes, the Kośala capital being moved from Ayodhyā to Śrāvastī and the Magadhan capital from Rājagṛha to Pāṭaliputra. Either the enhanced status of the *nagara* when it became a *mahānagara* grew with the maturing of the state and the description therefore relates to a somewhat later period, or else it would seem that the emergence of the state was a factor in encouraging commercial enterprise and thus indirectly contributing to the transformation of a *nagara* into a *mahānagara*. Ties between these cities are also indicated by references to wealthy *gahapati*s from the middle Ganga valley cities going to Taxila for professional training, as in the case of Jīvaka the physician from Rājagṛha.[131]

Trade within northern India extended over a wide geographical reach as is evident from the distribution of the Northern Black Polished Ware and related artefacts in the earlier phases of this culture. The degree to which commercial interests outside the Indian subcontinent acted as an incentive remains uncertain and would require further and more extensive excavations. In the north-west and particularly Gandhāra the demands of the Achaemenid empire may have laid the foundations for external trade, the fuller development of which dates to the Mauryan period. Another potential area would be Gujarat with its maritime connections extending into the Gulf area. The Assyrian empire in its twilight period may have had some trade connections with western India which are merely hinted at in the sources but require investigation. The revival of prosperity of Rangpur III (early first millennium B.C.) and the spread of the Lustrous Red Ware from Rangpur to Ahar, Navdatoli and Prakash may point to a possible linkage of coastal areas with a hinterland known for the availability of timber and semi-precious stones. Both these were commodities much in demand in west Asia.[132] The *Bāveru Jātaka* suggests a con-

[131] *Mahāvagga* I. 39; VIII. 1.4 ff., *Manorathapūrāṇi*, I. 216.

[132] Romila Thapar, 'A Possible Identification of Meluhha, Dilmun and Magan', *JESHO*, 1975, XVIII., pt., 1, p. 1ff.

nection with Baveru/Babylon which, in memory at least, probably dates to the pre-Alexandrine period when Babylon was still a major commercial centre. The importance of Bhṛgukaccha and Sopāra as ports on the west coast can only be explained in terms of a maritime trade with west Asia and with the emergence of the west coast from Sind to Sri Lanka as a circuit of trade with its own coastal network. The *dakṣināpatha* or the southern route going through Ujjain southwards was, whether it branched off at the Narmada or continued to Pratiṣṭhāna, aimed at linking the Ganga valley with the west coast, a link which probably was explored in this period although it developed to major importance later.

The city was demarcated in contemporary sources by its size. An average of thirty to fifty square kilometres was considered quite normal for a city[133] even though the size of the mounds today is often as small as five kilometres in circuit. Allowing for the fact that much of the original city may have spread well beyond the inner core,[134] which is probably all that is contained in present-day mounds, the tendency to exaggerate the size is evident. A rough approximation of settlements of the Northern Black Polished Ware period indicating the start of urbanization does suggest a noticeable rise in population and a larger size for the settlement.[135] Even if the measurement of the city is exaggerated the consciousness of differentiation in size is important.

Archaeology also points to the early phase of urbanization having a certain similarity in material culture. There is evidence of an improvement in living conditions, concentrations of people of a higher density than before and therefore the need for drains and refuse disposal.[136] Mud-brick was the main building material and probably this was augmented with timber buildings.[137] Kiln-fired bricks and stone occur more frequently in the subsequent period.

[133] E.g. The Ayodhyā of the *Rāmāyaṇa* I. 5. 6-7; A. Ghosh, *The City in Early Historical India*, p. 52. The city of Vaiśāli is described by Hsüan Tsang as extremely large although in ruins (Watters, *On Yuan Chwang's Travels in India*, II p. 63). Nevertheless it is not clearly defined as a *mahānagara* either in Buddhist or Jaina sources (J.C. Jain, *Life in Ancient India as Depicted in the Jaina Canon*, p. 257).

[134] *Mahāvastu* I. 271 refers to the suburbs as *bahira*.

[135] This was the case at sites in the Western Ganga valley such as Atranjikhera (A. Ghosh, *The City in Early Historical India*), and Hastinapur. B.B. Lal, 'Excavations at Hastinapur', *Ancient India*, nos. 10 and 11, 1954-5.

[136] A. Ghosh, *The City in Early Historical India*, p. 70.

[137] *Arthaśāstra* II. 36. Early Buddhist rock cut cave shrines carry traces of timber construction even where it was not necessary.

The extensively used black pottery might well have been luxury-ware and consequently an important item of trade.

The absence of a central market comparable to the Greek *agora,* highlights certain aspects of the lay-out of the middle Ganga town. It grew around the intersection of two main highways thus emphasizing the aspect of the four quarters, or along a river bank. The main roads became the spine of the urban centre linking it to rural areas and also providing the processional paths on ceremonial occasions, with the balconies of houses providing stalls for the audience, a scene so frequently depicted in Buddhist sculpture. Market areas or *nigamas* in the larger cities were located at the main gateways. Alternatively, transactions were carried out in areas where the commodity was produced. The *nigama* in large cities such as Rājagṛha and Śrāvasti may indicate an area which was once a market town before it was engulfed by the growth of the *mahānagara*. Monumental buildings, often listed as a characteristic feature of early cities, tend to be few and far between. This may have been in part due to the extensive use of wood for building,[138] or that neither political nor religious authority were powerful enough for prestige buildings during this period. There is little indication of a citadel or acropolis distinct from the residential area, a feature so characteristic of the towns of the Indus civilization. The cities built in the vicinity of Taxila have been horizontally excavated and a comparison of the early pre-Mauryan to Mauryan town of Bhir Mound with the later post-Mauryan town of Sirkap demonstrates the difference in the very lay-out of the cities.[139] It is difficult to differentiate the various areas of settlement at Bhir Mound whereas Sirkap is extremely well-planned. Admittedly Bhir Mound being the earlier settlement reveals the gradual evolution of the town whereas Sirkap represents a deliberately planned city. The absence of a citadel or acropolis at Bhir Mound or for that matter of any strikingly monumental building is very noticeable. The absence of large-scale warehouses or granaries in these towns again suggests that political authority was still relatively decentralized. The *gahapatis* have their own granaries, but state granaries are referred to only in the Mauryan period.

Commodities involved in the early trade included metals (iron, copper, tin, lead and silver) salt, pottery and textiles of a large

[138] A. Ghosh, *The City in Early Historical India*, p. 68.

[139] J. Marshall, *Taxila*, vol. I., Cambridge, 1951.

range among the more common items.[140] The elaboration of exchange on local circuits may have led to the marketing of the first two items. The distribution of luxury wares such as the Northern Black Polished Ware is doubtless what is later described as the wealthy potter owning five-hundred potteries and an equal number of boats for transporting the pottery to various river ports in the Ganga valley.[141] The quantity and volume of production and trade probably belongs to the subsequent period but the start of this pattern would date to the earlier period. Cotton-textiles and iron swords are especially remarked upon in Greek sources and remained associated with Indian trade for many centuries. More specialized items were woollen blankets from the north-west, particularly Gandhāra, ivory which was then abundant in the forests of the Ganga valley and the Himalayan foothills, and horses which came from Sind and Kamboja, and of which the chief market seems to have been at Kāśī.

The production of commodities for trade would involve the villages producing the raw material or even commodities (where villages had specialized craftsmen) and the sale of these at the market towns as well as to the merchants obtaining material and goods directly from the village either through exchange or through purchase. Certain commodities however, such as the finer textiles and more delicate ivory work among others are associated with skilled craftsmen in urban centres. Such artisans initially worked on their own, but gradually with the expansion of trade came to be organized into corporate bodies, the most commonly referred to being the *śreṇī* and the *pūga*, both names taken from the corporate assemblies associated with the *gaṇa-saṅgha* system. Included in the *śreṇī* were the artisans, and if the guild prospered then not only were assistants (*antevasika*) employed but also *dāsa-bhṛtaka*. In this period however there are few references to *dāsa*s employed by artisans or to advanced guilds. The *śreṇī* was gradually to evolve into a professional group bound by contractual ties. Its professional identity encouraged its evolution into a *jāti* and these were among the large number of occupational *jāti*s which were to be allotted a *śūdra* status in the *varṇa* system.

A distinction is made between the shopkeeper (*pāpanika)*, the retailer (*kraya-vikrayika*), the *vasnika* investing money, the small-

[140] Agrawala, *India as Known to Pānini*, p. 245 ff.

[141] *Uvāsagadāsao* (ed. R. Hoernle), Calcutta 1890, p. 184.

scale trader (*vaṇija*), and the *seṭṭhi-gahapati*.[142] The latter was essentially the banker or the investor interested in investing money and not involved in the actual production or transportation of commodities. The latter grew with the use of coined money, the evidence for which is available from the punch-marked coins found at various sites, most of which are associated with urban centres of this period.[143] The use of coined money although it had a wide horizontal spread is more frequently associated with urban centres; the excavation of rural settlements produce fewer coins at this level. Labourers in farms working for a wage would more likely have been paid in kind. Barter and the exchange of items prevailed on perhaps a larger scale elsewhere, as is suggested by the use of terms such as *nimāna* (value), *vasana* (that which is exchanged) and *go-pucha* (the value of one cow).[144] The coin of highest value in circulation was the silver *śatamāna* but the more standard coin was the silver *kārṣāpaṇa* and the copper *māṣa* and *kākaṇī*.[145] The *kārṣāpaṇa* is said to equal sixteen *māṣas* and was divided into a half (*ardha/addha*) and a quarter (*pada*). The *kākaṇī* was half a *māṣa* and the smallest denomination was the *ardha-kākaṇī*. The *kārṣāpana* or *kahapana* of the Pāli texts is also called the *paṇa*. The root *paṇ* provides a number of words connected with trade, as for example, *paṇya*, small-scale trade, *paṇāyitri*, a trader, etc. Punch-marked coins carry symbols which were the identification of the issuing authority, the combination and variety of symbols differing according to provenance and issuing authority. The issuing authority could either have been trading groups backed by the *rājās* of their lineage and identified by particular symbols, or professional groups affluent enough to issue their own coins. The question of whether punch-marked coins were issued by royalty remains controversial. Punch-marked coins were therefore a transitional

[142] Pānini III. 3.52; VI. 2.13; IV. 4.13.; *Ang. Nik.* I. 115; *Sam Nik.* I. 92.

[143] S.K. Chakravorty, *Ancient Indian Numismatics*, p. 56 ff.; J. Allan, *A Catalogue of the Coins of Ancient India*, Oxford, 1967; A.K. Narain (ed.), *Local Coins of Northern India*, Varanasi, 1966; A.K. Narain and L. Gopal (eds.), *Seminar Papers on the Chronology of the Punch-Marked Coins*, Varanasi, 1966. D.D. Kosambi's papers on punch-marked coins have recently been edited by B.D. Chattopadhyaya and published in a volume entitled D.D. Kosambi, *Indian Numismatics*, New Delhi, 1981.

[144] Pānini V. 2.47; V. 1.27; V. 1.19.

[145] Ibid. V. 1.29. The value of the *Kārṣāpaṇa* varied according to the metal in which it was issued. In this period silver and copper *kārṣāpaṇa*s are more frequently referred to. cf. *Manu* VIII. 1-36.

form between traders' tokens as units of value and legal tender issued by royalty. The backing of coins by the state is not referred to until the Kauṭilya *Arthaśāstra*.[146] Punch-marked coins from stratified levels of excavations and the comparative study of their symbols provides an indication of the trading links of that time. The introduction of coined metallic money, even if only in the urban markets, extended the geographical reach of trade as also the range of items traded and led increasingly to the computation of wealth in the form of coined money. Those who were wealthy were accorded a high status in urban life, which weakened the role of ritual status and, to a lesser extent, the monopoly of landownership as criteria of social rank.

Among the economic innovations associated with coined money which were to have far-reaching effects in the social life of the times were the introduction of the profession of money-lending and banking and as a further extension of this, activities associated with forward speculation. The new profession of financing trade and production was based on usury (*kuśīda, vṛddhi*) and attitudes to usury vary in the sources. The *Dharma-sūtra*s refer to a large variety of interest rates depending on the period for which the loan is taken and the purpose. The average rate is fifteen per cent per annum.[147] At the same time usury is regarded as a sin, *apātrīkarana* and the *brāhmaṇ* is prohibited from taking up this profession.[148] *Brāhmaṇ* usurers are to be treated like *śūdra*s. It is only permitted to *dvija*s if they derive an interest from those who are socially degraded. This was doubtless in part to discourage the *gahapati*s, particularly the *brāhmaṇ*s among them, from investing in trade at the cost of ritual prestations. Pāṇini describes usury as 'giving for a mean motive'.[149] This would be logical from the point of view of Vedic tradition since the accumulation of wealth was inimical to the furtherance of sacrifices and enabled the rich *gahapati* to invest his wealth in non-ritual activities. The encroachment of money into the lives of the *gahapati*s would of course have been restricted only to those who were wealthy, the same who in the brahmanical tradition should have been bestowing their wealth as *dāna* on *brāhmaṇ*s or as *yajamāna*s in sacrificial rituals. Certain *janapada*s are referred to as having fallen in status because they have ceased to perform the *yajña*s and not surprisingly those of the north-west along the *ut-*

146. II. 12. 24-5; D.D. Kosambi, *Indian Numismatics*, New Delhi, 1981.

147 *Baudhāyana D.S.* I. 5.10.22; *Gautama D.S.* XII. 29-42.

148 *Baudhāyana D.S.* I. 5.10. 23-5; *Vaśiṣtha D.S.* II. 40-2.

149 IV. 4. 30-2.(S.C. Vasu, tr.)

tarapatha are conspicuous in this regard.[150] As a counterpart to this the status of the *purohita* is sought to be enhanced by emphasizing the need for a permanent domestic priest.[151] Furthermore, the introduction of money would also tend to create a new set of impersonal professional ties not necessarily based on kinship nor subservient to the requirements of the ritual status of the *varṇa* hierarchy. Buddhist sources on the other hand endorse the status of the financier and carry no hint of disapproval of usuary. The *seṭṭhi-gahapati*s are highly respected and are frequently the more important patrons of the Buddhist *saṅgha*. The Buddhist sources depict the *gahapati*s in trade as an economic asset treated with respect by those in political authority.

The increasing complexity of trade may have led to the introduction of a script during this period. The earliest evidence of a script is that of the Aśokan *brāhmi* and *kharoṣṭhi* inscriptions. These assume literacy among at least the officers of the state. Regional variations in the language and the use of diverse scripts would suggest a literate tradition, no matter how limited, of at least a few generations. The compilation of a grammer, Pāṇini's, would also be indicative of the beginnings of literacy. Literate *gahapati*s would not have been viewed sympathetically by those who controlled the oral tradition and for whom literacy would be regarded as the preserve of the privileged.

It was from the families of the *gahapati*s that there emerged the *seṭṭhi*s who had the surplus from agricultural activities to invest in trade. The interchangeability of the *gahapati* and the *seṭṭhi* as members of the same family is supported from references to *gahapati*s who are also described as *seṭṭhi*s.[152] This inter-relation as a process is evident from later epigraphic sources as well.[153] It can also be observed in Buddhist texts, thus permitting extrapolation back to the preceding period. It is however necessary to emphasize that this link was common in the wealthier *gahapati* families and should not be seen as commerce replacing the income from agriculture or leading to a decrease in cultivation. The income from commerce would have been in the early stages a form of

[150] See ch. II. p. 52.

[151] *Baudhāyana D.S.* I. 10.18. 7-8.

[152] *Cullavagga* VI. 4.1; *Aṅg. Nik.* IV. 282; VIII. 1.16.

[153] *Epigraphia Indica* X. 1909-10, Luders List nos. 1056, 1062, 1073, 1075, 1121, 1127, 1209, 1281; G. Bühler, Bhattiprolu inscription, *Epigraphia Indica*, II. 1894, p. 323. cf. *Dīg. Nik.* II. 176.

augmenting the income from agriculture, and the transition to commerce as a profession was a gradual process.

The inclusion of trade as one of the activities of the *gahapati* contributed to the growth of towns but also brought about a change in the rural economy. The diversification of interest and investment in trade meant a diversification in the methods of cultivating the land owned by the richer *gahapati*s. Where the rich *gahapati*s began to invest in commerce, the direct control of cultivation through the employment of labourers and slaves would tend to be reduced gradually [154] and the land would be given out on a tenancy basis, either to erstwhile labourers or to other independent persons wishing to become tenant cultivators. Such changes are reflected in one of the rules in the *Dharma-sūtra*s that if a man has leased land from another and it fails to bear a crop that does not exempt him from payment to the owner, for he is still considered responsible for the crop and has to compensate the owner.[155]

The size of holdings seems extraordinarily large and in many cases would have required managers and tenants to make it worthwhile. A Licchavi *gahapati* renounced his wealth, retaining a small amount for his needs which in itself constituted five hundred ploughs, a hundred acres of land and forty thousand head of cattle.[156] Being a later reference this would date to the period after the breaking down of some clan holdings among the Licchavis and the emergence of the holdings of the *gahapati*s. Once land had been converted into private property, unless the rule of primogeniture was strictly applied, there would have been a continual subdivision of holdings through the generations with some sections of the family becoming impoverished.[157] Most sources refer to a fairly detailed partitioning of the estate, not necessarily in equal shares, among all the sons.[158] Drought and other calamities resulting in a poor harvest or none at all are also mentioned as leading to the impoverishment of landowners,[159] as also oppressive taxation. One source associates this with the Pañcāla *janapada*;[160] but may well relate to the subsequent period.

[154] The statement that the *gṛhapati* ploughs the land for a while and then gives the plough to the ploughman may reflect the employment of a cultivator or a tenant (*Kauśika-sūtra* 20. 1-24; *Baudhāyana D.S.* III. 2.2).

[155] *Āpastamba D.S.* II. 11.28.1.

[156] *Uvāsagadāsao*, I. 3 ff.

[157] *Vasiṣṭha D.S.*, XVII. 40 ff.

[158] *Baudhāyana D.S.* I. 5.11.11.ff; II. 2.3 2 ff.

[159] *Saṁ. Nik.* I.170-71; *Kāma Jātaka* no. 467; *Bilārikosiya Jātaka* No. 450.

[160] *Gaṇḍatiṇḍu Jātaka* no. 520.

The cultivation of land at this time can be classified into various categories. In some areas there was a continuation of clan holdings. In other areas, noticeably so in Kośala and Magadha, the pattern varied. Land could be cultivated by those who owned it either personally or with some help as was the case with the *gahapatis*. Land could be rented out to tenants who cultivated it and gave a share of the harvest to the owner, the latter most likely being a *gahapati*. Land could be brought under cultivation through the initiative of the state. The extension of land under cultivation as a source of wealth doubtless suggested the idea that the king should settle agriculturalists on waste land, converting it into arable land. Settlements established through the initiative of the state are mentioned in the *Jātakas*[161] and in Mauryan sources as one of the normal methods of extending agriculture but may have had their beginnings in the earlier period. The conquest of territory occupied by hunters, gatherers or primitive cultivators would, if brought under plough cultivation, have resulted in the conversion of such groups into castes and the agriculturalists would take on a peasant status. The sale of land is referred to very indirectly and that too in the context of a wealthy *gahapati* buying land to gift to the Buddhist *saṅgha*, as in the case of Anāthapiṇḍaka.[162] There is no clear testament of the sale of land in a generalized form, as for example in the *Arthaśāstra*.[163] The expansion of agriculture created a peasantry which worked the land neither as members of the kin-group owning the land nor as employees of the owners but on a contractual basis. The variation in landownership and tenures brought about a more complex stratification than had been known earlier. However, the relationship between the owner and the tenant was not necessarily entirely contractual, particularly where the tenants had earlier connections with the household. Both customary law and caste considerations tended to blur the sharpness of the change.

The emergence of the peasant is suggested in the use of terms such as *kassaka/karṣaka* which, together with *kṣetrika, kṛṣaka, kṛṣivāla*, became recognized terms for peasants even in later sources.[164] The peasant either owns the land he cultivates or rents it from the owner; he may cultivate it himself or with some assistance. He pays a tax to the state in the former case and a rent to the owner in the latter, for he is not an employee of either. The

[161] *Jayaddissa Jātaka* no. 513; *Arthaśāstra* II. 1.

[162] *Cullavagga* VI. 4.1.

[163] III. 10.9.

[164] *Dig. Nik.* I. 61: Pānini V. 2.112; *Manu* VIII. 241 ff.: IX. 53; X. 90.

tax is a stipulated amount, generally an agreed upon share of the produce or the equivalent which has to be paid at regular intervals and is treated as contract; obligations and dues may also be required in addition to the taxes. In one of the *Dharma-sūtras* it is stated that the cultivator should pay a tax of one-sixth of his produce to the king in return for the protection given by the king.[165] In another similar text the cultivator is required to pay the king a tax of one-tenth, one-eighth or one-sixth of the produce.[166] That this was not a rent is indicated by the subsequent statement that there should be a tax of one-fiftieth on cattle and gold and one-twentieth on the sale of merchandise. False evidence regarding land carries the threat of loss of caste.[167] It is also stated that the king has a preferential share in booty which otherwise should be equally divided.[168]

It would seem that the lineage system had not been completely converted into a peasant economy. It is significant that the payment is to be made not because the king claims to own the land but because the relationship between the king and the peasant symbolizes mutual rights and obligations. The question of landownership was to become a vexed one and contradictions in the sources of this early period suggest the probable co-existence of a variety of tenures varying from region to region. The emphasis here is less on the significance of the state claiming ownership and more on its entrepreneurial activity, an emphasis which is made more apparent in the major text on political economy, the *Arthaśāstra* of Kauṭilya. In this context there is much relevance in the statement, *kassaka gahapatiko kara karako rāsi vaddhako,*[169] the peasant who cultivates his land and the *gahapati* (both) paying taxes (i.e. performing their duties) increase the wealth. It is at this point that the peasant begins to crystallize as a social category quite distinct from the *gahapati*.

The epithet of *śūdra* in relation to cultivators would seem to mean the peasants. *Śūdras* employed in agricultural work were evidently small in number, judging from later Vedic literature, but by the Mauryan period *śūdra* agriculturalists come to mean peasants[170] and Megasthenes states that the cultivators are

[165] *Baudhāyana D.S.* I. 10.18.1.

[166] *Gautama D.S.* X. 24.

[167] *Baudhāyana D.S.* II. 1.2.4.ff.

[168] Ibid. X. 22-3.

[169] *Dīg. Nik.* I. 61; *PED.* p. 209; cf. *Ang Nik.* I. 229, 239, 241.

[170] *Arthaśāstra* II. 1.

numerically the largest of the seven 'castes' which he describes.[171] The more general references to *śūdras* included artisans and craftsmen as well, working both in, the villages and the towns. The economic importance of the *śūdra* made it necessary to define the *śūdra varṇa,* a definition which took the form of an elaboration of the *sankīrna jātis* in the *Dharma-sūtras*. The *varṇa* status of these *jātis* was kept low by arguing that it resulted from the polluting intermarriage between persons of the higer *varṇas* and combinations thereof: this was the counterpart in ritual status to the economic and social depression of both the peasant and the craftsman who had the most to lose with the erosion of kinship ties and the encroachment of contractual relations. The peasant was a new phenomenon tied to paying taxes instead of giving tribute and permitted little participation in the ritual. The peasant neither had the extra wealth nor did his status at the time allow him to participate more fully in ritual prestations.

Among the categories of *śūdras* reference is made to the *dāsasudda*. The term *dāsa* now carried the technical meaning of a slave characterized by an absence of legal status and rights.[172] The condition of a *dāsa* was to become a form of legal punishment, when an *ārya* had to serve as a *dāsa* for a stipulated period, particularly those unable to pay their debts.[173] Apart from prisoners-of-war and those born as slaves, another source of slaves would be debt-bondsmen although for a temporary period.

The hierarchical social stratification with a sharper consciousness of differentiated status in the middle Ganga valley, as compared to the earlier society of the western Ganga valley, derived from the more complex agrarian system and the commercial activities of the urban centres. The close control over land meant a clear distinction between indigenous populations and more recent settlers. Urbanization not only demarcated the umland from the city but also introduced a number of necessary although marginal occupations which were believed to be polluting and could only be carried out by uprooted groups. It is from these occupations and such groups that the untouchables in the main were drawn.

It has been suggested that untouchability arose from an urban

[171] *Strabo*. XV. 1.40.

[172] *Dīg, Nik*. I. 104; *Mahābhārata*, Sabhā Parvan, 54.12ff. *Papañcasudani* III. 409.

[173] Chanana, *Slavery in Ancient India*, p. 68; Pāṇini I. 4.35. *Mahāvagga* I. 47.

setting[174] which might explain why there is a noticeable increase in references to and the presence of excluded groups in the literature of the post-Vedic period. The *caṇḍāla*s are described as *bahinagare,*[175] literally living outside the town in separate villages as excluded groups. Their association with pollution is explicit in this literature. The daughter of a *seṭṭhi* washes her eyes on seeing a *caṇḍāla*[176] and a *brāhmaṇ* is worried that a breeze which blows past a *caṇḍāla* will blow on him as well.[177] These sources predate the reference to *caṇḍāla*s as *aspriśya*/untouchable, yet the sentiment is present. The *caṇḍāla* in these stories is said to have been the Buddha or a *bodhisatta*[178] in an earlier birth, an attempt perhaps to suggest that the Buddha did not differentiate as did other members of society between the excluded and caste groups. The same source refers to a king marrying a *caṇḍāla* woman and making her son his successor.[179] In the *Dharma-sūtra*s however they are included among the *sankīrna jāti*s[180] and there was evidently a hierarchy of impurity from the *śūdra* downwards. There seems to be a co-relation between greater stratification and the existence of untouchability, possibly because purity and pollution act as counterweights to each other, untouchability being the logical extension of a hierarchy which uses pollution as one criterion. Yet the more frequent references to the *caṇḍāla*s as untouchables, recognizably different by their dress, accessories and speech, comes from *Jātaka* sources where the recognition of the purity of the *brāhmaṇ*s was minimal. The notion of pollution is often found in non-urban societies, particularly those described technically as primitive, in which there are periods of time, situations and objects which are regarded as polluting. This may well have been the source of the idea. The strategy of using pollution as a method of segrega-

[174] Ç. von Führer Haimendorf, in the Foreword to S. Fuch's, *The Children of Hari*, Vienna, 1949.

[175] *Mātanga Jātaka* no. 497; *Amba Jātaka* no. 474.

[176] *Matanga Jātaka* no. 497; [177] *Setaketu Jātaka* no. 377.

[178] *Chavaka Jātaka* no. 309; *Uddālaka Jātaka* no. 487; *Citta-sambhūta Jātaka* no. 498.

[179] *Mahā-ummaga Jātaka* no. 546. This story is interesting as it refers to the *rājā* of Dvāravatī, Vāsudeva of the Kaṇhagana who married the Caṇḍāli Jambavatī and was succeeded by her son, Śivi who ruled at Dvāravatī. These links with Vāsudeva, Kṛṣṇa and the Vṛṣṇis is curious.

[180] *Baudhāyana D.S.* I. 8.16.8 ff; *Vasiṣṭha D.S.* XVIII. 1-6; *Āpastamba D.S.* II. 4.9.5.; *Gautama D.S.*, IV. 16 ff.

tion would have reinforced the existing distinctions based on other criteria and intensified with increasing stratification.

The middle Ganga valley witnessed a sequential but variant social formation from that predominant earlier in the western Ganga valley. The difference is also reflected in the range of religious ideas which were prevalent at this time. The links between historical changes and the rise of religious sects such as the Buddhists, the Jainas and the Ājīvikas have been suggested elsewhere.[181] Before the rise of these sects the two main strands of religious ideas in this area were either those of earlier Vedic texts or in the *gaṇa-saṅgha* territories the worship of *caityas* and *stūpas*. These as funerary monuments emphasized ancestral identity and lineage links, crucial to claims of rights over land but at a wider level providing a form for cosmic symbolism.

The leaders of the new sects preached to urban audiences in the main[182] and the tenets of their teaching held an appeal for such audiences although this did not exclude the village dwellers. Buddhism, for example, supports the investment of economic surplus in commercial enterprises rather than its consumption in rituals. The Buddha explains that a man should allot his income in the following manner : a quarter for daily expenses, a quarter to be put by as savings and the remaining half to be judiciously invested.[183] The patronage extended by the *gahapati*s to the Buddhist *saṅgha* and vice versa helped indirectly in forging new links which were not based on kinship. The Buddhist *saṅgha* with the monastery as its major institution supported by a lay following is, in itself, indicative of a changed socio-economic system in which, as the Buddha says, the village and the *nigama* were the mainstay of the monk.[184] The expenditure of wealth in this support was in exchange for a religious sanction which gave legitimacy to the pursuits of the *gahapati*s. Ritual prestations were replaced by *dāna* to the *saṅgha* which were said to be of enormous proportions as with the gifts of Jīvaka and Anāthapiṇḍaka.[185] Although *dāna* was ostensibly directed to non-economic channels, it went into the building of the *saṅgha* which, apart from bestowing status on its donors (as did

181 Romila Thapar, 'Ethics, Religion and Social Protest in the first Millennium B.C. in Northern India', in *AISH*, p. 40 ff.

182 In referring to places associated with the Buddha and his mission, the greatest number of references are to Rājagṛha, Śrāvasti and Kāśī.

183 *Dīg. Nik.* III. 188. 184 *Maj. Nik.* I. 369.

185 *Dīg. Nik.* I. 47; *Maj. Nik.* II. 112.

dāna through *yajña* in the earlier system), helped as an institution to provide a base and a network of contacts in new areas brought under the state system and across territorial boundaries. Such contacts were doubtless useful in places where clan and kinship ties were being slowly eroded and the ties built up on the basis of the *saṅgha-upāsaka* (lay follower) relations may have been seen as one among the possible replacements. With the increasing prosperity of the *saṅgha* as an institution, its social and political significance was also enhanced. Even more important was the implicit function of *dāna* : in order to obtain the surplus to give to the *saṅgha* it was necessary to lead a relatively austere life and invest one's wealth with care and caution. The Buddhist emphasis on investment was a boon to the commercial economy. Some of the new religious sects therefore provided an ethic in support of simple living and the investment of wealth. In an indirect manner royal patronage to Buddhist monasteries became a channel through which royalty could support the same ideology which the commercial groups supported, thus lending status to both the commercial groups (who otherwise had a low ritual status) and their religious ideology. Commerce as a new source of revenue[186], augmenting the taxes collected from agriculture, was doubtless one at least of the reasons for the encouragement of trade by royalty.

With the emergence of the monarchical state in Kośala there are distinctly fewer references to ritual prestations at the time of the *yajña* and more to the gifting of land to *brāhmaṇs*.The changes in the agrarian economy released a larger surplus and this was in turn matched by gradual changes in the concept of *dāna* and the content of ritual prestations. Gifting of land, particularly where it was waste land, would have had the added benefit of such gifts leading to the settlement and development of what was primarily the *āranya*. Gifts of land at this time did not carry any specific administrative rights.

The universalistic ethics of Buddhism, Jainism and similar religious movements extended to the entire range of castes in an effort to equate people not socially but at least at the level of ethical action. That the middle Ganga valley was generally outside the social pale by brahmanical norms and that these new religious sects had a susbstantial following, makes it a moot point whether they can be called the 'heterodoxy' in this area, although in terms of the

[186] *Suttavibhanga* II.2 2.2

Vedic religion they certainly took a heterodox stand. The emphasis on renunciation for example was in part a continuing tradition of those wishing to seek salvation by opting out of society, but in narrower social terms it also functioned as the containment of dissent. In the brahmanical system of *āśrama*s, renunciation came as a termination in the life cycle after the completion of all social obligations so that the risk of the social effectiveness of dissent was reduced. That there was a strong group of dissidents is evident not only from the attitudes towards social conservatism on the part of the heterodox sects, but more so from the view of the many radical groups referred to as Cārvākas and Lokāyatas. The monastery became the institution which brought together diverse persons in a new relationship. Within the monastic network there existed a potential of power in that well-endowed monasteries could become sufficiently independent of the state as to assume an almost parallel form. Of this potentiality Buddhist thinking was aware, but it chose to work in conformity with the state rather than in opposition to it. This is reflected in the relationship which it envisages between the Buddhist *saṅgha* and the government. In the historiography of Buddhism, written by Buddhist monks, there is a constant attempt to link the major events in the history of the religion with political authority. as for example linking the Councils of Rājagṛha and Pāṭaliputra with Ajātaśatru and Aśoka.[187] Not only this but in describing the establishment of the religion in an area an attempt is made to involve royalty with the event.[188] The association with the state doubtless derived from the fact that some, even rudimentary, state system was a prerequisite to the establishment of a *saṅgha* or monastery in an area. The attack on heretical groups by the staunchly brahmanical authors of the *Arthaśāstra* and the *Manu Dharmaśāstra*[189] were, apart from sectarian diatribes, also motivated by the fear that monastic networks could become extremely powerful and could divert royal patronage.

The *janapada* was no longer merely the territory identified by *kṣatriya* clans; it is now defined as including villages, market towns and cities, and involving administration and revenue,[190] which in a sense symbolize the complexity of the change. The kingdoms of

[187] *Mahāvaṃsa*, v. 234-42; *Dipavaṃsa*, VII. 36-49.

[188] This is evident from the description of the coming of the first Buddhist mission to Sri Lanka brought by Mahinda, the son of Aśoka Maurya, and welcomed by Tissa, the ruler at Anurādhapura.

[189] *Artha* II. 4.23; Manu v. 90; IX. 225.

[190] *Dīg. Nik.* I. 136; II. 349.

Kośala and Magadha were qualitatively different from those of the Kurus and the Pañcālas, even if the latter can be called kingdoms. The establishment of the state had many implications. Power was concentrated in the family of the rulers who were not necessarily of the highest status. The ruling family of Kośala was regarded as somewhat inferior in status by the *rāja-kula* of the Śākyas who refused their daughter in marriage to the king of Kośala.[191] Yet the Śākyas accepted the suzerainty of Kośala.[192] Pasenadi, the king of Kośala is also said to have performed all the required *yajña*s, such as the *aśvamedha, vājapeya,* etc., involving the slaughter of many hundreds of animals, [193] so that he was assured brahmanical sanction in claiming legitimacy as a king. These ceremonies were by now a formality as there was considerable wealth from agriculture and trade which remained untouched by sacrificial ritual. The comment in the text is that the slaves, servants and craftsmen involved in preparing the animals for the sacrifice were emotionally upset by the killing of so many animals; evidently they were not overawed by the destruction of animal wealth.

It is also said that when a rich *gahapati* of Kośala died intestate his wealth was attached by the king's treasury.[194] This would point to the collection of taxes being so well-established that the king's treasury had the power to appropriate wealth in such circumstances as well. It was doubtless the efficiency of tax collection which enabled Kośala to carry out a prolonged struggle with the kingdom of Kāśi which it finally annexed and which in turn brought it into conflict with Magadha. The earlier terms for prestations are now more often used as technical terms for taxes. *Bali* came to mean a tax but could also refer to an offering at a sacrifice.[195] *Bhāga* and *ardha* are clearly used as a share of the total which constitutes a tax.[196] *Śulka* is a customs duty levied on a consignment and presumably relates to the value of the consignment rather than its size or its contents; the notion of value linking it to its earlier meaning.[197] Pāṇini makes a special mention of the taxes paid in the eastern region, *kāra nāmni ca prācām halādau,*[198] which is glossed as a series of taxes on households as well as a tax on land. The significance of the latter to the prosperity of the *kośa* is evident.

A treasury built on regular tax collection and able to finance a

[191] *Maj. Nik.* II. 110, and 127; *Dhammapadaṭṭhakatha* I. 339 ff.

[192] *Aṅg. Nik.* I. 276; *Maj. Nik.* II. 124.

[193] *Saṃ. Nik.* I. 75.

[194] *Saṃ. Nik.* I. 89.

[195] Pāṇini II. 1.36; V. 1.13.

[196] Ibid., V. 1.48; V. 1.49.

[197] Ibid., V. 1.47; IV. 3.75.

[198] Ibid., VI. 3.10.

standing army was among the requisites of a state system. A standing army implied campaigns in which territory was annexed and these were qualitatively different from the raids of earlier times. A professional army was dependent on the recruitment and training of full time soldiers, the manufacture of armour which was often a state monopoly and a well-defined military administration. These aspects were to receive particular attention from the rulers of Magadha. An indication of the sea-change in relation to military activities is provided by certain technical innovations in weaponry at this time. In the Magadhan campaign against the Vṛjjis two new 'war machines' were apparently brought into use. One was the *rathamūṣala*, a chariot with knives pointing outwards fixed to its body, which when driven rapidly through enemy ranks would mow them down. The other was the *mahāśilakaṇṭika*, a giant-sized catapult for hurling heavy stones and rocks against the fortifications of a town under seige. The function of such weapons is a pointer to the change from raids to well-planned sieges and campaigns over long periods.

References in brahmanical sources to the Māgadha people describe them as of low caste, a *pratiloma jāti*,[199] although there is some difference of opinion among the *Dharma-sūtras* as to the combination which gave rise to the Māgadha.[200] The profession of the Māgadha is listed as that of the bard who composes eulogies on his patrons.[201] A later text describes it as that of trade, conducted on land routes.[202] Of the territory of Magadha, the early political centre called Girivraja, i.e. hilly pasture, gives way to a new capital adjoining the old and significantly called Rājagṛha, the dwelling of the *rājā*. Bṛhadratha is believed to have established a powerful kingdom at Magadha, such that his son Jarāsandha had to be vanquished before Yudhiṣṭhira could perform his *rājasūya*, and clearly Jarāsandha is regarded as the most powerful ruler. Of a later period, Bimbisāra was also called Māgadha, suggesting his link with the people of that name and *seniya/śreṇika* which would indicate the head of a *śreṇī* or corporate body, perhaps of the Māgadhas, which he might have used to establish his personal authority. His kingdom is said to have included eighty-thousand villages, the *grāminī* of which met in an assembly.[203] Its economic

199 *Gautama D.S.* IV. 17 ff; *Manu* X. 11-17.

200 *Baudhāyana D.S.* I. 9.17; *Gautama D.S.* IV. 17.

201 *Mahābhārata*, Ādi Parvan 175. 25; Udyog Parvan 36.53

202 *Manu* X. 47.

203 *Mahāvagga* V. 1.1 ff

potential is clearly referred to in the *Mahābhārata* where it is described as heavily populated, rich in cattle, flowing with water, because it was a land never avoided by the clouds, inhabited by the four *varnas*, boasting of opulent shops and its people holding in veneration a vast *caitya.*[204]

Magadha was in many ways ideally suited for the founding of a state. The land was fertile and naturally irrigated. The gentle gradient towards the Ganga prevented the formation of marshes and yet had the advantage of the Son valley catchment. The plain between the Ganga and the Vindhyan outcrops was subject to temporary inundation which could by a series of *bandhas* be converted into short-term reserves of water, making it possible to get a dry weather crop of rice in addition to the normal crop. The forests of the Rajmahal hills would have provided supplies of timber and elephants and to the south were located the major iron ore deposits of the region. Routes following the southern bank of the Ganga would pass through Magadha towards Aṅga or north to Vaiśāli. This doubtless motivated the eventual conquest of Aṅga and Vaiśāli by Magadha. The northern route via the Gandak also terminated at the Ganga bordering on Magadha. In a sense the Vṛjji confederacy controlling the *uttarapatha* and Magadha controlling the southern route, facing each other across the Gaṅgạ, were natural enemies. The conquest of Vaiśāli gave Magadha control over the most extensive segments of the two trade routes.[205]

The political stability of Magadha was sought to be established by Ajātaśatru, the son of Bimbisāra. He came into conflict with Kośala, the main rival to the west and the conflict was closed by a marriage alliance in which Ajātaśatru, according to Buddhist sources, married his mother's brother's daughter, his mother being the sister of Pasenadi, the king of Kośala.[206] Eventually Kośala was annexed to Magadha. Ajātaśatru's major success was the destruction of the Vṛjji confederacy. After a protracted campaign of sixteen years in which the Vṛjjis managed to stave him off, he finally sent his minister to live among them sowing dissension, which broke the unity of the confederacy and it fell to Magadha.[207] The sowing of dissension disguises faintly the real cause of the decline

[204] Sabhā Parvan, II. 19.1ff.

[205] D.D. Kosambi, *The Culture and Civilisation of Ancient India in Historical Outline*, London, 1965, p. 122.

[206] *Thusa Jātaka* no. 338.

[207] *Dīg Nik.* II. 72 ff.

of the Vṛjjis which was the break-up of the clan system. Significantly the name of the minister was Vassakāra, the rain-maker. As a result the northern route fell into the hands of Magadha and the *gaṇa-saṅgha* system of the middle Ganga valley gradually disappered.

The importance of Ajātaśatru is reflected in the description of him as a pious Buddist in Buddhist sources despite his unsavoury reputation of being a parricide.[208] In the historiography of Buddhism he is associated with the summoning of the Council at Rajagṛha[209] after the death of the Buddha, when the first differences over doctrinal interpretation beset the Buddhist *saṅgha*. Ajātaśatru epitomized the powerful king presiding over a newly established state system. Magadha became the nucleus of political power and expansion for the next couple of centuries.

208 Ibid., I. 85-6.

209 *Cullavagga* VII. 2.1–5; VII. 2.3–4 ff.; XI. 1.7.

IV. IDEOLOGY AND THE STATE

The state is distinct from society and from government; but the point at which the consciousness of a state comes into being and its functions are recognized, is the point when the nature of government and of society have also changed. Society sustains the form of the state, and government becomes the articulation of the state. The interrelation of these three facets is clearly set forth in the traditional theories on the origin of government in Vedic and Buddhist sources.

The evolution of government is ultimately traced to the appointment or election of one person in whom authority is vested and this also seems to be the point at which the idea of a state begins to germinate. In the brahmanical tradition the person assumes the office of a king. In the Buddhist tradition he is not actually referred to as a king but in effect rules as such, all authority being concentrated in the single person. This is in striking contrast to the many *rājās* of the *gaṇa-saṅgha* societies which influenced the concepts of early Buddhism. Variations in forms of government are recognized both in the differentiation between monarchies and chiefdoms as also within the latter category. The possibilities of alternatives may account in part for the insistence on kingship as the legitimate form of government in the *rājadharma* sections of the Manu *Dharmaśāstra* and the *Mahābhārata* which date to the period after the establishment of the state. Kingship in itself does not constitute the arrival of the state for the latter required a number of other features of which kingship was only one aspect. Kingship seems to have been viewed as an intermediary position reflecting the tendency towards the increasing power of the chief in the lineage system as well as the emergence of a pivotal office integrating the requirements of a state.

Vedic sources reflect a society in which government played a minimal role. The major concern is with explaining the origins of the status of chief and later the elements of divinity which were invested in this office and helped to gradually convert it into kingship. In the *Ṛg Veda* and the *Atharvaveda* human chiefs are compared to Indra, the hero among the deities.[1] The association of

[1] *Ṛg.V.* VIII. 35.17, VIII. 86.10-11; *Atharvaveda,* IV. 22. 4-5; VI. 87

deities with kingship is explained invariably in the context of wars between the *deva*s and the *asura*s, in which the latter were victorious and the *deva*s in desperation agreed to Indra leading them in battle.[2] In a situation where cattle raids and inter-tribal conflicts were frequent there would inevitably be an emphasis on the chief being a successful leader in battle.

In the period during which the state was in the process of emerging there is a noticeable change in the explanation for the origin of government. In the later theories the contractual element becomes more evident following on from a situation in which society itself has undergone a change. The earliest society is described as a utopian remote past in which there were neither kings nor laws nor social distinctions. But gradually virtue declined and this made it necessary for laws to be instituted and for authority to be vested in the *rājā*. The description of the decline of virtue varies from brahmanical to Buddhist sources in accordance with the perspective of each on social change.

In the Sānti Parvan, Bhiṣma explains how the status of the *rājyam* came about.[3] In the Kṛta-yuga there was no *rājyam*, no king, no authority, because people protected each other out of righteousness. With the decline of righteousness people became covetous, lustful and wrathful although we are not told why this happened. Distinctions between clean and unclean food disappeared, as also between right and wrong. (The former was important to the hierarchy of purity and pollution in the *varṇa* system). Finally with the disappearance of Vedas the *deva*s feared that all was lost and appealed to the god Brahma who in his infinite wisdom enunciated the concept of *puruṣārtha*, the balanced pursuit of *dharma*, *artha* and *kāma* leading to *mokṣa*. Brahma also expounded the concept of *rājadharma* or the law of government in which the notion of *daṇḍa*, authority backed by force, becomes important. The *deva*s then asked Viṣṇu to select one among the mortals to wield authority and Viṣṇu created a son. But most of his descendants became *ṛṣis* until finally Veṇa ruled, but ruled so unrighteously that the *ṛṣis* had to slay him. From his body they first churned Niṣāda who was expelled to the forest and then they produced Pṛthu who venerated the *brāhmaṇ*s, initiated agriculture and because he pleased the people he was called 'rājā'. (*ranjitāsca prajāḥ sarvāstena rājeti sabdyate* ...)

The 'disappearance of the Vedas' doubtless reflects the new ideas

[2] *Ait. Brāh.* I. 14; I. 24.

[3] *Mahābhārata*, Śānti Parvan, 59. 13 ff.

current in the middle Ganga valley and the falling off in the performance of ritual sacrifices. The expulsion of Niṣāda and the establishment of Pṛthu reflects the supersession of hunting and gathering by agriculture.[4] The etymology of *rājā* is generally unacceptable to scholars although it fits in with the story. Its purpose appears to be to explain the anomaly of power being concentrated in one person and carries an echo of the idea of the *rājā* being the most acceptable to all, a possible hint of earlier elections.

Further on in the text mention is made of the condition of *matsyanyāya*,[5] the law of the fishes when in a condition of drought the big fish eat the little fish, the analogy being to a condition of anarchy in human society which results from the absence of a king. Here the stress is placed on the king wielding the rod of authority, *daṇḍa*, with the power to punish offenders against social laws. It is then related that in times past when a condition of anarchy beset human society a few people assembled together and worked out a set of laws relating to mutual behaviour, respect for the family and protection of wealth. But eventually they appealed to the gods for a king and Manu was appointed. At first Manu was reluctant to take up this task of governance but eventually he agreed in return for receipt of one-tenth of the grain produced, one-fiftieth of the animal wealth, the most beautiful of the young women and a fourth part of the merit earned by his subjects. The condition of anarchy is characterized by an absence of family and property rights and the maintenance of law and order emerges from a contractual relationship between the king appointed by the gods and human society. Association with the gods is implicit in kingship.

On kingship itself perhaps the most explicit expression is to be found in the many versions of the story of Pṛthu (the son of the wicked Vena) who is remembered as the first righteous ruler.[6] Pṛthu is essentially the nourisher in the earlier versions of the story. Thus he pursues and milks the cow Virāj, provides grain and food for people and enables them to domesticate animals. He consolidates his domains and protects his subjects who in turn are so pleased with him that they call him *rājā*. His rule is characterized by uto-

[4] Romila Thapar, 'Origin Myths and the Early Indian Historical Tradition', in *AISH*, p. 294 ff.

[5] Śānti Parvan, 67.16; *Śat. Brāh.* XI. 1.6.24.

[6] *Atharvaveda* VIII. 10 ff; *Śat. Brāh.* V. 3.5.4; *Pañc. Brāh.* XIII.. 5.19. ff.; *Mahābhārata*, (Drona Parvan, 69, deleted in C.E.); Śānti Parvan, 29-129ff.

pian conditions; the earth yielded grain without cultivation, the cows gave milk, the trees bore luscious fruit and men were free from fear, old age, disease and calamities. Pṛthu ensured that the earth gave to each person whatever they required. Other versions of the story change the emphases and instead of the wealth going to whomsoever needs it, it is paid as tribute to Pṛthu.[7] It is also said that he was consecrated *rājā* by Viṣṇu, Indra and the *lokapāla*s (the guardian deities of the world) and Viṣṇu entered his body. A still later version has other details.[8] We are told that Veṇa obstructed the sacrifices and provoked the antagonism of the *ṛṣi*s, who in their wrath killed him with stalks of the sacred *kuśa* grass. But the absence of a *rājā* raised the threat of total anarchy. The *ṛṣis* churned the left thigh of Veṇa from which arose a dark, ugly short-statured man whom they called Niṣāda. Unhappy with what they had produced.they banished him and he became the ancestor of the *mleccha*s and the wild tribes of the forest. The *ṛṣis* then churned the right arm of Veṇa and from this there appeared a handsome man whom they accepted as *rājā*. His rule was righteous and he provided prosperity for his people and even the earth Pṛthvī bestowed her name on him and he came to be called Pṛthu.

The incorporation of Viṣṇu into the body of Pṛthu marks a major change from the earlier divine appointment of the *rājā* to his now actually assuming divinity. Later brahmanical texts maintain that the *rājā* was created from the particles of the gods, frequently the eight *lokapāla*s. This association served to underline the *rājā*'s function as protector since the *lokapāla*s were the protectors *par excellence* of the eight quarters of the universe. Thus the link with protection as a function had been raised to divine status. Once the element of divinity entered the notion of kingship it became a special category. Nevertheless it is worth emphasizing that the implication of this is not that the king is of divine descent but that the office of the king is sacred and divinity enters when the *rājā* is consecrated. The interlocking of divinity and the state system in the monarchical form provides the king with powers qualitatively different from those of the lineage based *rājā*. In the version of the story which mentions Nisāda and Pṛthu, a distinction is sought to be made between the food-gathering tribes of the forest and the

[7] *Mahābhārata*, Śānti Parvan 29.131; 59.115 ff.
[8] *Viṣṇu Purāṇa* I. 13.

agriculturalists where the left side is associated with the former and the right with the latter. It is also stated that the *sūta* and the *māgadha* (bard and panegyrist) emerge out of the sacrificial fire of Pṛthu adding further legitimacy to his rule.

Predictably the emphases of the Buddhist explanation of the emergence of the state are different.[9] The story begins with a pristine utopia where food was not required since the physical body was luminescent. People were not divided into families, there were no individual or group possessions and consequently there was no need for social laws. But some among the people tasted the earth, found it delicious and greed and craving entered the being of man. Their luminance faded and their bodies became solid. They now required food to nourish them and therefore rice appeared in forest clearings. In spite of its plenitude they began hoarding it. Eventually this led to the demarcation of the clearings into fields and theft of one man's rice by another and appropriation of each other's fields by fraud. (The demarcation of fields and their allotment to individual families was contrary to the clan ownership of land and was therefore seen as a deterioration of society. It may well have reflected the association of better times with the earlier clan system prior to the emergence of individual holdings.) Lust and passion required the setting up of families and ultimately possession led to conflict and disharmony. Finally they decided to select one among them, the most qualified, to sit in judgement over them and have the right to censure and banish those who deserved to be so treated. In return for this they agreed to give him a share of their rice. Since the person chosen was elected by all he was known as the Mahā-sammata. He was given the title of *khattiya* because he was said to be the lord of the fields and was called *rājā* as he charmed everyone. Subsequent to this there followed the *varṇa*s: the *khattiya*s were the lords of the fields; the *brāhmaṇa*s were those who went into the forest to remain away from immoral customs or else spent their time in studying the *Veda*s and lived by alms collected from the village, town or royal city; the *vessa*s adopted the married state and took to various occupations; and the *sudda*s were those who remained and took to hunting and other low occupations. The *śramaṇa*s were ascetics who came from any of the four groups.

In this version the question of ownership of cultivated land is the crux of the issue which leads to the necessity of a government.

[9] *Dīg Nik.* III. 80-98.

Authority is vested in a person who is selected by others and no appeal is made to any divine agency. The function of the elected person is clearly stated as also the contract of a share of the produce. Division of society into recognized social groups comes after this stage which is essentially the recognition of inequality.

In these and other similar theories of explanation of the origins of government the main aim is to prevent the fission of society or to indicate that a segmenting off is no longer a solution to the problems of tension within a society and that the tensions arose because of individual demands on property and persons; to have a system of authority with the right to be coercive both physically and legally and to empower this authority to maintain law and order and to expect it to consolidate functioning by upholding the social laws. These functions required not merely an explanation of government but a much fuller definition of what constituted the state. This is first expressed in the Kauṭilya *Arthaśāstra* and is described as the seven elements (*prakṛtis*) which constitute the state.[10]

The seven items are listed as *svāmi, amātya, janapada/rāṣṭra, durga/pura, kośa, daṇḍa/bala* and *mitra*. *Svāmi* refers to the king or the ruler. It is significant that *rājā* or its synonyms such as *bhūpati, bhogtā, nṛpati,* etc. are not used, but *svāmi* which carries a much stronger meaning of possession and ownership. A distinct change in the power and status of the king is reflected in the use of this term. *Amātya* refers not merely to the body of ministers but to the structure of administration which they control and assumes a functional group with specific powers. The third constituent of *janapada* or territory is defined as being agriculturally fertile with mines and forests and pastures, with perennial sources of water for irrigation, traversed by routes and maintenance of trade in commodities, with dedicated farmers (*karṣaka*) who together with the traders are capable of bearing the burden of taxes, and a high percentage of inhabitants of the lower *varṇa*s. The fort, *durga*,[11] is sometimes substituted by the fortified settlement, *pura*, but in both cases it comprises the royal capital together with sections of the city inhabited by artisans and guilds, clearly pointing to the major cities which have both a political and commercial base. It was around the king's palace and the treasury that the fortified capital was generally constructed. The treasury or *kośa* was where the revenue when

[10] VI. 1.

[11] Ibid; see also II.4.

collected was gathered and it was said that the *kośa* should be such that it should tide over periods of low revenue. *Daṇḍa* has been interpreted as the army or the access to legitimate physical force.[12] This is perhaps a somewhat narrow definition since in other texts it is treated more broadly as coercive power and relates even to the power of law and of authority. The definition of force would in itself have changed from the forays associated with cattle raids to the arbiter in social tensions among a more settled people. *Mitra* is the ally and is preferably one that has had a long tradition of alliance with the home state. These seven elements later come to be called the seven limbs, *saptāṅga*, of the body of the state.

The seven elements (*prakṛti*) or limbs (*anga*) can be recognized from the descriptions of governmental functioning in the texts. The *janapada* was no longer defined by the *jana* or clan land but by differentiated systems within the territory with the term *rāstra* coming into increasing use in preference to *janapada*. The inclusion of diverse clans, castes and languages pointing to an established heterogeneity required a controlling agency and the authority of the king (*svāmi*) was its symbol. *Rājyam* and *rāṣṭra* emphasized sovereign power rather than the control of clan lands. An important aspect of sovereignty was the claim to coercive legal authority which was required for the functions of government, namely, to prevent fission, to maintain law and order and to consolidate the claims to territory. The term *svāmi* should not be taken as referring to the divinity of kingship since the use of *svāmi* in the context of a deity is a late usage. The notion of divinity was not essential to kingship as such, but was an adjunct which in the western Ganga valley facilitated the trend from chiefship to kingship. Doubtless the consecratory rites were encouraged by the *brāhmaṇs* who might otherwise have been denied their *dāna* and *dakṣiṇā* with the decline of the lineage system. Dynasties of considerable power such as the Mauryas were not required to claim divine status. The existence of the state backing the king as its symbol was what enhanced the power of the king and divine kingship was not a precondition to the evolution of the state. However recourse to association with the deities was always a useful method of augmenting power.

The administrative framework, the rudiments of which were evident in the Vṛjji confederacy and in the kingdom of Magadha, now takes on major importance in the managerial and redistributive

[12] Śānti Parvan XIV. 14; cf. *Manu* VII. 14–20.

function of government. The earlier assemblies of the clans declined, *gaṇa, vidatha* and *samiti* becoming something of the past. Others evolved into advisory bodies such as the *sabhā* and the *pariṣad*. Membership was not by kinship but by selection and was open to non-kinsmen of the king, although restricted to the upper castes.[13] The employment of *brāhmaṇs* in the higher grades of administration where literacy was at a premium increased the acceptability of the state system among *brāhmaṇs*. Their induction as advisors and ministers led to their validating the new system since the access to power and the redistribution of wealth was still within their reach. A gradually perceptible distinction arose between *brāhmaṇs* performing priestly functions and those in managerial office. The former were regarded as superior and helped eventually in reviving the major Vedic sacrifices as avenues of legitimizing kingship as well as providing genealogical links and *kṣatriya* status to newly established dynasties.

The state controlled access to resources, particularly the forests which permitted control of both timber and animal wealth as well as clearance of land for cultivation. A distinction was maintained between waste land, land owned by the state and communal and private land. State land (*sītā*) was cultivated by agriculturalists who cleared it and established villages[14] under the initiative of the state. The extent to which this occurred would depend on the surplus which the state accumulated to invest in the development of new areas. There was thus an extension of the tenurial system in which the land was owned by the state but cultivated by peasants on the basis of prevailing tenures. Such cultivation was not conditioned by (*viṣṭi*) forced labour, or labour in lieu of taxation, and at the time of the Mauryas when the extension of agriculture took place on a larger scale than before mention is made of a variety of tenures including, apart from *viṣṭi*, share-cropping and a range of taxes.[15] Communal land was largely village pastures (*vrāja*). Privately held land was either cultivated directly by the owners who had a peasant status or by tenants who gave a percentage of their produce to the owners.

Taxes — their source, nature and definition — become a matter of serious discussion from the Mauryan period onwards. It is then that the technical meaning of *bali, bhāga, śulka, kara,* etc is given

[13] *Arthaśāstra* I. 8; I.15.47 ff.

[14] Ibid, II. 1. Cf. *Jayadissa Jātaka* no.513.

[15] Ibid, II. 24.16; J. Bloch, *Les Inscriptions d'Asoka* (Rummindei Inscription), Paris, 1950, p. 157; *Strabo* XV. 1.39-41; Arrian, *Indika,* XI.

currency and debated upon as part of the system of taxation and it is argued that revenue symbolized in the *kośa* is of the very essence of the state. Prior to that there is a groping towards an arrangement of taxes, since the principles of taxation are recognized. What earlier were prestations, shares and ritualized offerings are transformed into taxes. *Bali* and *bhāga* were now used to mean regular taxes. *Bhāga* is mentioned more frequently and as the share of the produce is computed at one-sixth. *Bali* may have been a nominal tax and *bhāga* the more substantial one.

The definition of *bali* as a tax, which has been variously interpreted, remains a little uncertain. Originally a voluntary offering of wealth, it may have retained its association with wealth and when wealth came to be linked with land, *bali* could have been used to mean a tax on land. It would thus relate to the area of land under cultivation whereas *bhāga* remained a share of the produce from land. *Bali* would be paid by all those who cultivated an area of land they owned. Thus when the Rummendei inscription comemoraitng the visit of Aśoka Maurya to the village of Lumbīnī where the Buddha was born,[16] records that Aśoka exempted the village from *bali* (*udbalika*) and reduced the amount of *bhāga*, the former would have affected only those who owned the land they cultivated, the latter would have applied to all cultivators. Alternatively *bali* could also have been a generalized tax on the area of land cultivated by each cultivator. This might have led to the confusion in the mind of Megasthenes, who states that the land belongs to the king because a tax is paid on it by those who cultivate it.[17] The payment of a land tax does not presuppose state ownership of land since it is in the nature of a tax on property. The measurement of land under cultivation as described in the *Jātakas* would also suggest the prevalence of land tax.[18]

The *Dharma-sūtra* of Gautama states that the king can impose *bali* because he protects the people,[19] even though in the theoretical justification for the origin of government it is *bhāga* which is collected as a fee for protection. It is also argued elsewhere that taxes are the wages of the king as stipulated in the original contract drawn up with Manu when he agreed to become the first king.[20] Oppressive taxation is cautioned against in the advice frequently

[16] J. Bloch, *Les Inscriptions d'Asoka,* p. 157. [18] *Kurudhamma Jāt*. no. 276.

[17] Strabo XV. 1. 39-41; Arrian, *Indika,* XI. 1 ff [19] X. 28.

[20] *Mahābhārata,* Śānti Parvan, 67 and 70 ; *Baudhāyana Dharma-sūtra* I. 10.18.1; *Arthaśāstra* I. 13;

given that taxes should not hurt those from who they are collected. It is suggested that wealth should be gathered in the manner of the bee taking honey from the flower.[21] It is also said that wisdom lies in placating the wealthy since the prosperity of the kingdom depends on the taxes which they provide,[22] an echo of the earlier statement of the *vaiśya*s being the *balihṛt*. The terminology need not change but the context and the connotation are different. *Bali* was no longer a prestation or oblation except on religious occasions; it was now used to finance the protection of the state and its well-being.

The production of commodities and the organization of their sale was also directed in part towards providing a tax to the state although this was not realized to the same extent as from agriculture in the initial stages. The use of non-kin labour, the *dāsa-bhṛtaka*s and the *karmakara*s, was gradually being extended to centres of craft production and trade, and helped in furthering specialization. Since commerce was a lucrative source of revenue the state came to be associated with entrepreneurial activities as well, although this was not a state monopoly.

The managerial and redistributive functions of the administration were therefore largely those concerning the extension of agriculture and the collection of revenue from both agricultural and craft activities together with the maintenance of an army and public servants. The older system of tribute and prestations continued but became increasingly marginal to economic activity and took on the symbolic role which characterized such actions in later periods. The wealth expended on *yajña*s and *saṃskāra*s became a smaller percentage of the wealth produced. The more substantial source of income was from the taxes, rents, tolls and customs dues collected from land and commerce, and directed towards the central treasury[23] (*kośa*). Those exempted from taxation[24] consisted of the learned *brāhmaṇ*, the ascetic, women, children, the sick and the infirm and the *śūdra* in the service of another person. In short, all those whose activities could not be regarded as directly economically productive. The treasury in turn became the hub of the redistributive function. The king and the ministers not only controlled this function but the channelizing of this income increased disparities in society. There is growing evidence of greater ap-

[21] *Mahābhārata*, Udyog Parvan, 34. 17-18.

[22] *Mahābhārata*, Śānti Parvan, 87. 25-33; 89. 25-6.

[23] *Āpastamba D.S.* II. 10.26.9.

[24] Ibid., II. 10.26. 10-17.

propriation by a smaller number. The capital city becomes the nucleus of redistribution. The existence of the *kośa* points to a changed attitude to wealth. It was not to be entirely consumed in prestations and rituals nor was it to be in substantial degree redistributed or even invested by the state in alternative entrepreneurial activities. Wealth was to be carefully accumulated and judiciously used for maintaining the state system. Should such maintenance coincide with entrepreneurial activities then these would be encouraged but a sizeable part of the revenue went into financing the administrative framework to ensure the flow of income, of goods and of services, and into the maintenance of a standing army (*bala/daṇḍa*) for the enforcement of claims to territory. The larger the claim the greater the force required to consolidate the claim.

The emergence of the state leads to the state taking over the function of integrating the ruler and the ruled and this gradually is extended to include all social relationships. This is done largely by the state monopolizing legal force through which it seeks to regulate social relations. In this sense *daṇḍa* can be rendered not merely as physical force but carries with it the sanction of coercion and authority. It is frequently translated as the rod of chastisement, punishment being an important aspect of *daṇḍa*. But the staff was also the symbol of the renouncer and the ascetic, the man whose authority may not have been tangible but was nevertheless effective enough to frighten even the rulers. The authority of the ascetic derived from his removing himself from society, even if notionally, and claiming immunity from social obligations and regulations. As such he could not only claim sanctions which were extra-societal, but could also become the source of a counter-culture.[25] Hence the fact that he was regarded with awe by those in political authority. Added to this was the popular image of the renouncer associating him with austerity, control over the physical body and the creation of energy or magical power. The symbiotic relationship between the renouncer and the community gave greater force to the image of the renouncer. The symbol of *daṇḍa* would therefore not have been restricted to coercion but would appear to represent all forms of authority.

Daṇḍa provides the support to the extension of *dharma*, the ordering of society in which caste as a theory of stratification

[25] Romila Thapar, 'Renunciation: the Making of a Counter-culture?' in *AISH*, p. 63 ff.

became one of the mechanisms by which the state was made acceptable in areas where no state had existed earlier: the state legitimizing the new society. The *Dharma-sūtras* formalized not only the laws of *varṇa* in stating the obligations of each *varṇa* to society and the regulations regarding practices but also formalizing those customary laws which could not be ignored. Custom (*ācāra*) became an important component of legal functioning and cut across any easy method of introducing a uniformity of laws for all. The concession to customary law did serve the purpose to begin with of preventing confrontations and fission since the emphasis was on consensus. One of the authors of a *Dharma-sūtra*, clearly an enthusiastic supporter of customary law, states that countries, castes, and families, together with cultivators, traders, herdsmen, money-lenders and artisans have the authority to formulate rules for themselves, provided such laws are not in opposition to those of the *Dharma-sūtras*.[26] Customary law would carry with it the use of ordeals, curses and analogous means as dispensers of law as well as the strength of supernatural sanctions in curbing conduct which met with social disapproval. In a society emphasizing ritual mores, actions resulting in ritual uncleanliness (as many socially disapproved actions were perceived to be) would require expiation rather than punishment — hence the increasing importance of *prāyaścitta*. In the early texts this was required of those who travelled to the *mleccha-deśa*, frequently places where the sacrificial ritual was on the decline or had not been introduced or where heterodoxy was in evidence. Even when legal institutions were recognized as the means of settling disputes, these were less often distinct bodies serving a legal function and more often existing bodies of deliberation which took on legal functions as well. Such a situation clearly militated against the over-despotic state. This doubtless changed as the state became more powerful and was able to impose impersonal laws through the efficacy of its right to *daṇḍa*, and to its being the chief arbiter. Compilation of the *Dharma-sūtras* would in itself indicate a society in which even custom come to require the backing of authority, although not necessarily political authority. It would also point to an inter-mixing of groups where norms for communities, professions and castes had to be stipulated. Such an attempt to regulate norms would be in keeping with the developing power of the state. Although the *Dharma-sūtra* literature was not

[26] *Gautama D.S.* XI. 20-2

seen as a system of civil laws *per se*, it did all the same reflect the views of those in authority.

That the notion of authority assumes considerable importance is in part a reflection of the tendency towards the centralization of power but also of the growing disparities of high and low in society. Disparities between the various *varṇa*s is strikingly noticeable in the *Dharma-sūtra*s.[27] Whereas in the *Ṛg Veda* there was a generalized payment or wergeld of a hundred cows (*śatadeya*) which was to be paid by one who killed another irrespective of their status, the *Dharma-sūtra*s maintain a hierarchy of payment in cows in accordance with the *varṇa* of the person killed.[28] Furthermore, the cows are not to be given to the kinsfolk of the dead man but to the king or to a *brāhmaṇ*. Punishments are also varied in accordance with *varṇa* status. In such a system *śūdra*s had the worst deal and paid the maximum penalty in most cases.[29] That the *Dharma-sūtra*s may have been prone to a little exaggeration in this matter, perhaps to make the point more strongly is suggested by Buddhist sources in which the *varṇa* disparities are not so sharp.[30] It may be argued that since Buddhism had less use for *varṇa* status it may have tended to be milder in making *varṇa* discriminations. Most sources are in agreement that the condition of the *dāsa*, even as a domestic slave, is not to be envied. *Dāsa*s are described as being afraid of their masters who took to beating them when angry.[31] References to kindliness and consideration towards slaves tend to be individualized and the Buddha expresses the need for this when he speaks of the duties of the *gahapati*.[32] The ill-treatment of slaves is a generalized description and is virtually taken for granted, in references to the beating, binding and even killing of slaves.[33] The *Dharma-sūtra*s seem to identify the *dāsa*s with the *śūdra*s on the question of disabilities of social groups and the real antagonism should perhaps be seen as between the *dāsa-bhṛtaka* and the *gahapati*, rather than the *brāhmaṇ* and the *śūdra*.

The last of the elements or limbs of the state was the ally (*mitra, suhṛta*) to which the *Arthaśāstra* adds as a corollary, *ari*, the enemy.[34] The need for an external policy involving either the con-

[27] R.S. Sharma, *Śūdras in Ancient India*, p. 122. ff.

[28] *Baudhāyana D.S.* I. 10. 19. 1-2; *Āpastamba D.S.* I. 9.24. 1-4.

[29] *Gautama D.S.* XXII. 14-16; *Āpastamba D.S.* I. 5.16.22; II. 10. 27.9.

[30] *Maj. Nik.* II. 88.

[31] *Maj. Nik.* I. 344; *Dīg. Nik.* I. 141; *Saṁ. Nik.* I. 76;

[32] *Aṅg. Nik.* II. 207-8; *Dīg. Nik.* III. 180-93.

[33] *Mahābhārata*, Śānti Parvan, 254, 38-9.

[34] VI. 1. 13-14

quest of the neighbour or a consciously worked out and carefully nurtured friendship became inevitable when the process of fission as the answer to internal tensions was no longer feasible. The breaking away of the segment of the clan was possible if there was enough land and other resources available in the vicinity. With the increase in numbers of *gaṇa-saṅghas* and kingdoms this became more difficult since in the case of the latter erstwhile frontier zones would have been claimed, protected and defended. The need to expand access to resources both in terms of fertile land and busy trade routes encouraged the conquest of neighbours. But the conquest of neighbours was through a systematic campaign as that between Magadha and the Vṛjji confederacy, and not through sporadic raids. There is a noticeable decrease in cattle raids, except along frontier areas where such activities were to be continued and permitted as part of a buffer zone strategy.[35] Whereas the lineage system profited by intermittent raids and warfare the state system required a limitation on locations given to warfare — the fields of battles and of campaigns — with a substantial area of stability and peace. This was necessary to prevent the disruption of agriculture and trade. Neighbours were therefore envisaged in a network of either hostile or friendly alliances, sometimes expressed in the theory of *maṇḍala* — a construct of the state within a concentric series of states. Significantly, Kauṭilya includes this in the discussion on the seven elements of the state.[36]

The subjects of the king are referred to less as members of the same *janapada* (*sa-janapada*) and more as *prajā*, a word which originally meant progeny but eventually came to mean subjects and citizens as well. The notion of progeny carried over traces of kinship links but at the same time the paternal authority of the king was stressed. The duties of the king revolved around the protection of the *prajā* but this was seen not merely as protection from external danger; it was also the maintenance of the internal structure eventually symbolized in the expression, 'the upholding of the *varṇāśramadharma*.'

The preservation of internal order had its counterweight in attitudes to revolt and protest. The question of the legitimacy of revolt is discussed in sources of the post-Vedic period. The

[35] Romila Thapar, 'Death and the Hero', in S.C. Humphreys (ed.), *Mortality and Immortality: the Anthropology and Archaeology of Death*, London, 1982.

[36] *Arthaśāstra* VI. 1.

legitimacy of revolt is conceded should a king fail to protect his subjects.[37] However, with the growing association of divinity with the office of kingship the logical development of the alternative view gradually gained strength, that the killing of a king by his subjects was not to be permitted as he is the equivalent of a god.[38] It is further argued that the king's *karma* will take care of his unrighteousness and the subjects should not therefore take the law into in their own hands.[39] The fear of chaos in a situation where the king has been removed is held out as a threat against assassination.

The banishment of a king is alluded to.[40] Assassination is referred to symbolically in the *Mahābhārata*[41] and more realistically in the *Jātakas*.[42] The actual act of killing is carried out either by *brāhmans* or by gods. In the case of Veṇa it was only the *ṛṣis* who could kill him and that too with stalks of the sacred *kuśa* grass. At the same time kings are warned against oppression lest their subjects revolt and express their resentment in various ways. The migration of *brāhmaṇs* brought humiliation but the migration of peasants was much more effective as it reduced the revenue and is therefore feared. Clearly the memory of groups migrating to ease tension was still fresh. Buddhist texts, needless to say, have a more matter of fact assessment of protest and revolt since the contractual basis of their theories on the origin of government provided a certain theoretical freedom for those contemplating the removal of the ruler.

The transition from lineage to state can be seen as a strand running through much of the literature which is included in the category of *itihāsa-purāṇa* and which is referred to as the ancient Indian historical tradition. Compiled by the *sūta* and the *māgadha* (bards and panegyrists) it grew out of the eulogies on heroes victorious in raids and the generous donors of wealth to the bards. Vedic literature has scattered fragments of a historical tradition in which the hero-lauds and narratives of the *nārāśaṃsīs*, *gāthās*, *dāna-stutis* and *ākhyānas*,[43] were preserved partially because they are incor-

[37] *Mahābhārata*, Anuśāsana Parvan, 60. 18.20; Śānti Parvan, 79.42-3

[38] *Nārada* XVIII. 20-2.

[39] Manu VII. 19 ff.

[40] *Mahāsutasoma Jātaka* no. 537; *Khaṇḍahāla Jāt.* no. 542; *Mahābhārata*, Vana Parvan, 3.1.1; *AV* III.3-5; *Tait. Sam.* II. 3.1.

[41] *Mahābhārata*, Śānti Parvan, 59. 100 ff; Udyog Parvan, 11.1 ff. 16.1 ff.

[42] *Saccamkira Jāt.* no. 73; *Manicora Jāt.* no. 194; *Padakusalamānava Jāt.* no. 432.

[43] *Vedic Index*, I, pp. 445, 350-1, 224, 52.

porated into the ritual of the *yajñas*. The *ākhyānas* were the stories and ballads recited on ritual occasions incorporating some element perhaps of actual events, but substantially reflecting the assumptions of that society and the process by which these were established as social custom. Thus the story of Śunaḥśepa[44] is quoted as an *ākhyāna* and has as one of its elements, the adoption of a non-kinsman into the clan of Viśvamitra. These are essentially compositions eulogizing the prowess, valour, generosity of the hero, the chief of the clan. None of them depict the hero as the key person in a state system, nor for that matter is there a reference to what might be the background to a state.

Central to these early sections of the *itihāsa-purāṇa* tradition was the genealogical data. This was crucial in a society where kinship links determined status, land-rights, wealth, marriage relations and the preservation of tribal identity. The genealogies form the core of the tradition. It has been suggested that these as they appear in the *Purāṇas* were originally recorded in Prākrit and were later rendered into Sanskrit[45] when the *brāhmaṇ* editors of what became the Purāṇic texts took over the tradition from the *sūtas* of earlier times. This would indicate the possible inclusion of both a pre-Vedic tradition (perhaps even going back to Harappan times and doubtless in a somewhat garbled fashion), as well as material conforming to contemporary needs, so that the texts could be used for contemporary purposes as well. A similar process can be suggested for the editing of the epics in their present form from earlier bardic sources. In memorizing the oral tradition various mnemonic devices would be used and legends commonly incorporated. Since the editing of the oral tradition in the form of the Purāṇic texts was done by *brāhmaṇs* (probably the Bhṛgu *brāhmaṇs*), the nature and function of the *Purāṇas* would also have undergone a change. One of the more apparent functions of these texts would be to legitimize the *kṣatriya* status of non-*kṣatriya* families by linking them to the older established lineages,[46] through fabricated connections.

Of the descent lists as given in the Purāṇic texts, the depth is such that they can hardly be regarded as authentic. The artificial lengthening of genealogies is a frequently observed phenomenon by those working on genealogical data. This happens particularly

[44] *Ait. Brāh.* VII. 18.

[45] F.E. Pargiter, ...*Dynasties of the Kali Age*, p. 77 ff.

[46] Romila Thapar, 'Social Mobility in Ancient India with special reference to Elite Groups', in *AISH*, p. 122 ff.

when attempts are made to show a long-established settlement by a clan in an area. The occasional name may be remembered from the past but for the major part it is the pattern of the records which can reveal more than the actual lists.[47] The descent list is sought to be fleshed out occasionally bý the inclusion of a myth involving one of the persons in the list. This can again act either as a mnemonic device or as stating certain assumptions about the lineage or can indicate the assimilation of a more recent tradition.

Apart from the Purāṇic texts, the *itihāsa-purāṇa* tradition includes the two epics, the *Mahābhārata* and the *Rāmāyaṇa*. The genealogical and mythical sections are not identical but similar and the epics probabiy contain the earlier versions of the edited material, before it was finalized into the form of the *Purāṇa*s. The transition from non-state to state is indirectly represented in both epics. The earlier sections of both texts depict a society which is closer in spirit to the lineage system described here. The later additions would date to a period when the lineage system had declined and the state had emerged.[48] In so far as these are texts legitimizing a changed situation their analyses have generally been limited to viewing them as bardic literature converted to religious purposes. Yet this was neither accidental nor is it the sole aspect of the texts as sources of legitimation. That Kṛṣṇa and Rāma are *avatāra*s of Viṣṇu has its own interest but they also represent other facets of society.

Many of the narrative sections[49] of the *Mahābhārata* represent the period just prior to the emergence of state systems. The structure of the Kuru *janapada* resembles the features which have been discussed here with reference to the western Ganga valley. Political institutions are as much kin-based as social relationships, the major ritual remains the *yajña* in various forms, and a pastoral-cum-agrarian economy is evident, with an emphasis on clan holdings rather than the breaking up of land into private holdings. The succession to the Kuru realm is among the *rājanya* lineages and this is firmly maintained even though neither of the contenders are actually related by blood to the Kuru lineage. The genealogical contortions necessary to establish the links and the recourse to divinity en-

[47] Romila Thapar, 'Genealogy as a Source of Social History,' in *AISH.*, p. 326 ff.

[48] Romila Thapar, 'The Historian and the Epic', *Annals of the Bhandarkar Oriental Research Institute,* 1979, LX, p. 199 ff; *Exile and the Kingdom: some thoughts on the Rāmāyaṇa,* Bangalore, 1978.

[49] As for example, the Sabhā Parvan and the Āranya Parvan.

courages the suspicion that this segment was artificially added onto the lineage which strictly terminates with Bhīsma.[50] Even if this was the case it is important that such lineage links were regarded as essential to the narrative. The activities of the Yādava tribe are even further away from a state system. The Andhaka-Vṛṣṇi were the ruling clan among them and Kṛṣṇa a prominent chief within the group. As the incarnation of Viṣṇu, Kṛṣṇa is outside the struggle for succession, and plays the role of the sympathetic kinsman. Śiśupāla has to be killed because he objects to clan connections determining status. The role of Kṛṣṇa as the charioteer in the battle, apart from its complex symbolism, and the frequency of face-to-face combat among the protagonists, is more suggestive of the earlier system than are the complicated battle formations. Post-Vedic society is clearly depicted in the didactic sections of the text[51] where the existence of the state is taken for granted. This is in itself a subtle endorsement of the state since monarchy is described as the ideal system and is axiomatic to the major didactic tracts such as the *rāja-dharma* and *mokṣa-dharma* sections. A characteristic of lineage society which is noticeable in the *Mahābhārata* is the resort to migration to ease tension and conflict, particularly in relation to political power. Thus the Pāṇḍavas build a new capital at Indraprastha and a segment of the Andhaka-Vṛṣṇis migrates from Mathurā to Dvārkā. In a sense the frequency of exile is also partially associated with fission since the need for exile arises out of crises concerning legitimacy and power both in the *Mahābhārata* and the *Rāmāyaṇa*.

In terms of the confrontation between non-state and state systems, the *Rāmāyaṇa* encapsulates the conflict more clearly and is essentially a statement in favour of the monarchical state.[52] Viṣṇu is reborn as the heir-apparent and ultimately becomes the initiator of the epitome of the monarchical state in the concept of *rāma-rājya*. Rāma's greatest virtue is that he upholds the duties of the king. Kośala is the ideal monarchical state and the descriptions are such that they could only have been based on Kośala in the post-Vedic period. The houses of the citizens of Ayodhyā are well-stocked with rice.[53] Families are said to be wealthy in cattle, horses

[50] Romila Thapar, 'The Historian and the Epic', *ABORI* 1979, LX, p. 199 ff.

[51] As for example, the Śānti Parvan.

[52] Romila Thapar, *Exile and the Kingdom : some thoughts on the Rāmāyaṇa*.

[53] I. 5.17. It is stated that the rice was the excellent *śāli* quality.

and grain.[54] Rāma questioning Bharata on his governing of Kośala reiterates some of the requirements of the *saptāṅga* theory.[55] The descriptions of the city of Ayodhyā in the *Bāla-kāṇḍa* seem to refer to the city after the mid-first millennium B.C.[56] There is a concentration of power in the king, an administrative hierarchy, a clearly defined territory with some notion of boundaries, a capital in which the main action of the earlier section of the epic takes place, a treasury, a regularly constituted army and a range of allies and foes. Kośala and Videha are treated sympathetically by the author and represent a society conforming to the mores of a transition to monarchical culture.

The contrast between state and non-state is most effectively shown in the deliniation of the *rākṣasas*. They are not bound to any territory, roam where they will and are present in virtually every area mentioned in the story. Rāvaṇa is more a chief than a king and is constantly advised by his kinsmen. There is no administrative hierarchy in Laṅkā and again the decisions are taken largely by the kinsmen of the chief. Laṅkā is the capital and although it is described as encrusted with gold and gems and boasting of considerable wealth none of these come through any system of taxation or revenue. The army of Rāvaṇa consists more of terrifying figures than of a well-trained professional force and his friends and foes are individuals whose relationship with Rāvaṇa is determined largely by goodwill and marriage alliances. Whereas Ayodhyā is described as replete with rice there is little mention of grain in Laṅkā.[57] Kośala is dotted with gardens and fields, only gardens are mentioned in the description of Laṅkā. The contrast between the two societies is highlighted by the confrontation. Whatever the original kernal of the epic events may have been, by the time it was rewritten as a *kāvya*, the differences between the state and the non-state were implicit in the rewriting.

The *Rāmāyaṇa* therefore became among other things an epic legitimizing the monarchical state. This is in part indicated by the many versions and adaptations of the *Rāmāyaṇa* in various languages in the Indian sub-continent and in south-east Asia. The adaptation frequently coincides with the establishment of monarchies based on indigenous power. The variants on the original text often relate to the particulars of the local situation in terms of kin-

[54] I. 6.7. [55] II. 94. [56] I. 5, 6 and 7.

[57] D.R. Chanana, *The Spread of Agriculture in Northern India*, New Delhi, 1963.

ship, economy and religion, all of which tend to strengthen the idea that the text as such validated the monarchical state. Whereas in the *Rāmāyaṇa* the difference is projected in the depiction of two entirely different societies, in the *Mahābhārata* the change is interpolated into the same society but is evident in the difference between the narrative and didactic sections. In the *Rāmāyaṇa* the epic hero becomes the archetypal figure representing the past and changes which may have occurred gradually over time are consolidated and attributed to him.

The transition from one sytem to another is demonstrated, apart from the epics, in some of the Purāṇic texts as becomes evident from a careful analysis of the *vaṃśānucarita* (genealogical) tradition contained in the major *Purāṇa*s. The *Viṣṇu Purāṇa* is often described as the exemplar among these texts since it is characterized by the five standard components (*pañca-lakṣana*) of the genre. These are described as *sarga,* the evolution of the universe from a first cause, *pratisarga,* the recreation of the universe at the end of each *kalpa* or cycle of time, *vaṃśa,* the genealogies of gods and *ṛṣis*, *mānavāntara,* the cycles of aeons in which mankind is created afresh from the ancestral Manu,. and *vaṃśānucarita,* the descent lists of those who are said to have ruled from earliest times. The structure is that of a book of genesis describing in an orderly fashion the view on the past. The genealogical section setting out the genealogical history of early times is contained in Book IV. An attempt is made to construct the past in terms of the history of lineages. The question of whether or not the reconstruction is historically authentic is not central to our argument. In the past genealogical lists have been used for calculating chronology on the basis of collating the diverse lists and attempting to assign a regnal period to each generation.[58] This is almost an exercise in futility. Such genealogies are notorious for not being exact since chronological exactitude is not their function. It would seem more purposeful to derive a different type of information from this data which would be more enlightening on lineage forms, geographical distribution and to some extent political perspective. What is important is to analyse why the information was put together in this particular way. The *Purāṇa* was probably composed sometime in

[58] S.N. Pradhan, *Chronology of Ancient India,* Calcutta, 1927; R. Morton Smith, *Dates and Dynasties in Earliest India,* Delhi, 1975. For an analytical study of this question see D.P. Henige, *The Chronology of Oral Tradition,* Oxford, 1974.

the Gupta period since the 'prophecies' regarding the dynasties ruling in Jambudvīpa terminate at this point. This was a period of considerable historical change in northern India and as such the *Purāṇa* represents a looking back on the past to construct an image of the past, of providing the past with a framework and at the same time preparing for the past to be used as a legal charter for contemporary and successor political systems. The *vaṃśānucarita* section therefore becomes a book of origins to be used by those seeking political legitimacy.

The authorship of the *itihāsa-purāṇa* tradition as collated in the *Purāṇa*s has some bearing on its function. It is said to have been compiled and edited by Vyāsa,[59] thus in a sense giving it the status of the Vedic texts and the *Mahābhārata*. It is in fact sometimes referred to as the fifth *Veda*. There was however a crucial difference in that the *itihāsa-purāṇa* tradition was taught by Vyāsa to his fifth disciple, the *sūta* (bard) Lomaharṣana who was of course not a *brāhmaṇ*. The latter divided the tradition into six parts each of which he taught to his six disciples who were all *brāhmaṇ*s. In addition, Lomaharṣana also taught the tradition to his son, Ugraśravasa who, being a bard, recited it for a living. Clearly there is an ambivalence on whether the tradition should be ascribed to *brāhmaṇ* authorship or to the bards and chroniclers. It is also suggestive of a shift in the maintenance of the tradition from bards to *brāhmaṇ*s. Most existing *Purāṇa*s claim the stereotype origin common to many *itihāsa* texts that they were revealed by a god to a *ṛṣi* who then recited the text at a sacrifice. Status is conferred on the tradition by linking it to a ritual event, and *brāhmaṇ* connections doubtless grew when the tradition was required for legitimation. The shift in status would also be indicated by the suggestion that the tradition was originally oral and probably composed in Prākrit but was converted to Sanskrit when it came to be maintained by the *brāhmaṇ*s and was recorded in writing.

As an oral tradition it would have been kept initially by the *sūta* and the *māgadha*. *The sūta* as a professional person was of high status and close to the chief. In later Vedic literature the *sūta* is one of the eight *vīras* (heroes) and one of the eleven or twelve *ratnin*s (jewels) and therefore associated with the *rājā* on ritual occasions.[60] In order of precedence the *sūta* follows the *mahiṣi* (chief queen) and precedes the *grāmaṇī*. He is described as being *ahantya* (inviolable)

[59] Pargiter, *Ancient Indian Historical Tradition*, p. 21 ff.

[60] Ibid., p. 16 ff

which may indicate that he was also the emissary. The origin of the *sūta* and the *māgadha* is linked to the consecration of Pṛthu when the two emerged out of the sacrificial fire and immediately began reciting the lineage of Pṛthu and a eulogy on his activities (*praśasti*). Pṛthu thereupon appointed them hereditary chroniclers to the eastern lands including Magadha. The link with Magadha and Aṅga is again curious and reflects either a late origin for the story or an association with the people of the middle Ganga valley, an association which would indicate a low status since these were *mleccha* lands. The hint of low status is suggested by the connection between the *māgadha* and the *vrātya* made in the *Atharvaveda*.[61] To this may be added the strange etymology of the word *sūta*. If it derives from the root **su* as is generally believed, then it can mean, 'to impel' or 'to give birth to'. That this refers to the sacrifice and the emergence of the *sūta* is to stretch the etymology; similarly to explain it on the basis that the *sūta* gave birth, metaphorically, to genealogies and lineage records is far-fetched. It might be more appropriate to consider the possibility of deriving it as a Prākrit form from either *sūtra* or *śruti*: the former meaning a thread would symbolize descent as a thread running through lineage and the latter referring to that which is heard or the oral tradition. If either of these derivations are feasible they would support the idea of the original record being in Prākrit. The meaning of *sūta* as a charioteer, would indicate a function which placed him close to the chief and consequently to the activities of ruling families.

The value of the *Purāṇa*s as historical records is circumscribed by their having been rewritten or edited at a period subsequent to that of the events described and that the rewriting was done not by the earlier custodians of the tradition but by *brāhmaṇ*s whose perspective would be very different from that of the *sūta*. Nevertheless their value lies in the fact that they did become the texts of a certain perception of the past in which a particular world view is articulated. As such they are important documents to the historiography of the tradition. Further, the perception of the past was linked to contemporary needs and the *vaṃśānucarita* section recording descent lists of lineages came to be regarded as especially significant.

[61] xv. 2. 1-4.

The structure of this section has its own interest. We are told that originally the world was ruled by a succession of Manus[62] and during the period of the seventh Manu there was a devastating flood created by the gods to punish man. This is described in some detail in the *Matsya Purāṇa*[63] since it is Viṣṇu in his *matsya-avatāra* (fish incarnation) who saves Manu and the seven *ṛṣis*, by advising Manu to seek refuge in a boat which he ties to his horn and swimming through the deluge lodges it safely on a mountain until the flood subsides. Manu returns home and performs sacrifices to obtain sons and continue the lineage. His many sons become the founding fathers of various lineages. The eldest Ikṣvāku, founds the Sūryavaṃśa or Solar lineage and it is this lineage which is eulogized in the *Rāmāyaṇa.* Manu's youngest child, occasionally described as a hermaphrodite or else as one who takes a male and female form alternately, becomes in its female form, Ilā, the ancestress of the Candravaṃśa or Lunar lineage whose members are the protagonists of the events described in the *Mahābhārata.* A substantial part of the *vaṃśānucarita* section lists the descendants of the various lineages covering geographically the whole of northern India. All the surviving lineages participate in the Mahābhārata war, after which the text takes on the future tense, speaking as if prophecying the events to come.[64] Mention is now made of dynasties and there is a concentration on the dynasty at Magadha which is clearly regarded as the most important and continues to be until well into historical times when other dynasties are also mentioned. Whereas for the earlier period the descent lists merely gave the succession of *rājās* there is now a significant change in that the regnal years, no matter how exaggerated in some cases, are given for each ruler and the total length of reign of a dynasty is also mentioned. There is clearly a historical change which is sought to be recorded.

That genealogies were maintained is evident from the statement of Megasthenes[65] that there was a count of one hundred and fifty-three/four kings prior to the coming of Alexander to India, and their reigns covered a period of six thousand four hundred and fifty-one years. As with most genealogical records the process of 'telescoping' events and generations must certainly have resulted in some confusion and deviation from an authentic record of events. Telescoping is in effect the pruning of the list in order to make its

[62] *Viṣṇu Purāṇa* III. 1.

[63] *Matsya Purāṇa* I. 10-33; II. 1-9.

[64] *Viṣṇu Purāṇa* IV. 21; F.E. Pargiter, *Dynasties of the Kali Age,* p. 14.

[65] Frag. L.C., Pliny, *Historia Naturalis,* VI. 21.4-5; Solin 52.5

preservation more manageable. Nevertheless the structure of the genealogy has its own importance.

The reference to the earliest Manus is the most vague and would suggest a period of remote antiquity or even mythical kings. The Flood acts as the first time-marker since floods symbolize the washing away of what went before and a new beginning with the receding of the flood and 'the abolition of profane time'.[66] The break is not complete since the lineages of the second period are the progeny of the Manu who survived the flood, via their eponymous ancestors. These lineage lists are said to be the *kṣatriya*s in power at the time. The form which they take are suggestive of their being the clans or the chiefships of the period prior to the emergence of the state. In some cases the names in the descent lists are identical with the names of the *jana*s or tribes as given in other sources which develop into territorial names, such as the five sons of Bali—Aṅga, Vaṅga, Kaliṅga, Puṇḍra and Suhma. In other cases they are individual names of chiefs. The genealogies from the *Purāṇa*s do not necessarily always tally with those from the epics or from Vedic literature. Genealogical depth in Vedic literature tends to be shallow in comparison with the epics and even more so when compared to the Purāṇic lists. But some of the names do get repeated in the later sources although their place in the descent may differ.[67] Nor should the number of generations listed in the *Purāṇas* be taken too literally since lists can be conflated merely to emphasize a longer period of time. It is a moot point whether synchronization of the texts was really important to the compilers. Had it been so then an effort would have been made to rewrite these sections in conformity with the data in the epics or vice versa. Considering that the original compilers, the *sūta*s and the *māgadha*s, as well as the later editors, were the same for each category of text, such a synchronism would not have been difficult. It might be more apposite to view these descent lists as indicators of social forms rather than as factual records.

The two major lineages are constructed on two differing principles. The senior lineage descended from the eldest son of Manu, Ikṣvāku, records only the senior line of descent in each generation, among the descendants of Iksvāku. The Kośala lineage is regarded

[66] M. Eliade, *Cosmos and History*, New York, 1959, p. 5ff.

[67] F.E. Pargiter, *The Ancient Indian Historical Tradition*. Pargiter has attempted some comparative study both between the *Purāṇa*s and with the epics in an effort to establish synchronisms, but the variants are too many.

as the most important and is given in the greatest detail. The emphasis is on primogeniture, an issue which is of the utmost importance to the narrative of the *Rāmāyaṇa* as well. The descendants of the youngest child of Manu, the Ailas, are recorded as a series of segmenting lineages. The seniormost lineage, that of the Yādavas, is exiled to western India; *madhya deśa* (essentially the Ganga-Yamuna *doāb* and its fringes) is inherited by the juniormost, that of Puru, the disruption of primogeniture being explained by the famous story of Yayāti postponing his old age.[68] The descendants of the intermediate sons of Yayāti are listed up to a point but soon these lists peter out and ultimately the Candravaṃśa is the record of the Pūru and Yādava lineages.[69] The segments are obviously not all related by blood and the record includes those who were assimilated into the lineage through conquest and through marriage alliances. The lineage lists are therefore also documents recording migrations, the assimilation of other groups and alliances. The emphasis is on legitimacy through claiming lineage links and hereditary sucession is not crucial, as is demonstrated in the links sought to be made between the Puru lineage and the Kauravas and the Pāṇḍavas. The importance of lineage links was both to claim *kṣatriya* status as well as to assert rights over territory and land. In the more settled agricultural society of the middle Ganga valley inheritance would have been an important issue from an early period with clearly defined rules for succession; but in the less hospitable areas of western and central India with large groups of pastoral-cum-agricultural peoples, rights to succession would still have been aspired to and fought over by the senior lineages.

The Mahābhārata war can be seen as the second time-marker in the structure of the *vamśānucarita* section. Virtually all the major *kṣatriyas* of the Candravaṃśa and many others gather together to take part in the war. What might have been an inter-tribal conflict

[68] *Viṣṇu Purāṇa* IV. 10.

[69] The lineage is essentially concerned with the Pūrus and their descendents in the watershed area and the upper Doāb and with the Yādavas in western India. I have made an attempt to discuss the possible archaeological identity of these two descent groups by comparing their settlements with those of the Painted Grey Ware and the Black-and-red Ware, but the identification remains very tentative and uncertain. 'Purānic Lineages and Archaeological Cultures', in *AISH*, p. 240 ff. Curiously the two regions which became the geographical focus of these two groups were the areas where the Late Harappan developed and overlapped with post-Harappan cultures. This makes it feasible to argue that some of the material included in the tradition may go back to Harappan times.

over succession takes on the dimensions of the end of an epoch. This is precisely what it is; the end of the epoch of *kṣatriya* chiefships and in a sense the war clears away this system as the dominant political system and makes way for the monarchical state of the middle Ganga valley. That the latter clings to some aspects of the earlier system is evident from the insistence that ideally kings should be of the *kṣatriya varṇa*; however, in fact many were not and some sought a *kṣatriya* status through a fabricated genealogy. Significantly, the location of the battle is associated with the pre-eminent among the *kṣatriyas*—the land of the Kurus. It is also significant that the battle occurs in the western Ganga valley and not in the middle Ganga valley since the latter area was to witness an easier transition to state formation. The intrinsic sorrow of the battle at Kurukṣetra is not merely at the death of kinsmen but also at the dying of a society, a style, a political form. The concept of the present as Kali-yuga combines a romanticization of the earlier society with the sense of insecurity born of a changing system and every fresh change of a major kind leads to the reiteration of the fears of the Kali-yuga.

The transition to a monarchical state in Kośala is reflected not only in the form in which the lineage is recorded in the *Purāṇas* but also and more so in the *Rāmāyaṇa* itself. The same transition in Magadha remains without an epic to eulogize it. This may in part be due to the inclination of the rulers of Magadha towards the heterodox sects, where, in the chronicles of early Buddhism, the epic as it were, of the rulers of Magadha is to be found in the *Dīpavamsa* and the *Mahāvamsa*, chronicles of the early history of Sri Lanka. It may also be because the central core of the *vaṃśānucarita* tradition becomes in fact the dynastic history of Magadha.[70] In any case the eulogy of the emergent state required a form different from the epic.

After the rise of Bṛhadratha the rulers of Magadha are listed together with their regnal years and the focus is on the succession in this region.[71] This is particularly stressed since the form of this record is prophetic and the intention is clearly to suggest that Magadha was the most important state to emerge after the *Mahābhārata* war. With the establishment of the monarchical state, these alone are considered worthy of record, even when the dynasties are not of *ksatriya* origin and are as low as *śūdra* as in the case of the

[70] *Visnu Purāna* IV. 23.

[71] Ibid., IV. 23-4.

Nandas.[72] References to chiefships are excluded in these lists, the *gaṇa-saṅghas* of the middle Ganga valley being either ignored or referred to obliquely by the inclusion of some names in a descent list. Thus Śākya is a name in the Ikṣvāku genealogy, whose son is Śuddhodhana and his son Rāhula is the father of a Praśenajīt — a good example of telescoping![73] The exclusion of the *gaṇa-saṅghas* of this period is in contrast to their being mentioned where they existed in northern and western India in the period prior to the war, and serves to emphasize the significance of the monarchical state in the eyes of the compilers of the *Purāṇas*.

The *vaṃśānucarita* section was not merely an attempt to record the past, it was also the clearing house of the genealogical material for contemporary political use. In the continual process of state formation which was accelerated with the establishment of new settlements serving both to extend agriculture and subsequently often also to encourage trade, new rulers had to be legitimized and this was frequently done by providing lineage links with earlier lineages recorded in the Purāṇic tradition. In the transition from *jana* to *jāti,* families of chiefs would often claim *kṣatriya* status. This was not only an expression of sanskritization and acculturation but was also an effective means of demarcating those families which could claim rights over land (the equivalent of the earlier *rāja-kulas*) and those who gradually subsided into the lesser categories of the *vaiśya* and *śūdra varṇas*. That succession lists are crucial to all those claiming status and property is evident not only from these lineages but also from the succession lists of teachers maintained by the Buddhist monasteries which could on occasion be substantial property holders.[74].

The Purāṇic evidence suggests, if looked at analytically, that prior to the rise of the dynasties, the recording of *kṣatriya* descent groups was important since power resided in the lineages. The system came to an end in the western Ganga valley and this termination was represented in the description of the Kurukṣetra war. The emergence of dynasties which was a major change in the socio-political form, took place in the middle Ganga valley and doubtless posed a threat to the lineage system. Thus Jarāsandha is the natural enemy of the Vṛṣṇis since he portends the birth of the new state and they represent the continuance of the *gaṇa-saṅgha* system.

[72] Ibid., IV. 24.
[73] Ibid., IV. 22.
[74] This is demonstrated in R.A.L.H. Gunawardana, *The Robe and Plough*, (Arizona, 1979), describing the process for the monasteries of Sri Lanka.

If the above analysis is acceptable then it suggests that the *itihāsa-purāṇa* tradition in some of its facets does make an attempt to represent a semblance of the past, if not as authentic history then at least as an authentic pattern of changing social relations. The same tradition is picked up by Buddhist authors and more fully developed in a Buddhist context. This in itself makes a worthwhile point of contrast.

The seeds of the Buddhist historical tradition may be located in the *itihāsa-samvāda,* the dialogues incorporating stories reminiscent of the dialogue hymns of Vedic literature but formulated in a recognizably Buddhist context and included in the *Sutta Piṭaka*[75]. Some of the *sutta*s are similar to the *ākhyāna*s but are used to illustrate Buddhist doctrine and often focus on an event connected with a well-known person. There is also reference to the legend of the life of the Buddha and his more important disciples. In the early texts the distinction between the biography of the Buddha and the history of the religion tends to merge. The *Sutta Nipāta* contains elements of the biography of the Buddha[76] and the *Jātaka* stories soak up a floating tradition, some of which is found in the *Rāmāyaṇa* and the *Mahābhārata* as well. The *Jātaka* stories echo the revised versions of the epics where frequently stories illustrate a moral, except that the *Jātaka* stories do so more invariably. The opening of the story carries a distinct historical flavour in that it often refers to a place, a period of time and a person. Those with an *itihāsa-purāṇa* connection are usually associated with the *Rāma-kathā* and the *Bharata-kathā* or else with themes from the epics such as the exile theme used so effectively in the *Vessantara Jātaka.*

Links with the *itihāsa-purāṇa* tradition are more evident in the two chronicles the *Dīpavamsa* and the *Mahāvamsa,* in the sections dealing with the history of Sri Lanka prior to the coming of Buddhism. There are lengthy lineage lists of Indian ancestors extending over many centuries and covering practically all the then known geographical regions. Vijaya and his entourage are the first humans to settle on the island and although their ancestry is from eastern India they sail from a port in western India.[77] Since Vijaya has no son his brother's son, Pāṇḍuvāsudeva is sent for. The name is almost archetypal and obviously suggests a

[75] M. Winternitz, *History of Indian Literature,* vol. II Calcutta, 1933, p. 34.
[76] Nalaka sutta III. 11; Pabbajja sutta III. 1; Padhana sutta III. 2.
[77] *Mahāvamsa* VI.

Pāṇḍava-Kṛṣṇa connection, perhaps an attempt to find links with the pre-eminent clans of the Yādavas. The link is further underlined by the story of Pāṇḍukabhaya the grandson of Pāṇḍuvāsudeva whose early life resembles that of Vāsudeva Kṛṣṇa to such a degree that it could not have been coincidental. The child is hidden at birth and brought up by relatives. There is also a conflict with the maternal uncle whom he destroys. It may be argued along the lines of Otto Rank that this story carries the stereotype myth of the birth of the hero[78] but the incidents are too similar for the similarity to have been accidental. Evidently the story was not only popular but carried some status. The frequency with which the Yādava lineage crops up along the west coast and in the peninsula would suggest that in the proximity of Sri Lanka it was the most respected lineage.[79] As if the Yādava status was not sufficient the wife of Pāṇḍuvāsudeva was said to have been a Śākya princess. Thus the ancestry of the earliest rulers of the island is traced back to or associated with the highest antecedents — the Śākya family to appease Buddhist sentiment and the Yādavas as part of the Candravaṃśa lineage of the *itihāsa-purāṇa* tradition.

The Buddhist Pāli canon was put together some centuries after the events which it records. The two main themes of Buddhist historiography can both be traced to these texts : the life of the Buddha and other important members of the *saṅgha* which was to become the nucleus of the *carita* or biographical tradition and the need to record the history of the *saṅgha* together with the sectarian conflicts and differentiations which emerged in time. The *Vinaya Piṭaka*, among other things, describes the formation of the Buddhist community and attempts a chronological narrative of these events. Commentaries on this text discussed the various sectarian differences. Another text, the *Kathāvatthu* of the *Abhidhamma Piṭaka* claimed by the Theravāda sect as a history of the *saṅgha* is not acceptable to some other sects, a difference of opinion which is of considerable historical significance. The historical material was built into the Canon almost accidentally through the sheer necessity of maintaining a record of the controversies and disputations.

The concern with historicity (whether factual or not) is a striking feature of the Buddhist historical tradition. The need to maintain a

[78] O. Rank, *The Myth of the Birth of the Hero*, New York, 1959.

[79] Romila Thapar, 'Purānic Lineages and Archaeological Cultures', in *AISH*, p. 240.

record of sectarian changes was doubtless due to control over property through monastic establishments and donations to the *saṅgha*. Close association with royal patronage made these records more imperative. Added to this was the fact that from the third century B.C., after the Council at Pāṭaliputra, the proselytizing mission of Buddhism was actively propagated with a number of missions being sent to various parts of the subcontinent and beyond. A record of these had to be maintained, particularly when in later periods the increasing sectarian rivalries sought sanction from the past. That the tradition took a systematic form may have originated in its hinging around a precise point in time and space, the historic person of the Buddha. This was also to provide the chronological starting point in the date of the Buddha's *parinirvāna*, a date which even though under dispute is nevertheless the commencing date in Buddhist history. At a wider level there were other factors which encouraged a more historical perception: the monks maintained a literate tradition in which the maintenance of records was a normal activity and the initial establishment and expansion of Buddhism was related to an urban context and was closely associated with the founding of the major state of Magadha.

The history of Magadha is narrated in some detail in the Buddhist Chronicles particularly the *Dīpavaṃsa* and the *Mahāvaṃsa*. This was both because it was the most powerful state and its kings were therefore the most prestigious, and because it was the crucible of the Theravāda/Sthaviravāda sect and therefore its history became a part of the sacred history of this sect. Linked to this was the fact that the first missionary to Sri Lanka, Mahinda, the son of Aśoka Maurya, was sent on his mission after the Council at Pāṭaliputra. It is possible that the events as narrated are correct but it is also plausible that the link with the Mauryas was an afterthought to enhance the prestige of the Theravāda sect. These histories were essentially accounts of the evolution of certain doctrines and the growth of particular monasteries, in well-defined kingdoms. The *Dīpavaṃsa* is the history of Buddhism in the island and the *Mahāvaṃsa*, the history of the major monastery, the Mahāvihāra. Interest lies in the manner in which the narrative brings into play the political authority at the time with the sacred history. These are not necessarily contemporary records and are frequently reflections on potential connections in a period after the arrival of Buddhism. Thus the *Dīpavamsa* and the *Mahāvaṃsa* were compiled in their present form in the mid-first millennium A.D. which allowed the idea of seeking to link the *saṅgha* with the state to mature.

The *Dīpavaṃsa*, the more archaic of the two texts demonstrates many of these facets of Buddhist historiography. It drew on various oral traditions[80] and among these were the *Sīhala-ṭṭhakathāmahāvaṃsa* and the *Porāṇā*. The Buddha not only visits Sri Lanka but also predicts the coming of Buddhism to the island, thus sanctifying the history of Buddhism in that area.[81] Another section, the *rāja vaṃsa,* traces the descent of *rājā*s and *khattiya*s from Mahāsammata which is here taken as the name of the first ruler. This extensive descent list borrows names from both the Ikṣvāku and Aila lineages, but is substantially a different list.[82] (Elsewhere, the Buddha's family is said to be of the Ikṣvāku *vaṃsa*.) The list continues down to Rāhula the son of Siddhartha. The last few verses mention the kings Bimbisāra and Ajātsatru as contemporaries of the Buddha.[83] The two councils at Rājagṛha and Vaiśāli are described and the seccessionist sects resulting from these are listed. This is followed by a succession list of the Theras of the *saṅgha,* the chronology of which is related to the succession of ruling monarchs at Magadha, a useful method of associating chronological information with reigning kings.[84] Since the age and years of ordination of the Theras is given[85] the cross-reference to kings seems unnecessary and suggests a conscious attempt at bringing in a political focus. Aśoka Maurya's biography though brief is embellished with details since he was the father of Mahinda.[86] Events leading up to the calling of the Third Council at Pāṭaliputra after the dissident monks have been expelled are narrated and this is attributed to the initiative of Aśoka.[87] It is of great importance since the pre-eminence of the Theravāda sect (dominant in Sri Lanka) was established at this council. The subsequent chapter deals with the various missions which were sent out as a result of this council, including Mahinda's mission to Sri Lanka.[88] The identity of the mission having been invested with the highest religious

[80] F. Perera, *The Early Buddhist Historiography of Ceylon*, unpublished Ph.D. thesis, Gottingen, 1976.

[81] *Dīp.* I and II. [82] *Dīp.* III [83] III. 55-59.

[84] IV. 55-7. [85] IV. 83-96. [86] VI. 1 ff.

[87] *Dīp.* VII. This is made even more explicit in the *Vaṃsatthapakāsinī*.5.228 ff. G.P. Malalasekara, *Vaṃsatthapakāsinī*, London 1935.

[88] *Dīp.* VIII.

and political credentials, there follows then the history of Buddhism in the island. The narrative has occasional flashes of similarity with the Purāṇic tradition as for example in some of the echoes of stories associated with the Yādava lineage[89] and the chronological co-relation of events in Sri Lanka with the rulers of Magadha continues, though briefly. The final few references are incidental, embedded in what is essentially the history of Sri Lanka in the latter half of the text.[90]

The transition from the lineage system to the state is reflected in the narrative of these Chronicles as well as in other Buddhist sources on which the narrative draws.[91] The Śākyas for example bear all the marks of a lineage society. Their ancestry goes back to the Ikṣvāku line or Okkāka as it is called in Pāli sources. They originate in the exile of the four sons and five daughters of Okkāka who settle in the Himalayan foothills near the hermitage of Kapila where they build their city of Kapilavastu. Four brothers marry four sisters and become the progenitors of the Śākyas by giving birth to sixteen pairs of twins. The origin myth of the Kolya clan links them to the Śākyas stating that the Kolyas married the Śākya women who were their maternal uncles' daughters. The new group in each case migrates away from the old and establishes its own *janapada* with its capital. The name of the clan provokes the etymological imagination as in deriving Śākya from *śaknoti* (to be able) or the *śaka* tree. The insistence on sibling twins as the procreators of the *jana* has to do with maintaining the purity of the lineage and tracing lineage origins back to those of identical blood. There is also a deliberate attempt to associate cross-cousin marriage with elite groups which also emphasizes kinship links among the *gaṇa-saṅgha* clans of the middle Ganga valley. The bearing of sixteen pairs of twins seems indicative of the *rāja-kula*, a symbolic diffusion of power into a small but effective social group. The *kṣatriya* status of the clan is evident from the Ikṣvāku connection which was high even by Purāṇic standards. Curiously the Purāṇic sources are either silent about these clans or cursorily mention a few names. Clearly Purāṇic authors did not approve of them, probably because they maintained a non-monarchic system.

Many of these elements are carried over in the *Mahāvaṃsa* as

[89] *Dīp.* X, XI. 1-4.

[90] *Dīp.* XI. 8-40; XII. 1-8, 50 ff; XV. 6-7, 83-94; XVI. 1-23; XVII. 81-6.

[91] Romila Thapar, 'Origin Myths and the Early Indian Historical Tradition', in *AISH*, p. 309 ff.

noticed earlier in the descriptions of the origins of Vijaya who first colonizes Sri Lanka.[92] The transition to the state system is again associated with the region of Magadha, and by the time of the Mauryas when the major events take place in relation to the arrival of Buddhism in Sri Lanka, the state is well-established in Magadha. At an underlying level the linkage is also sought through maintaining that the Maurya clan was an off-shoot of the Śākyas. However with the introduction of the Mauryas the vestiges of lineage society tend to be shed and the *saṅgha* has to face the emergent state.

The Buddhist endorsement of the state was in some ways a contradiction. The organization of the *saṅgha* borrowed its form from the *gaṇa-saṅgha* system and led the *saṅgha* to see itself as a contrast to monarchy and insisted on a separate identity. Perhaps its success in setting up a parallel system drew it towards the idea of further strengthening its position by accepting royal patronage and ultimately moving towards a close association with political authority. Thus in some areas it becomes the source of legitimizing the state, as is evident from the history of Buddhism in Sri Lanka. Association with political authority also had the advantage of the *sangha* reflecting in the 'glory' of 'great kings' as the association of Aśoka with the despatch of Buddhist missions would suggest.[93] Such an association is also important in ousting dissidents and here the *saṅgha* borrows the wielder of the *daṇḍa* to perform this role. The expulsion of dissidents is sought to be justified in terms of keeping the *saṅgha* pure, but it is in effect the underlining of authority. The first council is appropriately held at Rājagṛha, the capital of a powerful kingdom with its king, Ajātaśatru extending his patronage. The breakaway group of the Vajjiputtaka monks was established at the Council at Vaiśāli, the capital of the Vṛjjis. These monks were regarded as dissidents,[94] a curious parallel to the political relationship between Magadha and the Vṛjjis. The Theravāda sect which claims to represent the original teaching of the Buddha is associated with the Mauryan state through the statement that Aśoka was instrumental in calling the Council at Pāṭaliputra.(Even the later Sarvāstivāda sect associated with the northern school of Buddhism links itself with the Kuṣāṇa state through the tradition of the Council held at Kashmir to establish its status.) The

[92] *Mahāvaṃsa* VI.

[93] E. Frauwallner, *The Earliest Vinaya and the Beginnings of Buddhist Literature*, Rome, 1956.

[94] *Mahāvaṃsa* IV. 9 ff; *Cullavagga*, VII. 4.1 ff; XII. 1.1. ff.

association of Aśoka with the Buddhist *sangha* as described in the Ceylon Chronicles can be seen as the *saṅgha* conceding that Aśoka had authority over its activities. Aśoka at the same time claimed the right to adjudicate in the ecclesiastical matters of the *saṅgha*. This is clearly stated in the famous Schism Edict inscribed at various centres of Buddhist importance such as the monasteries at Kauśāmbi, Sārnāth and Sanchi in which he calls for dissident monks and nuns to be expelled from the monastic centres.[95] Such a concession to political authority by the *sangha* was the logical culmination of its connection with political power. The need to hold councils was also a pointer to the entry of secular power into the calculations of the *saṅgha* since controls of various kinds had now to be adjusted and balanced. That the role of Aśoka was viewed differently in the later and northern Buddhist tradition which did not share the historiography of the Theravāda sect, is apparent from the *Aśokāvadāna*.[96] Here the ruler is depicted largely as an enthusiastic royal patron of Buddhism who expresses his enthusiasm through magnanimous donations, some of which are on such a scale as would embarrass any government. He is also shown as suffering in the end for his support of the *saṅgha* since he is deprived by his ministers and successors of the power to give this support. The intention of the *Aśokāvadāna* may well have been moralistic, that even rulers have their time of troubles or that donations are not conditioned by the wealth of the donor and that the truly generous man gives even if he has only half a mango to give; but perhaps the moral is more subtle and relates to the problems of religious sects becoming enmeshed in politics.

The Buddhist *saṅgha* supporting the state system was useful to early states in that it provided an ideological framework for the integration of diverse groups. The network of monasteries could become either a series of supporting institutions backing the state, or alternatively, there was equal danger of their becoming a network of opposition. Initially monasteries were established in the vicinity of towns and large villages since the monks were dependant for alms on the lay community. Later when endowments of land were made to the monasteries then these institutions would act as centres of agrarian activity in areas newly opened up by the state. It was probably at this stage that the link with political authority

[95] Bloch, *Les Inscriptions d'Asoka*, p. 152 ff.

[96] J. Przyluski, *La Legende de l'Empereur Açoka*, Paris, 1923.

became a factor of consequence to the Buddhist tradition. At a wider level the universalistic ethics of Buddhism would appeal to a variety of social groups cutting across lineage and caste ties. This was more evident in the membership of the *saṅgha*. Concessions to political authority were however made, as for instance in the rule that slaves and debtors were not to be recruited as monks,[97] since many of them would have treated the monastery as a refuge from the inequities of society. At the ideological level the Buddhist concern with a transient universe justifies the propagation of change. The doctrines of *karma* and *saṃsāra* (actions and transmigration) as doctrines of retribution in which the cycle of rebirth accounts for social injustices had their use in weakening protest.[98]

With the break-up of the lineage society new alignments were sought. For the monk the *sangha* provided a changed set of relations and a different identity. The initial schism of the Mahāsaṅghikas came from the Vajjiputtakas, those monks who had been associated with the Vṛjji *gaṇa-sangha*, and therefore different from the system prevalent in Rājagṛha or Śrāvasti. Doubtless some older ties of kinship and political associations persisted in the sects of the *saṅgha* which took on the character of local factions. Interestingly the central problem at the Council of Vaiśāli was whether or not the monks were to be permitted to accept monetary donations as alms on which there was a sharp difference of opinion. The monks of Vaiśāli who supported the acceptance of donations of money were defeated and broke away. Other questions related to the kind of food which could be accepted as alms, seating arrangements and procedure in discussion within the monastery. These were questions relating to protocol, hierarchy and property.

The Buddhist support for the new order did not arise merely out of the wish to associate with authority. The egalitarian society of the *saṅgha* was possible only when the state system came into being and monastic institutions could be maintained. A parallel monastic society can only survive when there is a well-ordered agrarian system and trade to provide the surplus since the monastery for its daily needs has a parasitical relationship with society. Hence the statement of the Buddha that good government requires the invest-

[97] *Mahāvagga*, I. 40.1 ff.

[98] Romila Thapar, 'Ethics, Religion and Social Protest in the first millennium B.C. in Northern India', in *AISH*, p. 40 ff.

ment of seed to the cultivators, of capital to the traders and of food and wages to those who work for the government.[99] The insistence on *ahimsā* would also be endorsed by groups such as peasants or traders who required peace and stability for purposes of production. Recurring violence was inimical to the interests of societies in a state system. The harshness of the state was ameliorated in the concept of the *cakkavatti/cakravartin*, the universal ruler whose reign is synonymous with law, order and justice. Significantly it is the wheel of law which rolls across his domains and not the *daṇḍa* of chastizement.

The Buddhist view of this dual relationship also revolves around the role of the king and the *bhikkhu*. The king provides law and order, the *bhikkhu* breaks away from law and order and enters a new domain with its own rules and which is in theory at least beyond society, although in practice it has a close link with society. The *bhikkhu* therefore is in a middle position between the two polarities of the king and the ascetic. The king is in origin the Mahāsammata and aspires to be a *chakkavati* : the aim being the universality of law and order. The *bhikkhu* emulates the Buddha and supports the universality of the doctrine and the ethic. The king has to be seen as the hub of society, the *bhikkhu* of the *saṅgha*. Society moves from a pristine, casteless, egalitarian body to a stratified caste society. The *sangha* excludes stratified caste society and tries to recapture the pristine, egalitarian society.[100] The dual relationship between the *saṅgha* and the state is captured in a later phase of Buddhism in the mirror image of the *bodhisatta* and the *cakkavati*, where the *bodhisatta* is either an earlier incarnation of the Buddha or works towards this through his concern for the welfare of people.

The importance of the *bhikkhu* was not merely in terms of his relationship with the king, but even more so with the lay community. The *bhikkhu* ideal lay not in the monkhood or priesthood but in the mendicant wanderer who had renounced the world but was not cut off from the community. The etymology of *bhikṣu* from the root **bhaj* suggests asking for alms in the sense of sharing: presumably the sharing of the householder's wealth. To this extent the *bhikṣu* was still adhering to the ideals of the earlier system of sharing wealth. The definition of *bhikkhu* in the later Pāli sources

[99] *Dīg. Nik.* I. 135.

[100] S.J. Tambiah, *World Conqueror and World Renouncer*, p. 15 ff, Cambridge, 1976. See also *Dīg. Nik.* III. 101; *Suttanipāta*, 554.

changes noticeably where it refers to one who has cleansed himself of the stains of worldly existence and who is apprised of the horrors of rebirth.[101] That the notion of the *bhikkhu* was initially rooted in renunciation and mendicancy is apparent from the link between the *bhikkhu* and the *śramaṇa/samana*. The mendicant aspect of the *bhikkhu* which is emphasized in the code of behaviour enunciated for Bhuddhist *bhikkhu*s requires that he lives off the alms collected from the lay community. This presupposes the proximity of a lay community willing and able to give alms and also a constant interaction with the lay community. The *śramaṇa* was more of a recluse and an ascetic who had the option either of being a mendicant or living in isolation in the same way as the *saṃnyāsin*s.

The proximity to or distance from the lay community remains an essential feature of the religious sects of this time and goes back to the dichotomy between the *brāhmaṇ*s and the *śramaṇa*s, a dichotomy which was so sharp that Patañjali refers to it as synonymous with the relationship of the snake to the mongoose or the cat to the rat.[102] It is reiterated by Megasthenes who divides the caste of philosophers into Brachmanes and Sarmanes and also by Asoka who calls for the honouring of *bammana* and *samana*.[103] The *brāhmaṇ*s are deeply embedded in the community and cannot exist as a category outside it. The *śramaṇa*s and *samnyāsin*s deliberately opted out of society as is reflected in the *Upaniṣad*s and the *Āranyaka*s where their main intention was to think and act away from social obligations. Distance was further maintained by restricting the membership of such groups by and large to the upper castes and by taxing the mind with enigmatic discourses.

The renouncers of the middle Ganga valley — the Nirgranthas, Ājīvikas, Buddhists and other sectarian groups preferred a middle course in this dichotomy. At one level they were renouncers but at another level they returned to society and were dependent on the lay community.[104] In fact the lay follower (*upāsaka*) in the Buddhist scheme of things played a major role both in supporting the *saṅgha* and in return being ministered to by the *bhikkhu*s. The need for an institutional base, the monastery, made the dependence on the lay community even greater and in this there was competition

[101] *Visuddhi-magga* 3.16.

[102] *Vyākaraṇa Mahābhāṣyam* II. 4.9, I. 476.

[103] Bloch, *Les Inscriptions d'Asoka*, p. 126.

[104] Romila Thapar, 'Renunciation: The Making of a Counter-culture?', in *AISH*,

among the various new sects as well as between them and the *brāhmaṇs*. The antagonism was both at the ideological level as for instance in the sarcasm with which the Buddha treats the views of other sects[105] as well as at the more mundane level of competing for patronage. The ire of most was directed against the Cārvāka and the Lokāyata sects since they mocked even the efficacy of monkhood and sought to question the entire structure of explanation.

These sects are generally located in the cities of the middle Ganga valley suggesting that even the capitals of the *janapada*s of the western Ganga valley were an insufficient background to such movements. The qualitative difference can be seen in the *Dharmasūtra* instructions to include dicing in the assembly hall,[106] whereas in the middle Ganga valley there were *kutūhala-sāla*s or places for relaxation and debate. These were not merely shelters for the peripatetic teacher during the rainy season, for they attracted an audience of citizens. Urban life released a degree of curiosity and free thinking which was made use of by some of these *śramaṇa*s, and far from isolating themselves in the wilderness they were anxious to address large audiences. The teaching was open to everyone and because it was aimed at a large audience was perhaps less esoteric than the discourses of the forest dwellers. The importance of a teacher was recognized by the size of his following as much as by the theories which he expounded. Such sizeable followings were more available on the fringes of large urban centres. The subjects debated were varied but the basic questions centred on the universality of human experience, knowledge and intuition. The halls were often located in parks and were demarcated by rows of trees, reminiscent of the forest. The *kutūhala-sāla*s were the successors to the forest retreats.

The *kutūhala-sāla*s were maintained by wealthy citizens or through royal patronage and were clearly important locations for debating a variety of doctrines. Most references to them mention discourses on matters of religious and ethical importance but inevitably the discussion must also have included other concerns. Apart from the general interest in the new religious sects the encouragement of such discussion would also arise from the changed historical situation. It is repeatedly said that many of those who

p. 63 ff.

[105] *Dīg. Nik.* I. 27; I. 55.

[106] Āpastamba, II. 10.25.12.

frequented the *kutūhala-sālas* whether *brāhmaṇs* or *śramaṇas* were highly respected and had large followings.[107] Their popularity would lead those in power to treat them with respect. The gatherings at the *kutūhala-sālas* were doubtless also one avenue of assessing which sects should receive patronage. This is not to suggest that those with large followings were the leaders of popular opposition. There is in fact a remarkable lack of direct political statement on the increasing power of the state. Whatever questioning there was, has to be culled from the cynicism and satire of the wanderers. Nevertheless ethical systems are not constructed in a social vacuum and the questioning of existing mores by the Cārvāka and Lokayata teachers for example, could have been taken to a logical conclusion, namely, the direct questioning of the new political order. It is perhaps as well to keep in mind that the only evidence on revolts in the literature of this period comes from Buddhist sources and is generally in the form of citizens in the capital overthrowing the king or expressing their discontent with the oppression of the officials. The *Jātaka* literature has generalized references to such occurences.[108] In another text the revolt of the citizens of Taxila against Mauryan officials is described more than once.[109]

The centrality of philosophical disputation and the appeal to analytical thinking is at the ideological level reflective of a shift away from the security of the group towards the cutting edge of individual intellectual endeavour. Doubtless the *kutūhala-sālas* encouraged the group audience in that rhetoric, oratory and sophistry were all at a premium. But in effect it was the force of an individual's conviction and power of argument which drew the audience and eventually the following. The argument may not have been entirely logical but claimed frequently to be so and the theory propounded may well have been, as the descriptions suggest, often an attempt at an ambitious *tour de force*. Nevertheless, the appeal to the individual at an impersonal level was an important contribution and tied to similar changes in other spheres of life.

[107] *Dīg. Nik.* I. 179; *Maj. Nik.* II. 2; *Saṁ. Nik.* IV. 398.

[108] *Khaṇḍahāla Jātaka* no. 542; *Manicora Jātaka* no. 194; *Padakusalamānava Jātaka* no. 432.; Romila Thapar, 'Dissent and Protest in the Early Indian Tradition', in *Studies in History*, 1979 vol. I, no. 2, p. 177. ff.

[109] *Divyāvadāna* C. 372, p. 234; C. 407, p. 262.

V. ERGO

An attempt has been made in the previous chapters to trace the gradual movement from a lineage based society to the emergence of a state system in the mid-first millennium B.C. The awareness of change is amply reflected in the texts of the period, where there is a recognition of the absence of a state for the earlier beginnings. Thus the Śānti Parvan declares:[1]

> *naiva rājyam na rājāsinna daḍo na ca dāṇḍikaḥ dharmenaiva prajāḥ sarvā rakṣanti ca parasparam*
>
> (Once there was no ruling authority, no king, no coercion and no coercer, for people took care of each other out of a sense of righteousness).

The same sentiment is echoed in Buddhist texts. Some of this sentiment arose from locating a utopia in the past and therefore regarding antiquity as an ideal society not requiring the discipline of a state. The transition was from chiefships to kingships and inevitably with a considerable overlap between the two.

In suggesting the need for pointing to the differentiation it has been argued that although the terminology may not have changed, its connotation underwent substantial changes: thus *rājā* in Ṛg Vedic society had a different meaning from its use in the Kuru-Pañcāla period or from the *gaṇa-saṅgha* use of the term or for that matter its meaning in Buddhist sources. The definition in the *Sutta Nipāta*[2] that ' he who enjoys an income from land or from a village is a *rājā* ', would have been unrecognizable to the cattle-raiding *rājā*s of the Purus and Bharatas. Many of the terms discussed are carried over from the one society to the other, since there are rarely any sharp breaks in such change. But their connotation has to be viewed in the context of the change. There have been many reasons for the extrapolation back of the meanings of these terms from later sources to earlier periods. Often the reason was historiographical, especially when nationalism demanded that a supposedly more sophisticated society be presented for Vedic beginnings. But equally often it was the relative fullness of the

[1] *Mahābhārata*, Śānti Parvan, 59.14.

[2] *Sutta Nipāta*, Vaseṭṭhasutta, 26.

evidence from later sources and paucity from earlier ones which encouraged the assumption that the meaning of the term had not undergone any substantial change.

A further aspect is the examination of traditional concepts in relation to their own evolution. Thus the constituents of the *Saptāṅga* theory are noticeably absent in the earlier society. Of the seven elements, the *rājā* and *janapada/rāṣṭra* are referred to although the concentration of power in the office of the *rājā* and the notion of a defined territory remain vague. There is in Vedic literature little reference to the capitals of the *janapada*s and had the towns of Hastināpura, Ahicchatra and Kāmpilya, not to mention others, been the nucleii of power at this time they would surely have featured more prominently. The concept of a treasury, a standing army as well as a body of ministers appears to be altogether absent. Nor is there much evidence to suggest the awareness of the *maṇḍala* theory with its almost mathematically balanced diplomacy. Here again it would be incorrect to pose an insurmountable dichotomy between lineage and state since this would be unreal. There is a considerable shading off from one to the other. There were intermediate positions and one among these was undoubtedly the slow transformation of the chief into the king. These positions have also to be seen in the totality of a changing situation.

The movement from lineage to state registers changes at many levels. One among them is reflected in the *itihāsa-purāṇa* tradition. In trying to demonstrate the relevance of the tradition to these changes and the form given to the tradition by these changes, there is an implicit suggestion that the historical interpretation of early Indian society could now move away from the preoccupations of the historiography of the colonial period and seek an analysis which might take into consideration, at least in broad outline, the *itihāsa-purāṇa* view of the early Indian past. Such a view may not record factual history but may well provide pointers to historical actuality. The pattern of change reflected in the *itihāsa-purāṇa* tradition seems to synchronize with the argument supporting a change from a lineage society to a state system in the middle Ganga valley; a system which later evolved into a variety of states, each deriving its form from the region where it took shape and the degree to which it incorporated facets of the earlier lineage society. This would inevitably lead to a review of some of the theories which have been used to describe the early Indian past.

It would be impossible to pinpoint any single factor as crucial to the evolution of the state in the middle Ganga valley. The ecological niches of Ṛg Vedic times did not develop into a state system since there was less of confrontation and more of symbiosis. The resolution of conflict arising through stratification or demographic increase was not achieved by changing the system but by the migration of people which eased the tension, with migrating groups reproducing the structure and organization of the earlier society. The absence of geographical barriers encouraged this process. Land was available in the western Ganga valley and was more easily settled than in the marshlands and the monsoon forests of the middle Ganga valley. The need to defend the settlement was constant but external conflict did not require major changes in the administration of resources, since it was limited by and large to skirmishes, cattle-raids and the defence of fortified settlements. Pitched battles were not of frequent occurrence and when they did take place they were regarded as special events. In the middle Ganga valley rice agriculture and irrigation were initially important but probably were not sufficient causes. However they sharpened stratification between those who owned the land and those who laboured on it. The imminence of internal tension made the possibility of control through a state system feasible. The recognizable state emerges when the stratification is much more widespread both socially and geographically. This takes the form of the transformation of the *gahapati/gṛhapati* from a household head within a clan system to a landowner, and subsequent to this, as a participant in trading activities and in its counterpoise in the transformation of the *śūdra* into the peasant cultivator and the artisan.

These changes were by no means universal but were large enough to affect the overall system. Settlements were nucleated and became the foci of political power and exchange, some eventually developing into towns. Because of the greater concentration of wealth and power in such settlements they were required to be defended. External conflict was no longer a cattle-raid but a calculated campaign for acquisition of territories and towns. The concentration of wealth at the court and in the commercial towns is qualitatively different from the wealth obtained by chiefs and distributed as booty or as sacrificial offerings. Under the impact of trade the item which was a gift in the lineage system became a commodity when exchanged.[3] Whereas earlier the *kṣatriya* gave gifts to the *brāhmaṇs* in exchange for the abstract notion of status and legitimacy, in the new system the gift included immovable property. Thus the gift was transmuted into property and the concept of exchange also underwent a transformation.

In some areas the ethnos is replaced by the polis. The pivot of the community shifts from the clan to the town. The *janapada* is the territory of the clan and is identified as such but the concept of the *paurajanapada* introduces the urban settlement. The slow change to *rāṣṭra* is self-explanatory since the term *rāṣṭra* is said to derive from **rāj*, to rule. *Rāṣṭra* would therefore suggest territory in the political sense and not in the tribal sense as would *janapada*. Although again *rāṣṭra* manifests a difference of nuance from the Vedic to the later period. The importance of the town is also evident in the new category of *nāgarika*, the townsman, often used in the sense of citizen. Qualifications for citizenship which in the *gaṇa-saṅgha* system required high descent and claim to ownership of land through descent, were gradually eroded and by the time that the state is well established, the *nāgarika* includes all town dwellers although by implication the more influential are those who are highly placed by birth and by wealth.

These changes were more evident in urban society which was in any case a small percentage of the whole. Nor was the distinction between urban and rural a sharp divide. Yet rural society carried a larger component of lineage forms than did urban society. Land and produce changed from usage to property rights. Pasture land hardly required demarcation and was commonly owned. Cultivated land changed from clan ownership where it was worked by household units to ownership by the *gṛhapati* as the head of the household. Whether the *gṛhapati* was a *kṣatriya* or a *vaiśya,* lineage connections would have provided lateral links especially where ownership was vested in the family. The *kṣatriya* links being those of the senior lineages were the more effective and lasting. The *viś* as the lesser lineages would tend to disintegrate faster.

The question of class antagonism in relation to the lineage system[4] has produced a lively discussion. It has been argued that the distinction between senior and junior lineages where the latter pro-

[3] C. Meillassoux, 'The Social Organisation of the Peasantry: the economic basis of kinship', in D. Seddon (ed.), *Modes of Production*, London, 1978, pp. 159 ff.

[4] Ibid; G. Duprée and P.P. Rey, 'Reflections on the Relevance of a Theory of the History of Exchange', in Seddon (ed.), *Modes of Production*, pp. 171-208; P.P.

vided the prestations and the former asserted authority and presided over the redistribution processes, was sufficient to result in class antagonism. The senior lineages also controlled marriage relations, demographic reproduction, the induction of slaves and the exchange of élite goods. Neverthless it is probably more correct to maintain as it-has been said, that all this indicates at most a class function rather than an actual class. Since the major source of power was control over kinship (actual or fictive) it is difficult to accept the emergence of class at this stage. In the evidence considered here it was the gradual evolution of private ownership of land and the possibility of the alienation of land as well as the trend towards a commercial economy which encouraged the decline of the lineage system in the area under discussion. This released the *gahapati* into the ranks of landowners and traders and *śūdra* labour moved from the confines of service inherent in the householding system to a slow crystalizing into artisan professions and tenurial peasants. The *gahapati* may be said to approximate a class since the *gahapati* could be from any of the *dvija varṇa*s. The counterpart to the *gahapati* was, at the narrowest level, the *dāsa-bhṛtaka* and at the wider level the more dependant sections among *śūdra* peasants and artisans. At this point incipient classes become feasible.

The pattern of state formation and the particular factors which went into its making influenced the specific form it was to take. But even the evolved state was not frozen and in turn underwent substantial changes reflecting wider historical change. A distinction may be made not only between primary and secondary states but between varieties of states. Magadha is an example of a primary state and it has been argued that secondary states are formed by primary states conquering non-states.[5] This may not be an automatic sequence. What is crucial is that the area conquered must be economically restructured and integrated into the conquering state. In the case of Magadha, even after conquering a wide area including the Ganga valley there were substantial parts which were not integrated. Some of the Magadhan conquests included existing primary states but elsewhere the territory brought under control did not have a state system. Hegemony was extended over a range of differentiated systems — hunter-gatherers, chiefships, a variety of peasant tenures and exchange relationships extending

Rey, 'Class Contradiction in Lineage Societies', in *Critique of Anthropology*, 1979, 4, nos. 13 and 14, pp. 41-60.

[5] Cohen and Service (eds.), *Origin of the State*, p. 6 ff.

from barter to nascent market systems. Many of these survived the conquest and continued as before. Even after the conquest by the Nandas and Mauryas which included central India and Rajasthan, the *gaṇa-saṅghas* of these areas seem to have continued. Despite its size and administrative control, the Mauryan state does not appear to have attempted a restructuring of all the areas under its control. Possibly a distinction has to be maintained between what might be called the metropolitan state in such a system which would be the core region or the area which initiates conquest and control of the peripheral regions subservient to the metropolitan state but substantially continuing much as before.[6] The metropolitan state would be organized on a unitary, centralized basis. Its control over the peripheral areas would be through administration, the upper levels under central authority and the lower levels under local authority. This bifurcation would be possible if the major concern of the metropolitan state was to collect tax and tribute and even plunder during campaigns but not to restructure the economy of the peripheral areas in an attempt to integrate it and bring it into a uniform pattern. Tax and tribute would be collected not only from cultivators but from a variety of professions utilizing a range of resources : in fact from every conceivable human activity with which the state could be associated, as seems apparent from the *Arthaśāstra*. Major economic change would then be limited by and large to the metropolitan state and to potentially rich areas likely to provide a sizeable revenue. But the maximum development of the latter areas was not envisaged at this stage. The decline of states would be related among other things to the availability of finance to support the state structure. If the metropolitan state was in the main collecting revenue without extending, on a large scale, the activities leading to revenue then its income would hardly meet the expenses of such a structure. (Incidentally this might also help explain the remarkable paucity of monuments from the Mauryan period. Apart from the buildings at the site of Kumrahar there is little else to prove the grandeur of an empire. This is particularly noticeable when compared to the monuments of the Achaemenids or even to those of a single ruler, Shi Huang Ti.) Here might also be an explanation of why the *Arthaśāstra* tradition, even though it had known an empire as extensive as that of the Mauryas, visualizes a

[6] Romila Thapar, 'The State as Empire: the Mauryan case', in H. Claessen and P. Skalnik (eds.), *The Study of the State*, The Hague, 1901, p. 409 ff.

relatively small state in its discussion on how a state is to be administered. Or why Aśoka takes no grandiloquent titles and on occasion even confines himself to the simple title of *rājā māgadhe* (*rājā* of Magadha).[7] There is no reference, neither in his own edicts nor in the descriptions of the Mauryan state in the Ceylon Chronicles, to an empire as a new and distinctive category in the state system. This is not to suggest that there was no empire but rather that the control was flexible and that the metropolitan state was seen to be the most important element. The *itihāsa-purāṇa* tradition also maintains that the Mauryas ruled a kingdom but no distinction is made in terms of its being an empire.[8] What the tradition records in each case are the dynasties which ruled the metropolitan states. The concept of the *cakravartin* however does suggest control over a vast territory although it has been suggested[9] that the concept is not so much that of ruling a geographically vast territory as of centring control, as it were, firmly and securely in a hub of power. The symbolism of the wheel does suggest a differentiation between power at the centre of the circle and at the rim. The domain need not be restricted to the political for in the Buddhist concept the spiritual domain is also open to the *cakkavatti.* The *maṇḍala* theory may also have had its origins in a kaleidoscopic relationship between the metropolitan state and the peripheral areas, a relationship which would be characterized by concerns of friendship and hostility with the metropolitan state playing the role of the *vijigīṣu.*

Restructuring of the economy seems more evident in the post-Gupta period when there are many more nucleii of metropolitan states and when areas of land previously regarded as waste and isolated were brought under cultivation. There was then either a smaller range of differentiated systems or alternatively a condition where the less developed systems were more marginal to a larger component of complex agrarian structures and commercial networks. The metropolitan area tends to invest in the more complex systems often by encouraging their expansion, not directly, but through intermediaries. The question of restructuring the economy hinges on the wider question of landownership which has remained controversial in the context of early India.

The question of the ownership of land by the state cannot be

[7] J. Bloch, *Les Inscriptions d'Asoka*, p. 154.

[8] Pargiter, *The Purāna Text of the Dynasties of the Kali Age*, pp. 26-7.

[9] Gonda, *Ancient Indian Kingship*, p. 123 ff.

answered with a clear negative or affirmative, since ownership patterns changed over time and varied in different regions. For the early period of Indian history there cannot be an all-inclusive answer which would be applicable to the entire subcontinent. Even during the Mauryan period there was no uniformity in landownership. There are references to state-owned lands (*sīta*) as well as to the private ownership of land and its alienation by the owners. With the decline of clan ownership and of the householding economy there was a change to a tenurial system and the gradual emergence of a peasant economy. This was not based on cultivation through forced labour. The state did collect revenue from the cultivators and various supplementary taxes, of which only one is listed as *viṣṭi*. It is mentioned in the *Arthaśāstra*[10] in connection with those villages, among a large category of others, that provide *viṣṭi* in lieu of taxes. Evidently the state's claim to *viṣṭi* was not universal. New land was brought under cultivation and deserted areas resettled through the agency of the state; mention is made in the Mauryan period to the settling of agriculturalists and the deportation of prisoners-of-war to such areas. The *Arthaśāstra* clearly states that families of *śūdra* agriculturalists should be drafted from over-populated areas or induced to migrate from foreign *janapadas*.[11] This suggests a very different scene from the enslavement of clans and their employment in cultivation through a system of forced labour. One of the edicts of the Mauryan king Aśoka speaks of the deportation of prisoners of war after the campaign in Kalinga,[12] and it is presumed that they were used in establishing new agricultural settlements.[13] If this was the case then they were removed from their homelands and taken as colonists to new areas. In each of these cases, where the changed situation is brought about by the state, it results not in transforming agrarian relations in the existing settlements but in creating fresh settlements where the cultivators are in a direct relation with the state. These activities on the part of the state did not eliminate the independent owners and peasants. The question of which type of cultivation predominated remains without a conclusive answer, but possibly the short duration of large-scale state systems and the continued availability of new lands until recent centuries would suggest that forced settlements by the

[10] *Arthaśāstra*, II. 35.1.

[11] Ibid; II. 1.1.

[12] J. Bloch, *Les Inscriptions d'Asoka*, p. 125 ff.

[13] D.D. Kosambi, *Introduction to the Study of Indian History*, Bombay, 1956, p. 189 ff.

state were not the predominant system. The evidence on state enterprise in irrigation works is also limited. There are so far only the single examples of the Nandas building a canal in Kalinga and the Mauryas constructing a dam in Saurashtra. The *Arthaśāstra* provides no details for such state supervised irrigation systems. It suggests the abolition of the water cess on those who provide their own irrigation facilities and strongly urges the encouragement of such private enterprise.[14] This would amount to a fairly limited effort by the state at restructuring the economy. The location of the two irrigation works are in areas geographically peripheral but agriculturally rich and this would point to some state initiative. However, the evidence of only two examples is not very impressive or extensive in terms of the area covered by the Mauryan empire.

The major form of peasant protest against oppressive taxes was not revolt but migration to new lands outside the control of the state to which the peasants belonged.[15] There are enough authors who warn the king against oppressive taxation lest the peasants migrate,[16] as there are also instances of such migrations. This would again point to the availability of access to land for fresh settlements. Such protestors were doubtless welcome in neighbouring kingdoms for their migration would have meant additional revenue to the states where they settled. Possibly this is what Kauṭilya was referring to in his advice that *śūdra* agriculturalists should be induced to come from foreign kingdoms or that deserted lands should be resettled. It is more than likely, however, that peasant protesters would settle in forested areas or take to brigandage. The continuation of independent clan systems juxtaposed with areas of peasant economies would also suggest that state entrepreneurship in agriculture was not a uniform system throughout the territory held by a particular state.

A recent suggestion that the model of the segmentary state as developed for the Alur in Africa might be more purposeful for the Indian state would also posit a situation very different from that described in earlier models.[17] Perhaps the most positive contribution of this theory is the notion of territorial sovereignty being recognized by degree in various zones of control. Areas under direct

[14] *Arthaśāstra*, II. 1. 20-4; II. 24. 18; III. 9. 32-8; III. 10. 1-2.

[15] E.g. *Gaṇḍatiṇḍu Jātaka*, no. 520.

[16] *Manu* VII. 111; *Artha*, XIII. 1. 20-1; VII. 5; *Mahābhārata*, Śānti Parvan, 88. 35-8.

[17] A. Southall, *Alur Society*, Cambridge, 1956, p. 248 ff; B. Stein, *Peasant State and Society in Medieval South India*, Delhi, 1980.

state control were differentiated from peripheral areas of limited control and from spheres of influence. The form of administration at the centre tended to be repeated in miniature at the periphery. However the monopoly of force at the centre was restricted at the periphery. Peripheral units therefore have the flexibility to change allegiances. Political sovereignty and ritual sovereignty was kept distinct with the latter relating to the process of legitimization. Although the theory of the segmentary state may not be largely acceptable in the context of the early Indian situation, there are, nevertheless, elements of the system which can be noticed from time to time, particularly in areas and periods where lineage systems were moving over to state systems. The theory also raises the question of the possible variation on the unitary state which has long been the model for early Indian society.

The discussion on ownership of land has tended to cloud the reality of the early Indian state as one essentially interested in revenue collecting functions and less concerned with claims to ownership as is indicated in the *Arthaśāstra* of Kauṭilya. It would therefore be more meaningful to inquire into the range and variation of peasant tenures. This would require some discussion of the concepts of the village community and the peasant economy as developed for the colonial period of Indian history and their application to the early period.

The village community was believed to be a community of equals and economically self-sufficient. However, as we have seen, from the earliest period for which there is evidence, stratification is noticeable in the village community. The tension between the *rājanya* and the *viś* from the Vedic period becomes more acute in the hierarchy of the *kṣatriya* , the *gahapati* and the *śūdra* in the subsequent period. Sharper stratification emerges with the breaking up of the clan system and landownership taking the form of private holdings with grants to religious beneficiaries and peasant tenures that included independent cultivators, tenants and sharecroppers. The closed economy of the village community has been over-emphasized for it is observable only in those areas and those periods of Indian history in which the *jajmāni* system based on service relationships rather than on payment for services was the norm.[18] This varied in time and place. Artisans central to the village

[18] T.O. Beidelman, *A Comparative Analysis of the Jajmani System*, New York, 1959; W.H. Wiser, *The Hindu Jajmani System*, Lucknow,1958; S. Epstein, 'Productive Efficiency and Customary Systems of Rewards in Rural South India', in

economy such as carpenters are said to be working on daily wages.[19] Wages could be in kind or in cash and monetary salaries are mentioned in the *Arthaśāstra* and the *Jātaka*s. Nevertheless at this time too there is a variation, for in those areas where the use of coined metallic money had not been introduced or there was an absence of market centres, there service relationships and exchanges in kind would have persisted. Service relations or *jajmāni* relations reflecting a system of exchange of services in accordance with a recognized hierarchy could have had their genesis in a householding economy. The ritual status of the *yajamāna* in such a system would extend to mundane matters as well. The function of the *śūdra* to serve the higher *varṇa*s is explicit in the theory of *varṇa* and such service was not defined as based on wages. Service relations are distinct from the *jajmāni* system as such and the existence of the former does not necessarily imply the presence of the latter. However the *jajmāni* system would have evolved historically from *jajmāni* relations. It was supported by the hierarchy of ritual status and in turn reinforced it. This was not an idyllic, mutually supportive system but was based on power deriving from ownership of land and expressed economic disparities. The self-sufficiency of the village in the early period was encroached upon by itinerant professionals and by villages providing for merchants and markets outside the village. Even for later periods the degree to which self-sufficiency may have been eroded by horizontal links through local markets and fairs, networks of religious centres playing an economic role as well and trade in essential items brought by itinerant herders, artisans and traders, remains to be examined with greater precision.

The constituents of a peasant economy (as distinct from the existence of peasants as cultivators), are that roughly half the total population should be engaged in agriculture and that this should form approximately half the working population; that there should be a state and a ruling hierarchy, a separation of town and country, and that the unit of production and consumption should in the main comprise of peasant households.[20] Of the seven categories listed by Megasthenes in his description of Indian society,

Themes in Economic Anthropology, ASA 6, London, 1967.

[19] V.S. Agrawala, *India as Known to Panini*, pp. 236-7.

[20] D. Thorner, 'Peasant Economy as a Category in Economic History', in T. Shanin (ed.), *Peasants and Peasant Society*, Harmondsworth, 1971, p. 202 ff.

he writes that the cultivators are the largest in number and considering the small size of at least three, the philosophers, overseers and councillors, out of the seven, they were evidently above half of the working population.[21] The presence of towns as commercial centres is evident from Buddhist sources. The peasant household has been defined as one that cultivates its own allotment of land with or without slaves and wage-labourers, includes some production of handicrafts and indulges in petty trade. These characteristics were present in the peasant households of this period. As units of consumption the peasant households function without the mediation of markets,but presumably where markets exist even marginally some production would be geared towards these markets. The state and the ruling hierarchy control the administration of revenue. On the basis of this definition it can be argued that a peasant economy emerged with the establishment of the state in the Ganga valley.

Changes in the perception of society are reflected in the post-Vedic sources. The economic categories are however more easily distinguishable in the Buddhist texts since they reflect a wider social reality than the brahmanical literature of the time. Social categories even in Pāṇini are more often discussed in terms of *jāti* rather than *varṇa*, the currency of the former being in any case post-Vedic. The etymology of the two terms are distinct and separate and *jāti*s are described as having evolved out of the common bonds of mutual kinship.[22] Buddhist sources rank *jāti*s into a high and a low category, a dual division which is commonly adopted in Buddhist classifications. The frequency of reference to *jāti* as compared to *varṇa* would suggest that the *jāti* became the more evident category of social perception and *varṇa* the more theoretical. As an endogamous group *jāti* conserved elements of the lineage system. It is interesting that Megasthenes uses the term *genos,* in referring to caste and states that its essential characteristics are endogamy and hereditary occupation. He does however exclude the philosophers (Brachmanes and Sarmanes) from having to conform to endogamy, perhaps a reference to *gotra* exogamy.

[21] Diodorus II. 40.

[22] PED, p. 281 Pāṇini, V. 4.9; cf. VI. 3.85; II. 4.6. S.C. Vasu mentions that the term *jāti* is used to mean genus in Indian logic, *The Aṣṭādhyāyi of Pāṇini*, Delhi, 1962, I. p. 310. This has a significance for the use of the term as a social category. V.S. Agrawala, *India as Known to Panini*, p. 93, quotes the Kāśikā as saying that *jāti* is in itself an invisible entity which achieves concrete form only through its component parts or *bandhus* (kinsmen).

In the transition from lineage to monarchical states, *varṇa* as a theory assisting this process gradually becomes evident over time. The *brāhmaṇa* legitimizes the new political roles in the monarchical state and provides those in high office with religious sanctions and appropriate genealogical connections. In return for this the *brāhmaṇa* not only retained the highest ritual status but also had access to prime economic resources through the grants of land and other wealth. Gradations both ritual and economic within the *varṇa* were however apparent as only a few *brāhmaṇas* could aspire to these benefits, many being content with lesser prestations as village priests and performers of ceremonies. Not all rituals drew sanction from Vedic or Purānic sources; some were survivals of indigenous, local forms and were to be maintained by non-*brāhmaṇa* castes acting as *pujāri*s and performers of rituals. A distinction was to develop between those who were of high social status and ministrants to the high gods via the high culture and those who were of low social status and were the practitioners of cults dedicated to local deities. One of the avenues of upward mobility relates to the rise of such local cults to high status, often through their patrons becoming politically powerful.

The *kṣatriya varṇa* was reserved for those who had earlier been ruling clans and were converted into the royal families of the monarchical state, or else were those of obscure origin who, having come to power required the appropriate connections, the latter being acquired often through latching onto the ancient established lineages such as the Sūryavamśa and Candravamśa. The extended kin groups would also acquire status and become landowners, the economic rank depending on the amount of land owned. *Kṣatriya* status was important in the early stage of the transition from lineage to state. With the establishment of the latter, political power became more open and even *śūdra*s were recognized (although grudgingly) as kings, after the advent of the Nanda dynasty. The bi-polarity between the lineage and the state system is perhaps expressed in the harking back to facets of the lineage system by those who performed Vedic sacrifices to acquire legitimacy and who claimed *kṣatriya* status as against others such as the Mauryas who ignored Vedic rituals, supported the 'heterodox' sects and were relegated to the status of *śūdra*s and described as *adharmaḥ*. The continuance of the former into the centuries A.D. would indicate attempts to seek connections with the traditional sources of validation.

The status of the *vaiśya* although ritually lower varied in accordance with economic actuality. The *śreṣṭhins* and the *jyeṣtha*s of the *śreṇīs* commanded respect whereas others had a lower status. The *śūdra*s and the *caṇḍāla*s had less access to resources and at this level lowness of ritual status tended to conform to a low economic status as well. There was, it would seem, some flexibility in the *śūdra* ranks, some of which as *jātis* were added on when professions became more specialized and the existing stratification became inadequate. References to *śūdra*s as artisans and peasants increase when craftsmen and cultivators began to get separated from clan holdings and the householding economy. In the classification of the *śūdra*, the *jāti*s are usually associated with an occupation, locality, cult or tribe. The occupational aspect was clearly more important than in the case of the *dvija varṇa*s where the occupation is defined briefly and in a more generalized fashion. For the *śūdra*s and lesser groups, occupation was more central to status than lineage. By the same token new social groups identified by occupation were often accorded a *varṇa* status of *śūdra* even when they became affluent.

With the proliferation of lower caste groups the extremes of pollution also get extended further from *śūdra*s to *caṇḍāla*s and various other similar groups. Separation is not limited to a general bifurcation. There develop degrees of separation on the axis of purity-pollution with an eventual demarcation even between clean *śūdra*s, unclean *śūdra*s and untouchables together with a hierarchy within each of these. Thus the notion becomes embedded in every sizeable group. Pollution as a concept is not discussed in any of the sources, only its observances are listed. Pollution in theory relates to moments of contact with bodily discharges and dead bodies, and those constantly in contact with these were permanently polluted. Participation in rituals requires a state of purity and those professionally involved in rituals would tend to be regarded as purer than others. Segregation became essential for those who were performing rituals and the counter-weight to them had to be a group regarded as impure. Ritual segregation became a useful mechanism for keeping certain socially low status groups permanently servile. This may also have been a counterpoint to the heterodox theories of the fundamental ethical equality of all.

In the late-first millennium B.C. there was therefore no exact corelation between *varṇa* status and economic status. The *varṇa* hierarchy arose in and related to a lineage-based society but was adapted to a state system. Within each *varṇa* there were recognized gradations, some of an economic nature but not excluding ritual functions or even ethnic distinctions. The gradation within each *varṇa* was in accordance with access to resources as well as a traditional sanction which was slowly built up and which facilitated this access using among other things the notion of hereditary occupations and insisting on a close control over expertise. The importance of *varṇa* as ritual status had primacy where the *yajña* and *gṛhya* rituals were of central importance. Where they had ceased to play a central role the hierarchy of the *varṇa*s changed, as in the middle Ganga valley in Buddhist and Jaina sources. The building of institutional bases in the form of monasteries for these religious sects required a far greater economic outlay and the interlinkage of politics and religion, which is one aspect of the spread of these sects, takes on a new dimension. If *varṇa* is not to be defined as a system of economic status then it takes on the characteristics of a theory not entirely divorced from reality but at the same time not mirroring reality. For purposes of historical analyses each group has to be located both in terms of ritual rank and economic status although the two points need not necessarily have coincided. However, correspondence was frequent among some groups of high ritual status and virtually predictable among those of the lowest strata. Middle-level groups remained ambiguous and were probably the most mobile in terms of actual status; a movement which nevertheless would have had some restrictions emanating from ritual ranking. As a theory epitomizing a social form the continuity of *varṇa* had to be adhered to and this might explain the relative lack of major change in the theoretical formulations on the functioning of *varṇa*. Because of the centrality of marriage and kinship rules such a society carried along with it one of the essentials of the lineage system, thus ensuring the survival of some elements of lineage society even in a situation where much had changed. To this was added the concept of segmentation. The proliferation of a caste was either through fission where a new caste emerged on migrating away from an established caste or from taking on a new profession or from the assimilation of a new segment. Ethnic coherence therefore became less reliable within the *varṇa* although it was possibly retained to a greater degree in the *jāti*. Sometimes the ethnic coherence was claimed irrespective of the reality: a convenient fiction to establish a niche in the local hierarchy. Historically it would be worthwhile to locate and identify the hierarchy of economic status as a parallel system and investigate whether at some points in history the two systems would either cohere or modify each other; or for that matter consider the possibility that in the actual working of a caste society the role of *varṇa* is less important than has been made out so far.

The theory of *varṇa* furthered horizontal networks reminiscent of the lineage system. This was expressed through ritual ranking and identities which acted as links across territory. To some extent this modified the more vertical dimensions of the *jāti* framework. Like lineage, *varṇa* was a mechanism for assimilation and arises with stratification but pre-dates the conditions conducive to a possible class society. It may therefore be said to have an intermediate position between stratified and class societies. The assimilation is frequently through fission: a segment is recognized as breaking off from the existing *varṇa* (often because of changes in occupation), it claims higher status and if it can defend its claims or has adequate patronage, it moves into higher status, a process reminiscent of lineage systems. This appears to have been the case with some at least of those who became members of the ruling class and then claimed *kṣatriya* status.[23] Those who were economically well off but failed in their claim to high status asserted that they had belonged to a *dvija varṇa,* but because of the non-observance of some ritual taboo had been demoted. Ritual categories remain static even though the occupations carried out by their members may change. Thus *brāhmaṇas* could be priests and at a later period administrators or even horse-dealers.[24] Kṣatriyas moved from being warriors to becoming landowners or religious teachers. *Varṇa* therefore acts as a bridge between lineage systems and society under a state. The continuity of *varṇa*, would partially account for the contours of the state in the Indian polity being sometimes dimly perceived by those participating in its functions. This further permitted brahmanical sources to emphasize the greater relevance of *varṇa* as they saw it and to project it as the reality of Indian society, a viewpoint which seems partial and requires correction. As a corollary to this it becomes necessary to examine the changes which caste itself

[23] B.D. Chattopadhyaya, 'Origin of the Rajputs...' *IHR*, July 1976, III. 1, pp. 59-82.

[24] G. Bühler, 'The Peheva Inscription from the Temple of Garibnath', *Epigraphia Indica*, I. pp. 184-90.

underwent and which were occasioned by wider historical change. Thus even though the *varna* terminology is retained, the composition, role and function of members of a *varṇa* is seen to differ in time. The history of *varṇa* is not static. The four orders of the *varṇa* remained constant and represented an idealized theory of social functioning but the actual functioning of their members could deviate from the theory.

The articulation of economic status followed on the emergence of two changes, the peasant economy and the rise of towns and commerce. Both these changes in the mid-first millennium B.C. helped in weakening the lineage system and consequently the importance of ritual status in societies dominated by brahmanical values as well as in the static power of the ruling clans in the *gaṇa-saṅgha* system. The commercial economy in a sense prised economic status out of the earlier system. Trade and urbanization were not the sole causative factors in the emergence of the state but were of significance in changing the social structure of the time. Theories of state formation applied to India, such as that of the Asiatic Mode of Production and the segmentary state, tend either to ignore or underplay the importance of the commercial economy as a factor in historical change.

The lineage system did not die out with the emergence of the state. Population pressure was concentrated on areas of optimum economic activity so large tracts of less than optimum areas retained a *gaṇa-saṅgha* or a clan system for many centuries. Such areas did not change even under Mauryan hegemony and as late as the Gupta period Samudragupta boasts of uprooting various ruling clans.[25] The extension of intensive agriculture in the post-Gupta period through a system of land grants and the frequency of fresh states being consolidated in new areas was often as the result of the conversion of clan systems into the state system. The juxtaposition of the two remains therefore a continual feature of Indian history until well into the second millennium A.D.

Even where the lineage system was absorbed into the state its identity was not entirely eliminated. Administration, except at the higher levels, remained a local concern and the absence of impersonal recruitment to office meant that kinship ties were still effec-

[25] Allahabad Posthumous Pillar inscription of Samudragupta; J.F. Fleet, 'Inscriptions of the Early Gupta Kings and their Successors', *Corpus Inscriptionum Indicarum*, III., Varanasi 1970 (reprint), p. 6 ff.

tive. Legal codes drew substantially on customary law and incorporated local practices. Legitimacy was frequently expressed through rituals pertaining to the lineage system such as the Vedic sacrifices of the *aśvamedha, vājapeya, rājasūya* and *abhiṣeka,* or through conversion of clan deities and their rituals into the religious expression of the state, where the domain of the deity and its clientele would be fused into equivalent loyalty to the new state.[26] These became increasingly symbolic in the post-Gupta period but nevertheless acted as a link with the lineage system. Various lineage forms were reflected in the functions of *jāti*. Although occupation on occasion contradicted *varṇa* rules, nevertheless it would be worth investigating whether there was a weakening of the notion of the state where *varṇa* cohered with economic status. Thus it was not so much that the state was a segmentary system with a concentration of power at the centre shading off into ritual hegemony at the periphery as that the state system in itself was not a unitary, monolithic system restructuring the entire territory under its control but rather that it had a margin for flexibility in relation to peripheral areas.

The continuation of some aspects of the lineage system also required the continuation of the records of its history as well. Thus the *itihāsa-purāṇa* tradition remained the constant source of the earliest history. Nor is it strange that much of the tradition was preserved in the Purāṇic texts since these were also the sources which were drawn upon for validating *varṇa* status in the form of fabricated lineage links and myths of origin. Such validation was especially pertinent to the *kṣatriya varṇa.* The recourse to the *itihāsa-purāṇa* tradition as an introduction to a history was in part the usual search for legitimacy in tradition as well as the attempt to use tradition to disguise innovations. This technique was widely used in literature with a historical purpose. The genealogical material was central to the tracing of genealogical relationships irrespective of whether they were real or fictional and genealogical relationships were indicators of power. The persistence of some aspects of lineage society in many areas made the record of genealogical data an essential part of any process of political legitimation. The transition of royal status in a state system required genealogical support which could ultimately be provided by the *itihāsa-purāṇa* tradition.

Even when the *itihāsa-purāṇa* tradition gave rise to some new forms such as historical biographies and regional histories (as for

[26] H. Kulke, *Jagannātha-Kult und Gajapati-Königtum*, Weisbaden, 1979, p. 223 ff.

example, Bāṇa's *Harṣacarita*, Bilhaṇa's *Vikramāṅkadevacarita* and Kalhaṇa's *Rājataraṅginī*), it had its roots in the earlier tradition and some of the texts of this tradition were re-edited but not superseded. The rise of these new forms of the *itihāsa-purāṇa* tradition is linked to the establishment of states whose legitimacy was centred on brahmanical ideology. The state system itself underwent a change in that the states of the late first millennium A.D. registered a more pervasive activity on the part of the state and the monarch even if through intermediaries. The monarch was the symbol of the state and his biography became part of historical legitimation. The culmination of this process was the recognition of territory within which the restructuring had occurred as crucial to the definition of the state and in this context regional histories began to be written.

An analysis of state formation in early Indian history can be seen as a process of change from social formations which may broadly be classified as lineage systems to those dominated by a state system, but the nature of the domination does not fall easily into any of the existing models and its dynamics require a fresh-reworking. Nor is the change from one social formation to the other a clear-cut transformation for there is much that survives from the earlier to the later and many overlaps. Apart from the interpretational preconceptions of many theorists on pre-modern India, it is also these overlapping forms which have often helped to maintain the inter-links between ritual and economic status, leading to the clouding over of the one by the other and thus effectively hiding both the essential points of historical change and the complexities of Indian society in its early history.

BIBLIOGRAPHY

Adams, R.McC., *The Evolution of Urban Society*, Chicago, 1966.

Agrawal, D.P., and S. Kusumgar, *Prehistoric Chronology and Radio-Carbon Dating in India*, New Delhi, 1974.

Agrawal, V.S., *India as Known to Panini*, Varanasi, 1963 (revised ed.)

Aitareya Brāhmaṇa, ed. K.S. Agashe, Poona 1896, tr. A.B. Keith, H.O.S. xxv, Cambridge, Mass., 1920.

Allan, J., *A Catalogue of the Coins of Ancient India*, London, 1967.

Allchin, B. and R., *The Birth of Indian Civilization*, Harmondsworth, 1968.

Altekar, A.S., *State and Government in Ancient India*, Banaras, 1949.

Altekar, A.S., and V. Misra, *Report on the Kumrahar Excavations, 1951-55*, Patna, 1959.

Andersen, P., *Lineages of the Absolutist State*, London, 1974.

Aṅguttara Nikāya, ed. R. Morris and E. Hardy, P.T.S., London, 1885-1900; tr. F.L. Hare, 'The Book of Gradual Saying', P.T.S., London, 1932-6.

Āpastamba Dharmasūtra, ed. G. Bühler, Bombay 1894; tr. G. Bühler, SBE, vol. II. O.U.P., 1879.

Āpastamba Gṛhya Sūtra, ed. Chinnaswami Shastri, Benaras, 1928.

Āpastamba Śrauta Sūtra, ed. R. Garbe, Calcutta, 1882-1902.

Apte, V.M., *Social and Religious Life in the Grihya Sūtras*, Bombay, 1954.

ASA Monographs 2, *Political Systems and Distribution of power*, London, 1965.

ASA Monographs 6, *Themes in Economic Anthropology*, London, 1967.

Āśvālayana Gṛhya Sūtra, ed. A.G. Steuzler, Leipzig, 1864.

Āśvalāyana Śrauta-Sūtra, ed. Ganesh Shastri, Anandasrama, Poona, 1917.

Atharvaveda, ed. R. Roth and W.D. Whitney, Berlin, 1856; *Atharvaveda-Saṃhita* tr. W.D. Whitney, H.O.S. VII., Delhi, 1971 (2nd rpt).

Baden-Powell, B.H., *The Indian Village Community* (London, 1896), New Haven, 1957 (rpt).

Banerji, S.C., *Dharma-sūtras, A Study in their Origin and Development*, Calcutta, 1962.

Bareau, A., *Les Sectes Boudhiques du Petit Vehicule*, Saigon, 1955.

Barua, B.M., *Pre-Buddhistic Indian Philosophy*, Calcutta, 1921.

Basham, A.L., *The History and Doctrine of the Ājīvikas*, London, 1951.

Baudhāyana Dharma-Sūtra, ed. E. Hultsch, Leipzig, 1884; tr. G. Bühler, SBE, vol. XIV., Oxford, 1882.

Beal, S., *Romantic History of Buddha*, London, 1907.

Bechert, H., 'Beginnings of Buddhist Historiography', Ceylon Studies Seminar, 1974, series no. 2 (mimeographed).

Beidelman, T.O., *A Comparative Analysis of the Jajmani System*, New York, 1959.

Belshaw, Cyril S., *Traditional Exchange and Modern Markets*, New Delhi, 1969.

Benveniste, E., *Indo-European Language and Society*, London, 1973.

Bhāgavata Puraṇa, ed. V.L. Pansikar, Bombay, 1920; tr. M.N. Dutt, Calcutta, 1895.

Bloch, J., *Les Inscriptions d' Asoka*, Paris, 1950.

Bose, A., *Social and Rural Economy of India*, Calcutta, 1942-5.

Boserup, E., *The Conditions of Agricultural Growth*, London, 1965.

Bougle, C., *Essays on the Caste System*, tr. D. Pocock, Cambridge, 1971.

Bṛhad-devatā, ed. A.A. MacDonell (pts I and II), HOS V, Delhi, 1965 (rpt).

Brohier, R.L., *Ancient Irrigation works in Ceylon*, Colombo, 1934.

Brough, J., *The Early Brahmanical System of Gotra and Pravara*, Cambridge, 1953.

Buddhaghoṣa, *Visuddhi-Magga*, ed. Dharmananda Kosambi, Bombay, 1940.

Buitenan, J.A.B. van, *The Mahabharata*, vols. I, II, III, IV, Chicago, 1973; 1975.

Burrow, T., *The Sanskrit Language*, London, 1965.

Burrow, T. and M.B. Emeneau, *Dravidian Etymological Dictionary*, Oxford, 1961.

Cardona, G., *et al.* (ed), *Indo-European and Indo-Europeans*, Philadelphia, 1970.

Carneiro, R.L., 'A Theory of the Origin of the State', *Science*, 1970, 169, pp 733-8.

Chakrabarty, D.K., 'The Beginning of Iron in India', *Antiquity*, 1976, 50, pp. 114-24.

Chakrabarty, D.K., 'Distribution of Iron Ores and Archaeological Evidence of Early Iron in India', *JESHO*, 1977, XX, pt. 2, pp. 166-85.

Chanana, *Slavery in Ancient India*, New Delhi, 1960.

Chāndogya Upaniṣad, ed. & tr. O. Bohtlingk, Leipzig, 1889.

Chaudhuri, K.A., *Ancient Agriculture and Forestry in Northern India*, Bombay 1977.

Claessen, H.J.M. and P. Skalnik, *The Early State*, The Hague, 1978.

Cohen, R., and E.R. Service (eds.), *Origins of the State*, Philadelphia, 1978.

Coulanges, Fustel de, *The Ancient City*, New York.

Cullavagga, qv. *Vinaya Piṭaka*.

Dalton, G. (ed.), *Primitive, Archaic and Modern Economics: the Essays of Karl Polanyi*, New York, 1968.

Damle, Y.B., *Caste: A Review of the Literature on Caste*, M.I.T., 1961.

Deshpande, M.M., and P.E. Hook, *Aryan and Non-Aryan in India* (Michigan Papers on South and South East Asia, no. 14, 1978), Ann Arbor, 1979.

Dhammapada, ed. S.S. Thera, P.T.S., London, 1914; ed. & tr. Mrs. Rhys Davids, SBB, London, 1931.

Dīgha Nikāya, ed. T.W. Rhys Davids and J.E. Carpentier, P.T.S., London, 1890-1911; tr. T.W. Rhys Davids, 'Dialogues of the Buddha', SBB, London 1899, 1910, 1921.

Dikshit, K.N., 'Exploration along the Right Bank of River Sutlej in Punjab *Journal of History*, 1967, 45, pt II, pp. 561-68

Dīpavaṃsa, ed. and tr. H. Oldenberg, London, 1879; ed. B.C. Law, *The Ceylon Historical Journal,* VII, 1959, nos. 1-4.

Divyāvadāna, ed. E.B. Cowell and R.A. Neil, Cambridge, 1886.

Drekmeier, C., *Kingship and Community in Early India*, Bombay, 1962.

Dumezil, G., *Flamen-Brahman*, Paris, 1935.

Dumezil, G., *Mythe et Epopée*, vols. I, II, Paris, 1968, 1971.

Dumont, L., *Homo Hierarchicus*, Paris, 1966; trans., London, 1972.
Dutt, N., *Early History of the Spread of Buddhism and Buddhist Schools*, London, 1925.
Dutt, N., *Early Monastic Buddhism*, Calcutta, 1973.
Dutt, S., *Early Buddhist Monachism*, London, 1924.
Eliade, M., *Cosmos and History*, Paris, 1949; New York, 1959.
Eliade, M., *Shamanism*, Princeton, 1974.
Engels, F., *The Origin of the Family, Private Property, and the State*, London, 1940.
Fick, R., *The Social Organisation in North East India in Buddha's Time*, trans. S.K. Mitra, Calcutta University, 1920.
Finley, M.I., *Ancient Slavery and Modern Ideology*, London, 1980.
Flannery, K.V., 'The Cultural Evolution of Civilisations', *Annual Review of Ecology & Systematics*, 1972, 3, pp. 399-426.
Fleet, J.F., *Inscriptions of the Early Gupta Kings and their successors*, Corpus Inscriptionum Indicarum, vol. III., Varanasi, 1970.
Fortes, M., *Kinship and the Social Order*, Chicago, 1969.
Frauwallner, E., *The Earliest Vinaya and the Beginnings of Buddhist Literature*, Rome, 1956.
Fried, Morton H., *The Evolution of Political Society*, New York, 1967.
Fuchs, S., *The Children of Hari*, Vienna, 1949.
Garaudy, R., *Sur le 'Mode de Production Asiatique'*, Paris, 1969.
Gautama Dharma-Sūtra, ed. ASS, Poona; tr. G. Bühler, SBE, vol. II, Oxford, 1897.
Geiger, W., *The Dipavamsa and Mahavamsa and their Historical Development in Ceylon*, Colombo, 1908.
Gerth H.H. and C.W. Mills, *From Max Weber*, London, 1947.
Ghosh, A., and D.P. Agrawal (eds.), *Radio-Carbon and Indian Archaeology*, Bombay, 1972.
Ghosh, A., *The City in Early Historical India*, Simla, 1973.
Ghoshal, U.N., *A History of Hindu Political Theories*, Calcutta, 1923.
Ghoshal, U.N., *The Agrarian System in Ancient India*, Calcutta, 1930.
Ghose, B., Amalkar and Z. Hussain, 'The lost courses of the Sarasvati river in the Great Indian Desert: new evidence from Landstat Imagery', *The Geographical Journal*, 1979, 145, pt 3, pp. 446-51.
Ghose, B., Amalkar and Z. Hussain, 'Comparative Role of the Aravalli and Himalayan River Systems in the Fluvial Sedimentation of the Rajasthan Desert', *Man and Environment*, 1980, IV., pp. 8-12.
Ghose, R.L.M., *et al.*, *Rice in India*, ICAR, New Delhi, 1960.
Gobhila Gṛhya Sūtra, ed. Chintamani Bhattacharya, Cal. Sans. Series, Calcutta, 1936; tr. H. Oldenberg, S.B.E., vol. XXX, Oxford, 1892.
Godakumbara, C.E., *Sinhalese Literature*, Colombo, 1955.
Godelier, M., *Perspectives in Marxist Anthropology*, Cambridge, 1977.
Goldman, I., *Ancient Polynesian Society*, Chicago, 1970.
Gonda, J., *Ancient Indian Kingship from the Religious Point of View*, Leiden, 1969.
Gonda, J., *Selected Studies*, IV. Leiden, 1975.
Goody, J., *Comparative Studies in Kinship*, London, 1969.
Gunawardana, R.A.L.H., 'The Analysis of Pre-Colonial Social Formations in Asia

in the writings of Karl Marx'. *Indian Historical Review,* 1976. II, no. 2, p 365 ff.

Gurdip Singh, 'The Indus Valley Culture', *Archaeology and Physical Anthropology in Oceania*, 1971, vol. 6, no. 2, pp. 177-89.

Gurdip Singh, *et al.*, 'Late Quarternary History of Vegetation and Climate of the Rajasthan Desert, India', *Philosophical Transactions of the Royal Society of London*, 1974, 267, pp. 467–501.

Hara, M., 'A Note on the Sanskrit Word *Jana*', *Pratidānam*, p. 256 ff, The Hague, 1968.

Haswell, M.R., *The Economics of Subsistence Agriculture*, London, 1967.

Heesterman, J.C., *The Ancient Indian Royal Consecration*, The Hague, 1957.

Held, G.J., *The Mahabharata: An Ethnological Study*, Amsterdam, 1935.

Henige, D.P., *The Chronology of Oral Tradition*, Oxford, 1974.

Hiraṇyakeśin Gṛhya-sūtra, ed. J. Kirste, Vienna, 1889; tr. H. Oldenberg, SBE, XXX Oxford, 1982.

Hopkins, E.W., 'Pragathikani', *JAOS*, 1896, 17, p. 84.

Horton, R., and R. Finnegan, (eds.), *Modes of Thought*, London, 1973.

Humphreys, S.C. (ed.), *Mortality and Immortality: the anthropology and archaeology of death*, London, 1982.

Jain, J., *Life in Ancient India as depicted in the Jain Canons*, Bombay, 1947.

Jayaswal, K.P., *Hindu Polity*, Bangalore, 1943 (first ed. 1924).

Jātaka ed. V. Fausboll, London, 1877–97; tr. E.B. Cowell, vols. I-VII, Cambridge, 1895–1907.

Jayatilleke, K.N., *Early Buddhist Theory of Knowledge*, London, 1963.

Jha, H.N., *The Licchavis*, Varanasi, 1970.

Joshi, J.P., 'Interlocking of Late Harappan Culture and Painted Grey Ware Culture in the Light of Recent Excavations', *Man and Environment*, 1978, vol. II, pp. 100-3.

Kane, P.V., *History of Dharmaśāstra*, Poona, 1943 ff.

Kangle, R.P., *The Kautilya Arthaśāstra*, Bombay, 1965.

Kāṭhaka Saṃhitā, ed. Von Schroeder, Leipzig, 1900-11.

Kātyāna Śrauta-sūtra, ed. Vidyadhara Sharma, Benaras, 1933-7.

Kauśika Śrauta-sūtra, ed. M. Bloomfield, 1889

Kauṣītaki Upaniṣad, Allahabad 1925.

Kauṭilya, *Arthaśāstra*, qv. Kangle.

Kosambi, D.D., 'Brahman Clans', *JAOS*, 1953, 73, pp. 202–8.

Kosambi, D.D., *Introduction to the Study of Indian History*, Bombay, 1956.

Kosambi, D.D., *The Culture and Civilisation of Ancient India in Historical Outline*, London, 1965.

Kosambi, D.D., 'The Vedic "Five Tribes"', *JAOS*, 1967, 87 pp. 33-9.

Kosambi, D.D., *Indian Numismatics*, New Delhi, 1981.

Krader, L., *Formation of the State*, New Jersey, 1968.

Krader, L., *The Ethnological Notebooks of Karl Marx*, Assen, 1972.

Krader, L., *The Asiatic Mode of Production*, Assen, 1975.

Krishna Deva and V. Mishra, *Vaiśāli Excavations, 1950*, Vaisali, 1961.

Kulke, H., *Jagannātha-kult und Gajapati Königtum*, Weisbaden, 1979.

Kunāla Jātaka, ed. W.B. Bollee, London, 1970.

Lakatos, I., and A. Musgrave (eds.), *Criticism and the Growth of Knowledge*, Cambridge, 1970.

Lambrick, H.T., *Sind: A General Introduction*, Hyderabad, 1964

Law, B.C., *Kṣatriya Clans in Buddhist India*, Calcutta, 1922.
Law, B.C., *A History of Pali Literature*, 2 vols., London, 1933.
Law, N.N., *Aspects of Ancient Indian Polity*, Oxford, 1921.
Lloyd, G.E.R., *Magic, Reason and Experience*, Cambridge, 1979.
Lowie, R.H., *Primitive Society*, New York, 1920.
Lakṣman Sarup, *Nighantu tathā Nirukta*, Delhi, 1967.
Macdonnel, A.A., and A.B. Keith, *Vedic Index of Names and Subjects*, vols. I and II, Delhi, 1967.
Mahābhārata (Critical Edition), Ādi Parvan, ed. V.S. Sukthankar, Poona, 1927-33.
Mahābhārata, Sabhā Parvan, ed. F. Edgerton, Poona, 1943-4.
Mahābhārata, Udyog Parvan, ed. S.K. De, Poona, 1937-40/47
Mahāvagga, qv. *Vinaya Piṭaka.*
Mahāvaṃsa, ed. W. Geiger, London, 1908; tr. W. Geiger, London, 1912.
Maitrāyanī Saṃhitā, ed. Von Schroeder, Leipzig, 1881-6.
Majjhima Nikāya, ed. V. Trenckner and R. Chalmers, 3 vols., London, 1887-1902; I.B. Horner, 'The Middle Length Sayings', P.T.S. London 1954.
Malalasekara, G.P., *The Pali Literature of Ceylon*, London, 1928.
Mānava Dharmaśāstra, ed. J.R. Gharpure, Bombay, 1920.
Mānava Dharmāsastra/Manu Smṛti, G. Bühler, *The Laws of Manu*, SBE, XXV, Oxford, 1886.
Mankad, D.R., *Puranic Chronology*, Anand, 1951.
Marshall, J., *Taxila*, Cambridge, 1951
Marx, K. and F. Engels, *On Colonialism*, Moscow, 1968.
Matsya Purāṇa, ed. ASS, Poona, 1907.
Mauss, M., *The Gift*, London, 1954.
Megasthenes, J.W. McCrindle, *Ancient India as described by Megasthenes and Arrian*, London, 1877.
Mehta, R.L., *Pre-Buddhist India*, Bombay, 1939.
Meillassoux, C., 'From Reproduction to Production', *Economy and Society*, 1972, I, no. 1, pp. 93-105.
Meillassoux, C., 'Historical Modalities of the Exploitation and Over-exploitation of Labour, *Critique of Anthropology*, 1979, 4, nos. 13 and 14, pp. 7-16.
Middleton, J. and D. Tait, *Tribes without Rulers*, London, 1958.
Morton-Smith, R., *Dates and Dynasties in Earliest India*, Delhi, 1975.
Mukherji, P.C., *Antiquities of Kapilavastu*, no. XXVI, pt 1, Calcutta, 1901 (rpt, Delhi, 1969).

Nadel, S.F., *A Black Byzantium*, London, 1942.
Narain, A.K. (ed.), *Local Coins of Northern India, c. 300 B.C. to 300 A.D.*, Varanasi, 1966.
Narain A.K. and L. Gopal (eds.), *Seminar Papers on the Chronology of the Punch-Marked Coins*, Varanasi, 1966.
Narain, A.K., and T.N. Roy, *The Excavations of Prahladpur*, Benaras, 1968.
Narain, A.K. and T.N. Roy, *Excavations at Rajghat*, Benaras, 1976.
Naroll, R. and R. Cohen, *A Handbook of Method in Cultural Anthropology*, New York, 1970.
O'Callaghan, M., *Sociological Theories: Race and Colonialism*, UNESCO, 1980.
Oppenheimer, F., *The State*, New York, 1975 (rpt).
Pāli-English Dictionary, ed. by T.W. Rhys Davids and W. Stede, London, 1966.

Papañcasudani, ed. J.H. Woods and D. Kosambi, London 1922.
Pañcaviṃsa Brāhmaṇa, ed. A. Vedantavagisa, Calcutta, 1869-74.
Pande, G.C., *Studies in the Origins of Buddhism*, Allahabad, 1957.
Pāṇini, *Aṣṭādhyāyī*, ed. S.C. Vasu, Delhi, 1962.
Pargiter, F.E., *The Purana Texts of the Dynasties of the Kali Age*, Oxford, 1913.
Pargiter, F.E., *Ancient Indian Historical Tradition*, London, 1922.
Patañjali, *Vyākaraṇa Mahābhāṣyam*, ed. F. Kielhorn, vols. 1 and 2, Poona, 1962.
Patañjali, *Vyākaraṇa Mahābhāṣya*, ed. S.D. Joshi, Poona, 1968.
Pleiner, R., 'The Problems of the Beginning Iron Age in India', *Acta Praehistorica et Archaeologica*, 1971, 2, pp. 5-36.
Pliny, *Natural History*.
Polanyi, K., *The Great Transformation*, Boston, 1957.
Polanyi, K., *Trade and Markets in the Early Empires*, Glencoe, 1957.
Polanyi, K., *Dahomey and the Slave Trade*, Seattle, 1966.
Pradhan, S.N., *Chronology of Ancient India*, Calcutta, 1927.
Pusalkar, A.D., *Studies in the Epics and the Puranas*, Bombay, 1955.
Raikes, R.C., 'Kalibangan: death from natural causes', *Antiquity*, 1968, pp. 286-91.
Ramaswamy, C., 'Monsoon over the Indus Valley during the Harappan Period', *Nature*, 1968, 217, pp. 628-9.
Rāmāyaṇa, Bālakāṇḍa, ed. G.H. Bhatt, Baroda, 1960.
Rāmāyaṇa, Ayodhyakāṇḍa, ed. P.L. Vaidya, Baroda, 1962.
Rank, O., *The Myth of the Birth of a Hero*, New York, 1959.
Rey, P.P., 'The Lineage Mode of Production', *Critique of Anthropology*, Spring 1975, no. 3, pp. 27-9.
Rey, P.P., 'Class Contradiction in Lineage Societies', *Critique of Anthropology*, 1971, 4, nos. 13 and 14, pp. 41-60.
Ṛg Veda, ed. F. Max Muller, Oxford, 1890-2; tr. R.T.H. Griffith, 2 vols., Varanasi, 1963.
Rhys Davids, T.W., *Buddhist India*, London, 1903.
Rockhill, W.W., *Life of Buddha*, London, 1907.
Samantapāsādikā, ed. N.A. Jayawickrama, London, 1962.
Samyutta Nikāya, ed. L. Freer, 5 vols. PTS, London, 1884-98; tr. Mrs Rhys Davids and F.L. Woodward, 'Book of Kindred Sayings', PTS, London, 1913.
Sankalia, H.D., *Prehistory and Protohistory of India and Pakistan*, Poona, 1974.
Sānkhyāyana Gṛhya Sūtra, tr. H. Oldenberg, SBE, XXIX, Oxford.
Śatpatha Brāhmaṇa, ed. A. Weber, London, 1885; tr. J. Eggeling, pts. I-V, SBE, Oxford, 1882.
Scott Littleton, C., *The New Comparative Mythology*, Berkeley, 1972.
Seddon, D. (ed.), *Relations of Production*, London, 1978.
Senart, E., *Le Mahāvastu*, Paris, 1882-97.
Senart, E., *Caste in India: The Facts and the System*, tr. D. Ross, London, 1930.
Service, E.R., *Origins of the State and Civilization: The Process of Cultural Evolution*, New York, 1975.
Shanin, T. (ed), *Peasants and Pesant Society*, Harmondsworth, 1971.
Sharma, A., 'An Analysis of the Epithets applied to the Śūdras in Aitareya Brāhmaṇa', XVIII, pt 3, pp. 300-18.
Sharma, G.R., *The Excavations at Kauśāmbi*, 1957-9, Allahabad, 1960.
Sharma, G.R., *The Beginnings of Agriculture*, Allahabad, 1980.
Sharma, J.P., *Republics in Ancient India*, Leiden, 1968.
Sharma, R.S. *Light on Early Indian Society and Economy*, Bombay, 1966.

Sharma, R.S., *Aspects of Political Ideas and Institutions in Ancient India*, Delhi 1959/1968.

Sharma, R.S. 'Forms of Property in the Early Portions of the Ṛg Veda,' Essays in Honour of Prof. S.C. Sarkar, New Delhi, 1976, pp. 39-50.

Sharma, R.S., 'Class Formation and its Material Basis in the upper Gangetic Basin', c. 1000-500 B.C., *IHR*, July 1975, II, no. 1, p. 1 ff.

Sharma, R.S., *Śūdras in Ancient India*, Delhi, 1980.

Singh, R.L., *Regional Geography*, Varanasi, 1971.

Sinha, B.P., and B.S. Verma, 'Preliminary Report of Chirand Exacavations for the year 1969', *Patna University Journal*, July 1978, 23, no. 3, p. 97 ff.

Southall, A.W., *Alur Society*, Cambridge, 1956.

Spate, O.H.K., *India and Pakistan*, Landon, 1964.

Spooner, B., 'Politics, Kinship and Ecology in S.E. Persia', *Ethnology*, 1969, I, pp. 139-52.

Spooner, B. (ed)., *Population Growth*, Cambridge, Mass, 1972.

Srinivasan, D., *Concept of Cow in the Rig Veda*, Delhi, 1979.

Srivastava, B., *Trade and Commerce in Ancient India*, Varanasi, 1968.

Stein, B., *Essays on South India*, New Delhi, 1976.

Stein, B., *Peasant State and Society in Medieval South India*, Delhi, 1980.

Steward, J.H. *Theory of Culture Change*, Urbana, 1955.

Sumaṅgala Vilāsinī, ed. T.W. Rhys Davids and J. Carpenter, P.T.S., London, 1886.

Suraj Bhan, 'Excavation at Mithathal 1968 (Hissar)', *Journal of Haryana Studies*, 1969, I, no. 1, pp. 1-15.

Suraj Bhan, and J.G. Shaffer, 'New Discoveries in Northern Haryana', *Man and Environment*, 1978, II, pp. 59-68.

Suraj Bhan, *Excavation at Mithathal (1980) and other Explorations in the Sutlej-Yamuna Divide*, Kurukshetra, 1975.

Sutta-nipata, trans. E.M. Hare, Colombo 1944.

Sutta-vibhaṅga, ed. Mrs. Rhys Davids, P.T.S. London 1904.

Taittirīya Brāhmaṇa, ed. R. Mitra, Calcutta, 1855-70.

Tambiah, S.J., *World Conqueror and World Renouncer*, Cambridge, 1976.

Terray, E., *Marxism and 'Primitive' Societies*, New York, 1975.

Thapar, Romila. *The Past and Prejudice*, New Delhi, 1975.

Thapar, Romila., 'A Possible Identification of Meluhha, Dilmun and Makan', *JESHO*, 1975, XVIII, PT 1, p. 30 ff.

Thapar, Romila, *Ancient Indian Social History: Some Interpretations*, New Delhi, 1978.

Thapar, Romila, *Exile and the Kingdom: Some thoughts on the Rāmāyaṇa*, Bangalore, 1978.

Thapar, Romila, 'The Historian and the Epic', *Annals of the Bhandarkar Oriental Research Institute*, 1979, LX, pp. 199-213.

Thorner, D., 'Peasant Economy as a Category in Economic History', *Deuxieme Conferènce Internationale de' Histoire Economique*, Aix-en-Provence, 1962, vol. 2, pp. 287-300, Mouton; rptd. T. Shanin (ed.), *Peasants and Peasant Societies*, pp. 202-18.

Thorner, D., 'Marx on India and the Asiatic Mode of Production', *Contributions to Indian Sociology*, 1966, no. 9, pp. 33-66.

Trautmann, T.R., *Kauṭilya and the Arthaśāstra*, Leiden, 1971.

Trautmann, T.R. (ed.), *Kinship and History in South Asia*, Michigan, 1974.

Tripathi, V., *The Painted Grey Ware, An Iron Age Culture of Northern India*, Delhi, 1976.

Upaniṣads, ed. and tr. S. Radhakrishnan, *The Principal Upanisads*, London, 1953.

Uvāsaga Dasāo, ed. R. Hoernle, Calcutta, 1890.

Vājasaneyi Saṃhitā, ed. A. Weber, London, 1935.

Vamsatthapakāsinī, ed. G.P. Malalasekara, London, 1935.

Varma, S., *The Etymologies of Yāsaka*, Hoshiarpur, 1953.

Varma, V.P., *Early Buddhism and its Origins*, Delhi, 1972.

Vasistha Dharma-sūtra, ed. A.A. Führer, Bombay, 1916; tr. G. Bühler, SBE, vol. XIV, Oxford, 1892.

Vāyu Purāṇa, ed. R. Mitra, 2 vols., Calcutta, 1880-8.

Vubata Piṭaka, ed. H. Oldenberg, P.T.S., London, 1879-83; tr. T.W. Rhys Davids and H. Oldenberg, SBE, Oxford, 1881-5.

Viṣṇu Purāṇa, ed. J. Vidyasagara, Calcutta, 1882, tr. H.H. Wilson, 5 vols., London, 1864-70.

Viṣṇu-smṛti, Madras 1964

Wagle, N., *society at the Time of the Buddha*, Bombay, 1996. (2nd edition)

Watters, T., *On Yuan Chwang's Travels in India*, New Delhi, 1973 (rpt).

Wilhelmy, H., 'Das Urstromtal an Ostrand der Indusebens und dar Saraswati Problem', *Zeitschrift fur Geomorphologie*, Supplement Band, 1969, 8, pp. 76-93.

Wittfogel, K., *Oriental Despotism*, New Haven, 1957.

E.V. Winans, *Shambala*, Berkeley, 1962.

W.H. Wiser, *The Hindu Jajmani System*, Lucknow, 1958.

Yadav, B.N.S., 'The Kali Age and the Social Transition', *IHR*, 1978-9, v, nos. 1 and 2, pp. 37-8

Yājñavalkaya Smṛti, ed. ASS, Poona, 1903-4; tr. G.R. Gharpure, Bombay, 1936

INDEX

Abhidhamma Piṭaka, 144
abhiṣeka, 172
Ābhīra, 50
Achaemenid, 97
Adams, R.M., 9
administration, 121 ff, 81
Agni, 70
Agrawal, D.P., 71
Agrawala, V.S., 87, 100, 165, 166
agriculture, 32, 37 ff, 76 ff, 106 ff, 121
Ahicchatra, 91, 156
ahiṃsā, 151
Aitareya Brāhmaṇa, 22, 23, 26, 33, 38, 40, 41, 43, 53, 59, 62, 93, 117, 131
Ajātaśatru, 111, 114, 146, 148
Ājīvika, 85, 109, 152
ākhyāna, 130ff, 143
akṣavapa, 60
Allan, J., 90, 101
Allchin, B. & R., 23
Altekar, A.S., 3, 71
Alur, 163
amātya, 121 ff
anarchy, 118
Anderson, P., 3
Andhaka-Vṛṣṇi, 45, 70, 82, 133, 142
Aṅga, 96, 114, 137, 139
Aṅguttara Nikāya, 16, 76, 81, 85, 87, 89, 92, 101, 103, 106, 112, 128
Anu, 47
Āpastamba Dharma Sūtra, 88, 104, 108, 125, 128, 153
Āpastamba Gṛhya Sūtra, 16, 23, 56, 88, 89
Āpastamba Śrauta Sūtra, 53
Āraṇyaka, 15, 66
archaeological evidence, 21ff, 68-9, 71 ff, 94ff, 98ff
army, 113
Arrian, 123, 124
Arthaśāstra/Kauṭilya, 16, 41, 44, 69, 98, 102, 105, 106, 111, 113, 121, 123, 124, 129, 160, 162, 165
artisans, 85, 89, 165
ārya, 22, 28, 39-40, 42ff, 45, 49, 53, 83
Asiatic Mode of Production, 3, 171
Aśoka (Maurya), 111, 145 ff, 152, 161, 162
Aśokāvadāna, 149
āśramas, 111
assemblies, 55 ff, 82
asuras, 24, 43, 44-5, 47, 117
Āśvalāyana Gṛhya Sūtra, 42, 44
Āśvalāyana Śrauta Sūtra, 53
aśvamedha, 28, 63, 66, 172
Atharva Veda, 15, 23, 25, 26, 27, 28, 35, 36, 38, 40, 41, 43, 54, 55, 56, 57, 65, 93, 116, 118, 137
Atranji Khera, 27
Austro-Asiatic, 27
authority, 126 ff
Ayodhyā, 71, 74, 91, 96, 97, 133, 134

Bailey, H.W., 43
bali, 32, 33, 40 ff, 112, 123-4
balihṛt, 40, 125
balikṛt, 40
Bāṇa, *Harṣacarita*, 173
bard, 31, 136 ff
barley, 29
Baudhāyana Dharma Sūtra, 16, 17, 41, 42, 46, 54, 77, 80, 88, 93, 102, 103, 104, 106, 108, 113, 124, 128
Beal, S., 80
Beidelman, T.O., 164
Belan Valley, 72
Benveniste, E., 48
Béteille, A., 18
bhāga, 33, 40 ff, 112, 123-4
bhāgadugha, 40-1, 60
Bhāgavata Purāṇa, 49
Bharatas, 21, 25-6, 155
bhikkhu, 43, 151-2
Bhīṣma, 133
Bhṛgu, 52, 131
Bhṛgukaccha, 98
Bilhaṇa, *Vikramāṅkadevacarita*, 173
Bimbisāra, 113, 114, 146
Bipan Chandra, 3
Black-and-red Ware, 71 ff 140
Bloch, J., 123, 124, 149, 152, 161, 162
bodhisatta, 108, 151
Boserup, E., 73
brāhmana, 31, 32, ff, 41, 45-6, 49, 52, 53 ff, 65 ff, 85, 87, 88, 102, 108, 110, 122 ff, 125, 128, 130, 131, 136, 152, 154, 158, 167, 170
Brāhmaṇas, 15
brāhmī, 103
Bṛhaddevata, 63
Bṛhadratha, 113 ff, 141
Brohier, R.L., 74
Buddha, 108, 109, 145, 146, 150
Buddhist monasteries, 111, 142
Bühler, G., 103, 170